Lonely Planet

LONELY PLANET'S
WHERE TO GO WHEN

THE ULTIMATE TRIP PLANNER FOR EVERY MONTH OF THE YEAR

CONTENTS

April

P80-103

Jordan
Panama
Luzon, Philippines
Rome, Italy
Hawke's Bay, New Zealand
Alps, France & Switzerland
Palau
California, USA
Belize
Lake District, England
KwaZulu-Natal, South Africa
İstanbul, Turkey
Yangtze, China
Taranaki, New Zealand
Vanuatu
South West Australia
Appalachian Trail, USA
Thailand
Nepal
Brussels, Belgium
Washington, DC, USA
Melbourne, Australia
Andalucía, Spain
Arnhem Land, Australia
St Lucia
Galápagos Islands, Ecuador
Hawaii, USA
Japan
Mauritius
Boston, USA

May

P104-127

Montenegro
Abruzzo, Italy
Bermuda
Samoa
Uzbekistan
Komodo & Flores, Indonesia
Réunion
Amalfi Coast, Italy
Peru
Morocco
North Island, New Zealand
Cornwall, England
Loire Valley, France
West Coast, Norway
Northern Queensland, Australia
Cappadocia, Turkey
Israel
Cuba
Orient Express, Europe
Newfoundland, Canada
Red Centre, Australia
Prague, Czech Republic
Southern Namibia
Route 66, USA
Inside Passage, USA & Canada
Galicia, Spain
Skye, Scotland
Deep South, USA
Costa Rica
Las Vegas, USA

June

P128-151

Iran
Albania
Netherlands Antilles
Slovenia
Armenia
Bazaruto Archipelago, Mozambique
Ningaloo Reef, Australia
Darwin, Australia
Normandy, France
Bali & Lombok, Indonesia
Malaysian Borneo
Arctic Norway
Hobart, Australia
Dubrovnik, Croatia
Pacific Northwest, USA
Canadian Rockies
Montana, USA
Rwanda
Cape Cod, USA
Sardinia, Italy
St Petersburg, Russia
Lisbon, Portugal
Yosemite National Park, USA
Bora Bora, French Polynesia
South Luangwa, Zambia
Greenland
Jamaica
Mount Cook, New Zealand
Orkney, Scotland
Verona, Italy

CONTENTS

4

October

P224-247

Vietnam
Fiji
Moab, USA
Bolivia
Great Southern, Australia
Costa Verde, Brazil
Piedmont, Italy
Oman
Seychelles
New Mexico, USA
Porto & the Douro, Portugal
Southwest China
Blue Ridge Parkway, USA
Darjeeling, India
Flinders Ranges, Australia
Coromandel Peninsula, New Zealand
Namibia
Bhutan
Manitoba, Canada
Copper Canyon, Mexico
Slovakia
Lyon, France
Northern Tanzania
Peloponnese, Greece
Southern Jordan
La Rioja, Spain
Liguria, Italy
Highlands, Scotland
Taiwan
New York City, USA

November

P248-271

South Africa
Goa, India
Cayman Islands
Simien Mountains, Ethiopia
Puerto Rico
British Virgin Islands
Grampians, Australia
Auckland & Northland, New Zealand
Ruta Maya, Guatemala, Belize & Mexico
Rajasthan & the Golden Triangle, India
Costa Rica
Tokyo & Honshu, Japan
Abu Dhabi, UAE
Valletta, Malta
Uruguay
Florida, USA
Oregon, USA
Barbados
Dunedin, New Zealand
Ruka, Finland
Nepal
Mexico City, Mexico
Hong Kong, China
Athens & Evia, Greece
Northern Thailand
Sunshine Coast, Australia
Mekong, Indochina
North Chile
Nicaragua
Madrid, Spain

December

P272-295

Arctic Sweden
Southern Amazon, Peru
Ethiopia
Ras Al Khaimah, UAE
Jasper, Canada
Tenerife, Spain
Bath, England
Alta, USA
Tasmania, Australia
San Sebastián, Spain
Similan Islands, Thailand
Glacier Express, Switzerland
Southern Patagonia, Chile & Argentina
Micronesia
Whanganui River, New Zealand
Breckenridge, USA
West Coast Malaysia
Senegal
Laos
Sierra Leone
Sahara Desert, Morocco
Andaman Islands, India
Havana, Cuba
Tallinn, Estonia
Rovaniemi, Finland
Southern Vietnam
Sapphire Coast, Australia
Trinidad
St Vincent & the Grenadines
Scotland
New Orleans, USA

INTRODUCTION

We'd so nearly booked to come in early June. I'd thought: that'll be nice, surely? Start of summer, decent weather before the crowds descend, no? Well, not quite. As we sat sipping grappa on a high, sunny terrace, with a view of the spiky Dolomites spearing a cloudless blue sky, I was glad we'd waited until the start of July. By now, unlike in early June, the salubrious, red-gingham mountain huts and handy cablecars were all open for business; the high passes were mostly free of snow; the multifarious activities were all available; the wildflowers were rampant. Yet it still wasn't busy. We raised our little glasses again. Saluti! A local toast to perfect timing.

Of course, if we were ski buffs, our timing would have been completely wrong. In that case, February or March would have been our months for these north Italian slopes; then, the winter chill is less fierce and the powder is at its best. But different strokes for different folks. Which is where this book comes in.

'Where to go when?' is the most important question in travel. Maybe there's an experience you're desperate to have, and you want to make sure you have it when the conditions and circumstances are just right. For instance, there's no point dreaming of Peru's Inca Trail, then turning up without a permit in February (when it's closed) or July-August (when it's busiest).

Or maybe you have set dates for your next holiday – stuck with two weeks in October? With such restrictions, you need to know which destinations will offer your desired sun, sights, surf or wildlife-sightings when you're free to visit (FYI, try Greece, Jordan, Fiji and Namibia respectively).

© Matt Munro / Lonely Planet

Either way, this book will give you options and advice – and maybe make you consider places you've never considered before. Indeed, it's particularly suited to the confused or inspiration-seeking traveller. The book is divided into 12 chapters, one for every month, and at the start of each, we've included a handy flowchart. Answer the questins and follow the strands to help drill down the type of trip you want: do you want to chill out or challenge yourself? Do you want to find cultural sites, active exploits or your inner self? Do you want a quiet beach or a crazy one? We'll give you a wealth of ideas.

We've selected 360 places that cover all bases, from family-friendly escapes to hardcore adventures and plenty in between. And we'll tell you when are the best times to visit each one: maybe because it's hosting a mustn't-miss festival; because it's cheaper and calmer before peak season; because it's when the manta rays/polar bears/butterflies are in town; because the weather is just so very good. Whatever type of trip you're looking for, whichever month you can get away, and whether you're a hammock-swinger, hiker, biker, gourmand, rail-lover, roadtripper or raver, we'll tell you exactly where to go.

By Sarah Baxter & Paul Bloomfield

(L) The Dolomites in summer; (R) Machu Picchu; rumba drummers in Havana

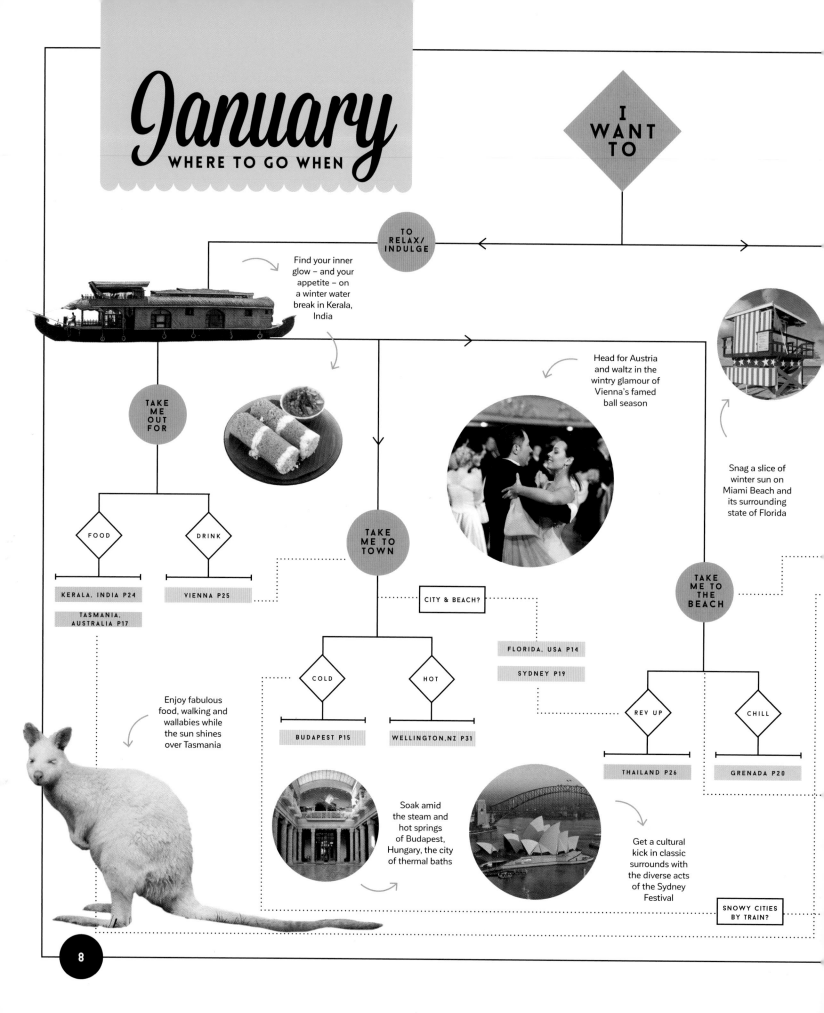

January
WHERE TO GO WHEN

I WANT TO

TO RELAX/INDULGE

Find your inner glow – and your appetite – on a winter water break in Kerala, India

Head for Austria and waltz in the wintry glamour of Vienna's famed ball season

Snag a slice of winter sun on Miami Beach and its surrounding state of Florida

TAKE ME OUT FOR

◇ FOOD

◇ DRINK

KERALA, INDIA P24

TASMANIA, AUSTRALIA P17

VIENNA P25

TAKE ME TO TOWN

CITY & BEACH?

◇ COLD

◇ HOT

BUDAPEST P15

WELLINGTON, NZ P31

FLORIDA, USA P14

SYDNEY P19

TAKE ME TO THE BEACH

◇ REV UP

◇ CHILL

THAILAND P26

GRENADA P20

Enjoy fabulous food, walking and wallabies while the sun shines over Tasmania

Soak amid the steam and hot springs of Budapest, Hungary, the city of thermal baths

Get a cultural kick in classic surrounds with the diverse acts of the Sydney Festival

SNOWY CITIES BY TRAIN?

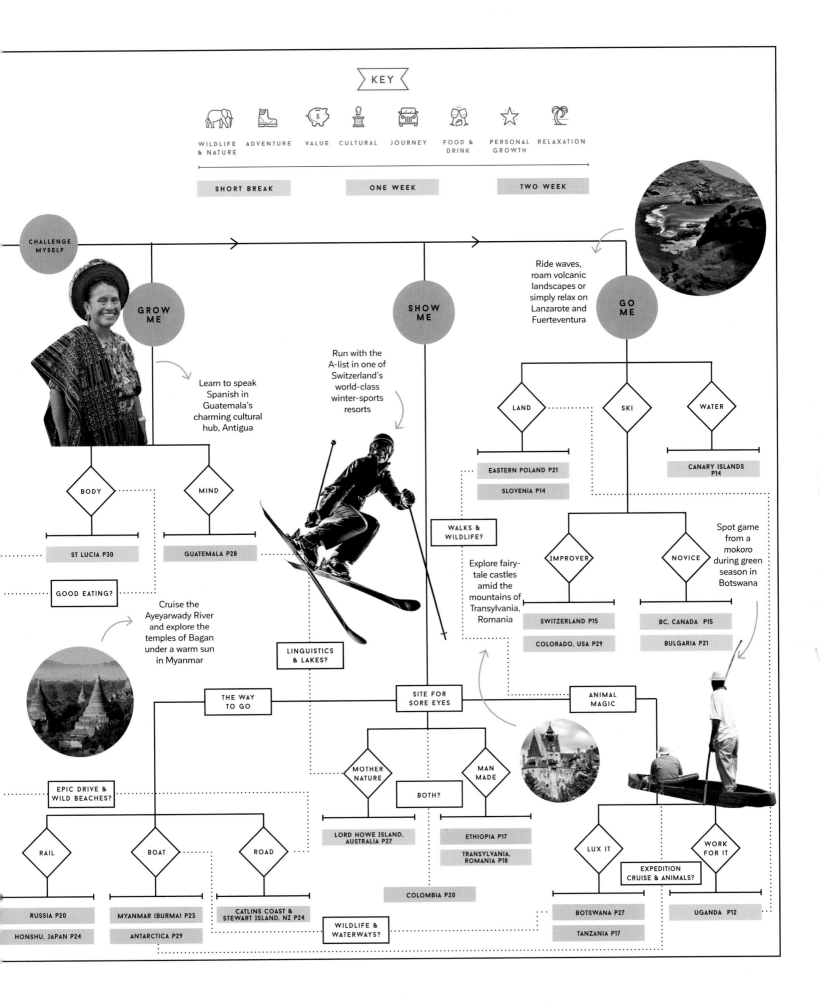

KEY

WILDLIFE & NATURE   ADVENTURE   VALUE   CULTURAL   JOURNEY   FOOD & DRINK   PERSONAL GROWTH   RELAXATION

SHORT BREAK   ONE WEEK   TWO WEEK

CHALLENGE MYSELF

GROW ME

SHOW ME

GO ME

Ride waves, roam volcanic landscapes or simply relax on Lanzarote and Fuerteventura

Learn to speak Spanish in Guatemala's charming cultural hub, Antigua

Run with the A-list in one of Switzerland's world-class winter-sports resorts

LAND   SKI   WATER

BODY   MIND

EASTERN POLAND P21

SLOVENIA P14

CANARY ISLANDS P14

WALKS & WILDLIFE?

ST LUCIA P30

GUATEMALA P28

Explore fairy-tale castles amid the mountains of Transylvania, Romania

IMPROVER   NOVICE

Spot game from a *mokoro* during green season in Botswana

GOOD EATING?

Cruise the Ayeyarwady River and explore the temples of Bagan under a warm sun in Myanmar

LINGUISTICS & LAKES?

SITE FOR SORE EYES

SWITZERLAND P15

COLORADO, USA P29

BC, CANADA P15

BULGARIA P21

ANIMAL MAGIC

THE WAY TO GO

MOTHER NATURE   MAN MADE

EPIC DRIVE & WILD BEACHES?

BOTH?

LORD HOWE ISLAND, AUSTRALIA P27

ETHIOPIA P17

TRANSYLVANIA, ROMANIA P18

LUX IT   WORK FOR IT

RAIL   BOAT   ROAD

COLOMBIA P20

EXPEDITION CRUISE & ANIMALS?

RUSSIA P20

HONSHU, JAPAN P24

MYANMAR (BURMA) P23

ANTARCTICA P29

CATLINS COAST & STEWART ISLAND, NZ P24

WILDLIFE & WATERWAYS?

BOTSWANA P27

TANZANIA P17

UGANDA P12

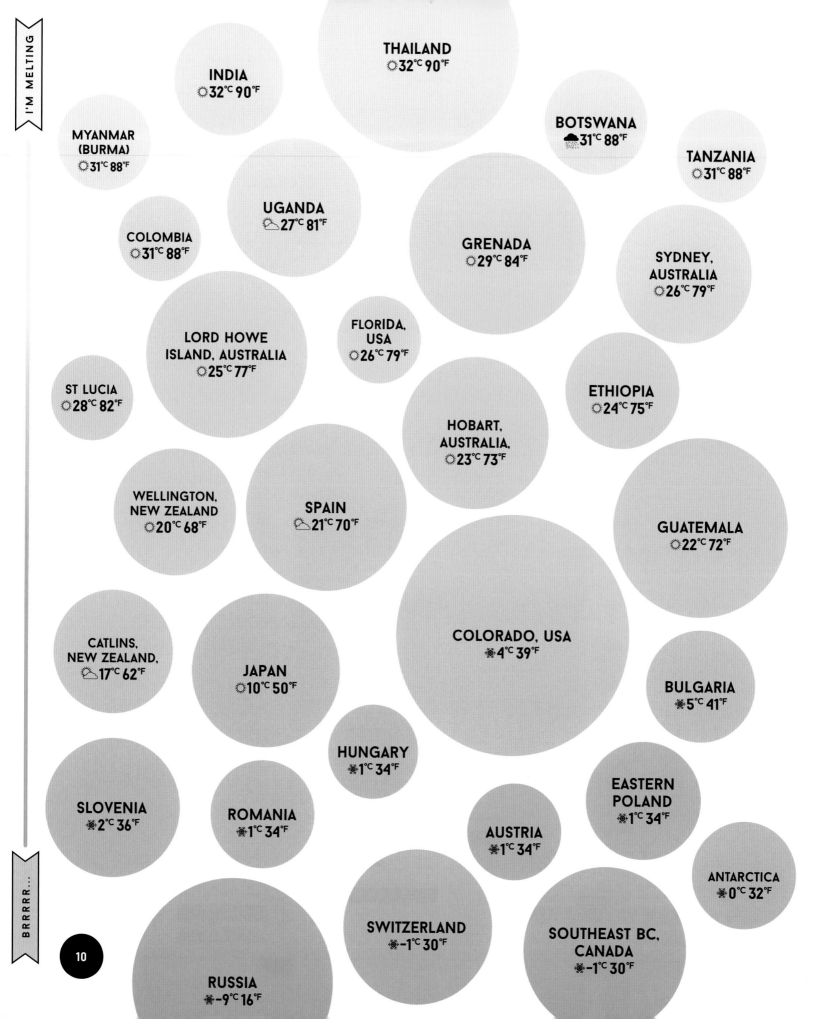

THAILAND
☀ 32°C 90°F

INDIA
☀ 32°C 90°F

BOTSWANA
🌧 31°C 88°F

MYANMAR
(BURMA)
☀ 31°C 88°F

TANZANIA
☀ 31°C 88°F

UGANDA
⛅ 27°C 81°F

COLOMBIA
☀ 31°C 88°F

GRENADA
☀ 29°C 84°F

SYDNEY,
AUSTRALIA
☀ 26°C 79°F

LORD HOWE
ISLAND, AUSTRALIA
☀ 25°C 77°F

FLORIDA,
USA
☀ 26°C 79°F

ETHIOPIA
☀ 24°C 75°F

ST LUCIA
☀ 28°C 82°F

HOBART,
AUSTRALIA,
☀ 23°C 73°F

WELLINGTON,
NEW ZEALAND
☀ 20°C 68°F

SPAIN
⛅ 21°C 70°F

GUATEMALA
☀ 22°C 72°F

CATLINS,
NEW ZEALAND,
⛅ 17°C 62°F

JAPAN
☀ 10°C 50°F

COLORADO, USA
❄ 4°C 39°F

BULGARIA
❄ 5°C 41°F

HUNGARY
❄ 1°C 34°F

SLOVENIA
❄ 2°C 36°F

ROMANIA
❄ 1°C 34°F

EASTERN
POLAND
❄ 1°C 34°F

AUSTRIA
❄ 1°C 34°F

ANTARCTICA
❄ 0°C 32°F

SWITZERLAND
❄ -1°C 30°F

SOUTHEAST BC,
CANADA
❄ -1°C 30°F

RUSSIA
❄ -9°C 16°F

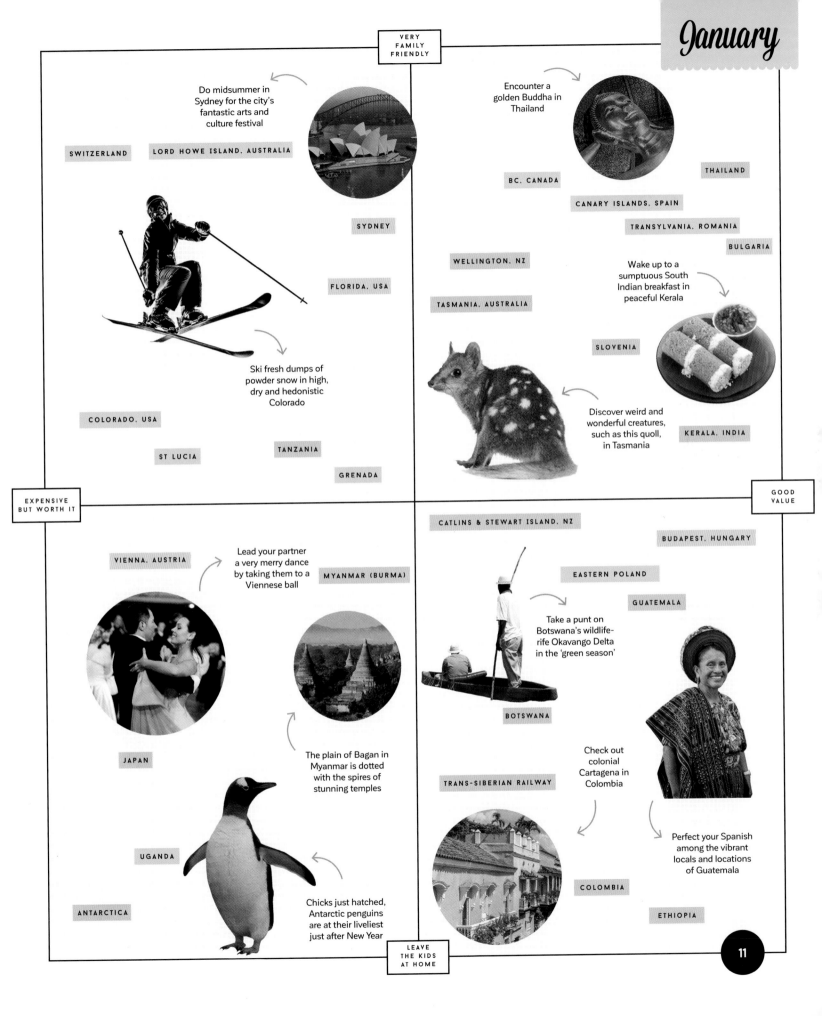

VERY FAMILY FRIENDLY

Do midsummer in Sydney for the city's fantastic arts and culture festival

SWITZERLAND

LORD HOWE ISLAND, AUSTRALIA

Encounter a golden Buddha in Thailand

BC, CANADA

THAILAND

CANARY ISLANDS, SPAIN

TRANSYLVANIA, ROMANIA

BULGARIA

SYDNEY

WELLINGTON, NZ

Wake up to a sumptuous South Indian breakfast in peaceful Kerala

FLORIDA, USA

TASMANIA, AUSTRALIA

SLOVENIA

Ski fresh dumps of powder snow in high, dry and hedonistic Colorado

COLORADO, USA

Discover weird and wonderful creatures, such as this quoll, in Tasmania

KERALA, INDIA

ST LUCIA

TANZANIA

GRENADA

EXPENSIVE BUT WORTH IT

GOOD VALUE

CATLINS & STEWART ISLAND, NZ

BUDAPEST, HUNGARY

VIENNA, AUSTRIA

Lead your partner a very merry dance by taking them to a Viennese ball

MYANMAR (BURMA)

EASTERN POLAND

GUATEMALA

Take a punt on Botswana's wildlife-rife Okavango Delta in the 'green season'

JAPAN

The plain of Bagan in Myanmar is dotted with the spires of stunning temples

BOTSWANA

Check out colonial Cartagena in Colombia

TRANS-SIBERIAN RAILWAY

UGANDA

Perfect your Spanish among the vibrant locals and locations of Guatemala

ANTARCTICA

Chicks just hatched, Antarctic penguins are at their liveliest just after New Year

COLOMBIA

ETHIOPIA

LEAVE THE KIDS AT HOME

UGANDA

Why now? Track the world's biggest primates in the dry(ish) season.
Gazing into the deep brown eyes of an endangered mountain gorilla is a precious experience: perhaps only 700 or so individuals survive, of which around half roam the dense forests of Uganda's Bwindi Impenetrable National Park. It's an experience you'll need to earn, tackling steep, muddy trails in altitudes up to 3000m, possibly for several hours. But if you snag one of only eight permits available for each of the park's nine habituated families, the rewards are luminous: an hour in the company of these gentle giants (a silverback male can reach 180kg) is unforgettable. The rest of the country holds its own, too. Nearby Queen Elizabeth National Park is renowned for tree-climbing lions, while you can track chimpanzees in Kibale National Park; beyond the far tip of Lake Albert, the Nile thunders over Murchison Falls, and there's fine trekking in the Rwenzori Mountains.

Trip plan: From Entebbe, Uganda's international airport, fly to Ishasha airstrip for Bwindi. Add time in Queen Elizabeth, Kibale and Murchison Falls national parks.

Need to know: Gorilla tracking permits valid for one day must be purchased in advance, currently US$600 for foreign non-residents (US$450 in April, May and November). Under-15s aren't permitted on gorilla-tracking excursions.

Other months: Dec-Feb & Jun-Sep – driest months, best for trekking; Mar-May – wet, good birding; Oct-Nov – wet, gorilla permits may be easier to obtain.

Wildlife & nature

Personal growth

Adventure

Worth every penny: seeing gorillas in Bwindi Impenetrable National Park

FLORIDA
USA

Why now? Snag a slice of warm sunshine.

Florida's gaudy, glamorous bill-topping star Miami is the picture-perfect antidote to grey winter. Powder pink and neon blue are the colours of the Art Deco Weekend at South Beach in mid-January: head to Ocean Dr and get your jazz hands ready to party like its 1929, with music, shows, talks, tours, alfresco movies and vintage shopping. But beyond the beaches and bars, the Latin-accented nightlife and no-holds-barred glitz, there's a rejuvenating calm to be absorbed. To the northwest, take a dip in Crystal River, where hundreds of manatees cluster around the warmer springs between November and March. Or grab a paddle and kayak through the tea-coloured waters of the Everglades, watching for alligators and profuse birdlife – and dealing with fewer biting bugs in the winter dry season.

Trip plan: Base yourself at South Beach to be in the heart of the art deco action.

Need to know: The Art Deco Weekend (www.artdecoweekend.com) runs for three days in mid-January.

Other months: Oct-May – pleasantly warm; Jun-Sep – summer, hot, humid.

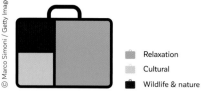

- Relaxation
- Cultural
- Wildlife & nature

LANZAROTE & FUERTEVENTURA
CANARY ISLANDS

Why now? Ride the waves (or just relax) under the sun.

The dramatic volcanic landscapes, sweeps of sand and rolling waves of the easternmost Canary Islands are at their most appealing in January, when the temperature is warm but not scorching (and when the rest of Europe shivers). Fuerteventura and Lanzarote are both playgrounds for surfers of all varieties: experienced wave-riders head to El Quemao (La Santa) and San Juan (Caleta de Famara) in Lanzarote's northwest, or Los Lobos on Fuerteventura, while kitesurfers and windsurfers are also spoiled for choice. Hiking and cycling opportunities across Fuerteventura's friable black lava fields and among Lanzarote's 300 rugged volcanic cones abound, too. There are beaches galore, naturally – choose from gold- or black-sand shores on Fuerteventura, or the chilled little islet of La Graciosa off Lanzarote's northern tip. Lanzarote also boasts wineries in La Geria region, and the innovative architecture of César Manrique.

Trip plan: It's easy to combine both islands – regular ferries make the crossing between Playa Blanca on Lanzarote with Corralejo on Fuerteventura in about 30 minutes.

Need to know: Wind and surf tend to be stronger on the west coasts than the east.

Other months: Jan-Jun & Sep-Dec fine weather; Jul-Aug – hot, crowded.

- Relaxation
- Adventure

SLOVENIA

Why now? Enjoy great-value snowsports.

It shouldn't come as a surprise that Slovenia's national sport is skiing: look at a topographic map and you'll see that the northern two-thirds of the country is heavily crinkled – dominated by a series of massifs extending east from the Julian Alps. With reliable snow from December to March, January is the sweet spot to carve the slopes without the crowds – after Christmas holidays and before the February half-term break. Resorts such as Vogel, Kranjska Gora, Mariborsko Pohorje, Krvavec and Kanin combine a range of pistes with gorgeous scenery – Slovenia is heavily wooded, with spectacular mountain landscapes dotted with churches and villages that look quite magical dusted with snow. It's not all downhill: snowboarders and cross-country skiers have plenty to get excited about, while sledding and snowshoeing are also on the menu. Prices are low compared with other alpine ski destinations and facilities for beginners and children are excellent.

Trip plan: Slovenia's compact size means it's easy to access all ski areas – none are over 80 miles from the airport at Ljubljana.

Need to know: If driving in the far northwestern mountains, be careful on the highest passes – Vršič Pass is often closed for long periods after heavy snow.

Other months: Dec-Mar – winter; May-Jun & Sep – warm, dry, great hiking, beach weather; Jul-Aug – beaches and lakes busy; Apr & Oct-Nov – cool, wetter.

- Adventure
- Value
- Food & drink

SWITZERLAND

⛄ ☆

→ **Why now?** Mingle with the A-list in one of the world's best winter-sports resorts.

To discover skiing at its best, come to where it all began. The ski holiday was born in St Moritz, in eastern Switzerland's Engadine valley, a little over 150 years ago. It's still arguably the world's best spot for winter sports, with 217 miles (350km) of slopes to tackle across three main areas: Corviglia, Corvatsch (with great glacier descents) and Diavolezza. Cheap, it isn't – this resort is a magnet for the wealthy and glamorous – but in January there's really nowhere better to barrel down a black run. Some 99 miles (160km) of groomed trails take cross-country skiers into the spectacular surrounding woodlands, and afterwards you can soak those weary muscles in a thermal spa bath. St Moritz also offers a near-unique opportunity to really test your nerves on the Cresta Run, the infamous three-quarter-mile (1.2km) ice toboggan track. The Cresta, built in 1884, is open from late December; even novices with nerves of steel can lie on a skeleton bob and hurtle down its bends.

Trip plan: The closest international airport is Zürich, about 125 miles (200km) and a scenic four-hour train ride away.

Need to know: Beginner slots on the Cresta Run are limited – book well ahead (www.cresta-run.com).

Other months: Dec-Apr – winter, snowy, skiing; May-Sep – warm, good sightseeing and hiking, snow on high passes until Jun; Oct-Nov – cold, grey.

Adventure
Personal growth

SOUTHEAST BRITISH COLUMBIA
CANADA

⛄ 🚙

→ **Why now?** Powder, powder, powder.

Sure, Whistler has the nightlife and the glamour, but there's more to skiing BC. In January, the southeast of the province revels in huge dumps of powder – over 8m in some spots – and with a range of resorts from quaint old-style towns to big family-friendly affairs, there are dozens of great reasons to explore the area. Rather than basing yourself in one resort, try a mobile ski safari. Head to Rossland, an old mining village, for a day or so on Red Mountain for challenging terrain. Nearby Nelson is the base for Whitewater, a small resort with similarly skimpy crowds. Then haul east for a day or two at Fernie, an attractive town framed by mountains on four sides, and with well over 100 runs plus varied terrain including good tree skiing. Then there's Revelstoke and Big White to the northwest… How long have you got?

Trip plan: A loop through the ski areas could start at Spokane over the border in Washington State (stop off at Schweitzer en route) or possibly Kelowna, near the huge, family-friendly Big White Resort.

Need to know: Crossing the mountains in snowstorms can be challenging – be sure to use winter tyres and carry chains.

Other months: Dec-Mar – winter; Apr-Oct – good hiking, snow lingers at altitude until Jun; Nov – cold.

Adventure
Journey

BUDAPEST
HUNGARY

🏛 🌴

→ **Why now?** Soak amid steam in the city of thermal baths.

Hungary's elegant capital won't leave you with cold feet. The land on which it's built is peppered with more than 120 hot springs, many open to the public as thermal baths – from the Turkish-style Rudas Baths to the art nouveau gem at the Gellért and vast Széchenyi. The city itself is glorious at any time, the medieval marvels of Buda's Castle Hill contrasting with the Secessionist glory of Pest. And with buzzing nightlife ranging from grunge-chic pubs to a performance at the magnificent neo-Renaissance State Opera House, there's plenty to keep you entertained through the long, dark evenings.

Trip plan: The main decision to make is whether to stay on the west bank of the Danube in Buda, dominated by the medieval sights of Castle Hill, or in art nouveau Pest on the opposite bank. Exploring is easy on the comprehensive metro, train and tram network.

Need to know: Not all baths open every day, and a few are men- or women-only on some days – check in advance. You're usually allowed to stay for two hours on weekdays, 90 minutes on weekends.

Other months: Jan-Jun & Aug-Oct – most pleasant; Jul-Aug – hot, busy; Nov-Dec – cold, wet.

Cultural
Relaxation

The waters of Dove Lake, backed by Cradle Mountain, Tasmania

16

© kjekol / Getty Images

(L) A lion watches for lunch in the Serengeti
(R) A worshipper at the church of Bet Amanuel, Lalibela

TASMANIA
AUSTRALIA

Why now? Enjoy fabulous food, walking and wildlife in the sun.

It may no longer be dubbed the 'Apple Isle', but Tassie is still a taste sensation, with artisan growers and producers packing market stalls and restaurants with local delicacies. The epicurean epicentre, Bruny Island, is a hop south of capital Hobart; come in January to roam its walking trails and swaths of empty beaches in the sunshine, working up an appetite for fresh oysters, cheeses and sausages, and tipples from Australia's southernmost winery. Keep an eye out for pademelons, quolls, potaroos and Bruny's famed white wallabies. Burn off more calories with active adventures further afield – from day hikes around iconic Cradle Mountain to multi-day treks including the Overland Track and recently opened Three Capes Track.

Trip plan: Flights from Melbourne, Sydney and Brisbane serve Hobart. Tasmania's best explored on a self-drive odyssey, visiting the haunting convict site Port Arthur, the sweep of Wineglass Bay, artsy Launceston, the Gordon River harbour at Strahan, and Cradle Mountain, returning via the historic settlements along the Heritage Hwy.

Need to know: In summer, ferries depart Kettering for Bruny Island (www.brunyislandferry.com.au) at least hourly from 6.30am to 7pm.

Other months: Nov-Mar – driest, sunniest, best for outdoors; Apr-Oct – cooler.

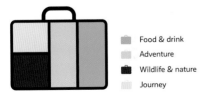

- Food & drink
- Adventure
- Wildlife & nature
- Journey

ETHIOPIA

Why now? Celebrate Christmas and Timkat among ancient sites in dry weather.

There's nowhere quite like Ethiopia: the religion, the languages, the food, the coffee – oh, the coffee… Even clocks and calendars throw up quirks: new year is 11 September, but it's on 7 January that Christmas (Leddet or Gena) is celebrated by throngs of devotees among the frescoed subterranean churches of Lalibela, carved into the solid rock in the 12th and 13th centuries. A bigger spectacle still is Timkat, commemorating Jesus' baptism; it's most dramatic among the 17th-century castles of Gonder, where priests march tabots – replicas of the Ark of the Covenant – to Fasildas' Bath for an overnight vigil followed by splashy baptisms. Away from the gladdened crowds there's space to explore Ethiopia's other wonders in this dry, cool month. North of Gonder loom the ancient *stelae* (obelisks) of Aksum, and trails meandering among gelada monkeys and precipitous ridges of the Simien Mountains, while to the south lies Lake Tana, lined with medieval monasteries.

Trip plan: Fly into capital Addis Ababa, from where domestic flights link Lalibela, Gonder, Aksum and Bahir Dar (for Lake Tana), allowing at least 10 days.

Need to know: Timkat is usually 19 January, but 20th in Ethiopian leap years.

Other months: Oct-Apr – largely dry; May-Sep – wet in many areas.

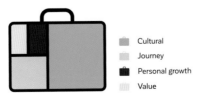

- Cultural
- Journey
- Personal growth
- Value

SOUTHERN SERENGETI
TANZANIA

Why now? Watch hundreds of thousands of grazing wildebeest.

If those images of wildebeest plunging through croc-infested rivers, or of lions stalking the herds across the vast Masai Mara have enticed you, think on this: each of those gnus came from somewhere. And that somewhere is their mother, who fattened up on the grasses of the southern Serengeti before calving in one of the world's great synchronised breeding events, producing up to half a million young each year. January is the time to explore this less-visited patch of Africa, watching herds of wildebeest and zebra as they munch their way across the short-grass plains, stocking up on calories before giving birth from late January – which is also when predator action can be thrilling. Perhaps 1.5 million gnus continue northwest on their cyclical migration around April. During the 'short rains', discounts may be found at some safari camps. You're also close to Olduvai Gorge, the famed 'Cradle of Mankind' known for finds of early hominid remains, and the wildlife-dense Ngorongoro Crater.

Trip plan: Fly into the Seronera airstrip from Arusha, and base yourself at a lodge in that zone.

Need to know: Most non-African nationals require a visa, usually available on arrival at major airports for US$50.

Other months: Dec-Feb – dry, wildebeest grazing; Mar-May – long rains; Jun-Sep – peak season, migration in north Serengeti and Masai Mara; Oct-Dec – short rains.

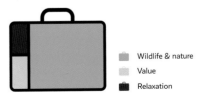

- Wildlife & nature
- Value
- Relaxation

Sydney's Opera House was completed in 1973

© Matt Munro / Lonely Planet

TRANSYLVANIA
ROMANIA

A shepherd tending his flock on hilltop pastures, Transylvania

Why now? Explore fairytale castles and track wolves amid mountains. For some, the castles and mountains of Transylvania are the stuff of fairytales; for others, vampire-plagued nightmares. Either way, a winter visit is the way to explore those fantasies in the most atmospheric conditions – magical for families. The 14th-century Bran Castle, sometimes touted as Dracula's lair (though connections with Vlad III Ţepeş, the historical Dracula, are slender), is at its dramatic best, while medieval cities such as Sibiu and Sighişoara (birthplace of Vlad III) are dusted with extra magic as snow frosts their rooftops. There are ample opportunities for burning off those Christmas calories, with snowshoeing, ski-touring or hiking excursions in the winter wonderland of the Carpathian Mountains, following wolf tracks in the glistening snow.

Romania offers great value, too, with a stay at its Hotel of Ice cheaper than a night in its Scandinavian or Canadian counterparts.

Trip planner: A week to 10 days provides time for a loop from Bucharest or Sibiu – the two most convenient airports – through Sibiu, Sighişoara, Braşov and Bran.

Need to know: Wrap up – the mercury can drop to -20°C (-4°F) in the high mountains in midwinter.

Other months: Dec-Feb – very cold, snowy; Jun-Aug – warm, dry, good hiking; Apr & Sep-Oct – mild, colourful flora; May – very wet; Mar & Nov – cool.

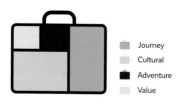

- Journey
- Cultural
- Adventure
- Value

SYDNEY
AUSTRALIA

→ **Why now?** Get a cultural kick with the diverse acts of the Sydney Festival.

Sure, it's hot, it's busy and it's brash – but Sydney in midsummer is also thrilling and plain gorgeous. January ushers in the hundreds of events comprising the Sydney Festival, three weeks of everything from circus and country to opera and film scores via dance performances, art installations, burlesque shows and family activities. Beyond the events and opera house, beaches and bridge, though, Sydney's natural wonders beg to be explored. Discover new perspectives on the harbour with a walk – the Manly to Spit Bridge route, perhaps – or head a little further to roam the lush forests, Aboriginal rock art and cool coastal breezes of Ku-ring-gai Chase National Park or Royal National Park (the world's second national park, gazetted in 1879).

Trip plan: After a few days enjoying the cultural and culinary delights of the city, branch out to explore the nearby parks – Ku-ring-gai Chase offers great hiking and mountain biking.

Need to know: You'll need an Opal Card to use public transport, including ferries – pick up and load a card with a minimum of A$10 at convenience stores across the city.

Other months: Dec-Feb – summer, hot, busier; Mar-Apr – autumn, more rain; May-Aug – winter, cooler, can be drier than summer; Sep-Nov – spring, dry, warm.

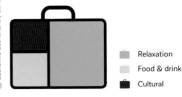

Relaxation
Food & drink
Cultural

TRANS-SIBERIAN RAILWAY RUSSIA

Why now? Visions of Siberia from a heated railway carriage.

Sure, it's cold outside – expect the mercury to dip to -26°C (-15°F) at Khabarovsk – but isn't that the point? You don't travel to Siberia for sun and sand: this is the land of fir forests and grasslands, both of which look better under a blanket of snow. Usually when folks talk about the Trans-Siberian, they mean the Trans-Mongolian, which loops south from Irkutsk through the Mongolian capital Ulaanbaatar before reaching Běijīng, providing glimpses of nomads' yurts on the steppe. But whichever route you choose, you'll spend most time crossing Siberia, stopping at Perm, Yekaterinburg and Irkutsk on the shores of Baikal. Bring a good book and a ready smile for the strangers with whom you'll share carriages (and bottles of vodka).

Trip plan: Choose between the 6152-mile (9900km), seven-night Moscow to Vladivostok Trans-Siberian Railway; the 4735-mile (7620km), six-night Trans-Mongolian to Běijīng; or the 5623-mile (9050km), six-night Trans-Manchurian to Běijīng via Harbin.

Need to know: As well as the clean public trains, several luxurious private services run the route – for example, the Golden Eagle.

Other months: Nov-Mar – very cold; Apr & Oct – slightly warmer, popular times; May-Sep – reliably above 0°C (32°F).

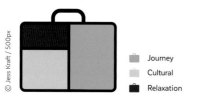

Journey
Cultural
Relaxation

COLOMBIA

Why now? Explore this diverse Latin American land in temperate days.

Latin America's most intriguing hotspot is beguiling in January, when the weather is warm and dry, and the Hay Festival adds a literary sheen with big-name authors speaking among the bougainvillea-clad balconies and cobbled alleys of Cartagena de Indias' old town. But this beauty by the Caribbean isn't the only appealing spot: capital Bogotá has its own colonial quarter, La Candelaria, while the coffee plantations of the central highlands offer opportunities to learn about traditional lifestyles in haciendas and farmstays. For a trip further back in time, delve into the Sierra Nevada de Santa Marta mountains of the north on a four-day trek to reach the 'lost city', Ciudad Perdida, built by the Tayrona people a millennium ago and rediscovered in the 1970s.

Trip plan: A two-week loop from Bogotá could take in the Zipaquirá Salt Cathedral, the Zona Cafetera, the beaches and jungles of Tayrona National Park, the trek to Ciudad Perdida and a few days in comely Cartagena.

Need to know: Many visitors, including those from the US, UK, Australia and New Zealand, receive a 90-day tourist visa on arrival. It's best not to bring in large amounts of cash.

Other months: Dec-Mar – warm, dry; Apr-Jun – some rain, regional variations; Jul-Sep – dry areas, busy; Oct-Nov – wet, low prices.

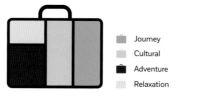

Journey
Cultural
Adventure
Relaxation

GRENADA

Why now? Get a taste of the 'spice isle' in the balmy dry season.

The island nation at the very southern tip of the Windward Islands is a tasty destination: known for its nutmeg heritage, today Grenada produces exceptional chocolate as well as a range of spices for which it's famed. Those spice plantations line fertile valleys and hillsides clad with rainforests, offering great hiking to remote waterfalls. But let's face it: most of us come to the Caribbean to loll, not lope, and Grenada's beaches – on the main island, particularly spectacular Grand Anse, plus the sleepy little isle of Carriacou to the northeast – are the big draw. But while a helping of winter sun is a treat, there are good reasons to stir from the sun lounger. Beneath the waves, kaleidoscopic coral reefs and the underwater sculptures of Jason deCaires Taylor make for terrific snorkelling and diving during the calm, clear days of January – visibility is usually over 15m, often closer to 30m.

Trip plan: Fly to Maurice Bishop International Airport in the southwest, close to most beaches and resorts.

Need to know: Grenada is at the southern edge of the hurricane belt, so is rarely affected by tropical storms.

Other months: Jan-May – dry and warm (Jan-Apr: busiest); Jun-Dec – heavy showers.

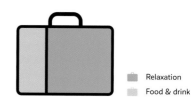

Relaxation
Food & drink

Spot elk and even wolves in the forests of Eastern Poland

EASTERN POLAND

→ **Why now?** Track wolves and lynx through epic wintry wilderness.

Here be giants: wisent, or European bison – the continent's largest land mammal – stand up to 1.8m high and can weigh nearly a tonne. Białowieża National Park, a sprawling reserve that's part of the primeval Białowieża Forest spanning the borders of Poland and Belarus, is the stronghold of the bison, reintroduced here in 1929 after wild bison became extinct in Europe in 1919; about 500 now live free in the Polish part of the forest. Midwinter is the time for a thrilling expedition tracking bison, wolf and elk (moose) footprints through the snow, and watching for boar, lynx and pine martens. If you don't catch a glimpse of wild bison, be awed by captive-bred beasts at the show reserve. Nearby Biebrza National Park is another winter wonderland, a marshy valley where the big draw is elk – head out to track one of the reserve's 600 residents and you might also enjoy

encounters with otters, boars or wolves.

Trip plan: Fly to Warsaw before going east to Białowieża and Biebrza national parks – allow at least four days for the trip to Białowieża alone, a week to include both parks.

Need to know: Temperatures average about -5°C (23°F) in January, and may drop much lower – pack warm clothes.

Other months: Dec-Feb – winter, snowy; May-Oct – warm, good wildlife-watching; Nov & Mar-Apr – cold, can be wet.

■ Wildlife & nature
■ Adventure

BULGARIA

→ **Why go?** Enjoy bang-for-buck ski action for beginners in the Balkans.

For a budget ski break it's hard to beat Bulgaria, when reliable snow combines with low costs. Accommodation is great value, food and drink are cheap, and a lift pass could set you back less than half the price of one in an Alps resort. Of course, that's not a like-for-like comparison as Bulgaria's three main ski areas – Borovets in the Rila Mountains south of capital Sofia, Bansko further south in the Pirin Mountains, and

Pamporovo to the east near Plovdiv – have fewer runs; the largest, Bansko, has only 47 miles (75km) of piste. Yet you get more than you pay for in this friendly country: affordable lessons, and fine red Mavrud wines and food combine for good après-ski. The churches and museums of Bansko's old quarter are worth exploring, and the perky capital, Sofia, demands a day or two to discover its Roman remains and Ottoman relics.

Trip plan: Borovets is just an hour's drive from Sofia Airport, Bansko two hours.

Pamporovo is best reached from Plovdiv.

Need to know: With few black runs, Bulgaria is less exciting for advanced skiers.

Other months: Jan-Mar – ski season; Apr-Sep – good for hiking and exploring cities; Oct-Dec – cold, wetter.

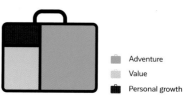

■ Adventure
■ Value
■ Personal growth

MYANMAR (BURMA)

→ **Why now?** Cruise the Ayeyarwady River and explore the temples of Bagan under a warm sun.

Myanmar is, it could fairly be claimed, Asia's warmest country. Not measured in celsius or fahrenheit, but in the smiles of its unfailingly welcoming people. Its roster of sights, sounds and smells is enticing, too: the 'winking wonder' of golden Shwedagon Paya in former capital Yangon; the pony-drawn carriages and strawberries of hill station Pyin Oo Lwin; the temples and leg-rowing fishermen of serene Inle Lake. The ideal 'road to Mandalay' is a ribbon not of tarmac but water: the Ayeyarwady (Irrawaddy) River, snaking between Yangon and that former royal capital, and in full flow in January. Board an old-style riverboat for a cruise past rural landscapes, villages and ancient sites – none more jaw-dropping than the vast plain of Bagan, studded with thousands of millennium-old stupas, pagodas and temples.

Trip plan: Yangon and Mandalay receive international flights. A two-week counterclockwise circuit from Yangon takes in the golden-boulder-balanced stupa at Kyaiktiyo, Inle Lake and hilltribes around Kalaw, Pyin Oo Lwin and Mandalay's temples and palace, before cruising downstream via Bagan and the Ayeyarwady delta.

Need to know: The entrance fee for Bagan Archaeological Zone, currently 25,000 kyat (about US$22), is valid for five days.

Other months: Oct-Apr – dry (Dec-Feb: peak season, cooler); May-Sep – rainy, hot, prices lower.

Cultural
Journey
Value

Young and old: a novice monk and crumbling pagodas at Shwe Inn Thein (R)

© Andrew Montgomery / Lonely Planet

CATLINS COAST & STEWART ISLAND
NEW ZEALAND

→ **Why now?** Explore New Zealand's wildest coastline and island.

New Zealand's not short of dramatic vistas – but the Catlins Coast is something else: a wild stretch of cliffs, temperate rainforest and the South Island's southernmost point. A midsummer road trip is the ideal way to discover its delights. Fill the tank and head off on the snaking Southern Scenic Route between Balclutha and Waipapa Point, pausing to watch for fur and elephant seals, whales, dolphins and yellow-eyed penguins en route. Just across the Foveaux Strait lies Stewart Island, known to Maori as Rakiura – 'Land of Glowing Skies'. Explore this luminous island, now 85% protected as national park, hiking the many trails and empty beaches, delving into lofty rimu forest and spotting day-dwelling kiwis and other birdlife. This is New Zealand at its more remote and unpopulated.

Trip plan: Allow at least two days for the road trip from Nugget Point – about 62 miles (100km) south of Dunedin – to Waiapapa Point, plus a few days on Stewart Island/Rakiura.

Need to know: Reaching Stewart Island/Rakiura involves a short (but often bumpy) flight from Invercargill or an hour-long (and also frequently rough) boat crossing from Bluff to Oban.

Other months: Dec-Apr – summer, dry weather for touring; May-Nov – cooler.

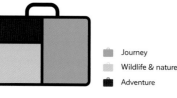
Journey
Wildlife & nature
Adventure

HONSHU JAPAN

→ **Why now?** For reduced crowds and prettier sights.

Japan's main island won't be warm in January, but it looks swell. Mt Fuji and the Japanese Alps are cloaked in snow, and low precipitation leaves skies clear and views at their most spectacular – you're more likely to be able to see Fuji's iconic cone from downtown Tokyo. Also, cultural highlights such as Kyoto temples are far less crowded. Days are short, but the bright lights of Tokyo will easily counter that. Warming up isn't a problem either: Japanese *onsen* (hot baths) and restaurants serving *nabe* (hotpot) and warm sake at *kotatsu* (tables with under-heating and blankets) will do the trick. Japan's excellent trains run without a hitch, and are super-heated, so you can glide across the country, sightseeing in the warmth as you go. And as this is off-season, room rates are lower, too.

Trip plan: With a JapanRail Pass, explore Honshu's highlights by *shinkansen* (bullet train). Link buzzing Tokyo with Kyoto, Osaka, Hiroshima and Takayama in the Japanese Alps. Fuji-Hakone National Park can be reached by train from Tokyo.

Need to know: JapanRail Passes must be bought before arrival in Japan.

Other months: Dec-Mar – cold, often clear and dry; Apr-May – cherry blossom, pricey; Jun-Jul – rainy; Aug – warm, busy; Sep-Nov – autumn colours.

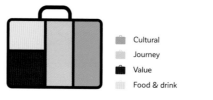
Cultural
Journey
Value
Food & drink

KERALA INDIA

→ **Why now?** Find your inner glow on a winter sun and yoga break in 'God's own country'.

Over the past couple of decades the beaches of Varkala and Kovalam have morphed from the peaceful preserves of fishermen and Hindu devotees into backpacker hangouts and on into full-blown resorts studded with exclusive hotels. But with serene stretches of sand still to be found here and there, you can take your pick of the trance parties, hot hotels and restful homestays. After the overindulgence of Christmas, Kerala offers opportunities for taking stock and detoxing on a yoga retreat, and exploring the backwaters on a rice barge or heading into the Western Ghats for cool air and wildlife-watching among the forested slopes and tea plantations.

Trip plan: Fly to Kochi via Delhi or Mumbai for the short transfer to Varkala, Kovalam or a homestay or retreat in the inland foothills. Alleppey is the starting point for most backwater cruises, while Munnar is a great hill-station centre for hiking and wildlife-watching in Chinnar Wildlife Sanctuary.

Need to know: Most visitors to India require a visa. Apply for an e-visa at least a week before travel.

Other months: Dec-Mar – dry, not too hot; Apr-May – very hot; Jun-Jul – very wet; Aug-Nov – slightly less rainy, heating up.

Relaxation
Cultural
Food & drink
Value

© Lottie Davies / Lonely Planet

VIENNA, AUSTRIA

→ **Why now? Waltz in the wintry glamour of the famed ball season.**
The Austrian capital enchants in any season, its melange of baroque and art nouveau, imperial grandeur and cafe culture endlessly appealing. But to admire the city resplendent in all its finery, visit during the peak ball season – January into February, when some 300-plus balls entertain tux- and gown-clad socialites waltzing the night away. And though events sport names such as Doctors', Lawyers' and Hunters' Ball, many are open to all – simply buy a ticket (well in advance), dress up for the occasion and prepare to be dazzled by the atmosphere and music. Of course, the city doesn't just wake at night – it continues to bustle under a wintry cloak of snow each day, with palaces, churches and museums to explore – don't miss the imperial Hofburg, Kunsthistorisches (Art History) Museum or the bling baroque palaces Schloss Schönbrunn and Schloss Belvedere. And with coffee and cake beckoning from charming cafes on every street corner, plus hip bars and restaurants lining streets around the city, it's a culinary delight, too.
Trip plan: Arrive, explore, waltz, eat and drink!
Need to know: Strict dress codes apply at most balls – tuxedo or dinner jacket for men, gowns for women. These may be hired at various stores in the city.
Other months: Year-round – busy; Jan-Feb – ball season; Jun-Aug – summer, busiest.

© Helen Cathcart / Lonely Planet

Sweet treats and a coffee at a Vienna cafe

Cultural

Food & drink

BEYOND VIENNA

BRATISLAVA, SLOVAKIA · 40 MILES (64KM) · Cafe culture in the 18th-century Old Town

KREMS & DÜRNSTEIN · 52 MILES (84KM) · Baroque houses and monasteries plus a ruined medieval castle

BUDAPEST, HUNGARY · 150 MILES (241KM) · Art nouveau masterpieces and steaming thermal baths

SALZBURG, AUSTRIA · 190 MILES (306KM) · The hills are alive with the sound of music...

ANDAMAN COAST
THAILAND

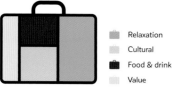

→ **Why now?** Soak up the rays and snorkel the seas during warm, dry days.

You come for the beaches, sure – and maybe that's enough, with a sprinkling of sundowners and tongue-tingling Thai dishes to round off the beach break. But there's plenty more to enjoy on Thailand's southwest coast in the shortish dry season. The photogenic karst-rock outcrops around Krabi call to climbers ranging from beginners to experts, and coral gardens and wrecks offer spectacular diving and snorkelling – Richelieu Rock (near the Myanmar border) and Hin Daeng off Ko Lanta are arguably the country's two best dive sites. With fine white-sand beaches and idyllic islands lining pretty much the whole coast, and accommodation ranging from backpacker shacks on Phi Phi to family-friendly and exclusive resorts on Phuket, you can find whatever kind of sun, sea and sand holiday appeals – peaceful or party-packed.

Trip plan: Who needs a plan? You could fly to Phuket or Krabi and just loll, or expand your horizons and add on some city action in Bangkok or Chiang Mai, both also dry in January.

Need to know: The Andaman Coast really gets hit by the monsoon between April and November.

Other months: Dec-Mar – warm and dry countrywide except Gulf islands; May-Oct – rainy on Andaman coast; Apr & Nov – shoulder, some rain.

Relaxation
Cultural
Food & drink
Value

LORD HOWE ISLAND
AUSTRALIA

→ **Why now?** Escape the hustle on a gorgeous, far-flung outpost of Australia.

Australia's beaches and cities seethe in January. Not so Lord Howe Island. This verdant, volcanic Unesco-listed speck, adrift in the southwest Pacific some 373 miles (600km) northeast of Sydney, allows only 400 visitors to stay at any time, so peace is guaranteed. As are terrific snorkelling and diving on the world's southernmost coral reefs and other sites, including Balls Pyramid – the world's tallest rock stack, soaring 1808ft (551m) from the waves – which might reward you with sightings of turtles, dolphins, double-headed wrasse and Galapagos whaler sharks. In January the water's a balmy 24°C (75°F), while sea breezes keep things cool on land. The island is laced with walking trails, notably the eight-hour trek up 2871ft (875m) Mt Gower, rewarded with a 360-degree panorama across the craggy island. Board-riders head to Blinky Beach for the 'champagne surf', and birdwatchers are blissful: among the 130-plus migratory and resident species are red-tailed tropicbirds – watch them perform their balletic courtship behaviour from the Malabar cliffs.

Trip plan: With only 400 tourist beds on the island, spots get booked up early. Daily flights from Sydney reach Lord Howe Island in under two hours.

Need to know: Embrace the digital detox – there's no mobile-phone coverage.

Other months: Year-round – seas warm (Sep-Jun: peak).

BOTSWANA

→ **Why now?** Enjoy a discounted luxury safari in the 'green season', among few other visitors

Botswana offers some of the world's most memorable wildlife experiences: you could spot bountiful game while gliding in a *mokoro* (dugout canoe) along the channels of the inland Okavango Delta, or be overwhelmed by gargantuan herds of elephant and buffalo in Chobe National Park. However, it's expensive: the policy of low-volume, high-cost tourism means safari prices are among the highest anywhere. The euphemistically named 'green season' brings costs crashing down by up to 40% – and though afternoon thunderstorms are common, you're unlikely to be rained out all day. And since the lush, verdant landscape is bustling with migratory birds, young animals and the predators that hunt them, it's also a great time to spot wildlife. Caveat: the annual flooding of the Okavango Delta actually happens in Botswana's dry season so *mokoro* safaris are limited to permanently full channels.

Trip plan: Fly from capital Gaborone to Maun, and combine stays in two lodges or camps in different parts of the delta.

Need to know: Some roads and tracks become impassable in the wet season, and camps and lodges may close.

Other months: Nov-Apr – 'green season', low prices; May-Oct – dry season (from Jun: Okavango floods arrive).

Krabi's coastal cliffs are a magnet for the world's rock climbers

- Relaxation
- Wildlife & nature
- Adventure

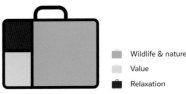

- Wildlife & nature
- Value
- Relaxation

A guide following ancient Mayan trails near Cruce Dos Aguadas, Guatemala

GUATEMALA

Why now? Learn Spanish in Guatemala's charming cultural hub, Antigua.

New year, new challenge, new language. If the gauntlet you've thrown down to yourself is to master Spanish, Guatemala's the perfect place, with countless good-quality schools – and now's the perfect time, in the midst of the dry season. Nestled between a trio of volcanoes, Antigua harbours many dozens of language schools in its cobbled, ochre-hued colonial streets; a week or two of one-on-one lessons (typically between two and six hours each day) will have you mastering the basics before heading off to test your new tongue among the ancient Mayan temples, high-altitude volcanic lakes and colourful markets. Add valuable practice with a homestay while you study – being forced to speak Spanish outside lesson time will boost your competence.

Trip plan: Antigua is half an hour by road from Guatemala City Airport by bus or taxi. Book accommodation and lessons before arriving in high season, including January.

Need to know: Though Antigua has the largest number of language schools, other popular destinations for learning Spanish include Quetzaltenango and Panajachel on Lake Atitlán.

Other months: Nov-Apr – dry, travel most comfortable; May-Oct – rainy (Jul-Aug: also busy).

Personal growth
Cultural
Journey

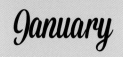

ANTARCTIC PENINSULA & SOUTH GEORGIA

→ Why now? Bask in near permanent daylight in this enormous white wilderness at the end of the world. High summer on the Antarctic Peninsula brings endless, warm days – well, it's all relative, isn't it? Temperatures 'soar' to freezing point or even a little higher in the middle of the austral summer. Certainly the locals appreciate it. In January you'll see – and hear – vast penguin colonies at their most raucous, with chicks (hatched at new year) demanding to be fed, and seal pups on South Georgia, while whale sightings rise towards the end of the month. Weather can't be guaranteed, of course, not least on the Drake Passage between Tierra del Fuego and the peninsula – you might get the 'Drake Shake' or just as easily the 'Drake Lake' – but at least in January you have a good chance of sailing among gargantuan icebergs and soaring cliffs while sunshine glints off water and ice.

Trip plan: Most cruises heading for the Antarctic Peninsula sail from Ushuaia on Tierra del Fuego, southern Argentina, and last around 11 to 14 days. Adding South Georgia increases duration by a few days.

Need to know: The Drake Passage crossing takes at least two days in each direction. It's possible to fly from Punta Arenas (Chile) to King George Island on one or both legs, avoiding the crossing.

Other months: Nov-Mar – summer, Antarctica accessible to tourist ships; Apr-Oct – winter, dark, cold, difficult to visit.

Victorian-era shopfronts in the ski haven of Silverton, Colorado

© Mark Read / Lonely Planet

COLORADO USA

→ Why now? Ski fresh dumps of powder snow in high, dry Colorado. If you absolutely, positively must get stuck into some deep, fresh powder in January, Colorado hits the mark. Known for its dry climate and reliable December dumps, the state boasts a whopping 25 ski areas, with plenty to offer for all levels (and pockets). Sure, the big names like Aspen, Vail and Telluride can sap your wallet, but there are other places that test the nerves more than the bank balance: try the lo-fi but challenging terrain at Silverton Mountain.

Elsewhere, beginners lap up gentle slopes at Buttermilk or family-friendly Powderhown and Cooper. The aprés-ski is distinctive in Colorado, too. With some 300 craft breweries across the state you can expect hop-tinged joy, and you can fuel up on hearty Mexican chow, gourmet burgers with swanky truffle fries or bone-in local lamb.

Trip plan: Pick your resort to match your expertise. Advanced? Consider Silverton. Families and beginners? Head for Purgatory or Buttermilk.

Need to know: Book ahead, particularly for weekends and during special events in January – Breckenridge's ULLR Fest and Wintersköl in Aspen, for example.

Other months: Nov-Mar – ski season; Apr-May & Sep-Oct – spring and fall, hiking weather; Jun-Aug – summer, hot, busy.

Journey
Wildlife & nature

Adventure
Food & drink
Personal growth

(L) Hiker looking out
to Petit Piton, St Lucia;
(R) Havana Coffee
Works, Wellington

ST LUCIA

🥂 ☆ 🌴

→ Why now? Enjoy a new year detox in the warm, dry Caribbean.

The emerald-green island of St Lucia, cloaked in rainforest and plantations, welcomes the dry season in January, along with holidaymakers looking to leave behind winter's chill and the vestiges of Christmas overindulgence. This volcanic island's fine beaches have garnered a glowing reputation, and with good reason – but now the range of novel spa treatments and fitness programs are bolstering the roster of attractions. As well as the familiar Ayurvedic massages, hot-rock treatments and yoga, you could slap on mud from the island's sulphurous hot springs, luxuriate in a cacao massage or embark on a holistic fitness program involving VO2 max testing, personal training and even a quadrathlon. Or you could just hit the beach…

Trip plan: Choose between the beaches of the northwest and the resorts around Soufrière bay in the southwest, with views of the Pitons.

Need to know: Most long-haul flights arrive at Hewanorra Airport, in the far south of the island; flights from other Caribbean islands tend to land at George FL Charles Airport near capital Castries and the northwest resorts.

Other months: Dec-May – driest, warm (late Dec-Mar: busiest); Jun-Nov – rainy season.

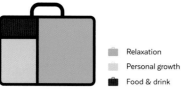

- Relaxation
- Personal growth
- Food & drink

© Justin Foulkes / Lonely Planet

WELLINGTON
NEW ZEALAND

→ **Why now?** Enjoy the warmest month in New Zealand's windy city.

New Zealand's capital welcomes *raumati* (summer in Māori) with a warmth to equal the rising mercury. From New Year's Day the Summer City vibe infuses Welly with a succession of events including free concerts in the Botanic Garden and the annual Pasifika Festival, celebrating the arts, music and food of the Pacific region. Add in perennial attractions – including some of the country's finest galleries and museums, particularly the 'box of treasures' that's Te Papa Tongarewa, and Zealandia eco-sanctuary – plus fine weather for exploring the beaches of the Miramar Peninsula and the forested hills hugging the city, or just enjoying cafe culture. And with a fair number of the country's finest eateries, you won't want for fuel.

Trip plan: Wellington has enough museums, galleries, shops, bars and restaurants to keep you busy for a few days, on top of outlying experiences such as Zealandia and winery tours.

Need to know: At least four ferries each day sail from Wellington for the three-hour voyage across the Cook Strait to Picton through the beautiful Marlborough Sounds, operated

© Pete Seaward / Lonely Planet

by Bluebridge (www.bluebridge.co.nz) and Interislander (www.interislander.co.nz).
Other months: Nov-Apr – pleasant temperatures; May-Oct – cooler, a little wetter.

- Cultural
- Food & drink
- Wildlife & nature

BEYOND WELLINGTON

MATIU/SOMES ISLAND · 5 MILES (8KM) · Historic lighthouse and quarantine station, native wildlife

KAPITI ISLAND · 37 MILES (60KM) · Rare birds, snorkelling and hiking

MARTINBOROUGH · 50 MILES (80KM) · Leafy old town, great wineries

NAPIER · 197 MILES (317KM) · Beautifully preserved art deco city

February

WHERE TO GO WHEN

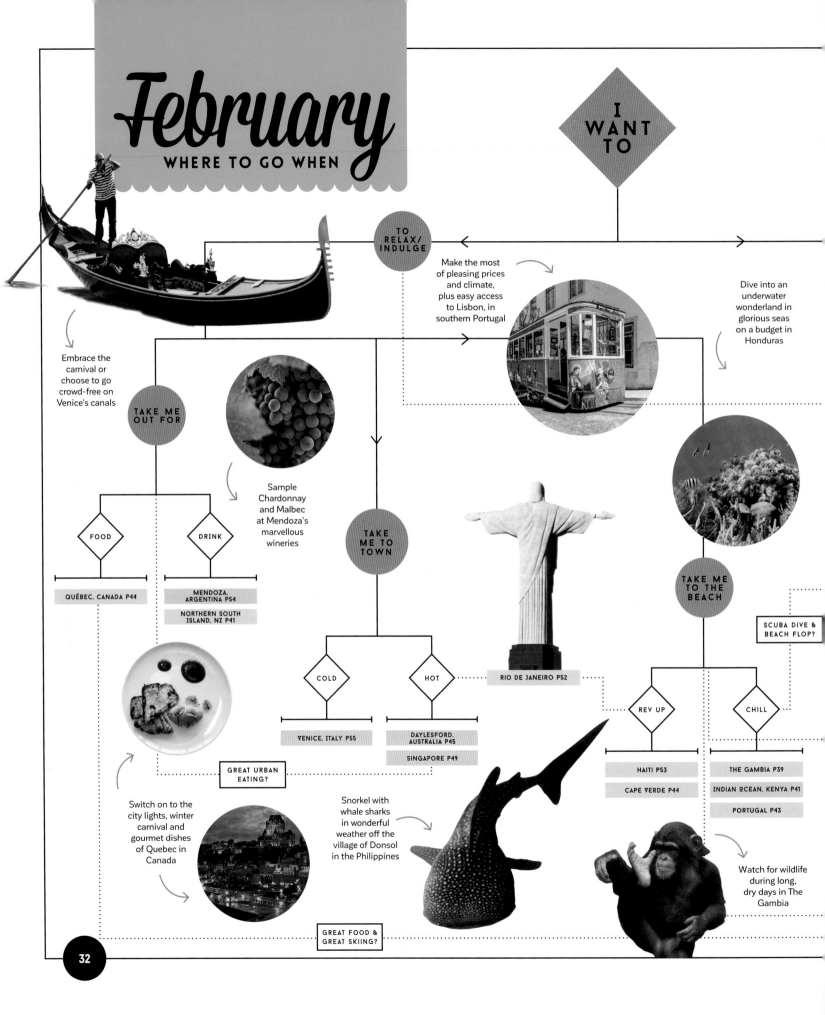

I WANT TO

TO RELAX/ INDULGE

Make the most of pleasing prices and climate, plus easy access to Lisbon, in southern Portugal

Dive into an underwater wonderland in glorious seas on a budget in Honduras

Embrace the carnival or choose to go crowd-free on Venice's canals

TAKE ME OUT FOR

Sample Chardonnay and Malbec at Mendoza's marvellous wineries

◇ **FOOD**

◇ **DRINK**

QUÉBEC, CANADA P44

MENDOZA, ARGENTINA P54

NORTHERN SOUTH ISLAND, NZ P41

TAKE ME TO TOWN

◇ **COLD**

◇ **HOT**

VENICE, ITALY P55

DAYLESFORD, AUSTRALIA P45

SINGAPORE P49

RIO DE JANEIRO P52

GREAT URBAN EATING?

Switch on to the city lights, winter carnival and gourmet dishes of Quebec in Canada

Snorkel with whale sharks in wonderful weather off the village of Donsol in the Philippines

TAKE ME TO THE BEACH

SCUBA DIVE & BEACH FLOP?

◇ **REV UP**

◇ **CHILL**

HAITI P53

CAPE VERDE P44

THE GAMBIA P39

INDIAN OCEAN, KENYA P41

PORTUGAL P43

Watch for wildlife during long, dry days in The Gambia

GREAT FOOD & GREAT SKIING?

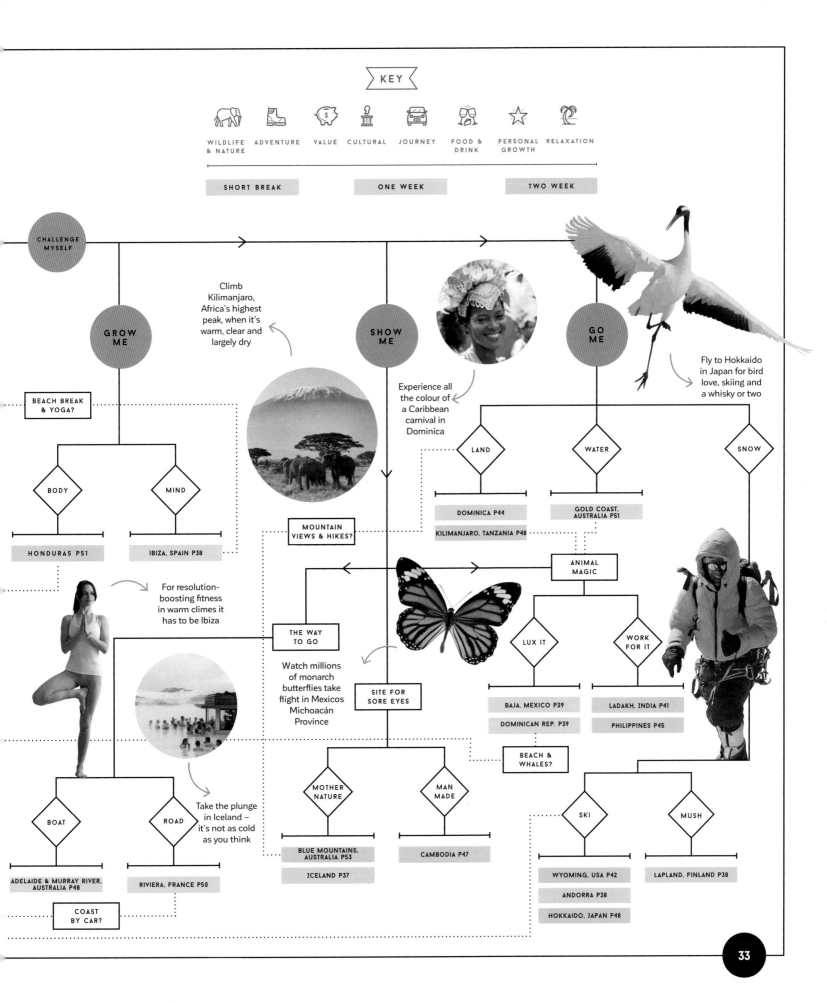

KEY

WILDLIFE & NATURE · ADVENTURE · VALUE · CULTURAL · JOURNEY · FOOD & DRINK · PERSONAL GROWTH · RELAXATION

SHORT BREAK · ONE WEEK · TWO WEEK

CHALLENGE MYSELF

GROW ME

BEACH BREAK & YOGA?

BODY → HONDURAS P51

MIND → IBIZA, SPAIN P38

For resolution-boosting fitness in warm climes it has to be Ibiza

THE WAY TO GO

BOAT → ADELAIDE & MURRAY RIVER, AUSTRALIA P48

ROAD → RIVIERA, FRANCE P50

COAST BY CAR?

Take the plunge in Iceland – it's not as cold as you think

Climb Kilimanjaro, Africa's highest peak, when it's warm, clear and largely dry

SHOW ME

Experience all the colour of a Caribbean carnival in Dominica

MOUNTAIN VIEWS & HIKES?

Watch millions of monarch butterflies take flight in Mexicos Michoacán Province

SITE FOR SORE EYES

MOTHER NATURE → BLUE MOUNTAINS, AUSTRALIA P53 / ICELAND P37

MAN MADE → CAMBODIA P47

GO ME

Fly to Hokkaido in Japan for bird love, skiing and a whisky or two

LAND → DOMINICA P44 / KILIMANJARO, TANZANIA P48

WATER → GOLD COAST, AUSTRALIA P51

SNOW

ANIMAL MAGIC

LUX IT → BAJA, MEXICO P39 / DOMINICAN REP. P39

WORK FOR IT → LADAKH, INDIA P41 / PHILIPPINES P45

BEACH & WHALES?

SKI → WYOMING, USA P42 / ANDORRA P38 / HOKKAIDO, JAPAN P48

MUSH → LAPLAND, FINLAND P38

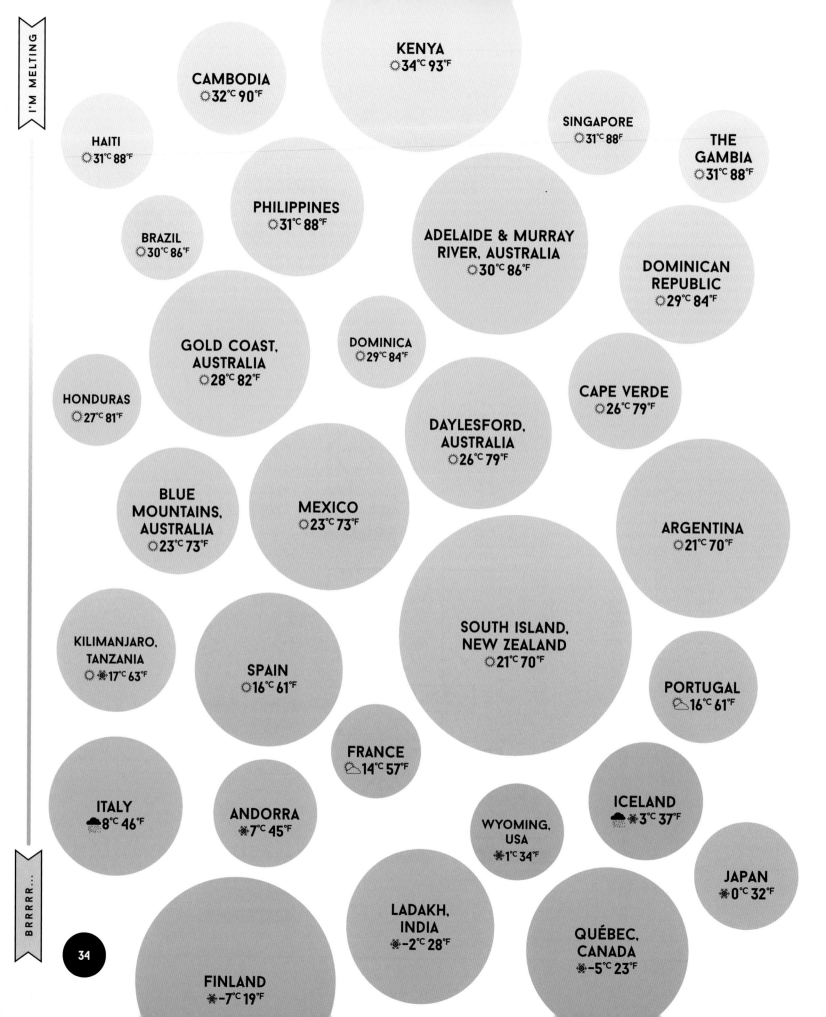

KENYA
☀34℃ 93°F

CAMBODIA
☀32℃ 90°F

SINGAPORE
☀31℃ 88°F

THE
GAMBIA
☀31℃ 88°F

HAITI
☀31℃ 88°F

PHILIPPINES
☀31℃ 88°F

ADELAIDE & MURRAY
RIVER, AUSTRALIA
☀30℃ 86°F

BRAZIL
☀30℃ 86°F

DOMINICAN
REPUBLIC
☀29℃ 84°F

GOLD COAST,
AUSTRALIA
☀28℃ 82°F

DOMINICA
☀29℃ 84°F

HONDURAS
☀27℃ 81°F

CAPE VERDE
☀26℃ 79°F

DAYLESFORD,
AUSTRALIA
☀26℃ 79°F

BLUE
MOUNTAINS,
AUSTRALIA
☀23℃ 73°F

MEXICO
☀23℃ 73°F

ARGENTINA
☀21℃ 70°F

KILIMANJARO,
TANZANIA
☀❄17℃ 63°F

SPAIN
☀16℃ 61°F

SOUTH ISLAND,
NEW ZEALAND
☀21℃ 70°F

PORTUGAL
⛅16℃ 61°F

FRANCE
⛅14℃ 57°F

ITALY
🌧8℃ 46°F

ANDORRA
❄7℃ 45°F

ICELAND
🌧3℃ 37°F

WYOMING,
USA
❄1℃ 34°F

JAPAN
❄0℃ 32°F

LADAKH,
INDIA
❄-2℃ 28°F

QUÉBEC,
CANADA
❄-5℃ 23°F

FINLAND
❄-7℃ 19°F

February

The dancing lights of the Aurora Borealis are on sparkling form this time of year

LAPLAND, FINLAND

Net freshwater crayfish on the rivers of South Australia in late summer

GOLD COAST, AUSTRALIA

ADELAIDE & MURRAY, AUSTRALIA

A gourmet feast after your town-centre ski? You must be vacationing in Québec City

QUÉBEC, CANADA

PORTUGAL

ANDORRA

DOMINICAN REPUBLIC

INDIAN OCEAN, KENYA

THE GAMBIA

Stay at the Chimpanzee Rehab Project on West Africa's 'Smiling Coast'

CAPE VERDE

SINGAPORE

SOUTH ISLAND, NZ

Revel in the costumes and calypso of the Dominica Carnival

MEXICO

Boost your sense of wellbeing at one of Ibiza's many yoga retreats

BLUE MOUNTAINS, AUSTRALIA

IBIZA

PHILIPPINES

Breathe-in the fresh Blue Mountain air from its panoramic cable car

DOMINICA

HONDURAS

DAYLESFORD, AUSTRALIA

RIVIERA, FRANCE

Enjoy Yellowstone's high slopes and hot springs minus the summer throng

The temples of Angkor astound beneath Cambodia's dry February skies

CAMBODIA

WYOMING, USA

VENICE

ICELAND

Carnival weekend is crazy, but otherwise Venice is all low-season calm

Ride with a gaucho before uncorking a Malbec in Argentina's wine country

LADAKH, INDIA

HOKKAIDO, JAPAN

Witness the majesty of the red-crowned crane on Japan's most northerly island

RIO, BRAZIL

Now's your chance to scale the mighty Kilimanjaro, towering over the African savannah

HAITI

KILIMANJARO, TANZANIA

MENDOZA, ARGENTINA

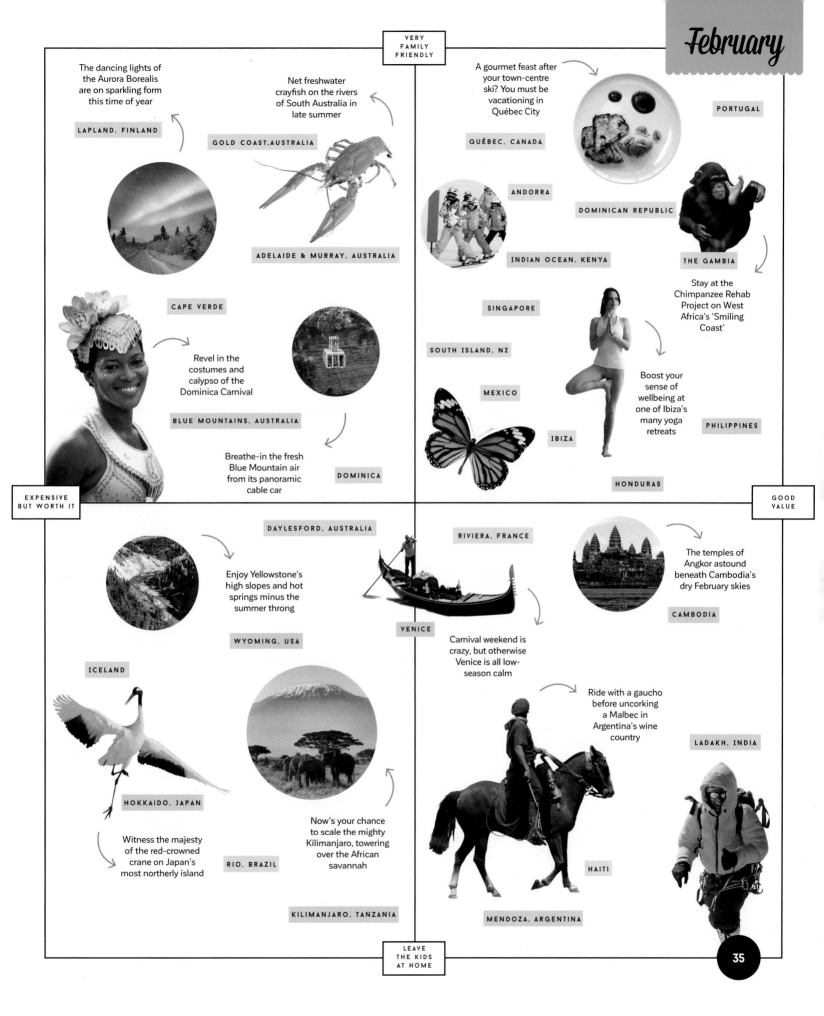

ICELAND

→ **Why now? It's not as cold as you think – but still very cool.**

Iceland in February might sound like a cold and gloomy prospect, but the truth is far from it. The Gulf Stream keeps this almost-Arctic island warmer than New York City (average: 37°F; 3°C) while, by month's end, the sun's up before 9am and doesn't set until after 6pm. Fortunately, this still leaves a good amount of darkness in which to (hopefully) see the Northern Lights. There are plenty of wintry activities on offer too: glacier hikes, snowmobile safaris, ice caving, superjeep drives across volcanoes. If you're careful, self-driving is still possible as the main ringroad is kept clear by snow-plough. You can even snorkel between the North American and Eurasian tectonic plates at Silfra – fed by glaciers, the water temperature varies little year-round, and you'll be snug inside a dry suit. If the cold does get too much, seek out one of Iceland's hot springs – maybe the fun-but-touristy Blue Lagoon or one of Reykjavík's cheaper public pools.

Trip plan: Arrange tours from Reykjavík. Spend a few nights away from the city lights for better odds of seeing aurora.

Need to know: Pack a swim suit so you can warm up in hot springs.

Other months: Oct-Mar – cold, dark, aurora possible; Apr-Sep – more tours, warmer.

◼ Adventure
◻ Wildlife & nature
◼ Personal growth
▦ Relaxation

Darkening skies envelop the dramatic Snaefellsnes Peninsula

LAPLAND
FINLAND

→ Why now? For dog-sleds and dancing lights.

The Arctic Circle sparkles at this time of year. The landscape is buried in snow and lakes are frozen. Polar night (the period of 24-hour darkness) is over, and the sun puts in ever-longer appearances. And the magical Northern Lights are quite likely to dance: according to the Finnish Meteorological Institute, the best time to look for aurora is February to March and September to October. This is also a great time for everyone – young, old, families, couples – to get into the great outdoors. Though still chilly, temperatures start to rise this month, and wilderness lodges offer full programs of activities: husky-sledding, snowmobiling, sleigh rides, snowshoeing, cross-country-skiing... All guaranteed to warm you up. If all else fails, a visit to a traditional Finnish sauna should do the trick.

Trip plan: Rovaniemi and Ivalo airports offer access to Finland's north. Spend four or more nights at a wilderness lodge to maximise chances of seeing aurora, and to pack in plenty of snowy fun.

Need to know: Many lodges offer 'aurora alerts' – a wake-up call if the lights emerge.

Other months: Dec-Apr – snow activities (Sep-Apr: aurora); May-Aug – long days, warmest; Sep-Nov – brief autumn, cooling.

ANDORRA

→ Why now? Good mid-season snow for beginners.

The titchy principality of Andorra, tucked into the Pyrenees between France and Spain, is basically all mountains. So it's no surprise that skiing is big here. Indeed, Andorra offers the best skiing in the range: it has modern chairlifts, a top-notch ski school, a good mix of accommodation and excellent slopes for beginners and intermediates. Being so small, all its main resorts are close, so you can easily move between them if you get bored – the two biggest areas, Soldeau and Pas de la Casa, are linked by lifts. Prices are reasonable too. February is a good choice – expect clear skies, and virtually guaranteed snow dusting the resort summits, which all top out at over 2500m. Away from the piste, the après-ski is lively and, thanks to low VAT, the shopping cheap.

Trip plan: Novices, head for Grandvalira, which has wide pistes, gentle gradients and some of the best ski schools.

Need to know: Andorra doesn't have an international airport – the best access is via Toulouse (France) or Barcelona (Spain).

Other months: Dec-Apr – ski season; May-Sep – warm, best for hiking/biking; Oct-Nov – cool, off-season.

IBIZA SPAIN

→ Why now? Resolution-boosting fitness in warming climes.

For the antithesis of Balearic hedonism, come to Ibiza now. This island, so well known for its wild summer clubbing scene, is a far quieter prospect off-season, and a good choice for a more cleansing, abstemious break. As devotion to New Year's resolutions starts to wane in February, boost it with a wellness-focused Ibizan escape, taking advantage of the relatively mild winter temperatures (around 10-16°C; 50-61°F). There are villas here that specialise in healthy holidays; they are often located near good running and cycling trails, and offer optional extras such as visits from fitness trainers and chefs who cook up creative, waistline-friendly dishes. There are also yoga retreats that operate year-round. Or you can work-out on your own: this beautiful island of pine forests, pretty coves, craggy clifftops and whitewashed hamlets is ideal for trail runs and downward-dogging out in nature. The February explosion of almond blossom is an added bonus.

Trip plan: Book a remote villa for a proper escape. Visit capital Ibiza Town, where many restaurants remain open and full of locals.

Need to know: Many bars and almost all nightclubs close October to May.

Other months: Jun-Aug – hot, busy; Sep-Oct – winding down, club closing parties; Nov-Mar – mild winters; Apr-May – spring.

Adventure
Wildlife & nature
Cultural

Adventure
Personal growth
Value

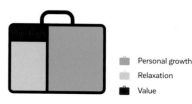

Personal growth
Relaxation
Value

© ostill / Shutterstock

THE GAMBIA

Why now? Long, dry, friendly days. This sliver of West Africa, blessed with a generous Atlantic coast and a wild, riverine interior, doesn't do cold. Average highs are around 30 to 34°C (86°F-93°F) year-round. But come in February (or, at least, November to May), and you can enjoy its beautiful, un-busy sands with barely a drop of rain, low humidity, few bugs, 10 hours of sunshine daily and a delightful sea breeze. There's extra kudos, though no risk, in picking this more offbeat beach retreat – it's a stable, friendly spot known as the 'Smiling Coast'. If you can, haul yourself from the sand to explore inland. Take a pirogue trip along the River Gambia's mangrove-fringed tributaries to see fishermen casting their jallo nets. Or venture deeper to stay at the Chimpanzee Rehabilitation Project, where over 100 chimps live on a cluster of islands. The birding is brilliant in February too.

Trip plan: Stick to the beach, adding day-trips to Tanji Fishing Village (for the lively market), Juffure's Slavery Museum and river cruises. Or combine the coast with wildlife-focused time upriver.

Need to know: The Gambia became a Muslim Republic in 2015, but other faiths remain free to practice.

Other months: Nov-Jun – dry (Feb-May: least humid); Jul-Oct – wet.

Relaxation
Wildlife & nature
Cultural

MICHOACÁN PROVINCE
MEXICO

Why now? Watch millions of monarch butterflies take flight. Visit Michoacán's forests on a sunny February morning and you'll witness an astonishing spectacle: hundreds of millions of orange-black wings flexing then fluttering as vast clouds of monarch butterflies take to the air. Each winter up to a billion of these incredible insects migrate thousands of miles from northeastern North America to the warmer climes of Mexico specifically, Michoacán Province's Oyamel fir forests, some of which are now protected as the Monarch Butterfly Biosphere Reserve; head to the El Rosario or Sierra Chincua sections. Here the monarchs breed before returning to their summer grounds far, far to the north.

Trip plan: The butterfly reserves can be visited on a day trip from Mexico City or Morelia, but better to stay nearby, perhaps in Angangueo or Zitácuaro. Another option is a clockwise circuit from Mexico City, taking in the butterflies, the colonial charm of Morelia, artsy San Miguel de Allende and the Toltec/ Aztec pyramid site of Tula.

Need to know: Wildlife fans travelling now could combine butterflies with whales – either humpbacks off Puerto Vallarta (Pacific Coast) or grey whales off Baja California.

Other months: Oct-Apr – butterflies present; May-Sep – wetter season, hot.

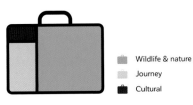

Wildlife & nature
Journey
Cultural

DOMINICAN REPUBLIC

Why now? For wind, whales and wonderful weather. The Dominican Republic is big enough to be all things to all comers. Occupying the eastern half of Hispaniola Island (Haiti covers the west), it offers backpacker digs in funky fishing villages, high-end honeymooners' retreats and family-friendly all-inclusives. More than that, it's home to the Caribbean's highest mountain (3098m Pico Duarte), one of its oldest towns (Santo Domingo), and even its own form of dance (merengue originated here). In February, the weather is lovely and dry for exploring all of these aspects, though special mention must go to two more: this is prime time for windsurfing at lively Cabarete, while thousands of humpback whales gather briefly in Samaná Bay to breed.

Trip planner: You could plonk yourself on a beach for two weeks. Alternatively, after a few beach days, head to Samaná for whales and remote sands, continue northwest to Cabarete, cut south into the mountains towards Jarabacoa for highland adventures, then finish with colonial culture in Santo Domingo.

Need to know: The Dominican Republic's main airports are at Santo Domingo (south), Puerto Plata (north) and Punta Cana (east).

Other months: Dec-Apr – dry, warm (whales Jan-Mar); May-Nov – wetter (Aug-Oct wettest).

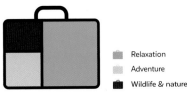

Relaxation
Adventure
Wildlife & nature

Dhow racing off Kenya's Indian Ocean coast during the Maulidi Festival

New Zealand's Marlborough region is home to more than 150 wineries

Rare snow leopards descend to the valleys to mate in February in Ladakh

NORTHERN SOUTH ISLAND
NEW ZEALAND

→ **Why now?** To feast with fewer people.

February is a New Zealand sweet spot. It's one of the hottest months (20-30°C; 68-86°F), yet Kiwi families have taken the kids back to school. This makes it a good month for popular, weather-sensitive places, such as Abel Tasman National Park – far better to walk, kayak and camp amid the golden sands and forested headlands here when it's sunny and quieter. While you're in northern South Island, tag on the Marlborough region too. It's home to more than 150 wineries, which will be thickening with grapes, before the March-May harvest; utilise February's good weather to tour between cellar doors by bike. And February is when the Marlborough Food and Wine Festival (in Blenheim) showcases the region's best produce: cherries, strawberries, apricots; Kaikoura cheese and Cloudy Bay clams; blue cod and green-lipped mussels from the Marlborough Sounds. There's also good eating at vineyard restaurants and chances to take seafood cruises to catch your own.

Trip plan: Combine activities in Abel Tasman with arty Nelson, Marlborough wine-tasting and whale-watching in Kaikoura.

Need to know: The ferry from the North Island docks at Picton, 62 miles (100km) east of Nelson, 19 miles (30km) north of Blenheim.

Other months: Dec-Feb – warmest, busiest; Mar-May – cooler, foodie, quiet; Jun-Aug – cold, wet; Sep-Nov – warming.

■ Food & drink
■ Wildlife & nature

LADAKH INDIA

→ **Why now?** For snow leopards and ice trekking.

Brrrrrr! It's not warm in the Himalayan heights of northwest India right now (days around 21°F; -6°C). But it's worth braving the cold for a couple of very special experiences. Wildlife fans should head for Hemis National Park, home to a 400-year-old monastery, and one of the few places on the planet where the elusive snow leopard isn't quite so elusive. During winter mating season – which peaks in February – the high-dwelling big cats descend to the valleys here to find mates, making them easier to spot. Alternatively, trekkers can check out the Chadar. This challenging winter hike starts near Leh, and uses the frozen Zanskar River as its path – walking on this icy meander is the only way to access the highland villages at this time. February is when the ice is at its most stable; the temperature is biting, but the snow-cloaked mountains spectacular.

Trip plan: Fly to Leh. Hemis is 6 miles (10km) south, where guided treks in the Tarbuns Valley may yield leopards. The Chadar hike starts in Chilling, 40 miles (65km) from Leh, and takes six days.

Need to know: Leh is at 11,483ft (3500m) so stay well-hydrated to help altitude acclimatisation.

Other months: Nov-Mar – cold, snowy (Jan-Feb: Chadar possible); Apr-May & Oct – quiet, cool; Jun-Sep – best for regular trekking.

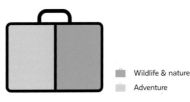

■ Wildlife & nature
■ Adventure

INDIAN OCEAN
KENYA

→ **Why now?** The air's hot, the water's gorgeous.

In a country blessed with some of the world's greatest game parks, it can be easy to overlook the coast. But Kenya's Indian Ocean shore is far from second-rate. The fine, soft sand is blinding white, the sea is a swirl of crystal-clear blues, and picturesque fishing dhows, swaying palms and women in rainbow-bright *kangas* add photogenic touches. There is a distinct, spice-infused Swahili Coast culture too – evident in the Arabic houses of Mombasa and the region's signature curries, fragrant and full of seafood. Development has occurred, but most hotels are low-key and well-spaced, and so don't interrupt the dreamy vibe. The snorkelling and diving are spectacular too, particularly in January and February, when the weather is hot and dry, and water visibility is at its best. Migrating whale sharks (February to April, September to October) also pass by.

Trip plan: Explore Mombasa's Old Town and Fort Jesus; if overlanding to Mombasa from Nairobi, break the journey with a safari in Tsavo. South of Mombasa, Diani offers traditional beach holidays; Watamu and Malindi, 75 miles (120km) north, are both protected by marine national parks.

Need to know: Check the security situation – the coast north of Malindi may be subject to travel advisories.

Other months: Jan-Feb – hot, dry, lush; Mar-May – long rains, very wet; Jun-Oct – dry, good game-viewing; Nov-Dec – short rains.

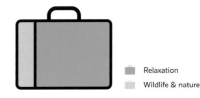

■ Relaxation
■ Wildlife & nature

(L) A thermal spring bubbles and steams in Yellowstone National Park

© Pete Seaward / Lonely Planet

WYOMING USA

→ **Why now? Hot slopes, hot springs.**
When snow cloaks the cowboy state, special things happen. Skiers and boarders will love the Teton Mountains resort of Jackson Hole, nicknamed 'The Big One' on account of its steep, squeaky-bum terrain and great powder (driest and deepest January to February). There are some baby slopes, but this is best for intermediates and pros. Après-ski is lively too. Then, further north, quite different thrills await in Yellowstone National Park. Heaving in summer, Yellowstone empties in winter. Park roads close, and the only ways to explore are via snowcoach, snowmobile, cross-country skis or snowshoes. Geysers and hot springs steam in the icy air, and animals congregate at the thermal areas for warmth. Also, grey wolves stand out against the snow-blanketed landscapes, and their tracks are

more easily followed – take a guided trip in the Lamar Valley for the chance of a sighting.
Trip plan: Jackson Hole keeps experienced powderhounds busy for weeks (nearby Snow King resort is better for beginners). It's a scenic drive north to Yellowstone; free ranger-led tours still run in winter, or book a wildlife or snow-sports package.
Need to know: Jackson Hole Airport is 7 miles (12km) north of Jackson, 56 miles (90km) south of Yellowstone's south gate.
Other months: Nov-Mar – skiing, Yellowstone winter; Apr-May & Sep-Oct – mild, uncrowded; Jun-Aug – hot, busy.

Wildlife & nature

Adventure

Find hilltop hamlets, fine wines and trees stripped for cork in Portugal's south

© Matt Munro / Lonely Planet

© Matt Munro / Lonely Planet

SOUTHERN PORTUGAL

Why now? Pleasing prices and weather, plus trees abloom.
Winter is fleeting and rarely harsh in mainland Europe's far southwest. The beaches of the wilder western Alentejo coast and the calm, southern Algarve might not be hot enough for swimming, but they'll be nicely uncrowded and even more picturesque, perfect for strolls or mountain-biking. There's the benefit of lower off-season prices too – which is saying quite a lot in this already great-value destination (beer less than US$2? Don't mind if I do...). Also, because February is so mild (average: 16°C; 61°F), spring comes early and already the almond blossom is blooming, beautifying the countryside. Indeed, this is a great time to explore southern Portugal's interior, which can be prohibitively sweltering in summer – places such as the hilltop village of Monsaraz, Moorish-medieval Évora and the cork-tree-dotted plains.

Trip plan: Fly to Lisbon or Faro. Base yourself at a pretty spot – Portugal has some excellent-value accommodation in converted *casas* and *quintas* (farmhouses) – or roam by car, bike or foot.

Need to know: Order *caldo verde*, a traditional winter-warmer soup typically served with pork sausage and cornbread.

Other months: Nov-Mar – cooler, off-season; Apr-Oct – warm/hot (Jul-Aug: busiest).

© Matt Munro / Lonely Planet

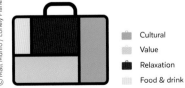

Cultural
Value
Relaxation
Food & drink

QUÉBEC CITY
CANADA

Why now? City sights, sports and celebrations.

One of North America's oldest settlements, part-encircled by 18th-century ramparts, Québec City is worth visiting at any time of year – but especially in February. Granted, it's freezing (-5°C to -15°C; 23-5°F), but the Québecois don't let that stop them, so neither should you. As well as admiring the old town under a shimmer of snow, go cross-country skiing in the city centre (the Plains of Abraham have tracks and ski rental); canoe across the ice-clogged St Lawrence River; book an ice room at the nearby Hôtel de Glace (January to March); and hit the slopes of Stoneham, 16 miles (25km) away. Also, held in early February, Winter Carnival is one of the city's most beloved events: two weeks of family-friendly fun with parades, snow-sculpting and ice games, plus plenty of *chocolat chaud* and hot Caribou (red wine, liquor, maple syrup and spice).

Trip plan: Book early if visiting during Carnival. Spend a few days in the 400-year-old city; combine with Montréal and the ski slopes of Mont-Tremblant.

Need to know: In cold winters, the spray from Québec's Montmorency Falls freezes to form a mountain at its base.

Other months: Dec-Mar – freezing; Apr-Jun – warming; Jul-Sep – hot, festivals; Oct-Nov – fall colours.

- Cultural
- Adventure
- Food & drink

CAPE VERDE

Why now? Be blown away by this Atlantic archipelago.

Part of Africa, historically influenced by Portugal and Brazil, and dubbed the 'new Caribbean', the 10-island archipelago of Cape Verde is quite unlike anywhere else. That's largely due to its location, adrift in the Atlantic Ocean, 621 miles (1000km) west of Senegal. Such remoteness means a distinct fusion culture thrives here – perhaps best expressed through Cape Verde's intoxicating *morna* folk music. There are also sandy beaches, lively bars (especially on São Vicente and Sal) and excellent hiking – notably on Fogo island's volcanic Pico and amid the mountains of Santo Antão. The islands' year-round warmth (26-30°C; 79-86°F) is especially appealing to northern hemisphere-dwellers seeking sun. As one of the breezier months, February is also ideal for sailors, surfers, windsurfers and kitesurfers – regular trade winds make it a world-class watersport destination.

Trip plan: Plan a twin-centre break to Sal and Boavista islands, for the best combination of beaches, nightlife and watersports. Flights link the islands.

Need to know: Sal, Santiago, Boavista and São Vicente have international airports.

Other months: Dec-Feb – dry, windiest, warm; Mar-Jun – warm, dry; Jul-Nov – rainy.

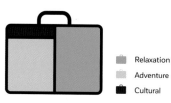

- Adventure
- Relaxation

DOMINICA

Why now? For a natural and cultural Caribbean adventure.

Dominica isn't really like the rest of the Caribbean. It does have some great beaches, though they're mostly black sand. Instead, it bills itself the Nature Isle, the country to choose if you want a Caribbean break with extra adventure and a whole lot of green. The rumpled island is almost entirely tucked under a blanket of lushness; it also has active volcanoes, a boiling lake, myriad waterfalls and – cutting across it all – the 124-mile (200km) Waitukubuli, the region's only long-distance hiking trail. The culture is intriguing too: Dominica's Kalinago Territory is home to some of the Caribbean's last remaining Kalinago (the region's first inhabitants), who continue to keep traditions alive. Talking of culture, February is a good month, not only for dry-season sunshine, but also Mas Dominik, Dominica's Carnival. Celebrations are held across the island, featuring irreverent Calypso contests and paraders in horned headpieces.

Trip plan: Relax by the sea, but plan excursions. Go canyoning in the interior, head to Wotton Waven for a tropical hot-spring soak or hike one of the Waitukubuli Trail's 14 sections.

Need to know: High-speed ferries connect Dominica to Guadeloupe, Martinique and St Lucia.

Other months: Dec-Apr – dry; May-Jun – rains begin; Jul-Nov – wettest, stormiest.

- Relaxation
- Adventure
- Cultural

DONSOL
PHILIPPINES

→ **Why now? Big fish in beautiful weather.**

Whale sharks are the world's biggest fish, growing up to 13m long. Snorkelling alongside one is more like finning with a slow-moving train than a living creature. Simply, it's up there with the greatest travel experiences. Donsol, a coastal village at the bottom of Luzon island, is one of the world's best places to do it. During whale-shark season, which runs November to June (peaking February to May), there might be more than 10 whale sharks in the water at a time. Plenty of eco-operators run boat trips that allow you to snorkel with the fish in a sensitive fashion. Being the middle of the dry season, this is also a good time to explore further – the Philippines has over 7000 islands to choose from!

Trip plan: Fly from Manila to Legazpi, near Donsol, for whale sharks. Then fly south for cultural Cebu, the 'Chocolate Hills' and wildlife of Bohol, and the dazzling beaches of Panglao.

Need to know: Before embarking on a whale-shark trip, you must attend a briefing on how to behave around them.

Other months: Nov-Apr – dry; May-Oct – wet.

It's peak whale-shark season off the Philippines' Luzon island, so dive in

© John Back / 500px

■ Wildlife & nature
■ Relaxation
■ Personal growth

DAYLESFORD AUSTRALIA

→ **Why now? Cool down with therapeutic waters.**

Want to escape the sizzling streets of Melbourne? Then take a short drive inland to the European Alps. Well, sort of. The town of Daylesford, tucked into Victoria's central highlands, was first settled by Italian Swiss gold-rush stampeders in the mid-19th century, and retains an old-world chocolate-box vibe. Having attracted an abundance of artisans and alt-lifestylers since, it also has thriving cultural and foodie scenes. All this makes Daylesford an idyllic escape, with cool swimming lakes, beautiful botanic gardens, galleries and antiques stores, farm-gate stalls and fancy restaurants. There are also rejuvenating mineral waters: 72 natural springs have been identified. Stroll a shady nature trail with an empty bottle to fill up at a remote pump; each spring is said to have a different mineral content and a different taste. Test your palate further at one of the local vineyards' cellar doors.

Trip plan: Daylesford is a 90-minute drive from Melbourne. Use it as a base for exploring the Macedon Ranges' countryside, villages and gold-rush history. Daylesford has spectacular accommodation options, ideal for a romantic escape.

Need to know: If it gets really hot, head up 3314ft (1010m) Mt Macedon, summer retreat of Melbourne's 19th-century elite.

Other months: Dec-Feb – hot; Mar-May – harvest, mild; Jun-Aug – cold, crisp; Sep-Nov – warming, blooming.

■ Relaxation
■ Food & drink

CAMBODIA

Why now? Skies are dry, the lake is still high.

The weather is dry and wonderful across Cambodia in February – right from the golden beaches of Sihanoukville to the temples of Angkor. Warmer than the early dry season (October to January) but not yet sweltering, this is a good month for exploring the vast, Unesco-listed complex. Long days of sightseeing are a more comfortable prospect in temperatures of around 27°C (81°F); and there's always shade to be found amid Angkor's stonework and jungly pockets. There's also just enough water left in Tonlé Sap Lake to take boat trips to floating villages that are still actually floating – as the dry season progresses, levels drop, leaving stilthouses marooned in mud and Kampong Phluk (the 'flooded forest') inaccessible.

Trip plan: Start in Siem Reap, granting Angkor the time it deserves. Then cruise on the Tonlé Sap Lake. Head south for the haunting museums of Phnom Penh before beach time in Kep or Sihanoukville; also consider hikes in the Cardamom Mountains.

Need to know: Angkor passes are available for durations of one (US$20), three (US$40) and seven (US$60) days.

Other months: Oct-Apr – dry; May-Sep – wet (Apr-Jun: hottest, most humid).

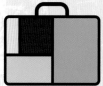

■ Cultural
▨ Value
■ Relaxation
▦ Journey/roadtrip

Monks wander the atmospheric ruins of Ta Prohm temple at Angkor

KILIMANJARO
TANZANIA

→ **Why now?** To climb Africa's highest peak when it's warm, clear and dry.
Lording it over the African savannah, 19,341ft (5895m) Kilimanjaro is the world's highest freestanding mountain, and a big, brooding beacon for travellers. This is a bucket-list climb, and a life-changing challenge – a mountain on which minds and bodies are tested by the terrain and the altitude, where firm friendships are made and world-views altered. Few other experiences are so tough yet so possible for so many. January to mid-March is the warmest time, with February generally quieter than new year. There may be daytime showers, but mornings and evenings are clear – perfect for summit night, when you'll set off around midnight, in time to (hopefully) make it to the top for sunrise. There are various routes up the volcano: Marangu is the only one with huts; the others require camping, though porters carry all equipment. For fewer fellow hikers, opt for the Lemosho or Rongai routes.

Trip plan: A Kili climb takes five to nine days – longer is better for acclimatisation. Add chill-out time in Zanzibar or a safari in northern Tanzania's game parks. Kilimanjaro has an international airport.

Need to know: A guide is mandatory.

Other months: Jan-Mar & Jun-Oct – dry, good climbing; Mar-May & Nov-Dec – wet.

- Adventure
- Personal growth
- Wildlife & nature

HOKKAIDO
JAPAN

→ **Why now?** For perfect powder, bird love and a whisky or two.
Hokkaido is Japan, but different. The northernmost of the country's main islands is a wild, mountainous region with spectacular wildlife and a reputation for some of the finest powder snow on the planet. Snowstorms from Siberia sweep across and dust the west of the island – head to Niseko in February for world-class powder, with three large ski areas and plenty of backcountry to explore, with ski, board or snowshoe. Naturally there are steaming *onsens* in which to soak those weary bones after a hard day on the slopes – and plenty of spots to sip the local Nikka whisky. Winter is also the time for two of Japan's most spectacular wildlife encounters. Head east across Hokkaido to Tsurui-Ito Tancho Sanctuary to witness the extraordinary courtship dance of the 5ft-high (1.5m) red-crowned crane and to the small town of Rausu to see hordes of white-tailed and Steller's sea eagle – with a wingspan of up to 8ft (2.5m), arguably the world's largest.

Trip plan: Fly to Sapporo for a few days on the slopes before crossing the island to explore the wilder reaches of the east.

Need to know: Refuel with Hokkaido cheeses or Ishikari *nabe* – salmon hotpot.

Other months: Dec-Mar – snow; Apr-May – spring, blossoms; Jun-Aug – warmest; Sep-Nov – fall colours.

- Adventure
- Wildlife & nature
- Food & drink
- Cultural
- Relaxation

ADELAIDE & MURRAY RIVER
AUSTRALIA

→ **Why now?** To mix a hot city and a refreshing waterway.
Artsy Adelaide averages around 30°C (86°F) in February, perfect for exploring the city's extensive parks, dining alfresco on Rundle St and embracing the eclectic Fringe Festival (February to March). You can always cool off in the galleries and museums of North Terrace or on the beach at Glenelg. However, for more of an escape, hire a houseboat on the nearby Murray River – think gentle breezes, iced drinks on deck and refreshing dips. The Riverland stretch is convenient (less than a two-hour drive from Adelaide) and scenic, twisting via river red gums, limestone cliffs, sandy beaches, vineyards and orchards, and settlements such as Blanchetown (founded in 1855) and Morgan, located on the Murray's Great Bend. Top tip: buy a hoop net to fish for yabbies (freshwater crayfish), which are best caught in late summer.

Trip plan: Adelaide warrants a few days. Then head to the Murray – houseboats can be hired from many riverside towns, for various durations; boats travel at around 4mph (7km/h).

Need to know: An unrestricted driving licence is required; foreign travellers should take an international licence.

Other months: Nov-Mar – hot; Apr-Oct – river quieter, water colder.

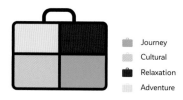

- Journey
- Cultural
- Relaxation
- Adventure

SINGAPORE

From its Gardens by the Bay to its urban skyline, Singapore is set to stun

Why now? For drier skies, cool gardens and great eating.

Loitering just one degree north of the equator, Singapore guarantees warmth year-round, with average temperatures a fairly consistent 27°C (81°F). February, however, is one of the driest months and – if you come after Lunar New Year (a national holiday) – it isn't crazy busy. Humidity is always high, but it's easy to find respite in a metropolis that's trying to rebrand itself as a 'City in a Garden'. Find shade downtown in the Botanic Gardens or the high-tech Gardens by the Bay, created in 2012. Or take a bus ride into the surrounding wildlife-rich rainforests. Perhaps the chief reason to visit, though, is to eat. Hawker centres serve up phenomenal food in cheap, canteen-like settings while top-end eateries are getting ever better – Michelin Guides launched its first Singapore edition in 2016. Seek out chilli crab, spicy *rendang* curry and a range of Nonya dishes, unique to the region.

Trip plan: Spend a few days sightseeing, and take a street-food tour to get a taste for less touristy neighbourhoods!

Need to know: Upcoming Lunar New Year dates are 28 January 2017, 16 February 2018, 5 February 2019, 25 January 2020.

Other months: Nov-Jan – wettest; Feb-Oct – hot, humid, drier.

- Food & drink
- Cultural
- Wildlife & nature

BEYOND SINGAPORE

PULAU UBIN · 1 MILE (1.6KM) · bike-friendly rural isle in the Johor Strait

MELAKA · 155 MILES (250KM) · Malaysia's historic Portuguese, Dutch, Chinese and Islam-influenced town

BANGKOK · 1140 MILES (1835KM) · Thai capital, via local trains or luxe Eastern & Oriental Express

SYDNEY · 3915 MILES (6300KM) · Australian metropolis in 10 hours, one of many options from well-connected Changi airport

CÔTE D'AZUR
FRANCE

Terracotta roofs hug the hills overlooking the French Riviera

→ **Why now?** It's quiet, mild and extra zesty.

How times change. Hitting the glitzy Côte d'Azur in February is now considered an off-season choice – a good time to avoid summer crowds. But it was winter visitors (such as Queen Victoria) who first made this Mediterranean stretch so fashionable in the 19th century. They came for the microclimate that gives the French Riviera – roughly, Menton to St Tropez – pleasantly mild winters (February averages 10°C; 50°F). They also came for the oh-so-blue waters, islands and dramatic hills; artists came for the clarity of the light. All these attractions remain, but the masses now prefer to wait for bikini weather. Let them keep it. Come now for crowd-free coves, emptier coast roads and quieter explorations of Nice's old town and Monaco's monied harbour. If it's crowds you want, add on Menton – every February the town hosts a two-week Lemon Festival, which involves floats and 145 tonnes of citrus fruit.

Trip plan: Fly to Nice to explore the Côte d'Azur by car – traffic/parking is less hellish in winter. Trace the Corniches (the Riviera's most scenic roads), cafe-hop in Cannes and visit hilltop St Paul de Vence.

Need to know: Nice is packed during its huge two-week Carnival every February.

Other months: Jun-Sep – glorious, heaving; Oct – changeable; Nov-Jan – some businesses close; Feb-May – quieter, warm.

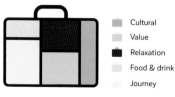

- Cultural
- Value
- Relaxation
- Food & drink
- Journey

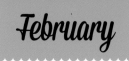

GOLD COAST
AUSTRALIA

→ **Why now? To get wet in a wealth of ways.**

The sandy strip of southern Queensland known as the Gold Coast is possibly the most developed 22 miles (35km) in all Australia. Lined with high-rises, theme parks and shopping malls, subtle it ain't. But it can be lots of fun. In February, it's still summer-hot for beach-lazing; the ocean is an inviting 25°C (77°F) and free of jellyfish, which don't generally float this far south). The kids are back at school too, so it's quieter. Rain is likely, but it doesn't matter if you're getting wet anyway, either surfing, swimming or riding the slides at Wet 'n' Wild. Find the flipside to this razzamatazz in the Gold Coast Hinterland. Springbrook and Lamington national parks heave with animals not people, and will be lush and threaded with waterfalls from the rains. It's cooler here too, ideal for walks through fern gullies and temperate rainforest. Don't miss a nighttime trip to Springbrook's Natural Bridge, where millions of glowworms glitter; their bioluminescence is best during the warmer, wetter months (December to March).

Trip plan: In a week, combine beaches and theme parks with hinterland exploration.

Need to know: Direct trains connect Brisbane Airport to stations on the Gold Coast (90 minutes).

Other months: Dec-Feb – hot, wet (busiest mid-Nov to mid-Dec, 'schoolies' weeks); Apr-May & Sep-Nov – milder; Jun-Aug – coolest but still warm, dry, whales.

◼ Relaxation
◻ Wildlife & nature
◼ Adventure

HONDURAS

→ **Why now? To dive on a budget, in glorious weather.**

Diving is about as close as a human can get to flying – learning to breathe underwater, master your buoyancy and explore another world is one of the great natural highs. The Bay Islands of Honduras (Utila and Roatán in particular) are brilliant places to do scuba courses. Not only are there many dive schools here, but this is renowned as one of the cheapest places to learn. The islands are also idyllic, with powdery white-sand beaches and clear Caribbean waters (visibility is best February to June). The marine life is incredible too, with species such as dolphins, hawksbill turtles, eagle rays and reef sharks present year-round, and whale sharks passing by February to May.

Trip plan: Fly or ferry to Roatán; an Open Water PADI course takes about four days. February (dry, cool) is also good for exploring other sites such as the Mayan ruins of Copán and Pico Bonito National Park.

Need to know: Most international flights to Honduras land at San Pedro Sula.

Other months: Feb-May – dry, warm; Jun-Nov – rainy; Sep-Jan – north coast wet, dry elsewhere.

◻ Adventure
◻ Personal growth
◼ Relaxation
◻ Value

© Shutterstock

© Celso Pupo / Shutterstock

RIO DE JANEIRO
BRAZIL

🏛 🌴 ☆

→ **Why now? Party!**
There is no party on the planet like Rio Carnival. Two million people sequinned-up, samba-ing, cavorting, dancing and drinking in one of the world's best-looking cities – celebrations don't come much brighter, brasher or rowdier, or more unforgettable. For some, joining this massive melee might sound like hell on earth; for others this is bucket-list stuff. Early booking is key, as is deciding how to participate: a ticketed seat in the Sambodrome grandstand, watching the parades? Signing up with a samba school to take part in the action? Joining the *blocos* (street parties) for more informal fun? Also consider different Brazilian cities, for a variety of Carnival vibes. Try Salvador's enormous African-influenced event, the traditional street parties of Recife and Olinda, or São Paulo Carnival – like Rio but less touristy by far.

Trip plan: Book well in advance if visiting Brazil during Carnival season. Add on recuperative beach time: Búzios (near Rio) or Ilha de Tinharé (near Salvador).

Need to know: Upcoming dates for Carnival Sunday are 26 February 2017, 11 February 2018, 3 March 2019, 23 February 2020.

Other months: Dec-Mar – Rio summer, hot (Carnival Feb-Mar); Apr-May – cooler, humid; Jun-Sep – mild winters; Oct-Nov – warm, uncrowded.

See spectacular samba or surf Ipanema during Rio's carnival season

© Michael Heffernan / Lonely Planet

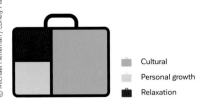
Cultural
Personal growth
Relaxation

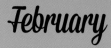

© Pete Seaward / Lonely Planet

HAITI

→ **Why now? The alternative Caribbean at the optimum time.**

Yes, this is the Caribbean. But few come to Haiti for its Caribbean beaches – sandy and palm-fringed though they may be. No, people come to experience the region at its most offbeat, its most African-influenced and its most resurgent. The 2010 earthquake devastated the country, but there is optimism for the future, and a thrilling destination awaiting those who visit. February is cool and dry across the island, and thus the best time to explore it all. Capital Port-au-Prince is a heady introduction, a mayhem of traffic, rubble, market vendors, voodoo rituals, gingerbread houses and a lively music scene. Jacmel is a more laid-back artsy-craftsy hub, with lovely beaches and a raucous February Carnival. Elsewhere, take a dip in the lagoons and waterfalls of Bassin-Bleu and hike (or donkey-ride) up to Citadelle Laferrière, an 18th-century fort that thrusts up like a battleship from the lush northern hills.

Trip plan: Allow at least 10 days to explore Haiti. Consider flying from Port-au-Prince to Cap-Haitien (for the Citadelle) to save time.

Need to know: Malaria is present, so take precautions.

Other months: Nov-Mar – coolest, dry (rainy in north Nov-Jan); Apr-Jun – hotter, rainy in centre; Aug-Oct – humid, wet, storms possible.

■ Cultural
■ Relaxation

BLUE MOUNTAINS
AUSTRALIA

The Three Sisters above Jamison Valley, Blue Mountains

→ **Why now? For a breath of fresh, eucalypt-tinged air.**

As a general rule, you can knock 2°C (4°F) off the Sydney temperature for every 984ft (300m) you climb into the nearby Blue Mountains. That makes hub-town Katoomba – 3281ft (1000m) up on the sandstone plateau – a refreshing 12°F (7°C) cooler than the New South Wales capital. Thus, when Sydney is sweltering in February, the highlands make a still-warm but refreshing escape. The Blue Mountains are also alive with wildflowers at this time, and romantic under the legendary blue haze created by their gum-tree canopy. Bushwalking, biking, kayaking and climbing amid the valleys and outcrops are available, as well as cultural forays to rock-art sites with indigenous guides. There are also panoramas available by steep scenic railway and cable-car. The Blue Mountains have a fine foodie reputation too – you will eat and drink well here.

Trip plan: Catch a train from Sydney to Katoomba (two hours) or Lithgow (2¾ hours) – it's possible to come for a day but much better to stay for several, allowing time for hikes and eating.

Need to know: Buses run between the main towns; a hop-on hop-off Blue Mountains Explorer Bus links key sites.

Other months: Dec-Feb – summer, warmest; Mar-May & Sep-Oct – colourful flora, cooler; Jun-Aug – cold.

■ Wildlife & nature
■ Adventure
■ Food & drink

MENDOZA
ARGENTINA

Why now? Raise a glass to the greatness of grapes.

This is the most intoxicating time to visit Mendoza, the heart of Argentinean wine country. Vineyards dominate here – every hillside is scored with vines – and in hot, sunny February they'll be healthily heavy with fruit in anticipation of the March harvest. A festive atmosphere reigns, with every bodega (and there are around 900) open for tours, tastings and celebrations. The leafy, plaza-dotted city of Mendoza makes a good base. Alternatively, some wine estates offer characterful accommodation amid the vines, with backdrops of the snow-capped Andes. Activities such as biking, hiking, horse-riding and golf are also readily available during this dry, sunny period, and doable in the knowledge that a beefy Malbec will be uncorked and waiting on your return.

Trip plan: It's a two-hour flight from Buenos Aires to Mendoza. Tour the vineyards, adding on walks and rides. Consider combining with the wineries of Cafayate, further north.

Need to know: The Vendimia (Harvest Festival) is held on the first weekend in March.

Other months: Dec-Jan – hottest; Feb-May – best for wine tours; Jun-Aug – cool, nearby skiing; Sep-Nov – spring blooms.

Mendoza's wine country with Mount Aconcagua in the background

Food & drink
Adventure
Relaxation

© Ksenia Ragozina / Shutterstock
© Matt Munro / Lonely Planet
© Matt Munro / Lonely Planet
© Matt Munro / Lonely Planet

VENICE
ITALY

🐷 🏛 🥂

→ **Why now? Embrace Carnival – or go crowd-free.**

February is a month of two halves in Italy's Floating City. In part, it's winter Venice: cold but entrancing, largely untouristed. It can be grey and bitingly cold, but the canals are enswirled by atmospheric mists, and cafes serving thick *cioccolata calda* offer refuge. Virtually free of cruise ships, this is when locals reclaim the place, while museums and churches remain open but empty. However, pick an alternative February weekend and it's all different: Carnival takes over. There are masked balls, parades and fireworks, and masked figures swish down the alleys. Photographers will be in heaven, as will anyone who's ever wanted to play dress-up in one of the world's most magical cities. It's busy but beautiful too. Note: most Carnival action stays central, so head to Venice's more residential areas (Cannaregio, for example) to find pockets of calm.

Trip plan: Venice deserves several days, to cover sights such as St Mark's Square as well as outlying islands (Burano, Murano). *Vaporettos* (watertaxis) run year-round.

Need to know: Book accommodation well in advance for Carnival. Upcoming dates: 18 to 28 February 2017, 3 to 13 February 2018, 23 February to 5 March 2019, 15 to 25 February 2020.

Other months: Nov-Apr – cold/cool, quiet; May-Jun & Sep-Oct – warm, not busy; Jul-Aug – hot, crowded.

© Mark Read / Lonely Planet

The ornate exterior of St Mark's Basilica in Venice

🟫 Cultural
⬜ Food & drink
⬛ Value

BEYOND VENICE

TREVISO • 20 MILES (32KM) • Historic city, quieter canals

PADUA • 25 MILES (40KM) • Awesome art galleries

CORTINA D'AMPEZZO, DOLOMITES • 99 MILES (160KM) • Winter skiing

ROME • 342 MILES (550KM) • Only three hours to the capital by high-speed train

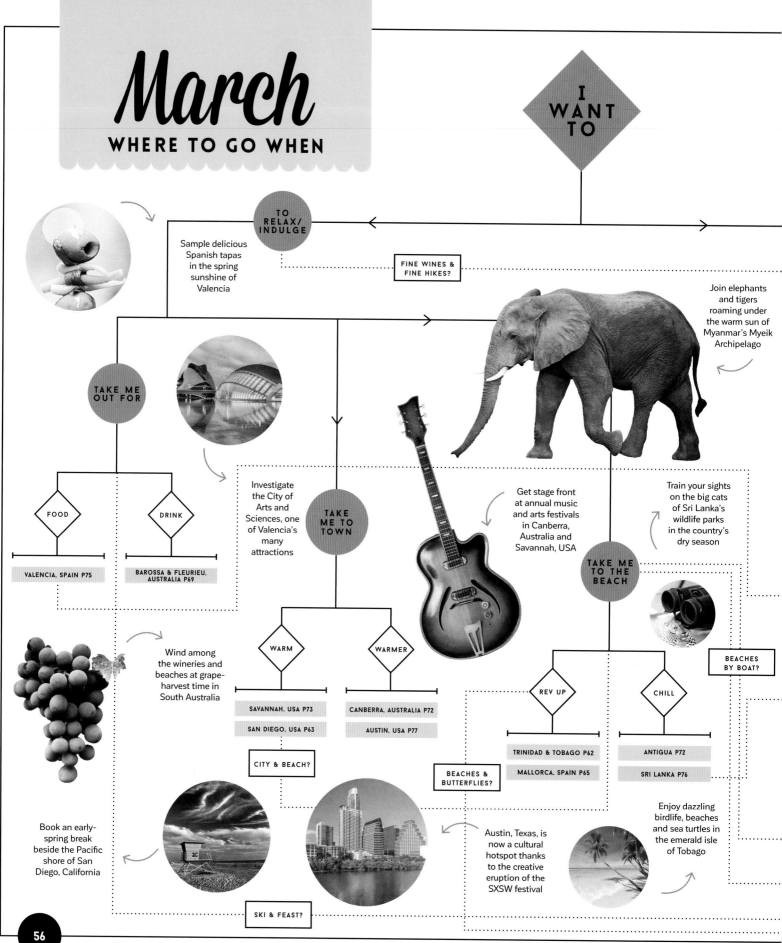

March
WHERE TO GO WHEN

I WANT TO

TO RELAX/ INDULGE

Sample delicious Spanish tapas in the spring sunshine of Valencia

FINE WINES & FINE HIKES?

Join elephants and tigers roaming under the warm sun of Myanmar's Myeik Archipelago

TAKE ME OUT FOR

Investigate the City of Arts and Sciences, one of Valencia's many attractions

TAKE ME TO TOWN

Get stage front at annual music and arts festivals in Canberra, Australia and Savannah, USA

Train your sights on the big cats of Sri Lanka's wildlife parks in the country's dry season

TAKE ME TO THE BEACH

FOOD

DRINK

VALENCIA, SPAIN P75

BAROSSA & FLEURIEU, AUSTRALIA P69

Wind among the wineries and beaches at grape-harvest time in South Australia

WARM

WARMER

REV UP

CHILL

BEACHES BY BOAT?

SAVANNAH, USA P73

SAN DIEGO, USA P63

CANBERRA, AUSTRALIA P72

AUSTIN, USA P77

CITY & BEACH?

TRINIDAD & TOBAGO P62

MALLORCA, SPAIN P65

ANTIGUA P72

SRI LANKA P76

Book an early-spring break beside the Pacific shore of San Diego, California

BEACHES & BUTTERFLIES?

Austin, Texas, is now a cultural hotspot thanks to the creative eruption of the SXSW festival

Enjoy dazzling birdlife, beaches and sea turtles in the emerald isle of Tobago

SKI & FEAST?

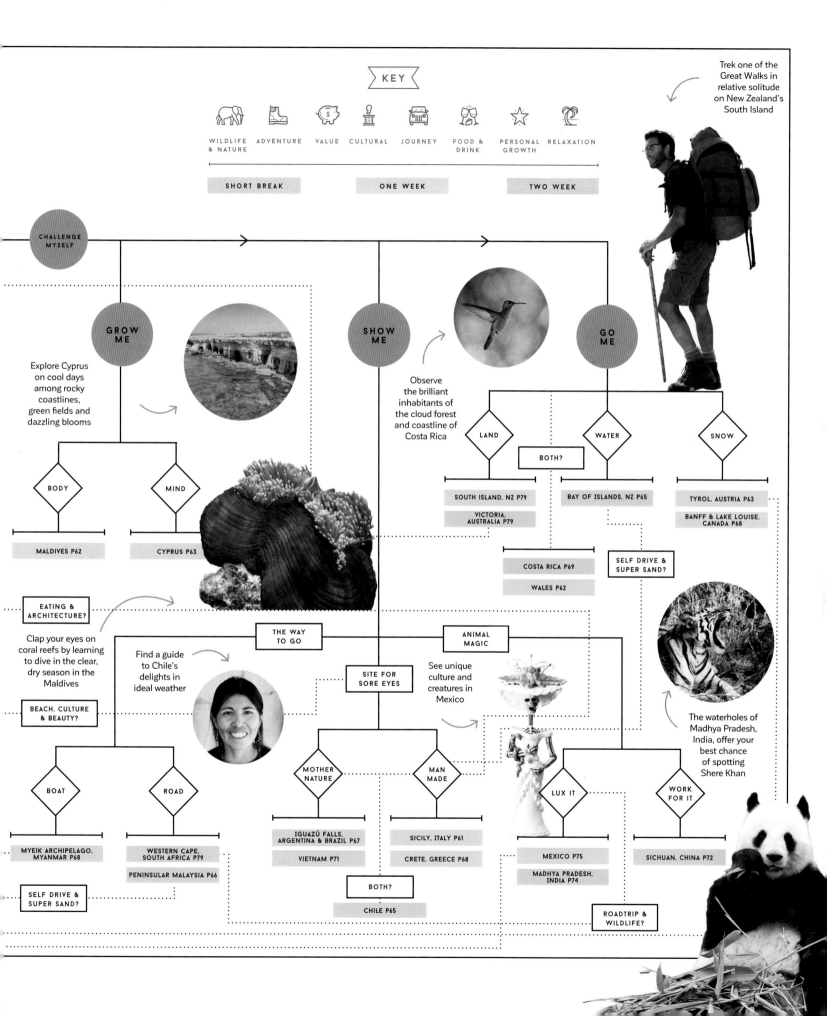

Trek one of the Great Walks in relative solitude on New Zealand's South Island

KEY

- WILDLIFE & NATURE
- ADVENTURE
- VALUE
- CULTURAL
- JOURNEY
- FOOD & DRINK
- PERSONAL GROWTH
- RELAXATION

SHORT BREAK   ONE WEEK   TWO WEEK

CHALLENGE MYSELF

GROW ME

Explore Cyprus on cool days among rocky coastlines, green fields and dazzling blooms

SHOW ME

Observe the brilliant inhabitants of the cloud forest and coastline of Costa Rica

GO ME

LAND — WATER — SNOW

BOTH?

- BODY
- MIND

SOUTH ISLAND, NZ P79

VICTORIA, AUSTRALIA P79

BAY OF ISLANDS, NZ P65

TYROL, AUSTRIA P63

BANFF & LAKE LOUISE, CANADA P68

MALDIVES P62

CYPRUS P63

COSTA RICA P69

WALES P62

SELF DRIVE & SUPER SAND?

EATING & ARCHITECTURE?

Clap your eyes on coral reefs by learning to dive in the clear, dry season in the Maldives

BEACH, CULTURE & BEAUTY?

Find a guide to Chile's delights in ideal weather

THE WAY TO GO

ANIMAL MAGIC

SITE FOR SORE EYES

See unique culture and creatures in Mexico

The waterholes of Madhya Pradesh, India, offer your best chance of spotting Shere Khan

- BOAT
- ROAD
- MOTHER NATURE
- MAN MADE
- LUX IT
- WORK FOR IT

MYEIK ARCHIPELAGO, MYANMAR P68

WESTERN CAPE, SOUTH AFRICA P79

PENINSULAR MALAYSIA P66

IGUAZÚ FALLS, ARGENTINA & BRAZIL P67

VIETNAM P71

SICILY, ITALY P61

CRETE, GREECE P68

MEXICO P75

MADHYA PRADESH, INDIA P74

SICHUAN, CHINA P72

SELF DRIVE & SUPER SAND?

BOTH?

CHILE P65

ROADTRIP & WILDLIFE?

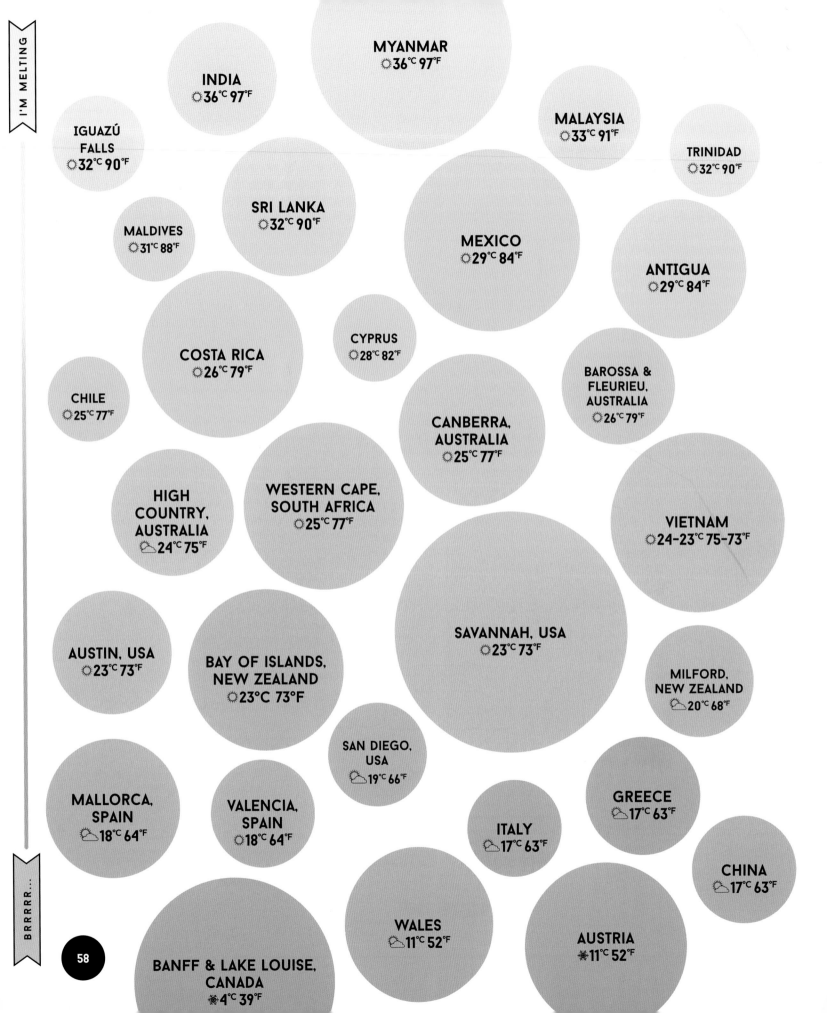

MYANMAR
☀36°C 97°F

INDIA
☀36°C 97°F

MALAYSIA
☀33°C 91°F

IGUAZÚ
FALLS
☀32°C 90°F

TRINIDAD
☀32°C 90°F

SRI LANKA
☀32°C 90°F

MALDIVES
☀31°C 88°F

MEXICO
☀29°C 84°F

ANTIGUA
☀29°C 84°F

COSTA RICA
☀26°C 79°F

CYPRUS
☀28°C 82°F

BAROSSA &
FLEURIEU,
AUSTRALIA
☀26°C 79°F

CHILE
☀25°C 77°F

CANBERRA,
AUSTRALIA
☀25°C 77°F

HIGH
COUNTRY,
AUSTRALIA
⛅24°C 75°F

WESTERN CAPE,
SOUTH AFRICA
☀25°C 77°F

VIETNAM
☀24-23°C 75-73°F

AUSTIN, USA
☀23°C 73°F

BAY OF ISLANDS,
NEW ZEALAND
☀23°C 73°F

SAVANNAH, USA
☀23°C 73°F

MILFORD,
NEW ZEALAND
⛅20°C 68°F

SAN DIEGO,
USA
⛅19°C 66°F

MALLORCA,
SPAIN
⛅18°C 64°F

VALENCIA,
SPAIN
☀18°C 64°F

GREECE
⛅17°C 63°F

ITALY
⛅17°C 63°F

CHINA
⛅17°C 63°F

WALES
⛅11°C 52°F

AUSTRIA
❄11°C 52°F

BANFF & LAKE LOUISE,
CANADA
❄4°C 39°F

VERY FAMILY FRIENDLY

COSTA RICA

BAY OF ISLANDS, NZ

SAN DIEGO, USA

MALLORCA, SPAIN

BANFF & LAKE LOUISE, CANADA

SRI LANKA

ANTIGUA

Enjoy the unique culture of Mexico

Skiing season starts to give way to challenging hikes in the Austrian Tyrol

CYPRUS

Costa Rica may only be a small country but it's one of nature's big hitters

TYROL, AUSTRIA

TRINIDAD & TOBAGO

NORTH WALES

CRETE, GREECE

MEXICO

The road east of Cape Town is lined with verdant forests and glorious shores

VICTORIA, AUSTRALIA

WESTERN CAPE, SOUTH AFRICA

MALAYSIA

Cycling Lake Burley Griffin is a prime way to spend an Aussie autumn day

CANBERRA, AUSTRALIA

SICHUAN, CHINA

Meet pandas and admire spring blooms in this varied Chinese province

SICILY, ITALY

The ancient sites and traditional towns of Sicily are as appealing as its food

EXPENSIVE BUT WORTH IT

GOOD VALUE

SAVANNAH, USA

IGUAZÚ FALLS, BRAZIL & ARGENTINA

VALENCIA, SPAIN

Where better to feast on paella than in the city that first served the Spanish dish?

VIETNAM

Gawp at the mighty waterfalls that border Brazil and Argentina

BAROSSA & FLEURIEU

This Australian peninsula is an oenophile's dream destination

Sapa in Vietnam is surrounded by enticing rice terraces and hill tribes

MYEIK, MYANMAR

AUSTIN, USA

Cruise among hundreds of idyllic tropical specks in the Myeik Archipelago

MADHYA PRADESH, INDIA

MALDIVES

Austin's SXSW has become the go-to festival for the music industry worldwide

The dry season in Madhya Pradesh is the peak time for tiger sightings

Huge *moai* watch over Easter Island, a five-hour flight from Santiago

CHILE

SOUTH ISLAND, NZ

LEAVE THE KIDS AT HOME

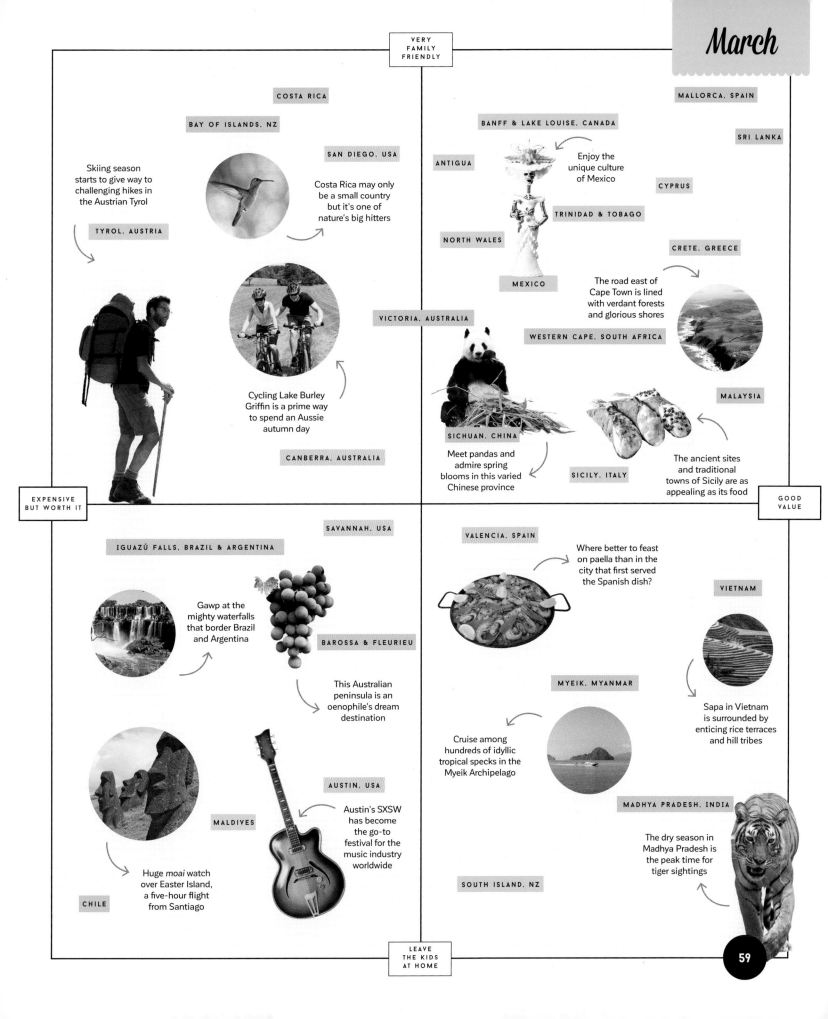

SICILY

→ **Why now? Tour ancient sites and traditional towns in peace.**

The largest island in the Mediterranean is Italian, but with an indefinable twang influenced by French, Spanish, Arabic, Greek and numerous other cultures that have come and gone over the millennia. Early spring's the time to explore its fascinating historic sites – the Greek theatre of Siracusa and temples at Agrigento, the medieval cathedral of Monreale, Roman mosaics, baroque towns and Norman relics – with days lengthening and warming, but without school and tourist groups. Prices tend to be lower, and March is ideal for hiking and biking (though higher reaches are still snow-dusted). Sicilian food is a treat, incorporating varied culinary influences, including a tang of the tropical: orange, lemon, palm and olive trees are ubiquitous.

Trip planner: Fly to Palermo or Catania, or take the short ferry voyage to Messina from the Calabrian mainland. Most attractions are on the coast, so you can trace a loop around the island from any of these starting points.

Need to know: The ski season on Etna extends into March – you can ski in the morning and soak up the sun in Taormina that afternoon.

Other months: Nov-Feb – many coastal resorts and islands closed; Apr-Jun – good weather, reasonable prices; Jul-Aug – beaches and historic sites busy; Sep-Oct – good value.

■ Cultural
■ Adventure
■ Food & drink
■ Value

Sicilian ice cream from Pasticceria Mandolfior in Noto

Cycling past Chiesa
di San Michele in
Scicli, Sicily

NORTH WALES UK

→ **Why now?** For outdoor activities among daffodils and spring lambs.

Springtime in Wales: lambs gambol on hillsides sprinkled with clusters of butter-yellow daffodils. For once, reality matches cliché – though sunshine is never guaranteed here, the Welsh countryside is glorious in March, which is a great time to dust off wintry cobwebs and explore some of the UK's less-visited countryside. The Dee Valley is a year-round destination for active adventures – the River Dee being one of the few that offers great whitewater year-round, with rafting, kayaking, bodyboating, even stand-up paddleboarding provide adrenaline highs. This region, including the Clwydian Range to the north, is packed with attractions and activities – hikes to ruined Castell Dinas Brân and Thomas Telford's Pontcysyllte Aqueduct, a ride on the steam-drawn Llangollen Railway, and zip lines, cave trampolines and an artificial surf wavegarden in Snowdonia just to the west.

Trip plan: Llangollen makes a great base for an active break in the Dee Valley and Clwydian Range; Snowdonia is 20 miles (32km) west.

Need to know: There's no train station at Llangollen – the nearest railway stop is 6 miles (10km) away at Chirk.

Other months: Mar-Oct – spring to autumn, driest, warmest; Nov-Feb – cold, short days.

© Georgette Douwma / Getty Images

- Adventure
- Cultural
- Food & drink

MALDIVES

→ **Why now?** Learn to dive in this clear, dry season.

It seems crazy to call this long archipelago of some 1200 islands, scattered across 500 miles (800km) of Indian Ocean within clusters of 26 atolls, a country. It's really some people and their homes perched atop patches of coral, peeking above the surface of the sea: fragile, diaphanous, beautiful. And the Maldives are at their most winsome around March, when humidity and rain are low, the air is clear and visibility below is great. The headline attractions – turquoise water and luxurious resorts – are undeniably magnetic, but beyond simply sunbathing and swimming, this is a fabulous place to learn to scuba-dive, with a wealth of experienced companies offering courses.

Trip plan: Your itinerary will depend on your need for relaxation or activity. In March, opportunities for diving with whale sharks and perhaps even manta rays are best at Ari Atoll – ask locally about the top sites for this season.

Need to know: Some resorts are particularly well set up for families, with friendly experts on hand to help kids understand the fragile ecology of the atolls.

Other months: Mid-Dec–Apr – driest, prices higher; May–mid-Dec – showers, prices lower.

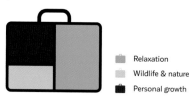

- Relaxation
- Wildlife & nature
- Personal growth

TRINIDAD & TOBAGO

→ **Why now?** Spot dazzling birdlife and watch nesting sea turtles.

This emerald isle afloat off the coast of South America is everything you'd expect from a Caribbean paradise – palm-fringed beaches, relaxed pace of life, sunshine – and plenty you might not expect. Rather than big cruise ships and package tourists, little Tobago attracts nature-lovers, snorkellers and divers. March has the fine weather you'd want on a beach holiday, but also brings nesting sea turtles – green, leatherback and hawksbill – who return to the patches of sand from which they hatched to lay their own eggs. Watch – with care – as the lumbering females haul themselves ashore, or join monitoring and conservation programs to help these threatened beauties. Sprawling across the eastern end of the island, Tobago Main Ridge Forest Reserve is bustling with birdlife – more than 200 species call the island home, including dazzling hummingbirds – and spectacular snorkelling can be enjoyed at various points around the coast.

Trip plan: Tobago's international airport is at its far western tip, and most beaches and resorts are along the southwest coast, though the natural attractions lie at the opposite (eastern) end of the island.

Need to know: All three species of sea turtle found on and around Tobago are in trouble – hawksbill turtles are critically endangered. Be careful not to harm or disturb nesting turtles.

Other months: Jan-May – warm, dry; Jun-Dec – heavy but usually short downpours.

- Relaxation
- Wildlife & nature
- Cultural
- Personal growth

REPUBLIC OF CYPRUS

Why now? Explore in cool days among green fields and dazzling blooms.

When the mountains and emerald-green hillsides are strewn with wildflowers, the sun bathes beaches such as Lara and Fig Tree Bay, and the skies are an unblemished azure, you know spring has arrived in Cyprus. March is a great time to visit: winter rains have subsided but comfortable temperatures have arrived – but not the crowds. Snow is melting from the trails in the Troödos Massif, offering heavenly hiking and cycling between traditional villages and the Byzantine frescoed churches of the central highlands. Many, though, come to Cyprus to wind down rather than rev up; a wave of yoga retreats has emerged beyond the popular beaches – and a terrace overlooking the Mediterranean is the perfect place to start the day with a sun salutation or six.

Trip plan: The Republic's international airports are at Larnaka and Pafos.

Need to know: Easter celebrations are joyful occasions for locals and visitors – but be aware that the Greek Orthodox Easter is often celebrated later than in Western churches (based on the Gregorian calendar).

Other months: Apr-Jun – warm but not too busy; Jul-Aug – high prices, crowded beaches; Sep-Nov – some rain, good hiking; Dec-Mar – snow on mountains, cool sunny days.

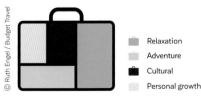

Relaxation
Adventure
Cultural
Personal growth

SAN DIEGO USA

Why now? A spring coastal break.

'America's Finest City' – or so the local claim boasts – is deceptively laid-back despite its size. And though summer is hotter and drier, March is still plenty warm, and also offers better value and shorter queues at its big attractions, of which there are many. There are the beaches, of course: Mission has its wooden rollercoaster, surfers head to Pacific Beach; Moonlight's a family favourite; La Jolla's the place for kayaking and snorkelling; hit Del Mar for peace and sweeping ocean views; and Coronado… well, it's just beautiful. Balboa Park, with its museums and zoo, is uncrowded in March, while the bars and restaurants of the Gaslamp Quarter are as lively as ever. Go north towards Carlsbad to be dazzled by the ranunculus flowers at the Flower Fields, or to Torrey Pines State Natural Reserve to hike clifftop trails – watch for dolphins and migrating grey whales between December and March.

Trip plan: San Diego's airport is absurdly (but conveniently) close to downtown – just a couple of miles from the Gaslamp Quarter, as the crow flies.

Need to know: Check dates for Spring Break, when school and college kids flood town.

Other months: Mar-May & Sep-Nov – warm weather, not too crowded; Jun-Aug – very hot; Dec-Feb – cool.

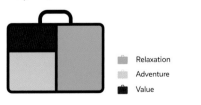

Relaxation
Adventure
Value

TYROL AUSTRIA

Why now? Some of the best late-season skiing.

Spring doesn't have to signal the end of skiing – at least in the high resorts of the Austrian Tyrol region. The valleys south and west of Innsbruck – the Stubaital, Ötztal, Tuxertal and Paznauntal, in particular – are blessed with glaciers and high, north-facing slopes that hold the snow well into March and beyond. There's variety here, too: the pretty, traditional village of Obergurgl has pistes suitable for beginners and intermediates, while nearby Sölden has more challenging runs and two glaciers, guaranteeing skiing into May; high-level Ischgl is known for its great terrain park and lively après-ski, while the slopes of the Stubaital include good off-piste options as well as traditional groomed runs. Oh, and the food and drink is high-calibre, too.

Trip plan: The international airport at Innsbruck, capital of the Tyrol, is well served by flights from across Europe, with good transport links to the resorts.

Need to know: If you absolutely, positively have to ski all year, Hintertux is the place to head – skiing on the glacier is possible 365 days.

Other months: Dec-Apr – ski season (some ski areas open to May); Jun-Sep – great hiking; May & Oct-Nov – cooler.

Adventure
Food & drink

March sees
Mallorca's almond
trees blossom

(R) One of many
moai heads on
Easter Island, Chile
(L) Waewaetorea
Island, New Zealand

© Mark Read / Lonely Planet

64

BAY OF ISLANDS
NEW ZEALAND

Why now? Late summer kayaking, swimming and sailing action.

Flecked with 144 jade outcrops, the stretch of water embraced by Cape Brett and the Purerua Peninsula is a marine playground. And March is a great month in which to roam its coves and inlets, without the crowds of high summer but still in long, warm days. However well you think you know New Zealand's history, the Waitangi Treaty Grounds just north of Paihia, where Queen Victoria's representative signed the important (and controversial) agreement with 43 Māori chiefs, are a fascinating place to visit. But get out on the water to get the most from your trip: kayak on calm waters, sail among the islands on the tall ship *R Tucker Thompson*, or take a dip with the dolphins – the bottlenose and common varieties are year-round residents of the bay, while orca and various whales visit at various times.

Trip plan: Paihia is the base for exploring the bay, with ample accommodation, eating and drinking options and activities providers, all close to the historic Waitangi Treaty Grounds. It's a three-hour drive north of Auckland.

Need to know: Swimming with dolphins isn't permitted when a pod has young calves – which can be at any time of year.

Other months: Dec-Mar – crowded; Apr-May – also pleasant; Jun-Aug – winter; Sep-Nov – weather unpredictable.

MALLORCA
SPAIN

Why now? Discover glorious coastlines, mountains and traditional villages in peace.

The 'snow of Mallorca' still blankets the hillsides in March. Not actual frozen-water snow, you understand; no, it's the pinky-white blossom of the countless almond trees that give Mallorca its distinctive icing-sugar coating at the start of the year. And as the blossoms disappear in early March, so the warm weather makes a visit a delight – before the arrival of masses of package tourists, but with plenty of sunshine to enjoy the beaches, roam traditional honey-hued towns and villages such as Deià, Fornalutx and Sóller, and hike the heights of the Serra de Tramuntana. Don't discount Palma, either; though sometimes unfortunately conflated with party resorts such as Magaluf nearby, the capital's old town is another proposition entirely, with wonderful palaces, museums, squares and the monumental cathedral.

Trip plan: Ample flights serve Palma, and with reasonable car hire and well-organised public transport, both a weekend break or a longer tour of the island are easy to organise.

Need to know: Mallorca is a cycling hotspot. Several pro teams train on its well-maintained mountain roads in winter – bring your bike and join them.

Other months: Year-round – mild winters (though with heavy showers), cooling sea breezes in summer.

CHILE

Why now? Wander in ideal weather among Rapa Nui's enigmatic stone heads and gorgeous lakes.

Chile stretches some 2700 miles (4345km) from its border with Peru and Bolivia in the north to Cape Horn, the very tip of the Americas, at 56° south – so finding the perfect time to explore can be tricky. Try March: a balmy time to be roaming the Lake District and the wineries (for the joys of the grape harvest), and it's the end of the Patagonian summer when crowds thin and prices simmer down. It's also good for a journey to that baffling ocean-lapped rock, Rapa Nui (Easter Island), adrift 2250 miles (3621km) from the mainland. The enormous *moai*, huge stone heads for which the island is famed, are just the most visible of the mysteries surrounding the culture of its first inhabitants. Make a circuit of the island's *ahu* (platforms bearing moai) and ponder the birdman cult at Orongo ceremonial village.

Trip plan: Latam Airlines (www.latam.com) makes the 5½-hour flight from Chile's capital Santiago to Rapa Nui several times a week.

Need to know: Occasional outbreaks of dengue fever on Rapa Nui mean covering up and using insect repellent is a wise strategy.

Other months: Jan-Apr & Oct-Dec – warmer and drier; May-Sep – rainier.

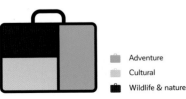

Adventure
Cultural
Wildlife & nature

Adventure
Cultural
Relaxation
Food & drink
Value

Cultural
Journey
Food & drink

© Pete Seaward / Lonely Planet

PENINSULAR MALAYSIA

A worker harvesting tea at the Boh plantation.

Water falling and mist rising at Iguazú Falls

→ **Why now?** Explore cities, beaches, islands and highlands in relatively dry conditions.

You'd expect a country as diverse as Malaysia to enjoy a varied climate – and so it does: those forests are watered by rains year round, with different monsoons bringing downpours to east and west coasts at different times. Visit in March to enjoy the best weather overall: largely dry, but with lush vegetation and gushing waterfalls. Soak up rays on beaches and islands east (Tioman and the Perhentians, with their glorious diving and snorkelling) and west (Langkawi and Penang). Active types can hike out around the tea plantations of the Cameron Highlands in relative dryness, and follow the snaking river into the steamy depths of Taman Negara's ancient rainforest on jungle treks and canopy walkways. The Chinese temples of Penang's old Georgetown and Portuguese colonial Melaka are at their most appealing, too – take the chance to sample tangy Nonya (Chinese-Malay) cuisine in those cities.

Trip plan: Trace a circuit from Kuala Lumpur (KL) north to the Cameron Highlands and Penang, pausing for a beach break on Langkawi or the Perhentian Islands before turning south to Taman Negara National Park and on to Melaka, a hop south of KL.

Need to know: Respect local sensibilities by not wearing skimpy clothing in public, particularly in more conservative areas such as Kota Bharu.

Other months: Feb-Apr – driest in most areas; Sep-Dec – heaviest widespread rain.

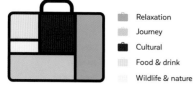

Relaxation
Journey
Cultural
Food & drink
Wildlife & nature

IGUAZÚ FALLS
BRAZIL & ARGENTINA

→ **Why now? Gawp at the mighty falls in full flow.**

A spectacle with a split personality – is it Iguazú or Iguaçu? – these hundreds of mighty cataracts arcing nearly 2 miles (3km) thunder 269ft (82m) down into a gorge dividing southern Brazil from a slender finger of Argentina. While January and February are hottest and most humid, they also bring most visitors from those two countries. By March, crowds have thinned, the weather is becoming more temperate and less damp, but the falls are still dramatically powerful. This isn't a point, shoot and leave kind of spot: the falls are surrounded by luxuriant rainforest, a national park with several excellent (and easy) walking trails bustling with wildlife and providing various views of the cataracts, most famously the Garganta del Diablo (the Devil's Throat), into which half the flow plunges.

Trip planner: Beyond the falls themselves, there's plenty to see on both the Brazilian and Argentinian sides of the national park, and a trip south alongside the Paraná River reveals the fascinating remains of 18th-century Jesuit missions. Cross the river to visit Paraguay and complete a week-long tri-country adventure.

Need to know: There are international airports on both the Argentine and Brazilian sides of the falls.

Other months: Jan-Feb – busiest, prices high; Mar-May & Sep-Oct – driest; Jun-Aug & Nov-Feb – wet.

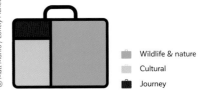

- Wildlife & nature
- Cultural
- Journey

CRETE GREECE

→ **Why now?** Get a taste of traditional Cretan life.

Dip a toe in this part of the Med in March and you'll find it a little chilly – unlike the reception. The character of much of Crete changes over winter, when package tourists vanish and a more authentic, traditional way of life takes hold. By March, daytime temperatures are warming (though a dip in the sea may still be a step too far), the hills are speckled with wildflowers, and nightlife is centred not around seafront cafes but trendy bars, non-touristy restaurants and cosy village tavernas, perhaps with a wood-burning stove or open fire. This is the time to admire the extraordinary frescoes of the Minoan palace at Knossos without the crowds, to delve into the Venetian-Ottoman quarters of Rethymno and Hania, and to hike Imbros Gorge.

Trip planner: The airport at Iraklio (Heraklion) doesn't usually receive international flights until April, but ferries sail frequently from Piraeus, Santorini and other islands.

Need to know: Some attractions and accommodation options are still closed in March, including the dramatic Samaria Gorge hike, which usually opens late April or early May.

Other months: Apr-Jun – fine weather, not too busy; Jul-Aug – hot, beaches crowded; Sep-Oct – pleasant weather, crowds thinning.

- Cultural
- Value
- Relaxation

BANFF & LAKE LOUISE CANADA

→ Enjoy late-season skiing in warmer days.

The Albertan Rockies rejoice in big dumps of snow late in the season – and as backdrops go, the mountain ridges and profuse wildlife of Banff National Park are hard to top, summer or winter; watch for elk, moose and bighorn sheep alongside the road. With three ski areas in touching distance – Lake Louise, high Sunshine Meadows and smaller Norquay, all accessible by free bus – Banff is a great base, with ample restaurants, brewpubs and bars. Accommodation prices tend to be lower in winter than in summer here, so there's good value to be found in the plentiful lodgings. Temperatures in March hover around or just above freezing with a dry climate, so the air feels pleasant. And if you do need to warm up post-ski, you can slip into the steaming thermal hot baths at Banff.

Trip plan: Banff is 85 miles (137km; a 90-minute drive) west of Calgary Airport.

Need to know: Many nationalities need to complete an Electronic Travel Authorisation (eTA) online before travelling to Canada (www.canada.ca/eta). Many facilities close during shoulder seasons.

Other months: Dec-Apr – ski slopes open, sometimes till May; May-Jun & Oct-Nov – cooler, hiking trails may be closed; Jul-Sep for good hiking.

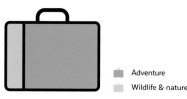

- Adventure
- Wildlife & nature

MYEIK ARCHIPELAGO MYANMAR

→ **Why now?** Cruise among hundreds of idyllic tropical specks under a warm sun.

Far off the beaten track there's a dock, and from that dock a boat sails even further from the modern world – to the long-isolated Myeik (or Mergui) Archipelago, off the southeast coast of Myanmar. This sprinkling of 800 or so rocky islands flecking the Andaman Sea only recently began welcoming foreign visitors, and is at its most beautiful in the early months of the year; in March the weather is dry and warm, with underwater visibility perfect for snorkellers and divers to absorb the varied marine life. Some islands, such as Lampi – a designated nature reserve – are blanketed with dense jungle in which tigers and elephants are reputed to roam. Others are studded with golden beaches and the stilted fishing villages of the Moken, the nomadic 'sea gypsies', who may have been the country's earliest inhabitants.

Trip plan: Several international tour operators organise sailing cruises, mostly departing from Kawthoung near the Thai border, or liveaboard dive trips from Phuket or other Thai islands.

Need to know: Burmese food is a blend of Indian and Thai; the traditional breakfast (and unofficial national dish) is *mohinga*, a spicy fish noodle soup.

Other months: Other months: Nov-Apr – driest months, best for sailing islands; May-Oct – monsoon.

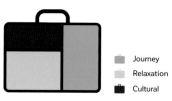

- Journey
- Relaxation
- Cultural

© Mark Read / Lonely Planet

COSTA RICA

Why now? Explore coast, cloud forest, volcanoes and whitewater rivers in the most pleasant season.

A tiny country with a huge range of landscapes and wildlife, Costa Rica also has plenty of weather – hence the lush rainforests. Come in March to hit the dry(er) season on both Pacific and Caribbean coasts and in the highlands (though showers are always likely). It's also after the peak US holiday period, so crowds are thinner. The biggest challenge is deciding what to do first: climb up and then zip line down the slopes of Arenal Volcano? Spot dazzling birdlife at the Monteverde Cloud Forest Reserve? Watch monkeys, sloths and iguanas in Manuel Antonio National Park, or caimans and manatees from a boat in Tortuguero National Park? Raft the whitewaters of the Pacuare River or surf the breaks? Tour a coffee plantation or just loll on a Caribbean beach?

Trip plan: Road distances between attractions are usually short in this compact country – a loop from capital San José, taking in Arenal, Monteverde and Manuel Antonio is comfortable in a week or so. Add more time to visit the Caribbean coast.

Need to know: Come prepared with insect repellent, heavy-duty sunscreen and an awareness of challenging driving conditions.

Other months: Dec-Apr – driest; May-Nov – wet, with regional variations, cheapest (Jun-Jul: slight lull in rain).

© Jonathan Gregson / Lonely Planet

Water flowing down the lower slopes of Arenal Volcano, Costa Rica

- Wildlife & nature
- Adventure
- Journey

BAROSSA VALLEY & FLEURIEU PENINSULA AUSTRALIA

Why now? Wind among wineries and beaches at grape-harvest time.

Come March, the grape-pickers are busy plucking bunches from the vines – and it's the perfect time to roam the rolling hills south of Adelaide. While the Barossa, northeast of the state capital, gets the bulk of the wine tourists, the Fleurieu Peninsula offers a diverse menu of fine vineyards – some 70-plus cellar doors, dominated by hearty Shiraz vintages – plus artsy towns such as Willunga, kitsch Victor Harbour, and a gorgeous coastline, with sandy shores along Gulf St Vincent and surf breaks such as those at Middleton and Christies Beach.

Trip plan: You could base yourself in Adelaide and explore from there, but better to noodle south and spend the night in McLaren Vale or at one of the beaches, roaming the wineries by day.

Need to know: If you're feeling active, the 750-mile (1200km) Heysen Trail winds from Cape Jervis at the tip of the peninsula to the Flinders Ranges – tackle a short stretch to justify another gourmet dinner.

Other months: Sep-May – spring to autumn most pleasant; Jun-Aug – winter.

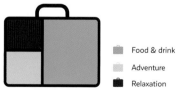

- Food & drink
- Adventure
- Relaxation

VIETNAM

Why now? Roam among karst outcrops, drift through the delta and meet hilltribes.

With three microclimates, and rain hitting different regions in different months, it's always a great time to visit somewhere in Vietnam – but damp in other spots. March, though, is fine pretty much across the board: it's a rare season when you can capture photos of the junks and karst outcrops of Halong Bay and Bai Tu Long against an azure sky rather than haze; when trekking up the country's highest peak, Fansipan (3143m), and among the hilltribes around Sapa is comfortably cool and dry; when wandering Hanoi's charming Old Quarter is a delight; and when the central coast and southern beaches such as Mui Ne or Phu Quoc are pleasantly warm and rain-free.

Trip plan: How long have you got? A fortnight allows time for a tour of the north, looping from Hanoi to Sapa and Halong Bay, possibly even down to Hue and Hoi An. Add more time and you can stretch your route south to Nha Trang, Dalat, Saigon, the Mekong Delta and those beaches. And maybe get off the beaten track, too.

Need to know: Visa regulations change often – check the latest requirements with a Vietnamese consulate before heading off.

Other months: South – dry Dec-Apr, rains May-Nov; central coast around Hue – dry Mar-Aug, rains Sep-Feb; north – cold Dec-Mar, wet Apr-Sep, dry and cool Oct-Nov.

- Cultural
- Journey
- Adventure
- Food & drink

(R) Postcards of Vietnam War propaganda posters (L) Two girls from Black Hmong tribe

SÌCHUĀN
CHINA

→ **Why now?** To meet pandas and admire spring blooms.

Spanning the Tibetan Plateau and the subtropical climes of the east, Sìchuān is a big province with diverse cultures and experiences. Early spring is the ideal time to take a vertical slice through the middle, with blooming flowers and blossoming pear trees. Capital Chéngdū has its share of temples and parks, but the panda has the strongest pull – specifically the giant panda, of which a chunk of the surviving population of around 1600 live in Sìchuān or the Qinling Mountains just to the north in Shaanxi province. Visit the Giant Panda Breeding Research Base 6 miles (10km) north of Chéngdū for an introduction, or head to Bifengxia Panda Reserve, which hosts 80 of the monochrome mammals in a larger area. Further north, Jiǔzhàigōu National Park may also harbour giant pandas, though you'd be lucky to spot one – you might, though, see golden monkeys as you walk among the forests, waterfalls and 114 turquoise lakes.

Trip plan: Fly to Chéngdū and visit Bifengxia to the southwest before making a loop north via historic Lángzhōng to Jiǔzhàigōu.

Need to know: It's possible to meet pandas on a volunteer placement at Bifengxia.

Other months: Nov-Mar – very cold at altitude; Apr-Jun – most pleasant; Jul-Aug – very hot and humid; Sep-Oct – autumn.

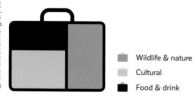

Wildlife & nature
Cultural
Food & drink

ANTIGUA

→ **Why now?** Bright Caribbean sunshine and cool breezes in the perfect season.

Antigua has a beach for every day of the year – or so the legend goes. Whether or not there are 365 separate stretches of sand on the island, it's true that you won't want for a patch of soft, golden-tinted shoreline on which to lounge. March sees a lull in tourist arrivals after the midwinter peak and before Easter, but the weather is still dry and hurricane-free. Antigua is a family-friendly paradise, too, with activities galore and a piratical air – venture to Nelson's Dockyard or the atmospheric, 18th-century Fort James for a bit of maritime history, snorkel the colourful reefs or try a bit of bodysurfing.

Trip plan: International flights serve VC Bird Airport in Antigua's north, near the capital, St John's; the other significant centre is around the dual coves and historic sites of Falmouth Harbour and English Harbour in the south. But with its compact 13-mile (21km) length and beaches all around the island, it's easy to access all parts of the island.

Need to know: March is towards the end of the mating season for frigate birds – look for the throat sacs of courting males at Codrington on neighbouring Barbuda, one of the world's largest breeding colonies.

Other months: Dec-Apr – driest; May-Jun – hot; Jul-Nov – showers; Jul – Carnival.

Relaxation

CANBERRA
AUSTRALIA

→ **Why now?** Roam the well-wooded capital and surrounds in its autumn finery.

Australia's capital, built pretty much from scratch over the past century, might be the orderly, well-planned centre of the country's civic life, but it's also a cultural hub and lively university town, with a world-beating arts scene. The verdant, tree-studded city is at its best in autumn: board a bike to complete a circuit of Lake Burley Griffin and tour the semi-subterranean Parliament House, moving Australian War Memorial, National Gallery and National Portrait Gallery, and (on Sundays) bustling Old Bus Depot Markets. Canberra reputedly boasts the highest number of restaurants per capita in the country; once you've finished sampling the city's culinary delights, head out on a road trip along the Poacher's Way, a lattice of meandering routes linking the dozens of vineyards, artisan food producers, galleries and craft studios around Bungendore, Hall, Gundaroo and Murrumbateman north and east of Canberra. Mmmm.

Trip plan: You'll need at least three days to drive the whole Poacher's Way, plus a couple of nights in Canberra.

Need to know: The Enlighten festival brings music, dance and other arts and interactive events to the capital during early March evenings (enlightencanberra. com.au).

Other months: Oct-Apr – spring to autumn most pleasant; Jun-Aug – winter.

Cultural
Food & drink

SAVANNAH USA

Admire spring blooms in a gracious old town.

To meet a grand southern belle in her prime, venture to Savannah in March. The azaleas and dogwoods are blooming, the air is warm but not too warm, the stately antebellum architecture of the historic district looks at its finest, and a string of events see melodies and harmonies drifting through the streets, parks and 21 historic squares. Either side of the renowned St Patrick's Day celebrations, Savannah Stopover hosts up-and-coming acts and the Savannah Music Festival at the end of the month brings top classical, world, country, jazz and other performers to the city. There's a chance to nose around some of those historic properties, too, with the Annual Savannah Tour of Homes and Gardens. But it's not all moss-draped oak avenues, riverboats and plantation houses; the student population keeps things lively with a great nightlife and a thriving arts scene.

Trip plan: The choice is really whether to coincide your visit with a festival, or enjoy thinner crowds between the big events. Check www.visitsavannah.com for dates and ideas for things to do.

Need to know: Savannah's spring appeal means it's a busy time to visit – book accommodation well in advance for stays after St Patrick's Day (17 March).

Other months: Mar-Oct – warm days, lush foliage, lots of events; Nov-Feb – mild, dry.

© Jeremy Woodhouse / Getty Images

Stately trees give shade in an urban park in Savannah

■ Cultural
▨ Relaxation

BEYOND SAVANNAH

🚙 **TYBEE ISLAND · 18 MILES (29KM) ·** Sandy beaches and a historic lighthouse

🚙 **JEKYLL ISLAND · 90 MILES (145KM) ·** Cycling, fishing and long sandy beaches

🚆 **CHARLESTON, SOUTH CAROLINA · 110 MILES (177KM) ·** More glorious antebellum architecture

🚙 **OKEFENOKEE NATIONAL WILDLIFE REFUGE · 130 MILES (209KM) ·** Vast swamp swarming with alligators and birds

Gray langur monkeys and roe deer are two species also keeping an eye out for tigers

MADHYA PRADESH INDIA

→ **Why now? For the best chance of spotting Shere Khan.**

If you want to encounter the world's biggest big cat, *Panthera tigris*, central India's the place to come – and March is the time, when the dry season has taken its toll on grasses, visibility is better and wildlife gathers at waterholes. Perhaps only 3000 (or even fewer) of these endangered carnivores survive across the 13 tiger range countries, of which two-thirds are in India. Take a few jeep safaris in the cluster of tiger reserves in Madhya Pradesh for a fighting chance of earning your stripes with a sighting. Bandhavgarh, Kanha, Tadoba-Andhari and Pench – reputedly the patch that inspired Kipling's *Jungle Book* – all harbour (relatively) healthy tiger populations, as well as species such as leopards, sloth bears, monkeys and profuse birdlife. Though tiger sightings are less reliable at Satpura, it's possible to walk and even kayak in this reserve – both electrifying experiences.

Trip plan: The most convenient airport is Nagpur. It's fairly easy to combine safaris in two or more of the reserves, and add on visits to the temples of Khajuraho (famed for erotic carvings) or even the palaces of Rajasthan and the Taj Mahal.

Need to know: Most tiger reserves, except Tadoba-Andhari, close to tourists during the monsoon, from mid-June to September.

Other months: Oct-Jan – dry, thick vegetation; Feb-May – dry, warming; Jun-Sep – monsoon.

■ Wildlife & nature
▨ Cultural

BAJA CALIFORNIA
MEXICO

→ **Why now? To meet a whale.**
The grey whales that congregate off this spindly, untamed Mexican peninsula are a friendly bunch. Around 10,000 of them migrate from the Arctic down the west coast of North America to over-winter in the Baja's Pacific lagoons, where they mate and calve; numbers peak February to April. In San Ignacio Lagoon in particular the whales are extremely curious, often bopping boats and courting cuddles. Eyeballing one of these barnacled leviathans is one of the planet's most emotional wildlife encounters. Even better, Baja's waters are chock-full of other species. The Pacific coast attracts still more whales, including humpbacks, plus dolphins and fur seals. On Baja's east coast, La Paz Bay is a whale-shark hangout while the Sea of Cortez is one of the world's best places to spot Bryde's and blue whales.

Trip plan: Expedition cruises heading south from San Diego offer the most comprehensive marine experience. Alternatively, take day-boat excursions from shore camps at San Ignacio, Cabo San Lucas (for the Sea of Cortez) and La Paz.

Need to know: Loreto is the closest international airport to the lagoons; Cabo San Lucas 10-hour drive) receives more flights.

Other months: Jan-Apr – main whale-watching season; Jul-Sep – rainiest; Sep-Dec – whale-shark numbers peak.

© Xavier Loh / 500px

The Ciudad de las Artes y Ciencias (City of Arts and Sciences), Valencia

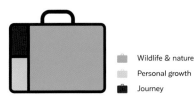

- Wildlife & nature
- Personal growth
- Journey

VALENCIA SPAIN

→ **Why now? Sample Spain's finest paella in the spring sunshine.**
Spain's third city heats up in March – meteorologically and culturally. This is the month when a legion of huge figures called *ninots* are constructed in the city centre, then burned in a vast conflagration accompanied by the fireworks and festivities of Las Fallas. Aside from the pyrotechnics, though, March is a great time to explore the city's culinary variety, reflecting the fertility of the surrounding *huerta* farmlands. This is the home of paella, and nowhere else is the rice feast prepared so magnificently – head to the wetlands of nearby Albufera National Park to see the lush rice fields, and take a cookery class to learn how to prepare the perfect paella yourself. Spare time to explore the old, warren-like Barrio del Carmen and admire La Ciudad de las Artes y Ciencias cultural complex, largely designed by renowned Valencian architect Santiago Calatrava.

Trip plan: Valencia is served by flights from most major European cities.

Need to know: Valencia gets full to bursting for the climax of Las Fallas (15 to 19 March) – it's a great time to be in town, but book transport and accommodation well in advance.

Other months: Jan-May – mild, pleasant temperatures; Jun-Sep – summer, very hot, busy; Oct-Dec – autumn, cooler and rainy.

- Food & drink
- Cultural
- Personal growth

SRI LANKA

→ **Why now? Chilling, culture, cetaceans and carnivores in the dry season.**

Sri Lanka is complicated – not least the weather: much of it gets hit by monsoons around May and October, while the north and east get soaked November and December. Come in March, when weather's good all over, wildlife at parks such as Yala and Uda Walawe – home to leopards, elephants, monkeys and more – comes out to drink at waterholes, blue and sperm whales cruise the coast, and hiking Adam's Peak is most pleasant. Hit the beaches of the west for gorgeous sweeps of sand, and the south for peace and surf, but be sure to explore inland – sacred city Kandy, with its Buddha tooth relic; the 'Lion Rock' topped with an ancient palace at Sigiriya; and the ruins of Anuradhapura and Polonnaruwa in the 'Cultural Triangle'. Make time to sample the glorious food, a blend of South Indian, Arab, Malay and Portuguese flavours.

Trip plan: Fly to capital Colombo and head south to the beaches around Galle for a few days' relaxation, then hire a car and driver or catch trains and local buses east to the wildlife reserves then north to the cultural attractions of the centre.

Need to know: Visitors require a visa; obtain an Electronic Travel Authorisation (ETA) online at www.eta.gov.lk/slvisa.

Other months: Jan-Mar & Jul-Aug – dry most places; Dec–mid-Jan – busiest; Apr-Jun & Sep-Nov – wet in southwest and centre.

- Relaxation
- Wildlife & nature
- Journey
- Food & drink
- Adventure

Animals spotted around waterholes include the elusive leopard

AUSTIN USA

Why now? To experience the creative eruption that is SXSW. Texas is normally associated with big oil and big bucks, not so much big creative ideas. Yet little Austin, till the mid-80s a modest but hip college town, bucks the trend. In 1987 it launched a new kind of festival, SXSW, not just to promote its vibrant music scene but the creative ideas buzzing around it. Now, for a few days in mid-March each year Austin is the music, film and interactive hub of the US, with top speakers, local and international acts and movie premieres. March is a great time to explore Austin's thriving music scene anyway, with countless venues staging live acts every night of the week. And after spending a pleasantly warm day in the surrounding countryside admiring desert wildflowers in bloom, head to the Colorado River before dusk to watch the spectacle of 1.5 million Mexican free-tailed bats emerge from their roost under the Congress Avenue Bridge – they arrive here each March.

Trip plan: If you're here for SXSW, register for your event badge and accommodation as far in advance as possible – ideally the previous August.

Need to know: Come back in early October, when Austin City Limits – a more straight-ahead music-focused festival – sees dozens of top acts hit town.

Other months: Mar-May – spring; Sep-Nov – autumn; Jun-Aug – extremely hot; Dec-Feb – cooler but mild.

© Kris Davidson / Lonely Planet

A street performer on South Congress Street, Austin

Cultural
Relaxation

BEYOND AUSTIN

BASTROP · 30 MILES (48KM) · 'Most Historic Small Town in Texas'

FREDERICKSBURG · 78 MILES (126KM) · German heritage, peach orchards and vineyards

SAN ANTONIO · 80 MILES (129KM) · The Alamo, historic hotels and Riverwalk nightlife

DALLAS · 200 MILES (322KM) · Spectacular dining and vast Arts District

Hiking the Routeburn
Track high above Lake
Mackenzie, New Zealand

Exploring the sands of
Amiston Beach in a dune
buggy, South Africa

VICTORIA'S HIGH COUNTRY
AUSTRALIA

→ Why now? Fine cycling along some of Australia's tastiest trails.

The heights around Bright in the northeastern corner of Victoria make a credible claim to being Australia's cycle epicentre, and March is an ideal time to saddle up – sunny, not too hot, just at the tipping point between summer and autumn. The region is laced with over 150 miles (241km) of safe off-road routes including the 72-mile (116km) Murray to Mountains Rail Trail, plus adrenaline-piquing mountain-biking, testing road rides and plenty of family-friendly routes. Pedal between historic gold-mining towns such as Yackandandah and Beechworth, stopping in at the bountiful cafes and cellar doors of notable wineries including Brown Brothers and John Gehrig. The region's riddled with foodie treats, too, from artisan food producers (try the wares of Milawa Cheese Company) to gourmet restaurants.

Trip planner: Bright, usually considered the gateway to the High Country, is a three-hour drive north of Melbourne. There are plenty of accommodation options, many of them charming historic B&Bs.

Need to know: If you don't bring your own bike, hire is available at most towns across the region; check details at www.victoriashighcountry.com.au.

Other months: Dec-Mar – summer; Apr-May – fine autumn foliage, harvest festivals; Jun-Sep – ski season; Oct-Nov – spring.

WESTERN CAPE
SOUTH AFRICA

→ Why now? For a sand and city break without the crowds.

The quirks of the African climate mean that during the austral summer, while much of the rest of the country soaks, South Africa's Cape region basks in warm sunshine. The peak of summer – from mid-December through January and into February – sees holidaymakers flock here, which is why March is the ideal time, with blue skies but without the crowds. Cape Town celebrates now, too: in March, the city and surrounding region sings and dances with festivals and events including its annual Carnival. Drive east from Cape Town on the N2, then duck off the highway and down to the coast to explore the gems of the forested-lined Garden Route. Discover glorious beaches and charming villages, surf with the dolphins of Plettenberg Bay, kayak the waterways of Wilderness National Park, wander pretty seaside towns, and roam the ancient forests of Knysna and Tsitsikamma National Park.

Trip plan: By flying into Cape Town and out of Port Elizabeth, or vice versa, you can plan a one-way route and avoid doubling back on yourself.

Need to know: For high-flyers, March is the end of the best paragliding season.

Other months: Nov-Mar – summer, dry, warm; Apr-Oct – cooler, rainy.

SOUTH ISLAND
NEW ZEALAND

→ Why now? Trek a Great Walk in relative solitude.

The four-day Milford Track hike through Fiordland National Park, from Glade Wharf to Sandfly Point, is among the world's most famous. It's also among the most popular, with bunks in the three DOC huts en route booked out many months in advance for high summer. Two solutions: hike outside the peak – March being arguably the optimal month, still enjoying pretty fine weather – or pick an alternative route, many of which boast similarly spectacular scenery but not the marquee status that attracts the crowds. Two other Great Walks in the same area, the Routeburn and Kepler, are also popular but not quite as busy; alternatively, pick one without Great Walk branding – perhaps the four-day Queen Charlotte Track near Picton, or the relatively new and little-known three-day Tuatapere Hump Ridge Track west of Invercargill.

Trip plan: Queenstown is the most convenient hopping-off point for the Milford, Kepler and Routeburn tracks, with shuttle services to trailheads (or connecting boats) for all three.

Need to know: Hut bookings during the Great Walks season (late October to late April) open the previous May or even earlier for the big-name trails. Consider booking with a guiding company for the Milford, for more comfortable huts and great food.

Other months: Nov-Apr – summer, early autumn, driest; May-Oct – colder, wetter.

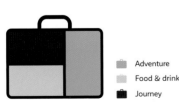

Adventure
Food & drink
Journey

Journey
Relaxation
Cultural

Adventure
Cultural

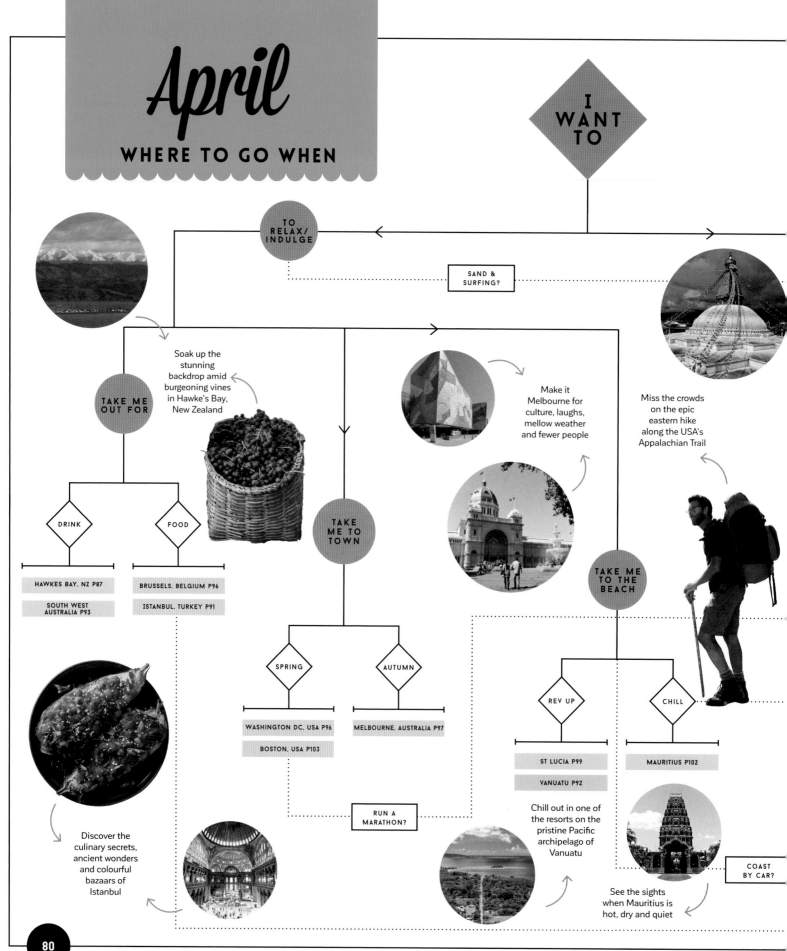

April

WHERE TO GO WHEN

I WANT TO

TO RELAX/ INDULGE

SAND & SURFING?

TAKE ME OUT FOR

Soak up the stunning backdrop amid burgeoning vines in Hawke's Bay, New Zealand

Make it Melbourne for culture, laughs, mellow weather and fewer people

Miss the crowds on the epic eastern hike along the USA's Appalachian Trail

DRINK

FOOD

TAKE ME TO TOWN

TAKE ME TO THE BEACH

| HAWKES BAY, NZ P87 |
| SOUTH WEST AUSTRALIA P93 |

| BRUSSELS, BELGIUM P96 |
| ISTANBUL, TURKEY P91 |

SPRING

AUTUMN

REV UP

CHILL

| WASHINGTON DC, USA P96 |
| BOSTON, USA P103 |

| MELBOURNE, AUSTRALIA P97 |

| ST LUCIA P99 |
| VANUATU P92 |

| MAURITIUS P102 |

RUN A MARATHON?

Discover the culinary secrets, ancient wonders and colourful bazaars of Istanbul

Chill out in one of the resorts on the pristine Pacific archipelago of Vanuatu

COAST BY CAR?

See the sights when Mauritius is hot, dry and quiet

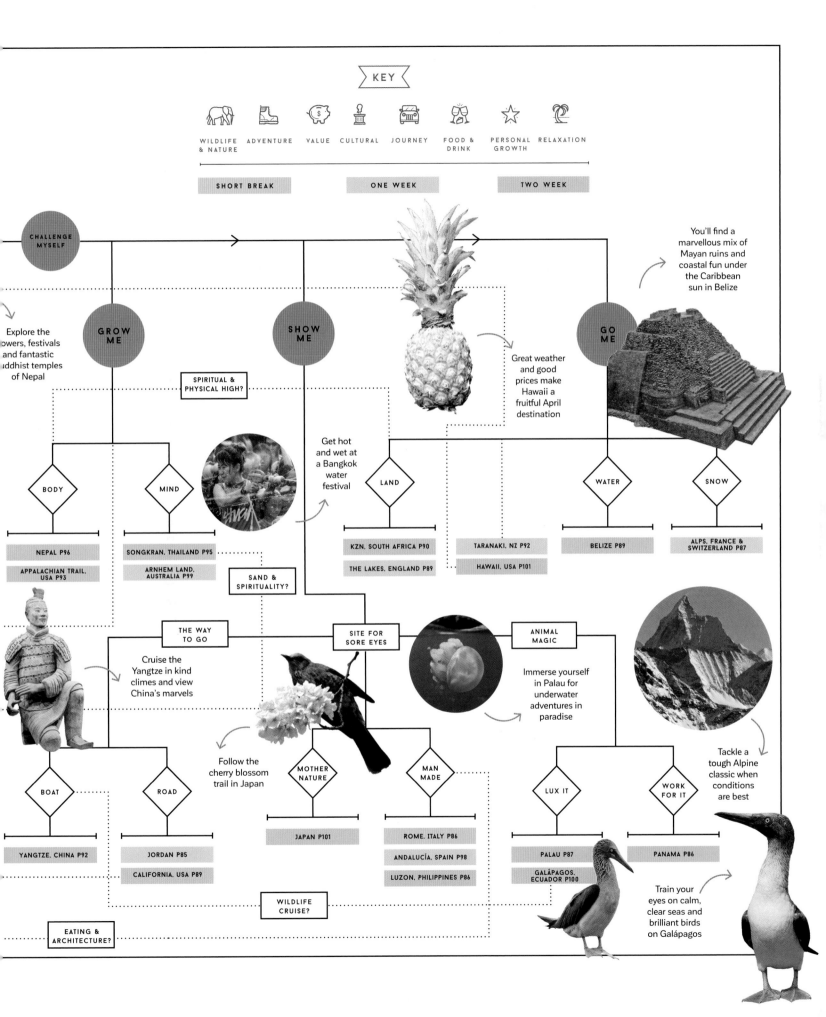

KEY

WILDLIFE & NATURE   ADVENTURE   VALUE   CULTURAL   JOURNEY   FOOD & DRINK   PERSONAL GROWTH   RELAXATION

SHORT BREAK   ONE WEEK   TWO WEEK

CHALLENGE MYSELF

GROW ME

SHOW ME

GO ME

You'll find a marvellous mix of Mayan ruins and coastal fun under the Caribbean sun in Belize

Explore the flowers, festivals and fantastic Buddhist temples of Nepal

SPIRITUAL & PHYSICAL HIGH?

Great weather and good prices make Hawaii a fruitful April destination

Get hot and wet at a Bangkok water festival

BODY

MIND

LAND

WATER

SNOW

NEPAL P96

APPALACHIAN TRAIL, USA P93

SONGKRAN, THAILAND P95

ARNHEM LAND, AUSTRALIA P99

KZN, SOUTH AFRICA P90

THE LAKES, ENGLAND P89

TARANAKI, NZ P92

HAWAII, USA P101

BELIZE P89

ALPS, FRANCE & SWITZERLAND P87

SAND & SPIRITUALITY?

THE WAY TO GO

SITE FOR SORE EYES

ANIMAL MAGIC

Cruise the Yangtze in kind climes and view China's marvels

Immerse yourself in Palau for underwater adventures in paradise

Tackle a tough Alpine classic when conditions are best

Follow the cherry blossom trail in Japan

MOTHER NATURE

MAN MADE

LUX IT

WORK FOR IT

BOAT

ROAD

JAPAN P101

ROME, ITALY P86

ANDALUCÍA, SPAIN P98

LUZON, PHILIPPINES P86

PALAU P87

GALÁPAGOS, ECUADOR P100

PANAMA P86

YANGTZE, CHINA P92

JORDAN P85

CALIFORNIA, USA P89

Train your eyes on calm, clear seas and brilliant birds on Galápagos

WILDLIFE CRUISE?

EATING & ARCHITECTURE?

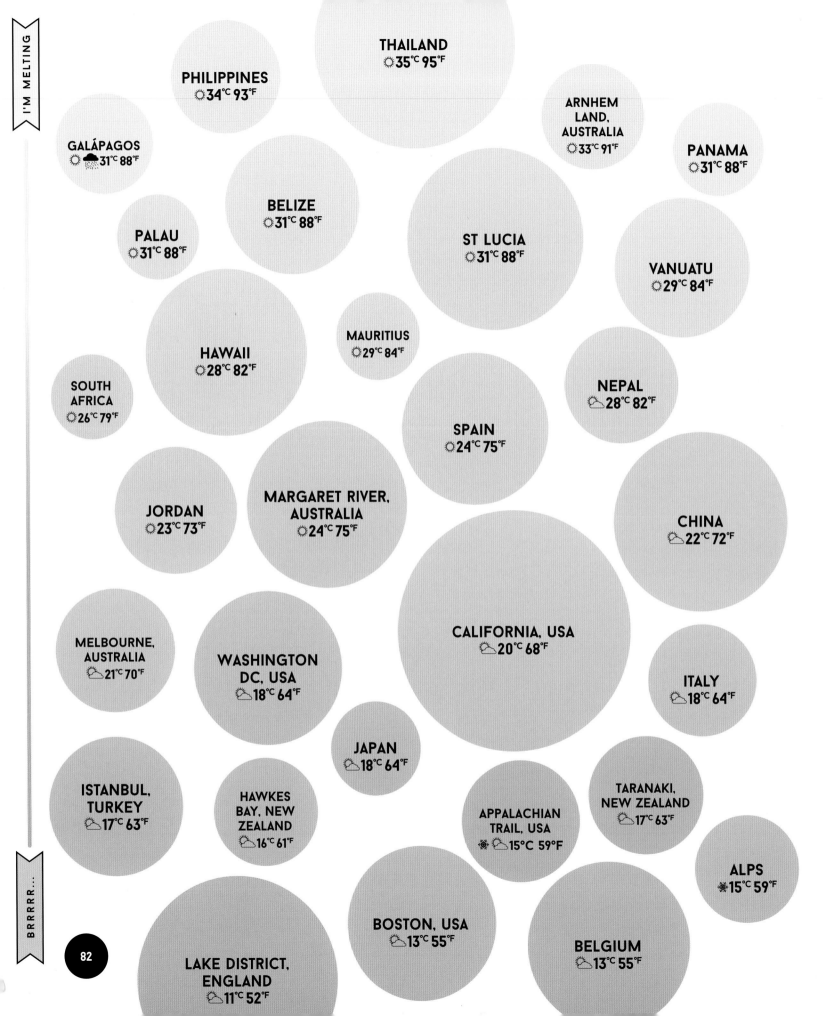

THAILAND
☀ 35℃ 95℉

PHILIPPINES
☀ 34℃ 93℉

ARNHEM
LAND,
AUSTRALIA
☀ 33℃ 91℉

PANAMA
☀ 31℃ 88℉

GALÁPAGOS
☀🌧 31℃ 88℉

BELIZE
☀ 31℃ 88℉

PALAU
☀ 31℃ 88℉

ST LUCIA
☀ 31℃ 88℉

VANUATU
☀ 29℃ 84℉

MAURITIUS
☀ 29℃ 84℉

HAWAII
☀ 28℃ 82℉

NEPAL
⛅ 28℃ 82℉

SOUTH
AFRICA
☀ 26℃ 79℉

SPAIN
☀ 24℃ 75℉

JORDAN
☀ 23℃ 73℉

MARGARET RIVER,
AUSTRALIA
☀ 24℃ 75℉

CHINA
⛅ 22℃ 72℉

MELBOURNE,
AUSTRALIA
⛅ 21℃ 70℉

CALIFORNIA, USA
☁ 20℃ 68℉

ITALY
☁ 18℃ 64℉

WASHINGTON
DC, USA
☁ 18℃ 64℉

JAPAN
☁ 18℃ 64℉

ISTANBUL,
TURKEY
⛅ 17℃ 63℉

HAWKES
BAY, NEW
ZEALAND
☁ 16℃ 61℉

APPALACHIAN
TRAIL, USA
❄☁ 15℃ 59℉

TARANAKI,
NEW ZEALAND
⛅ 17℃ 63℉

ALPS
❄ 15℃ 59℉

BOSTON, USA
☁ 13℃ 55℉

BELGIUM
☁ 13℃ 55℉

LAKE DISTRICT,
ENGLAND
🌧 11℃ 52℉

BELIZE

MELBOURNE,
AUSTRALIA

GALÁPAGOS

Check out the
blue-footed booby's
courtship dance on
the Galápagos

BOSTON, USA

CALIFORNIA, USA

JAPAN

Spring
temperatures
make sightseeing
at the Colosseum
comfortable

MAURITIUS

ROME, ITALY

Immerse
yourself in Palau
for underwater
adventures in
paradise

PALAU

HAWAII, USA

JORDAN

WASHINGTON
DC, USA

A huge waterfight
cools down
Bangkok's residents
during Thai New Year

THAILAND

The tropical US state
of Hawaii was once
the pineapple capital
of the world

LAKE DISTRICT, ENGLAND

The locals ride
Andalucian horses
during Seville's
Feria de Abril

ANDALUCÍA, SPAIN

NEPAL

ISTANBUL,
TURKEY

BRUSSELS, BELGIUM

TARANAKI, NZ

It's usually dry and
mild in Belgium's
captivating capital at
this time of year

PANAMA

It's the perfect
season to explore
Ifuago's vertiginous
terraces of rice

ST LUCIA

The Terracotta
Warriors are just one
essential stop-off on
a Yangtze cruise

LUZON, PHILIPPINES

YANGTZE, CHINA

VANUATU

You can island-hop
by kayak around San
Blas off Panama's
Caribbean coast

ARNHEM LAND,
AUSTRALIA

SOUTH WEST
AUSTRALIA

HAWKES BAY, NZ

KZN, SOUTH AFRICA

HAUTE ROUTE, ALPS

APPALACHIAN TRAIL, USA

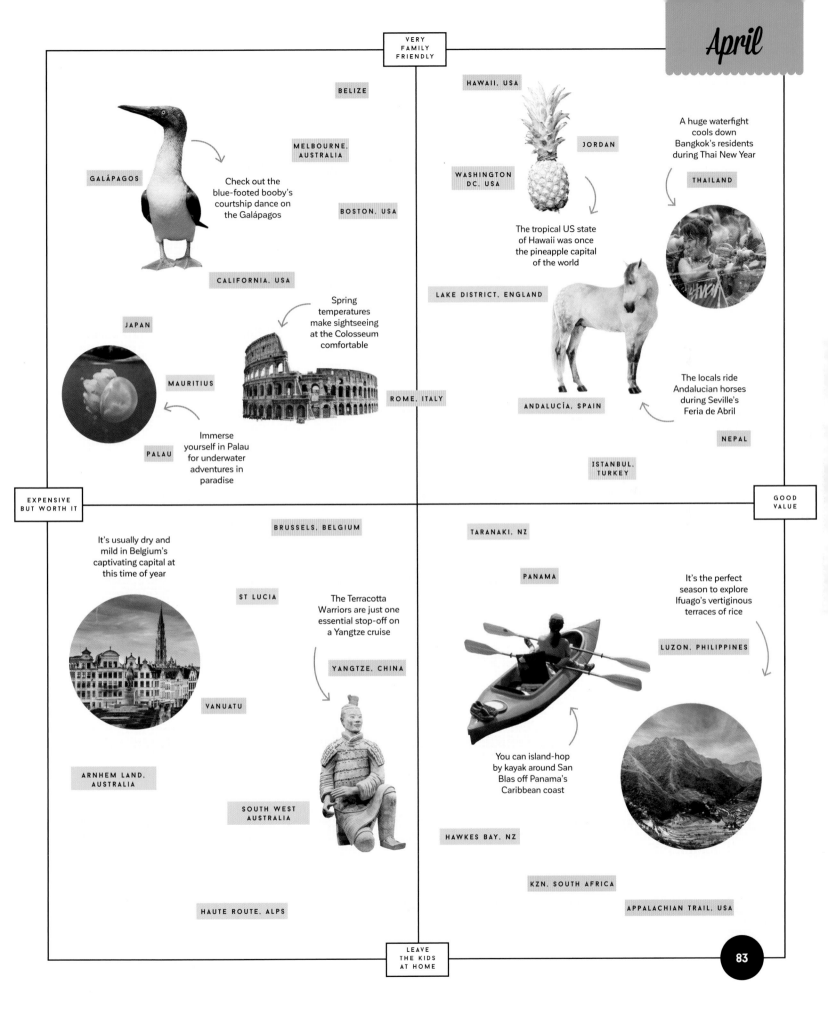

JORDAN

Why now? For Indiana Jones-ing in the kindest temperatures.

Compact Jordan is the complete package. Ancient wonders? Visit the 2000-year-old rock-hewn city of Petra or Kerak's Crusader castle. City sights? Try Roman Jerash or the souks of Amman. Jaw-dropping landscapes? Camp in the alien-esque deserts of Wadi Rum. Wildlife? Explore Dana Nature Reserve. Beach? Pick between the salty Dead Sea or snorkel-friendly Red Sea. More surprisingly, Jordan can also be very green – especially at this time. In April, humidity and rainfall are low, temperatures loiter delightfully around the low 20°Cs (68-73°F), the central valleys are lush from winter rains and there are wildflowers everywhere. In particular, Ajloun Forest is abloom with strawberry trees and rock roses and Dana's oases are bright with oleander and birds. Also, the vastness of Petra can be explored without breaking a sweat. In short, a beautiful time to travel across the country.

Trip plan: From Amman, nip north to Jerash and Ajloun before veering south towards Aqaba, stopping at the Dead Sea, Dana, Petra and Wadi Rum en route.

Need to know: The *khamseen* (hot, sandy wind) can hit Jordan in spring; it usually only lasts a few days.

Other months: Mar-May – springlike, ideal; Jun-Sep – very hot; Oct – fleeting autumn, pleasant; Nov-Feb – cold in many areas, Aqaba warm.

■ Cultural
■ Wildlife & nature
■ Journey

The moon rising over the desert landscape of Wadi Rum

PANAMA

LUZON
PHILIPPINES

ROME
ITALY

Why now? Combine Caribbean and Pacific in drier climes.

Tourism to the skinny isthmus of Panama is on the up. However, this is largely thanks to an increase in cruise-ship passengers, who sail through the country's famed canal without stepping foot elsewhere. That leaves much of the country invitingly empty – like Costa Rica without the crowds. Squarely in the tropics, Panama can get hot and sticky, so it's best to visit in the drier, sunnier period of December to mid-April. Showers can fall at any time but, outside the wettest months, are often short, sudden storms that quickly clear. It's worth braving any rain, though. Highlights include the Caribbean-side San Blas Islands, where you can island-hop by kayak and meet indigenous Kuna people; the cool highlands of Chiriquí, for adventures amid alpine forests and coffee plantations; and the offbeat Pacific beaches of Boca Chica, where surf swells are epic from April to November.

Trip plan: Arrive in Panama City, pass through the Panama Canal, escape the heat in the highlands, then finish with beach time on the Caribbean coast.

Need to know: Panama is a birding hotspot, with more than 950 species.

Other months: Dec-Apr – driest; Mar-May – sunniest; May-Nov – wet season (worst Sep-Oct).

Why now? Perfect weather, nice rice.

The rice terraces of Ifuago province, on the Philippines island of Luzon, are farming at its most fantastic. These fertile shelves hewn into the hills were first created over 2000 years ago, and are now listed by Unesco. The fields are planted in January and February, and are at their glorious greenest April to May; from June they turn spectacular yellows, but it's harder work exploring once the rains kick in. The amphitheatre of terraces around Batad is particularly impressive, and guided walks offer good views as well as visits to Ifugao villages and markets. This dry-season month is also ideal for exploring the nearby mountain-tucked town of Sagada. From here, hiking trails lead through the hills, and tours reveal the region's rather singular burial tradition: the practice of hanging coffins high up on the cliffs.

Trip plan: Fly to Manila and head north for Mt Pinatubo, Baguio market, Banaue and Sagada. Add on beach time at untouristy Pagudpud.

Need to know: The Philippines is inexpensive – midrange travellers can get by on around US$40 a day.

Other months: Nov-May – cooler, dry (Jan-Apr: best); Jun-Oct – wet.

Why now? Spring temperatures make for comfy sightseeing.

History buffs might like to visit Rome on its birthday. The Eternal City was founded on 21 April 753 BC, and every year it celebrates with events, illuminations and truck-loads of fireworks. Festivities aside, April to May is a delightful time to visit. Rome is a city for sightseeing, which is far better done on milder spring days (15-20°C; 59-68°F) than in the depths of winter or heights of summer with the largely shadeless Forum being particularly unforgiving in the latter. It's also less busy (and a little cheaper), though seasonal attractions are open; for instance, atmospheric after-dark tours of the Colosseum run April to October. To top it all, menus fill with good spring things, such as artichokes and asparagus. *Vignarola*, a Roman speciality combining peas, fava beans, lettuce and artichokes is the season's signature dish.

Trip plan: Rome warrants several days. As well as visiting its famed ruins and piazzas, take a walk along the Via Appia (the first Roman road), which is particularly handsome in spring.

Need to know: Free drinking water is available from *nasoni* (public fountains) across the city.

Other months: Apr-May & Sep-Oct – manageable weather, quieter; Jun-Aug – sweltering; Nov-Mar – cool, wet.

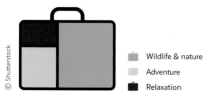

- Wildlife & nature
- Adventure
- Relaxation

- Cultural
- Wildlife & nature
- Journey
- Value

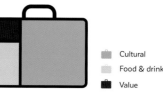

- Cultural
- Food & drink
- Value

© Shutterstock

HAWKE'S BAY
NEW ZEALAND

→ **Why now?** To bike amid burgeoning vines.

Hawke's Bay is the larder of New Zealand: apples, figs, peaches, squashes and, most notably, grapes. Hugging the east coast of the North Island, this is the country's oldest wine-growing region, and in April the grapes are being plucked: 4700 hectares of vineyards harvesting 45,000 tonnes of fruit. The serried vines begin to glow russet and gold under the autumn sun too. Still reasonably warm and dry, this is a great time to explore by bicycle. Hawke's Bay has New Zealand's biggest network of gentle cycle paths, many of which link wine estates, cafes and cellar doors. Try the flat, offroad 22-mile (36km) Wineries Ride, which navigates the grape-growing heartland of Bridge Pa, Gimblett Gravels and Ngatarawa Triangle. Napier, with its art deco architecture and Saturday Urban Food Market, makes a good base.

Trip plan: Enjoy the historic streets and fine eats of Napier and Hastings. Then follow a couple of easy cycle trails – perhaps one along the coast, another between wine estates.

Need to know: There are flights to Hawke's Bay daily from Wellington, Auckland and Christchurch.

Other months: Dec-Feb – warmest; Mar-May – wine harvest; Jun-Sep – winter, cool. Oct-Nov – spring produce, warming up.

ALPS FRANCE & SWITZERLAND

→ **Why now?** Tackle a tough Alpine classic when conditions are best.

The 75-mile (120km) Haute Route links Chamonix/Mont Blanc and Zermatt/the Matterhorn via some of the Alps' finest terrain. It ticks off two countries, skirts beneath most of the range's highest summits, crosses cols, traverses lakes and descends glaciers. Simply, it is the crème de la crème of ski-touring, and only for those with experience. Long days at high altitude (it tops out at 12,434ft (3790m) Pigne d'Arolla) make it a challenging prospect. The main Haute Route ski-touring season runs from mid-March to late April. This is when the glaciers are safely covered in powder, the weather is generally milder, and the mountain huts are open, heated and cooking up hearty hot meals. Don't ski? Come back in summer to do it on foot.

Trip plan: Skiing the Haute Route takes six days. Allow time in lively Chamonix and Zermatt too.

Need to know: You will need both euros (France) and Swiss francs (Switzerland).

Other months: Mar-Apr – best snow conditions; Jun-Sep – route hikeable; Nov-Feb & May – conditions not ideal for either.

PALAU

→ **Why now?** For underwater adventures in paradise.

The Micronesian nation of Palau looks pretty amazing above water: it's a sprinkle of 200-odd lush-green limestone outcrops, sheltered lagoons, white sands and blindingly turquoise seas. But it's under water where things become truly spectacular. This is the sub-aqua Serengeti, with 1500 fish species, soft corals and sea fans, sheer drop-offs and WWII wrecks. Palau is balmy year-round, and there's no really bad time to dive here. However, dry-season April, when seas are calmer and clearer, is a good choice. Also, whale sharks and manta rays are more likely January to April, while green and hawksbill turtles are most often seen April to July. The icing on the cake? Jellyfish Lake, a lagoon pulsating with a million translucent, stingless jellies – it's like snorkelling through the chorus line of an immense submarine ballet.

Trip plan: Keen divers should consider a liveaboard trip, to maximise dive options and ease access to the best sites (including Blue Corner and German Channel).

Need to know: Roman Tmetuchl International Airport is on Babeldaob island; it's a 1½-hour flight from Guam (which has US connections), four hours from Tokyo.

Other months: May-Oct – wet, typhoons more likely; Nov-Apr – drier, best diving.

Food & drink
Relaxation
Adventure

Adventure
Personal growth

Wildlife & nature
Relaxation

© Patryk Kosmider / Shutterstock

The Bixby Creek Bridge on California's scenic Pacific Coast Highway

(R) Duddon Valley, Lake District; (L) Mayan villager from San Antonio, Belize

CALIFORNIA
USA

Why now? Drive the most dramatic coast, traffic-free.

The Pacific Ocean and the US coast come to their most sensational blows at Big Sur. This 93-mile (150km) stretch, from Carmel-by-the-Sea to San Simeon, is scantily populated and wonderfully wild. Yet, somehow, Hwy 1 has been hewn into its cliffs and built over its crevices (see much-photographed Bixby Bridge), thus facilitating a truly dramatic drive. April is a great month to do it: clear, sunshiny skies, 20°C (68°F) temperatures and far less traffic than summer. You could cover Big Sur in a day, but don't. Dally on the headlands and beaches, and delve into the Santa Lucia Mountains, which rise a mile high, right from the ocean. Also, there are attractions at either end: south, hubristic Hearst Castle and Spanish missions at San Luis Obispo and Santa Barbara; north, charming Carmel-by-the-Sea and Monterey Bay, with its resident sea lions and sea otters.

Trip plan: With unlimited time, drive the entire west coast, from San Diego to the Canadian border. LA to San Francisco, including Big Sur, is 684 miles (1100km); allow two weeks.

Need to know: Non-drivers can board Amtrak's Coastal Starlight train, which hugs the coast for parts of its LA-to-Seattle run.

Other months: Mar-May & Sep-Oct – quieter, clear, warm; Jun-Aug – busy, hot, foggy; Nov-Feb – cool, cheaper (Dec-Apr: best for grey whales).

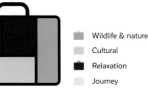

- Wildlife & nature
- Cultural
- Relaxation
- Journey

BELIZE

Why now? For a marvellous mix, under the Caribbean sun.

The best of Central America in microcosm? Maybe. Compact Belize squeezes Mayan ruins, wildlife-packed rainforest, paradisical islands, beautiful beaches, big fish, jungle lodges, jaguars, sacrificial caves, canopy zip lines, Creole culture and the world's second-largest barrier reef into its boundaries. All this, in a small space, coupled with a safe, traveller-friendly vibe and English-speaking locals, makes it very good for families. Kids will particularly love imitating the howler monkeys and snorkelling over technicolour corals. Speaking of which, warm, dry April is a prime time for getting in the water. Visibility is especially good, and whale sharks gather at Glover's Reef, off Palencia, April to May.

Trip plan: Got two weeks? Fly to Belize City, head to a jungle lodge and visit the Mayan sites of Lamanai and Xunantunich. Mount a cave-canoeing expedition, then hit the Mountain Pine Ridge for waterfall swimming. Follow the scenic Hummingbird Hwy to the beach at Palencia to snorkel/dive. Look for wildlife (including jaguars) in Cockscomb Basin before taking a watertaxi to finish on lovely low-key Caye Caulker.

Need to know: Follow responsible diving guidelines and do not buy coral products.

Other months: Dec-May – dry, warm; Jun-Nov – wetter, still warm.

- Adventure
- Wildlife & nature
- Personal growth

LAKE DISTRICT
ENGLAND

Why now? To see a host of golden daffodils.

Poet William Wordsworth loved the Lake District. He lived in Grasmere, at Dove Cottage (now open to visitors), and found inspiration in the surrounding fells, most notably in April: it was a daffodil-filled walk in April 1802 that provoked his most famous work, 'I Wandered Lonely as a Cloud'. Spring in the Lakes might make anyone feel lyrical. New-born lambs gambolling, Wordsworth's daffodils nodding, the hills an extraordinary shade of green. Services such as boats across the lakes are becoming more frequent, yet summer tourists haven't descended, so roads, campsites and honey-pot towns aren't heaving, and holiday cottages are more affordable. There's also plenty of great hiking and cycling. Yes, the weather can be unpredictable, but it always is. Prepare for cold and rain, hope for sun, set out to be inspired.

Trip plan: Base yourself at Windermere or Ambleside for Lake Windermere, Coniston Water and Grasmere. Keswick is the gateway to the northern Lakes and the valleys of Borrowdale and Buttermere. Scafell Pike, England's highest peak, is in the west.

Need to know: Lakeland peaks aren't high but shouldn't be underestimated – go prepared, and choose trails suited to your experience.

Other months: Apr-May & Sep-Oct – quieter; Jun-Aug – warmest, busiest; Nov-Mar – coldest, snow possible.

- Adventure
- Wildlife & nature

© Michael Heffernan / Lonely Planet

KWAZULU-NATAL
SOUTH AFRICA

(L) The Amphitheatre,
Drakensberg, KZN
(R) Aya Sofya, İstanbul

→ **Why now?** For stable weather, mighty mountains, moving history and massive mammals.

For an excellent South African all-rounder, look no further than KwaZulu-Natal. The province has golden Indian Ocean frontage, the country's highest peaks and brilliant big-game parks (including some of Africa's best rhino-spotting). Its earth is soaked with history too, most notably the bloody skirmishes of the 1879 Anglo-Zulu War, best appreciated on guided trips to the battlefield sites of Isandlwana and Rorke's Drift. Soak it all up in the austral autumn, when the weather is still warm (24°C; 75°F) and the skies dry. Conditions are generally stable in the spear-like Drakensberg Mountains too, opening a world of wonderful walking of all levels,

via geological amphitheatres, pools and waterfalls, imposing spires and San rock art.

Trip planner: Head inland from coastal Durban to the Drakensberg (Lesotho is an easy detour, country-tickers). Continue to the battlefields for guided tours. Finish with a safari in Hluhluwe-Imfolozi game reserve.

Need to know: : In Durban, try local speciality bunny chow, a hollowed-out loaf of bread filled with curry.

Other months: Sep-Nov & Mar-May – stable weather; Dec-Feb – hot, thunderstorms; Jun-Aug – cold, snowy.

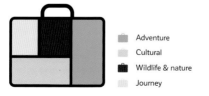

- Adventure
- Cultural
- Wildlife & nature
- Journey

İSTANBUL
TURKEY

→ **Why now?** Discover bazaars, ancient wonders and culinary secrets in peace.

You might debate which is the greatest treasure of the former Constantinople: the incredible 6th-century basilica-mosque-museum Aya Sofya? Sprawling, opulent Topkapı Palace? The domes, minarets and ornate azure tilework of the Blue Mosque? Wander among them to decide for yourself, by all means – and in April, as things are warming up at the end of the low season, you can enjoy discounts, smaller crowds and more forgiving weather. But save some time for the greatest legacy the Ottomans left the world: food, of course. Why do you think the Spice Bazaar is so huge and bustling? From simple kebabs to *meze* feasts and the luscious aubergine (eggplant) masterpiece, *imam bayıldı*, there are few cuisines that are as indulgent as Turkish. Over the past couple of decades a roster of excellent food-themed walking tours and cookery schools has sprung up in İstanbul, providing the opportunity to combine a spring city break with a culinary reboot.

Trip plan: Base yourself in the Sultanahmet district, on the west (European) side of the Bosphorus for easy access to the Grand Bazaar, Spice Bazaar and most historic sites.

Need to know: Two points of Turkish etiquette – don't point your finger or the sole of your foot towards anyone.

Other months: Apr-May & Sep-Oct – mild, quieter; Jun-Aug – hot, busy; Nov-Feb – cold, damp.

Cultural
Food & drink
Value

YANGTZE CHINA

Why now? To cruise in kind climes.
The world's third-longest river, the Yangtze oozes for 2237 miles (3600km) from deepest China to skyscrapered Shànghǎi. Few travellers follow the whole waterway, opting instead for a shorter float from Chóngqìng to Wuhàn. This includes the 99-mile (160km) Three Gorges stretch, where the river squeezes between bamboo groves, tranquil banks and the trio of titular ravines: steep-sided Xiling, the longest gorge; sinuous Wu, with its phalanx of high peaks; and limestone-lined Qutang, the most dramatic. Boats also stop at the Three Gorges Dam, the world's biggest construction project, and the 'ghost city' of Fengdu, part-flooded as a result of it. April is a comfy month for a Yangtze cruise – river weather is dry and cool. It's also pretty pleasant in Běijīng, Shànghǎi, Guìlín and Xī'ān, which are easily added on to make a classic China trip
Trip plan: Start in Běijīng (Forbidden City), move to Xī'ān (Terracotta Warriors), cruise the Yangtze, disembark near Shànghǎi and finish in Guìlín (rural China, rice terraces).
Need to know: All visitors to China must obtain a tourist visa prior to arrival.
Other months: Apr-Oct – cruise season; Nov-Feb – cold, cheaper.

TARANAKI NEW ZEALAND

Why now? Hike, surf, sip and savour under blue autumn skies.
It's a mystery why the 'Naki (as locals call this North Island nub nudging west into the Tasman Sea) isn't a stellar destination with travellers. It has the impossibly photogenic volcano, Mt Taranaki/Egmont, and verdant landscape pocked by distinctive lumpy hills. It has the surf – there's always at least one great break somewhere along the Surf Highway wrapped around its north, west and south coast. It has the culture, with the Govett-Brewster Gallery and the Len Lye Centre being the country's most provocative contemporary art space. The sunny days of April are ideal for exploring its hiking trails – especially the Pouakai Crossing on the flanks of Mt Taranaki, rivalling the Tongariro as the country's finest day walk. And there are excellent restaurants, cafes, music and sports venues to enjoy too.
Trip plan: Fly to New Plymouth direct from Auckland, Wellington or Christchurch. Shuttles run to the start and end of the Pouakai Crossing.
Need to know: World-music spectacular WOMAD comes to New Plymouth in mid-March, when the town is extra busy.
Other months: Nov-May – warm, largely dry; Sep-Oct – weather unpredictable; Jun-Aug – cold but often clear.

VANUATU

Why now? To chill out with the original bungy boys.
Around 80 pieces of paradise make up the Pacific archipelago of Vanuatu. Around capital Port Vila (on Efate island), the country has the sorts of resorts you could sink into for a fortnight, doing nothing but squishing sand between your toes and going for mind-blowing snorkels. But visit a traditional *kastom* (custom) village on an outer isle and you'll find a very different Vanuatu indeed. The vibrant, volcano-pocked nation is home to 100 indigenous languages, a cannibalistic past, blow-your-mind *kava* potions and many tribal rituals. For instance, head to Pentecost island on any Saturday, April to June, to see the *naghol*. Rickety land towers, 20m to 30m high (66ft to 98ft), are built from sticks, and young men leap from the tops, with only a vine tied round their ankles to break their fall. A fertility rite, it celebrates the yam harvest – and has inspired many a bungy-jumper since.
Trip plan: Fly into Port Vila and use internal flights or slow boats to access outlying islands. Pentecost is a 50-minute flight from Port Vila. Melanesian cruises, linking Vanuatu with the Solomon Islands, are possible.
Need to know: Port Vila is a 3½-hour flight from Sydney, 3¼ hours from Auckland.
Other months: Apr-Jul – warm, dry, land-diving; Aug-Oct – dry, busy; Nov-Mar – wetter, cheaper.

- Journey
- Wildlife & nature
- Cultural

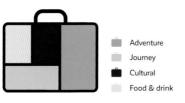

- Adventure
- Journey
- Cultural
- Food & drink

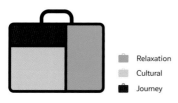

- Relaxation
- Cultural
- Journey

Margaret River in Western Australia is home to more than 220 wineries

Catherine Sutherland © Lonely Planet

SOUTH WEST AUSTRALIA

→ **Why now? To indulge under autumn sunshine.**

The bottom corner of Western Australia is a beaut. South from Perth – the country's sunniest city, by the way – lies a region of rippling vineyards, towering tingle and karri trees, dazzle-white beaches (where kangaroos like to chill) and cave-galleries of millennia-old rock art. Better, relative to the gargantuan size of the state, this is a compact chunk; you can actually get your head around exploring it at a sensible pace. It's also extremely intoxicating in the austral autumn, when temperatures are mild and the vines of Margaret River (home to more than 220 wineries) are heavy with fruit and ripe for tastings. There's also a raft of local producers creating excellent craft ales, cheeses, olive oils, honey, chocolate and more.

Trip plan: Spend a few days looping south from Perth. Head to Harvey for cheese-tasting and Bunbury to see dolphins in Koombana Bay. Drive amid Margaret River's vines; stop for tastings, fine dining and a winery stay. Walk amid the vineyards and huge karris at Pemberton and sample truffles at Manjimup before returning to Perth.

Need to know: Perth Comedy Festival usually runs from mid-April to mid-May.

Other months: Sep-Nov – flowers; Dec-Feb – hot, busy; Mar-May – autumn, harvest; Jun-Aug – dry, cooler.

■ Food & drink
■ Journey
■ Relaxation

APPALACHIAN TRAIL USA

→ **Why now? To miss the crowds on the epic eastern hike.**

You're going to need about six months and a lot of grit and stamina to complete the 2190-mile (3525km) Appalachian Trail. But, wow – just imagine if you do? Tackling one of the world's longest marked footpaths unravels 14-states-worth of impressive scenery, and spending that long carrying your kit, camping wild, and dealing with blisters and bears is also life-changing stuff. Most northbound thru-hikers start at Georgia's Springer Mountain between March and mid-April, to ensure they're finished before winter descends on the end of the AT, at Mt Katahdin, Maine. However, better is to start late April/early May, to avoid both the chances of late snow in the south and the log-jam of other thru-hikers all setting off at the same time.

Trip plan: Start slowly to avoid injury (around 7 miles, or 12km, a day), and build from there. Note: only one in four thru-hikers successfully completes the AT. If you're short on time, walk a section. Maybe 100 miles (161km) through Shenandoah National Park (Virginia)? Or a 2-mile (3km) hike to Anthony's Nose (New York), from where you can see the NYC skyline.

Need to know: Avoid starting on 1 April, the most popular start date; weekdays are typically less busy than weekends.

Other months: Mar-May – thru-hike start time; Jun-Oct – warm, snow-free (for short sections); Nov-Feb – largely cold.

■ Adventure
■ Personal growth

THAILAND

Why now? To get hot and wet.

All of Thailand sizzles in April – from the highlands of Chiang Mai to the islands of the south, the mercury is rising above 30°C (86°F). Sweaty stuff, but a great time to hit the beach. Ko Samet is an easy white-sand escape from Bangkok; further afield, try paddling around the James Bond karst rocks of Ao Phang Nga, diving off Ko Tao, watersporting on Phuket or simply lolling on offbeat Ko Kood. If you're stuck in the city, head to one of Bangkok's many rooftop bars for a bit of a breeze. However, come mid-month, cooling down gets easier. Songkran, Thai New Year, is held 13 to 15 April and is celebrated with the world's biggest water-fight. Traditionally, family members gently sprinkled each other for good luck; now water balloons and pump-action pistols are employed. It's all refreshing good fun. Chiang Mai and Chiang Rai are two of the best places to go for a festive drenching.

Trip plan: Leave boiling Bangkok for the southern beaches as soon as possible. For Songkran celebrations, head north from Bangkok to Chiang Mai (12 hours by train, 70 minutes by plane).

Need to know: During Songkran, don't wear white clothes or expensive watches; consider buying goggles.

Other months: May-Oct – rainy, southwest monsoon (Sep-Oct: wettest); Nov-Feb – cool (Oct-Jan: northeast monsoon); Mar-May – hot.

- Cultural
- Relaxation
- Food & drink

April is a great time to hit Thailand's many beaches

NEPAL

→ **Why now?** Flowers, festivals and on-foot exploration.

Quick! You can just squeeze in a trip to Nepal before the summer monsoon renders it hot, wet and treacherous. Indeed, March to April is a great time to explore the Himalaya: the rhododendron trees are in full and fabulous bloom, painting the land in incredible reds, pinks and purples, turning to white higher up. Long, warm days also make this an appealing time to hike. In particular, there's a buzz in the Everest region as hardcore mountaineers start gathering (most summit attempts are made mid-May); tackle the Everest Base Camp trek to rub shoulders with the climbing elite. The Kathmandu Valley is lively too – Bisket Jatra (Nepali New Year) is celebrated in mid-April, most exuberantly in Bhaktapur, where a god-toting chariot is dragged through streets and tug-of-war contests are held.

Trip plan: Fly to Kathmandu. Explore the temples and towns of the Kathmandu Valley, where there are also good short walks. Lukla, gateway to the Everest region, is a 35-minute flight from Kathmandu; the Base Camp trek takes 14 days.

Need to know: If trekking, take out travel insurance that covers you at higher altitudes.

Other months: Oct-Nov – clear, pleasant; Dec-Feb – cold; Mar-Apr – flowers, warm; May-Sep – hot, wet.

BRUSSELS
BELGIUM

→ **Why now?** Fine food and weather, without the crowds.

Despite being 'off-season', April is actually the driest month in the Belgian capital, and its mild days (peaking around 15°C; 59°F) are perfect for comfortable outdoors sightseeing. Wander the Grand Place (the 17th-century centre), the open-air antiques market of the Grand Sablon, and hip districts such as Rue Antoine Dansaert. Then sample the renowned eating and drinking scene. Brussels has arguably been world chocolate capital since 1912, when Jean Neuhaus invented the praline here. Now, there are chocolateries everywhere, and opportunities to buy, make and taste the stuff. If Easter falls in April, where better to be? Brussels does a good line in atmospheric cafe-bars too, so when spring evenings cool, hunker down in a smoke-stained art nouveau establishment with an excellent Belgian beer or two.

Trip plan: Spend a few days eating your way around Brussels. Add on cobbled, canal-riddled Bruges, another chocolate hub (70 minutes by train).

Need to know: Handmade chocolates contain few preservatives; they should be eaten within 21 days.

Other months: Other months: Mar-May & Sep-Oct – mild, shoulder; Jun-Aug – hotter, busy; Nov-Feb – cold (Christmas markets).

WASHINGTON
DC USA

→ **Why now?** Capital culture with added colour.

There's a lot to see in Washington, DC. Better, entry to all the major sites around the National Mall – including the Smithsonian museums, presidential memorials, White House and Capitol – is always free. No excuse not to visit them all. DC winters can be Baltic, summers sticky, but the mild days of spring (average highs of 18°C, or 64°F, in April) are ideal for exploring in comfort. This is also when the city's 3700 cherry trees (a gift from Japan) bloom. The natural spectacle is celebrated with parades and events during the National Cherry Blossom Festival (late March to mid-April); the average peak blooming date is 4 April. The trees line West Potomac Park's Tidal Basin; walk or cycle beneath the flowery boughs, or view them by paddleboat.

Trip plan: Allow several days for DC's sites. Intersperse museums with neighbourhood culture – historic Georgetown, trendy Shaw and U Street Corridor, diverse Adams-Morgan.

Need to know: White House tours are free but subject to application. US citizens must apply to their senator's office, foreign nationals to their embassy.

Other months: Mar-May & Sep-Nov – mild, good weather; Jun-Aug – humid, hot, busy; Dec-Feb – low-season, cold.

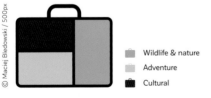

- Wildlife & nature
- Adventure
- Cultural

- Food & drink
- Cultural

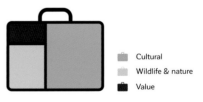

- Cultural
- Wildlife & nature
- Value

Get a ticket to ride
in Luna Park,
St Kilda

MELBOURNE
AUSTRALIA

→ **Why now?** For laughs, mellow weather and fewer people.

It's all happening in Melbourne in March. The city explodes with events: Fashion Festival, Food & Wine Festival, Formula 1 Grand Prix. Which is great – if you want to fight your way to the bar and pay a premium for your bed... Alternatively, wait until April and visit Australia's culture capital when there's more room to breathe. The Comedy Festival (the world's third-largest laugh-fest) runs to the middle of the month anyway; the pleasant autumnal weather continues (highs around 20°C; 68°F), but the city isn't so overrun. That means you'll have more space while browsing the creative laneways, walking in the Botanic Gardens (aflame with autumn colour), cycling the buzzy neighbourhoods of Fitzroy, Collingwood and Carlton, and strolling seaside St Kilda. If you do get some autumn rain, shelter in one of Melbourne's 100-plus art galleries or aboard the free City Circle Tram.

Trip plan: Allow at least three days. Make time to explore the inner-city suburbs, where the best bars and cafes are found. The vineyard-streaked Yarra Valley makes a lovely, easy escape, especially during autumn's grape harvest.

© Glenn Van Der Knijff / Getty Images

Need to know: Free wi-fi is available in public spaces, including in Federation Sq.

Other months: Dec-Feb – very hot; Mar-May – milder, festivals; Jun-Aug – cold, wet; Sep-Nov – mild, quieter.

■ Cultural
■ Food & drink
■ Relaxation

BEYOND MELBOURNE

WILLIAMSTOWN • 8 MILES (13KM) • Scenic ferry along the Yarra River into Port Philip Bay

MORNINGTON PENINSULA • 30 MILES (48KM) • Wildlife, wild beaches, trails, farms, fruits, wines

PHILLIP ISLAND • 85 MILES (137KM) • Rugged coast, little penguin parade

PORT FAIRY • 230 MILES (370KM) • Epic drive along the Great Ocean Rd

ANDALUCÍA
SPAIN

→ **Why now? Beautifully balmy for cities, hills and sea.**

There's a bit of everything for everyone in southern Spain in spring. The marvellous Moorish cities – Seville, Granada, Córdoba – are far better for sightseeing in this mild month, when temperatures average around 18°C (64°F). The cities might also put on a show – Semana Santa (Holy Week) can fall in April, as does Seville's Feria de Abril, a week of hardcore dancing, drinking and eating, where locals wear traditional costumes and ride fine Andalucian horses. Some, including families, might prefer to leave town to do their own riding, hacking out across the badlands of Tabernas (Europe's only desert) or the rippled Sierra Nevada. The latter will be lovely right now: fragrant with orange blossom, and the ideal temperature for walks amid the white villages and olive groves that rest in their folds. Finally, Andalucía's Mediterranean coast offers golden, family-friendly beaches without the summer crowds.

Trip plan: An Andalucian loop might lead from coastal Málaga to gorge-straddling Ronda, then Seville, Córdoba and Granada, the white villages of the Alpujarras mountains and back to the Med.

Need to know: Málaga has an airport and an excellent Picasso Museum.

Other months: Jun-Sep – baking hot; Nov-Feb – mild winters; Mar-May & Oct – warm, pleasant.

- Cultural
- Journey
- Food & drink
- Relaxation

© Pete Seaward / Lonely Planet

Palacio de Generalif, Granada, Andalucía

ARNHEM LAND
AUSTRALIA

→ **Why now?** For clear skies and indigenous encounters.

Arnhem Land's Bininj/Mungguy people call April 'Banggerreng' – the harvest month, when floodwaters recede, skies are clear and plants start to fruit. It's a lovely time to head to this remote top corner of the Northern Territory – dry weather makes it easier to navigate its 35,000 sq miles (91,000 sq km) of undeveloped wilderness, yet the landscapes are still lush from the rains. It's not the easiest place to travel, but Arnhem Land offers arguably the richest opportunities to engage with Aboriginal culture. Though the rugged coasts, rainforested hills, glowing escarpments and endless savannah seem utterly untouched, they sing with 40,000 years of human history. Enter caves resplendent with rock art, follow indigenous guides on bush-tucker walks, visit traditional craft workshops and hear didgeridoos being played (the instrument originated here). The wildlife is plentiful too, from saltwater crocs to brilliant birds.

Trip plan: Joining a tour is advised – accommodation is limited, distances are huge. Flights from Darwin and Cairns land at Nhulunbuy (northeast coast), which opens up the Gove Peninsula. The impressive rock-art site of Mt Borradaile is in western Arnhem Land.

Need to know: A permit from the Northern Land Council is required to visit Arnhem Land.

Other months: Oct-Mar – wet; Apr-Sep – cooler, dry (Apr-May: quieter).

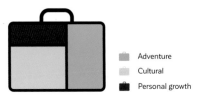

■ Adventure
□ Cultural
■ Personal growth

ST LUCIA

→ **Why now?** Sunshine, good times and potentially falling prices.

What's not to love about little St Lucia? As one of the Caribbean's most mountainous isles, its beaches come with ruggedly handsome backdrops. It's an ideal place to relax, but also offers potential for adventures – from zip-lining through rainforest to climbing Gros Piton, one the island's iconic twin peaks. St Lucia also offers a few unique experiences, including the region's best Friday-night fish fry, a 'drive-in' volcano and the chance to have a chocolate massage. Peak tourist season runs mid-December to mid-April, when the weather is driest and finest – a good choice, though the most expensive. However, as things get a smidgen wetter in late April and into May, prices drop accordingly – a great time for potential savings, and to catch the respected Jazz Festival, which sees international names and local stars perform island-wide.

Trip plan: Pick a base: the north (home to capital Castries) is busier and more developed, but has nicer beaches and more restaurants; the south is more scenic and serene, and has some exquisite hotels, but the beaches are mostly black sand.

Need to know: Hewanorra International Airport is in the south; Castries, 37 miles (60km) north, has a regional airport.

Other months: Dec-May – dry season, warm; Jun-Nov – wetter (Sep-Oct: hurricanes more likely).

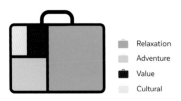

■ Relaxation
□ Adventure
■ Value
□ Cultural

A Sally Lightfoot crab crawls over a marine iguana, Galápagos

GALÁPAGOS ISLANDS
ECUADOR

→ **Why now?** Calm, clear seas and brilliant birds.

There's never a bad time to visit the Galápagos Islands. Straddling the equator, the archipelago never gets cold, and the wildlife – the main reason to visit – is always doing something wonderful. That said, March to April is particularly good. Rain is quite likely but the seas are at their calmest and clearest, and water temperatures high – all the better for snorkelling with turtles, marine iguanas, curious sea lions and the planet's northernmost-dwelling penguin. Some of the islands' most enchanting birds are in their best form too: waved albatross are returning to begin their balletic courtship; frigatebirds are mating, the males inflating their crimson throat pouches; blue-footed booby pairs are doing their comic dance. Giant tortoise eggs are hatching too – it's a wildlife-watching feast.

Trip plan: Fly from mainland Ecuador to Baltra. Explore the archipelago by expedition cruise (usually four or eight days). Boats follow set itineraries – pick one that visits Española (for albatrosses) and North Seymour (blue-footed boobies).

Need to know: If prone to seasickness, book a lower-deck cabin on a medium/large ship or opt for a land-based trip.

Other months: Jul-Nov – cool, dry, rougher seas; Dec-Jun – wetter, calmer, better for snorkelling.

■ Wildlife & nature
■ Journey
■ Adventure

HAWAII USA

Cherry blossom blooms in Kyoto, Toyko and Hiroshima in April

Why now? Good weather, good prices.

Hawaii's temperature varies little year-round: averages are a consistently warm (26-29°C; 79-84°F). What do vary are visitor numbers – tourists tend to seek out this tropical, volcanic, dramatic archipelago when it's cold where they are (mostly December to March) and during traditional vacation time (mostly June to August). This leaves April to May, which is also the start of the drier period, perfect weather-wise yet attractively off-season (lower prices, fewer people). Come now for hotel bargains and crowd-free beaches. Oahu is a good choice for families, especially gently sloping Kailua Beach, Dole Pineapple Plantation and Aulani Disney Resort. Big Island's must-see is Hawaii Volcanoes National Park. On Maui, drive the scenic Hana Hwy and go whale-watching – humpbacks pass by from December to May.

Trip plan: Don't try to visit more than one island a week. Stay on one or allow more time to island-hop – there's too much to see and do.

Need to know: Hawaii has only two inter-island ferries: Molokai-Maui and Maui-Lanai. Most inter-island flights go through Honolulu Airport (Oahu).

Other months: Apr-Oct – dry; Nov-Mar – rainy season; Dec-Mar & Jun-Aug – peak visitor numbers.

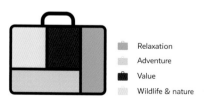

■ Relaxation
▨ Adventure
■ Value
▨ Wildlife & nature

JAPAN

Why now? It's blooming gorgeous!

No time of year excites the Japanese quite like spring, because it is *sakura* (cherry blossom) season. Across the country, people await the first blooms, which usually appear in the southern Okinawan islands by February, before spreading northwards, erupting in cities such as Kyoto, Tokyo and Hiroshima in late March and April; Hokkaido sees blossom into May. Not only is this the prettiest time to be in Japan, it is among the most festive. *Hanami* (parties under the blossom) are widespread in city parks. Families and friends roll out their tarps and eat beneath the trees; stores even sell *hanami* bento boxes, which contain seasonal produce, pink-tinged dumplings and veg cut into blossom shapes. Especially scenic *sakura* spots include

Kyoto's canal-side Philosopher's Path, Mt Yoshino in Nara and Kumamoto Castle.

Trip plan: A classic itinerary links Tokyo, Matsumoto, Takayama, Kanazawa, Kyoto and Hakone (for blossom by Mt Fuji).

Need to know: The Japan Weather Association issues cherry-tree opening estimates for the whole country; plan accordingly.

Other months: Feb-May – blossom spreads; Sep-Nov – fall colours; Dec-Jan – cold; Jun-Aug – hottest.

■ Wildlife & nature
▨ Cultural
■ Food & drink

The calm waters inside Mauritius' reef are a safe haven for water sports

MAURITIUS

→ Why now? It's hot, dry and not too busy.

When the gods were handing out weather, Mauritius pulled the long straw. This subtropical Indian Ocean island has an enviable climate year-round, with only minor fluctuations interrupting the gorgeousness. April to May is shoulder season between the hotter, more humid start of the year and the cooler austral winter. It's still pretty warm (27-28°C; 81-82°F), and largely dry, but also less busy, being outside typical school holiday times (which nudges down the prices of its swish resorts). Visibility in the dazzlingly blue sea is good too, ideal for exploring the fascinating underwater world of coral reefs and dramatic drop-offs. On land, there is brilliant birdwatching (Mauritius is home to some of the world's rarest species), great food (try the octopus *vindaye*) and plenty of scope for doing nothing at all.

Trip plan: Book a boutique beach stay, making time to snorkel or dive. Mauritius also works well as a relaxing addition to a South Africa safari (flight time from Johannesburg: five hours).

Need to know: English is the official language, and widely spoken, but French and Creole are most used.

Other months: Jan-Feb – wettest; Oct-Dec – hottest; Jun-Aug – busiest, cooler; Apr-May & Nov – shoulder seasons, quieter.

Relaxation
Adventure
Value

© Mark Read / Lonely Planet

Fenway Park is the home of the city's beloved baseball team, the Red Sox

BOSTON USA

© Michael Ivins/Boston Red Sox / Getty Images

→ **Why now? To spring into sporting action.**

On your marks, get set, go now! Boston is a city of sport fanatics – baseball, ice hockey, American football and basketball are all followed passionately in Beantown. Indeed, the Red Sox are as integral to the city as Paul Revere and *Cheers*, and to see a ball game at Fenway Park is an essential US experience. Fortunately, the baseball season pitches off in early April, just as the weather becomes less wintry and Boston's 'Emerald Necklace' of parks and green spaces begins to flourish. April (specifically, third Monday) is also when the Boston Marathon – the world's oldest city marathon – is held. Whether you run it, or cheer from the sidewalk, it's an inspiring, emotional sight. Refuelling is a pleasure here too: choose anything from New England seafood to creamy cannoli from Italian-influenced North End. Or try creative street eats from one of Boston's many, eclectic food trucks – food-truck season starts this month.

Trip plan: : Allow at least three days, and make sure the Red Sox have a home game when you're in town.

Need to know: MBTA subway trains link

Logan Airport to Downtown Boston in 10 to 15 minutes.

Other months: Mar-May – warming, flowers; Jun-Sep – hot, busy; Oct-Nov – milder, quieter; Dec-Feb – chilly, no baseball.

Adventure
Personal growth
Cultural
Food & drink

BEYOND BOSTON

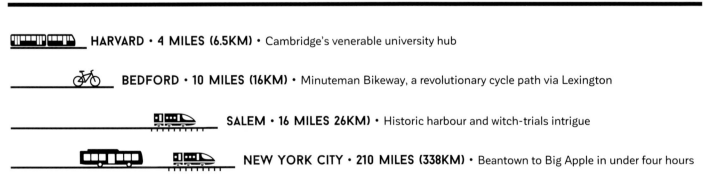

HARVARD · 4 MILES (6.5KM) · Cambridge's venerable university hub

BEDFORD · 10 MILES (16KM) · Minuteman Bikeway, a revolutionary cycle path via Lexington

SALEM · 16 MILES 26KM) · Historic harbour and witch-trials intrigue

NEW YORK CITY · 210 MILES (338KM) · Beantown to Big Apple in under four hours

May

WHERE TO GO WHEN

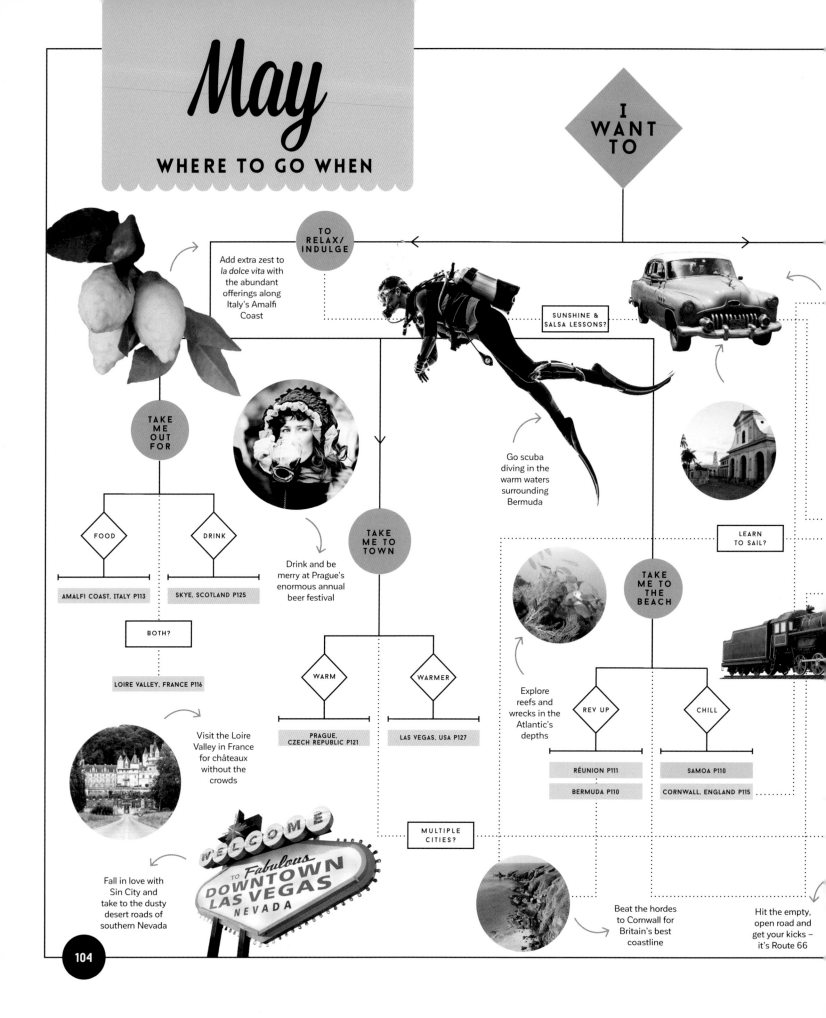

I WANT TO

TO RELAX/ INDULGE

Add extra zest to *la dolce vita* with the abundant offerings along Italy's Amalfi Coast

SUNSHINE & SALSA LESSONS?

Go scuba diving in the warm waters surrounding Bermuda

TAKE ME OUT FOR

FOOD

DRINK

AMALFI COAST, ITALY P113

SKYE, SCOTLAND P125

BOTH?

LOIRE VALLEY, FRANCE P116

Drink and be merry at Prague's enormous annual beer festival

TAKE ME TO TOWN

LEARN TO SAIL?

TAKE ME TO THE BEACH

Explore reefs and wrecks in the Atlantic's depths

Visit the Loire Valley in France for châteaux without the crowds

WARM

WARMER

PRAGUE, CZECH REPUBLIC P121

LAS VEGAS, USA P127

REV UP

CHILL

RÉUNION P111

SAMOA P110

BERMUDA P110

CORNWALL, ENGLAND P115

MULTIPLE CITIES?

Fall in love with Sin City and take to the dusty desert roads of southern Nevada

WELCOME TO Fabulous DOWNTOWN LAS VEGAS NEVADA

Beat the hordes to Cornwall for Britain's best coastline

Hit the empty, open road and get your kicks – it's Route 66

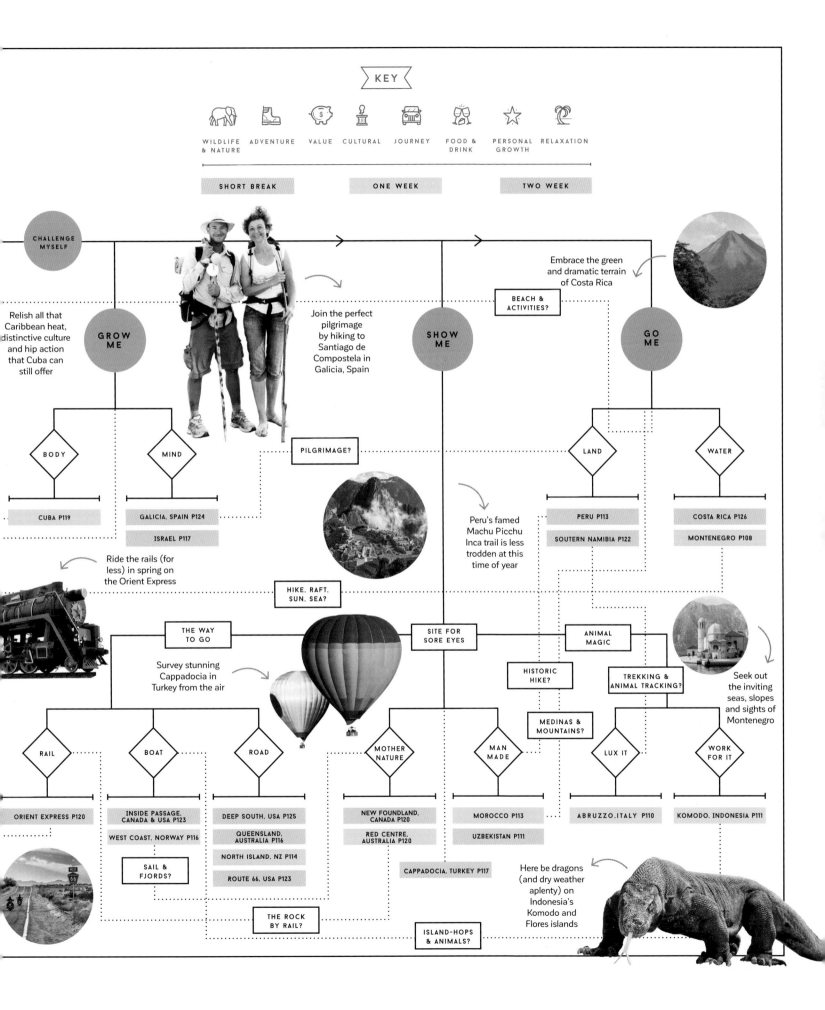

KEY

WILDLIFE & NATURE — ADVENTURE — VALUE — CULTURAL — JOURNEY — FOOD & DRINK — PERSONAL GROWTH — RELAXATION

SHORT BREAK   ONE WEEK   TWO WEEK

CHALLENGE MYSELF

Embrace the green and dramatic terrain of Costa Rica

Relish all that Caribbean heat, distinctive culture and hip action that Cuba can still offer

GROW ME

Join the perfect pilgrimage by hiking to Santiago de Compostela in Galicia, Spain

SHOW ME

GO ME

BEACH & ACTIVITIES?

BODY

MIND

CUBA P119

GALICIA, SPAIN P124

ISRAEL P117

PILGRIMAGE?

LAND

WATER

PERU P113

SOUTERN NAMIBIA P122

COSTA RICA P126

MONTENEGRO P108

Peru's famed Machu Picchu Inca trail is less trodden at this time of year

Ride the rails (for less) in spring on the Orient Express

HIKE, RAFT, SUN, SEA?

THE WAY TO GO

SITE FOR SORE EYES

ANIMAL MAGIC

Survey stunning Cappadocia in Turkey from the air

HISTORIC HIKE?

TREKKING & ANIMAL TRACKING?

Seek out the inviting seas, slopes and sights of Montenegro

MEDINAS & MOUNTAINS?

RAIL

BOAT

ROAD

MOTHER NATURE

MAN MADE

LUX IT

WORK FOR IT

ORIENT EXPRESS P120

INSIDE PASSAGE, CANADA & USA P123

WEST COAST, NORWAY P116

DEEP SOUTH, USA P125

QUEENSLAND, AUSTRALIA P116

NORTH ISLAND, NZ P114

ROUTE 66, USA P123

NEW FOUNDLAND, CANADA P120

RED CENTRE, AUSTRALIA P120

MOROCCO P113

UZBEKISTAN P111

ABRUZZO, ITALY P110

KOMODO, INDONESIA P111

SAIL & FJORDS?

CAPPADOCIA, TURKEY P117

Here be dragons (and dry weather aplenty) on Indonesia's Komodo and Flores islands

THE ROCK BY RAIL?

ISLAND-HOPS & ANIMALS?

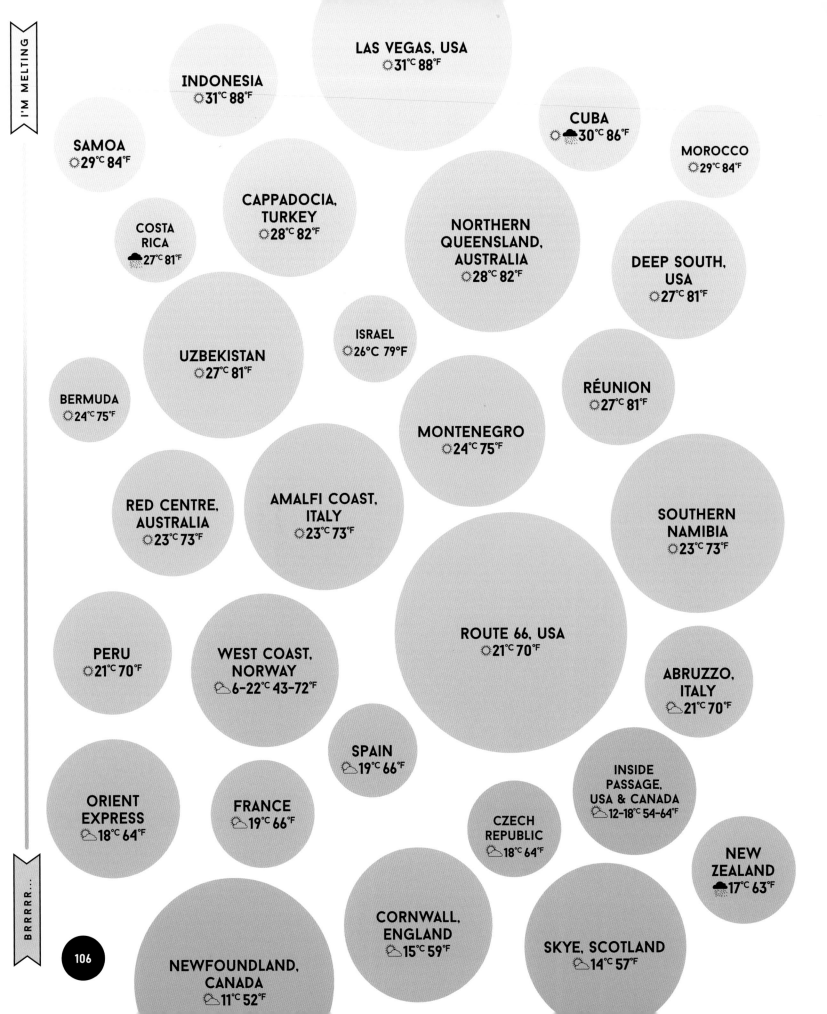

LAS VEGAS, USA
☀31°C 88°F

INDONESIA
☀31°C 88°F

CUBA
⛈30°C 86°F

MOROCCO
☀29°C 84°F

SAMOA
☀29°C 84°F

CAPPADOCIA,
TURKEY
☀28°C 82°F

COSTA
RICA
⛈27°C 81°F

NORTHERN
QUEENSLAND,
AUSTRALIA
☀28°C 82°F

DEEP SOUTH,
USA
☀27°C 81°F

ISRAEL
☀26°C 79°F

UZBEKISTAN
☀27°C 81°F

RÉUNION
☀27°C 81°F

BERMUDA
☀24°C 75°F

MONTENEGRO
☀24°C 75°F

RED CENTRE,
AUSTRALIA
☀23°C 73°F

AMALFI COAST,
ITALY
☀23°C 73°F

SOUTHERN
NAMIBIA
☀23°C 73°F

ROUTE 66, USA
☀21°C 70°F

PERU
☀21°C 70°F

WEST COAST,
NORWAY
⛅6–22°C 43–72°F

ABRUZZO,
ITALY
⛅21°C 70°F

SPAIN
⛅19°C 66°F

ORIENT
EXPRESS
⛅18°C 64°F

FRANCE
⛅19°C 66°F

INSIDE
PASSAGE,
USA & CANADA
⛅12–18°C 54–64°F

CZECH
REPUBLIC
⛅18°C 64°F

NEW
ZEALAND
⛈17°C 63°F

CORNWALL,
ENGLAND
⛅15°C 59°F

SKYE, SCOTLAND
⛅14°C 57°F

NEWFOUNDLAND,
CANADA
⛅11°C 52°F

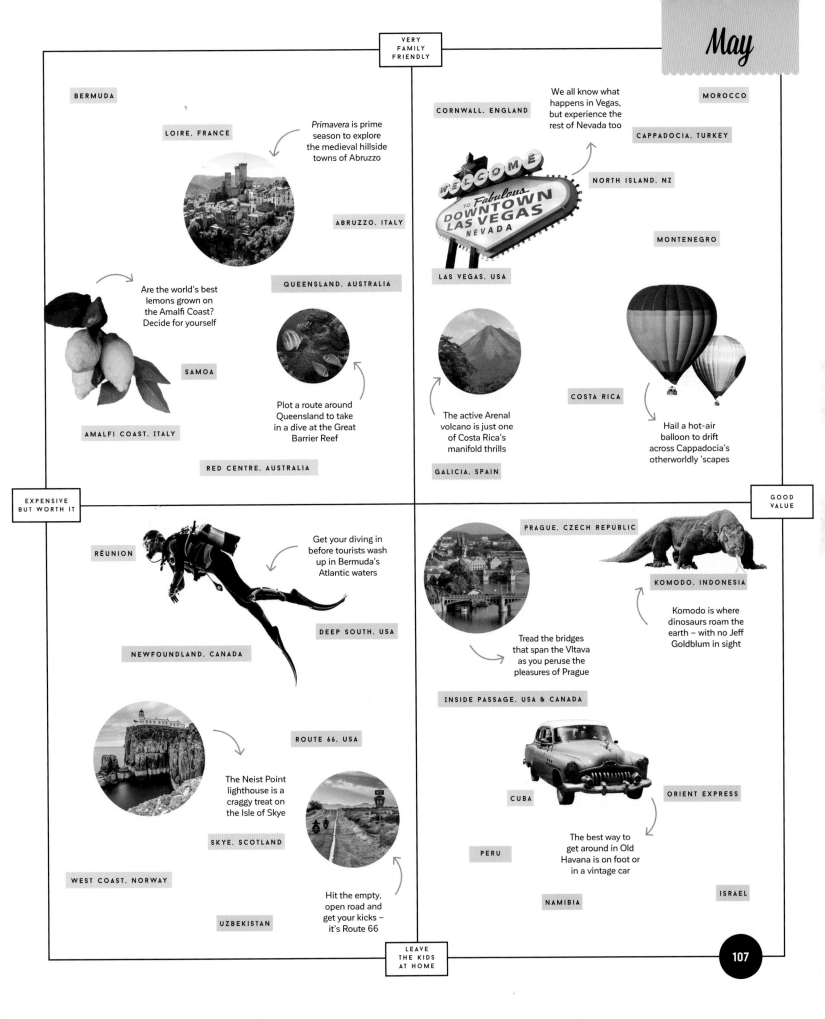

VERY FAMILY FRIENDLY

BERMUDA

LOIRE, FRANCE

Primavera is prime season to explore the medieval hillside towns of Abruzzo

ABRUZZO, ITALY

Are the world's best lemons grown on the Amalfi Coast? Decide for yourself

SAMOA

AMALFI COAST, ITALY

QUEENSLAND, AUSTRALIA

Plot a route around Queensland to take in a dive at the Great Barrier Reef

RED CENTRE, AUSTRALIA

CORNWALL, ENGLAND

We all know what happens in Vegas, but experience the rest of Nevada too

MOROCCO

CAPPADOCIA, TURKEY

NORTH ISLAND, NZ

LAS VEGAS, USA

MONTENEGRO

The active Arenal volcano is just one of Costa Rica's manifold thrills

COSTA RICA

GALICIA, SPAIN

Hail a hot-air balloon to drift across Cappadocia's otherworldly 'scapes

EXPENSIVE BUT WORTH IT

RÉUNION

Get your diving in before tourists wash up in Bermuda's Atlantic waters

NEWFOUNDLAND, CANADA

DEEP SOUTH, USA

The Neist Point lighthouse is a craggy treat on the Isle of Skye

ROUTE 66, USA

SKYE, SCOTLAND

WEST COAST, NORWAY

Hit the empty, open road and get your kicks – it's Route 66

UZBEKISTAN

GOOD VALUE

PRAGUE, CZECH REPUBLIC

KOMODO, INDONESIA

Komodo is where dinosaurs roam the earth – with no Jeff Goldblum in sight

Tread the bridges that span the Vltava as you peruse the pleasures of Prague

INSIDE PASSAGE, USA & CANADA

CUBA

ORIENT EXPRESS

The best way to get around in Old Havana is on foot or in a vintage car

PERU

NAMIBIA

ISRAEL

MONTENEGRO

→ **Why now? For rivers, seas and slopes at their most inviting.**
Mini-sized Montenegro squeezes a lot of good stuff into its compact proportions – all the more reason to visit before peak season, as there's limited space to go round. In May, temperatures on the coast reach the mid-20°Cs (70°Fs) and the sea warms up, so you can happily hit dazzling Adriatic spots such as cliff-hugged Kotor and medieval Budva before the crowds descend. This is also a good month for exploring mountainous Durmitor National Park. May sees the start of rafting season through Europe's deepest, longest canyon – the Tara River is full of snow-melt, lively but safe. There are also excellent walks here, which don't have to be taxing. As well as higher-level hikes over still-snowy passes, there are gentle valley walks to walnut groves and watering holes. Wild tortoises are an extra bonus.

Trip plan: Montenegro is a great choice for a multi-activity holiday, whatever your age. Mix glorious sea-kayaking with mountain-biking and hiking, rafting, wine- or honey-tasting and tours of historic towns.
Need to know: There are airports in Tivat and capital Podgorica. Buses run into Montenegro from Dubrovnik (Croatia).
Other months: Jul-Aug – very hot; Apr-Jun & Sep-Oct – warm, less crowded; Nov-Mar – cold, skiing possible.

- Adventure
- Wildlife & nature
- Relaxation
- Value
- Cultural

Looking down over the town of Kotor, in the spectacular Bay of Kotor

ABRUZZO
ITALY

Why now? It's *primavera* – prime time.

The central Italian region of Abruzzo is one of Italy's wildest. Spread alongside the central Adriatic coast – where beach resorts such as Pescara and Vasto can be found – it rises up to the rugged Apennines to offer a quite different holiday experience. The mountains are snow-speckled, sliced by valleys, dotted with *borghi* (medieval towns) and patrolled by wolves and bears. Spring – *primavera* – is ideal. Nature is reawakening, rivers are full and alpine meadows are riotous with butterflies and wildflowers. Guided nature walks in Majella National Park reveal gorgeous floral displays, and maybe chamois too. Visit the hills around L'Aquila for teetering castles and tiny hamlets stuck in time.

Trip plan: Fly to Pescara. Enjoy beach time before heading inland to an *agriturismo* (farmstay). The mountain-backed town of Sulmona makes a good base.

Need to know: Cocullo's extraordinary Snake Festival, when a statue is festooned with live snakes, is held on the first Thursday in May. Cocullo is near Sulmona.

Other months: Jul-Aug – very hot; Nov-Mar – cold, wettest; Apr-May & Sep-Oct – milder, nature at its best.

BERMUDA

Why now? Pre-peak perfection on this Atlantic outpost.

Bermuda is a magnificent oddball. It's marooned in the Atlantic, a two-hour flight from east coast USA and 994 miles (1600km) north of the Caribbean, yet it's owned by Great Britain. Expect red postboxes, afternoon tea, croquet and cricket. The weather's not so British, though. This semitropical island is springlike in winter (December to February: 16-20°C; 61-68°F), edging towards 30°C (86°F) in summer. May is a marvel – warm and sunny enough to lounge on Bermuda's family-friendly pink-sand beaches, but before tourist high-season kicks in. The water is warm too, ideal for reef snorkelling and excellent wreck dives. On land, cycle via pastel villages and hidden coves on the island-long Old Railway Trail or indulge at one of the island's spas.

Trip plan: Fly to Bermuda International Airport. Bermuda is an archipelago and it's possible to hire a boat to hop between islands. Mix beach time with visits to capital Hamilton, and historic St George.

Need to know: Visitors are not allowed to hire cars; scooters can be rented. Buses and bikes are the best options.

Other months: Jun-Sep – hot, high season (storms most likely Aug-Oct); May, Oct – warm, shoulder months; Nov-Apr – cool.

SAMOA

Why now? Drier, cheaper days in paradise.

Simmering away in the tropical South Pacific, the Samoa archipelago is a remote piece of paradise still embracing its traditional roots. The islands' culture – dominated by the tenets of *Fa'a Samoa* (the Samoan Way) – is as interesting as its seas are blue and its volcanic interior exotically profuse. Samoa is hot year-round (around 25-30°C; 77-86°F) with consistent trade winds providing cooling late-afternoon breezes. What does change is the rain: May to October offers a significantly drier experience. As a shoulder month, May offers good weather at cheaper prices than the June-to-September peak. That's more money to spend on exploring the islands, from the rainforest, beaches and lagoons of Upolu to tiny, car-free Manono, to the lava fields of Savai'i. Essential experience? Stay in an open-sided beach *fale* (thatched hut) and snorkel the balmy blue – the water is 28°C (82°F) all year.

Trip plan: Fly to Faleolo Airport on Upolu. Visit capital Apia's market and south-coast beaches. Bigger Savai'i (90 minutes by ferry) is home to the ancient Polynesian mound of Pulemelei and to volcanic action.

Need to know: Samoa is a five-hour flight from Sydney, 3½ hours from Auckland, five hours from Hawaii.

Other months: Nov-Apr – wetter; May-Oct – drier.

- Wildlife & nature
- Relaxation
- Cultural
- Food & drink

- Relaxation
- Adventure
- Journey

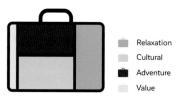

- Relaxation
- Cultural
- Adventure
- Value

© Shutterstock

UZBEKISTAN

Why now? For fine weather in a Silk Road showstopper.

Caravanserais. Silk Road. Spices. There's something undeniably romantic about travel to this 'Stan', which has been the cultural heart of Central Asia for millennia. This is especially true of Uzbekistan's trio of historic cities – Samarkand, Bukhara, Khiva – which glitter with mosaic-tiled mausoleums, mosques and *medressas* (religious schools) that still speak of ancient times; Bukhara's Silk and Spices Festival (late May) seeks to celebrate that legacy, showcasing the carpet weavers, wood-carvers, musicians and artists still practising traditional skills. Indeed, May is the perfect month to visit. Temperatures in the mid-20°Cs (70°Fs) make for comfortable sightseeing, while tulips and apricot blossom enliven the landscapes.

Trip plan: Fly to capital Tashkent. Overland, via the Kyzyl-kum Desert, to the walled city of Khiva, then Bukhara, to finish in Samarkand, home to the resplendent Registan Sq.

Need to know: Uzbekistan is one of the world's two double-landlocked countries (nations surrounded completely by other landlocked countries).

Other months: Apr-Jun & Sep-Oct – warm, lovely; Nov-Mar – cold, clear, quiet; Jul-Aug – uncomfortably hot.

- Journey
- Cultural

KOMODO & FLORES
INDONESIA

Why now? Here be dragons (and dry weather).

A real-life Godzilla, the Komodo dragon is the world's largest existing lizard – and it exists on only a handful of Indonesian islands. May is a great month to see them. Early in the dry season, the islands of Rinca and Komodo – the best places for sightings – are still green but less humid; it's before peak tourist season too. At this time, dragons are largely visible in open areas; however, mating season is just beginning – they retreat to forests, so are more elusive, but witnessing dramatic fights between males is possible. Aside from reptilian action, Komodo offers brilliant diving with manta rays, beaches (some with pink sand) and hikes up Gunung Ara (Komodo's highest point). Explore neighbouring Flores too, including the multicoloured crater lakes of Kelimutu and the traditional village of Bajawa.

Trip plan: Flores is accessible via air from Bali. Explore Flores, then sail to Rinca and Komodo; stay overnight for the best chance to see dragons (they're most active in the morning).

Need to know: Access to Komodo National Park is by boat from Labuan Bajo on Flores.

Other months: Apr-Oct – dry, lower humidity (Apr-May less busy); Nov-Mar – wet (wettest Jan-Feb).

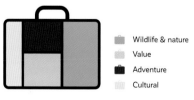

- Wildlife & nature
- Value
- Adventure
- Cultural

RÉUNION

Why now? To enter a Gallic lost world without the crowds.

Rugged Réunion is the most topographically phenomenal department of France. Thrusting up from the Indian Ocean, this volcanic outcrop is closer to Madagascar than Marseilles; more like Hawaii in its aesthetics; and a cultural mix of French, Creole, African and Asian influences. The result: a unique destination – with fabulous fusion food. May is a great time to visit. Falling between the wet, hot austral summer and cooler winter, the month sees low rain, low humidity and delicious temperatures in the high 20°Cs (low 80°Fs). Plus, holidaymaking crowds are absent and cheaper deals can be found. Beaches are available for relaxing on. Inland lie exploring opportunities aplenty: hikes around the dramatic *cirques*, where villages sit in the dormant calderas; paragliding, canyoning and mountain-biking adventures; and visits to Piton de la Fournaise, one of the world's most accessible active volcanoes.

Trip plan: Combine hikes to the three *cirques* with chill-out time (for example, at St Gilles-les-Bain) and eating.

Need to know: There are direct flights to Réunion from Paris and Johannesburg.

Other months: Apr-May & Oct-Nov – good weather, quieter; Dec-Mar – humid, wettest, cyclones possible; Jun-Aug – busy, cool.

- Wildlife & nature
- Adventure
- Cultural
- Food & drink

The picture-perfect town of Amalfi, Italy

The *Panacea prola* butterfly, one of the species found in the Peruvian Andes

A traditonally-dressed Berber man standing proudly in front of his home

© Philip Lee Harvey / Lonely Planet

112

AMALFI COAST ITALY

→ Why now? To add extra zest to *la dolce vita.*

The sparkling azure sea! The cliff-tumbling towns! The serpentine coast roads! The hellish traffic jams! Wait a minute... The Amalfi and Sorrentine coasts, south of Naples and in sight of Mt Vesuvius, ooze Italian seaside glamour; you'll picture 1950s starlets in catseye sunglasses wherever you look. But in high summer, the picturesque little roads grind to a standstill with chic-seeking tourists. Come in spring instead, when driving between honeypot towns such as Sorrento, Positano and Ravello is less onerous, but the weather is still a delight (24°C; 75°F). The rugged Sorrentine Peninsula is also famed for its luscious lemons (arguably the world's best), and the hillsides will be fruit-heavy, fragrant and cheerily yellow right now. Book into a traditional *agriturismo* (farmstay) to learn to make pizza dough and *limoncello*, and sleep within scent of the groves.

Trip plan: Enjoy the foodie delights of Naples (birthplace of pizza) before heading south to Amalfi, via Pompeii's astounding archaeology. For extra glitz, sail over to Capri.

Need to know: Naples to Sorrento takes about an hour by road or rail.

Other months: Jul-Aug – hot, heaving; Apr-Jun & Sep-Oct – pleasant, quieter; Nov-Mar – off-season, coolest, businesses close.

PERU

→ Why now? To beat the crowds to Machu Picchu.

Machu Picchu is probably the world's most bucket-listed site. Its precipitous location and mysterious purpose, coupled with the fact that it sat undiscovered for centuries, make for the most magical combination. It gets especially busy during Peru's drier season; permits for the four-day Inca Trail hike to Machu Picchu must be booked months in advance at this time. Unless you go in May. May is the first dry month, but is outside traditional vacation season. Ergo, the weather is good, but the trails and trains of the Peruvian Andes are less crowded. Dry days are good for countrywide sightseeing too, as well as visits to the Amazon, where rainfall is a little lower and wildlife easier to spot.

Trip plan: Fly from Lima to Cuzco. Explore the Sacred Valley and Machu Picchu (by train or trek). Take the Cuzco to Puno train to Lake Titicaca. Continue west to colonial Arequipa and deep Colca Canyon, returning to Lima. Add on a stay at a remote Amazon ecolodge.

Need to know: Only 500 people are permitted to walk the Inca Trail each day; quieter alternatives include the Salkantay and Choquequirao treks.

Other months: Jan-Apr – wettest (Feb: Inca Trail closes); May-Sep – dry, busy (Jun-Aug: busiest); Oct-Dec – rains begin gradually.

MOROCCO

→ Why now? It's perfect for peaks and petals.

Morocco is marvellous in May. The temperature is ideal countrywide: Marrakesh hovers in the high 20°Cs (low 80°Fs), not too oppressive for wandering the souks; coastal Essaouira is a refreshing 20°C (68°F); the Sahara is hot (30°C+; 86°F+) but far more manageable than July to August (40°C+; 104°F+). The Valley of the Roses, at the foot of the High Atlas Mountains, is particularly pretty during its mid-May flower festival. Now is also an excellent time to head into Morocco's Atlas range. The valleys are vibrantly green, the days often clear and temperatures – in the low 20°Cs (68-73°F), though chilly at night – are good for hiking. Morocco's zenith, Jebel Toubkal, measures 13,671ft (4167m) but is attainable by anyone of average fitness, either via a straightforward two-day climb or a longer, more immersive Toubkal Circuit trek. The mountain village of Imlil is a good base for shorter, family-friendly excursions into Berber country.

Trip plan: Explore Marrakesh before delving into the Atlas Mountains. Head to the walled city of Taroudant via the spectacular Tizi n'Test pass or drive to Imlil. Numerous walks are possible; mules can be hired to carry kit/kids.

Need to know: Check the dates of Ramadan (month of fasting); this can impact services.

Other months: Apr-Oct – good trekking; Nov-Mar – cool, winter hiking possible.

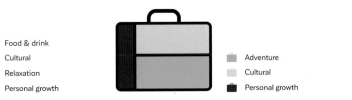

Food & drink
Cultural
Relaxation
Personal growth

Adventure
Cultural
Personal growth

Adventure
Cultural
Value

The sublime shoreline of Lizard Point, Cornwall

© Matt Munro / Lonely Planet

NORTH ISLAND
NEW ZEALAND

The interior of Bilbo and Frodo Baggins' house on the *Lord of the Rings* film set

→ **Why now? Save big on a steamy drive.**

Good, quiet, scenic roads; sleeping in out-of-the-way places; the chance to go wherever the mood takes you... There are few better ways to explore New Zealand than by campervan. High summer seems best for a road trip, but hiring a camper outside peak season can be up to 50% cheaper. Autumnal May is a good halfway house: lower prices but still not too cold, and better driving conditions than winter. Stick to the North Island, which will be warmer: 14°C (57°F) in Auckland versus 7°C (45°F) in Queenstown. It's also bubbling with geothermal activity: warm up at Rotorua and Lake Taupo's hot-spring complexes, or find wild-and-free thermal pools such as Kerosene Creek (near Rotorua), which has a hot waterfall. There's

also plenty of non-weather-dependent fun: blackwater raft through Waitomo's glowworm caves, shelter amid the Hobbiton film set, or walk beneath Waipoua Forest's towering kauri trees.

Trip plan: From Auckland, spend a week or two looping south to Wellington and back. With more time, add on Northland, north of Auckland.

Need to know: Distances can be deceptive, due to hilly, twisty roads – allow lots of time.

Other months: Dec-Feb – warmest, priciest; Mar-May & Sep-Nov – mild/cool, cheaper; Jun-Aug – winter, tougher driving.

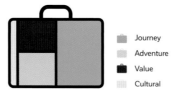

Journey
Adventure
Value
Cultural

CORNWALL
ENGLAND

→ **Why now? Beat the crowds to Britain's best beaches.**

Cornwall has been called a magnificent frame around an ugly picture, which is overly harsh on the county's interior, but emphasises how astounding its edges are. This is the English coast at its wildest, most cliff-soaring best. There are whale sharks, world-class walks, smuggling intrigue, Unesco-listed mining heritage, fishing villages, cream teas and pasties, castles, legends and beaches to suit all sorts – surfers, hedonists, loners, artists, kids. The only trouble is, it gets awful busy in summer. So visit in May, when the hedgerows are flower-bright and the days long but the hordes of tourists haven't descended. Pleasant temperatures should be warm enough for camping; if unsure, the county is big on 'glamping' so opt for yurts or bell tents that come equipped with duvets and woodburners.

Trip plan: Must-sees include arty St Ives town, Tintagel castle and Porthcurno's cliff-side Minnack Theatre, though the main joy is discovering your own favourite cove. Walkers should tackle the breathtaking Cornish section of the South West Coast Path.

Need to know: Cornwall is 300 miles (480km) west of London (six hours by train or car).

Other months: Apr-Jun – quieter, mild, flowery; Jul-Aug – hottest, crowded; Sep-Oct – warmest seas, food festivals; Nov-Mar – bracing, off-season.

Relaxation
Food & drink
Adventure
Value

115

LOIRE VALLEY
FRANCE

→ Why now? Castles without the crowds.

No river is as resplendent as the Loire. Draped in weeping willows, lined by vineyards and flanked by a parade of châteaux, palaces and pretty towns, it's in a class of its own. The history is rich – for instance, Joan of Arc links in Orléans, the royal tombs in Fontevraud Abbey. The wine and food is wonderful, from Michelin-starred restaurants to family *auberges* – plus, in May, markets are full of strawberries and asparagus. Any overindulgence can be offset by delightful canoe paddles and strolls or cycles along the riverbank. This calibre of destination attracts crowds, but May is much quieter than high summer, so you can admire the valley's cavalcade of castles – enormous Chambord, river-spanning Chenonceau, fairytale Ussé – with fewer other people.

Trip plan: Concentrate on the central Loire, from Orléans to Angers, packing in great architecture and eating en route. Include a night at a château hotel.

Need to know: Trains link the Loire Valley to Paris; Paris to Orléans takes one hour.

Other months: Jul-Aug – hot, crowded, river levels low; Nov-Mar – cold, damp; Apr-Jun & Sep-Oct – mild, quieter.

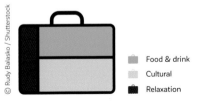

- Food & drink
- Cultural
- Relaxation

WEST COAST
NORWAY

→ Why now? To sail the fjords in sunshine.

Hurtigruten ferries ply Norway's 1491-mile (2400km) west coast, from southerly Bergen to Arctic Kirkenes, 365 days a year. They are a lifeline for people living along this wild, fjord-serrated seaboard, so they must depart, whatever the weather. That said, May to June is a good time to visit. The weather is generally mild and days are extraordinarily long. By mid-May, the sun doesn't set at all in far-north Tromsø – you can watch jaw-dropping scenery glide by all night long. Better weather and more light makes it easier to hop off for activities too. There are 34 ports of call; disembark to fish in the Lofoten Islands, meet Sami people at North Cape or hike near Geirangerfjord. Note, May is a month of festivals in pretty Bergen, so allow extra time here before you sail.

Trip plan: A Bergen-Kirkenes-Bergen round voyage takes 12 days; shorter cruises and numerous excursions are possible.

Need to know: Hurtigruten boats are no-frills – don't expect the amenities and entertainment found on big cruise ships.

Other months: May-Sep – best weather, long days (Jul-Aug: most expensive); Oct-Apr – cool to cold, aurora possible.

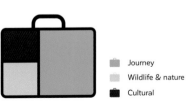

- Journey
- Wildlife & nature
- Cultural

NORTHERN QUEENSLAND
AUSTRALIA

→ Why now? Buckle up for a vibrant, varied road trip.

The 1243-mile (2000km) Great Tropical Drive is a dramatic and diverse road trip that links northern Queensland's best bits, from reef to rainforest. To fully embrace its tropicality, drive it in May. It's the first month of the dry season, which means little rain, slightly cooler temperatures (28°C; 82°F) and accessible roads, but landscapes that are still vigorously green. From the lively hub town of Cairns, the route loops north to pretty Port Douglas and historic Cooktown (Australia's first – albeit transient – European settlement) via lush Mossman Gorge. It backtracks south and inland to the fruit orchards of Mareeba, Undara's lava tubes and the gold-rush heritage town of Charters Towers. Then it rejoins the Pacific Coast, where you could sail to Magnetic Island, raft the Tully River, hike on Hinchinbrook Island, relax on Mission Beach and tour a tea plantation, before returning to Cairns. Great Drive, indeed.

Trip plan: This loop from Cairns takes around two weeks to do properly, though myriad detours are possible. Include Great Barrier Reef diving/snorkelling and indigenous-led tours in locations such as Cooktown and Echo Creek (Tully Gorge).

Need to know: Jellyfish are more prevalent off north Queensland November to May – seek advice before swimming.

Other months: Nov-Apr – hot, wet; May-Oct – drier, cooler.

- Journey
- Wildlife & nature
- Relaxation

CAPPADOCIA
TURKEY

Explore the chimney-like rock formations of Cappadocia by foot, balloon or horse

© Mark Read / Lonely Planet

→ **Why now?** The 'fairy chimneys' are warming up.

Mother Nature must have been in a whimsical mood when she sculpted the Central Anatolian region of Cappadocia. Here, the soft tuff rock has been carved into fantastical ravines, tablelands and turrets that would befit Mr Disney. It's a magical place to explore (kids especially will love it), and the warm-but-not-hot spring weather is ideal for activities. Hike along steep-sided valleys and explore underground cities where rock-hewn churches contain ninth-century frescoes; stay in budget and boutique cave hotels; and drift overhead in hot-air balloons. Winters can be cold – snowy even – but by May temperatures are pleasantly up (25°C; 77°F) and rainfall is low. Indeed, locals put their coal stoves away at the start of May, a portent for good weather.

Trip plan: Walk in the Ihlara Valley, explore the subterranean city of Kaymakli, visit Göreme Open Air Museum and take a cooking class. Combine with İstanbul (two-hour flight) or a beach flop on the Turquoise Coast (two-hour flight).

Need to know: Two airports serve Cappadocia: Kayseri (47 miles, or 75km, from Göreme) and Nevşehir (25 miles; 40km).

Other months: Apr-Jun & Sep-Oct – best weather; Jul-Aug – very hot; Nov-Mar – cold, snow possible.

- Wildlife & nature
- Adventure
- Cultural

ISRAEL

→ **Why now?** To explore and help out, with fewer people.

Israel is ideal in May. Visitor numbers are low, but averages of 26°C (79°F) and barely any rain are perfect for exploring everywhere, from the Dead Sea to the Sea of Galilee, from technicolour Makhtesh Ramon canyon to Jerusalem's Temple Mount. It's the best month for hiking the country-spanning Israel National Trail, as the hills and valleys are lush and the heat not punishing. It's also a good temperature for staying on a *kibbutz*. These communal farms welcome volunteers (Jewish or not) willing to help out with various tasks, including harvesting or planting. In exchange you get food, lodging and a great sense of camaraderie. As a bonus, Shavuot, a Biblical harvest festival, usually falls in May, which sees *kibbutzim* get into the festive spirit with dancing and parades.

Trip plan: From cosmopolitan Tel Aviv head to Jerusalem; cross the wall into Palestine to visit Bethlehem; head north to Nazareth and the Sea of Galilee; then follow the Mediterranean coast back to Tel Aviv.

Need to know: *Kibbutz* volunteers must be aged 18 to 35.

Other months: Apr-May – warm, green; Jun-Aug – very busy, hot; Sep-Nov – quieter, cooler; Dec-Mar – wet, cool.

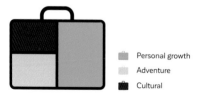

- Personal growth
- Adventure
- Cultural

CUBA

→ **Why now? For Caribbean heat and hip action.**

If you like it hot, in all manner of ways, choose Cuba in May. Technically, it's the first month of the wet, hot, low season on this coolest of Caribbean isles. But in reality, temperatures don't get uncomfortable until June, and heavy rains don't fall until late July. There are 'off-season' bargains to be found too. With the mercury around 30°C (86°F), this is a good month for sun-seekers – try the palm-swayed Varadero peninsula for all-inclusive resorts (many good for families), or head to one of Cuba's 900-odd white-sand cays. Combine beach time with sizzling salsa – there's nowhere better to watch or learn this hot, hip-shimmying dance. Go to the clubs of Havana or cobbled, colonial Trinidad. You'll be too busy mastering your steps to be bothered by the chance of rain.

Trip plan: Explore Old Havana, on foot and by vintage car; if you have time, take a salsa course. Varadero is two hours east of Havana.

Need to know: Cuba has two units of currency: Cuban peso (CUP, for locals) and convertible peso (CUC, used by tourists).

Other months: Dec-Apr – cool, dry, high season; May-Jun – shoulder months, temperatures rising, wetter; Jul-Nov – hotter, wettest (Aug-Oct: stormiest).

▮ Cultural
▮ Personal growth
▮ Relaxation
▮ Value

Havana's streets are famed for their many classic 1950s American cars

ORIENT EXPRESS
EUROPE

→ **Why now?** To ride the rails (for less) in super springtime.

It's the classic train route: the eastward journey from Paris to İstanbul, skimming across Europe via some of its grandest cities to reach the edge of Asia. Its very name evokes an era of wood-panneled glamour, when train travel was at its most romantic. Today, the Venice-Simplon Orient Express (which runs London–Venice) aims to recapture this romance – for those who have pots of cash. Alternatively, you could use a rail pass to chart your own version of the famed route, using much cheaper scheduled trains. Plan your trip for May, when you're likely to find lovely weather all along the way. Leave the springtime boulevards of Paris for pink-tinged medieval Strasbourg. Continue to beery Munich, the music halls of Vienna, art nouveau Budapest, grittier Belgrade and east-meets-west Sofia before reaching the shores of the Bosphorus in İstanbul. You might not get butler service, but the joy of watching the continent unfurl remains.

Trip plan: The Paris–İstanbul journey could be done in four days, linking trains, but allow longer to stop off and explore en route.

Need to know: Various types of rail pass are available; younger and older travellers are eligible for discounts.

Other months: Apr-Jun & Sep-Oct – good weather; Jul-Aug – very hot; Nov-Mar – cold.

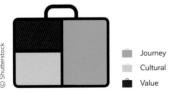

- Journey
- Cultural
- Value

© Shutterstock

NEWFOUNDLAND
CANADA

→ **Why now?** Watch an onslaught of icebergs.

They call the waters off Newfoundland & Labrador 'Iceberg Alley'. In spring, great hunks of Arctic ice – mostly cast-offs from the glaciers of western Greenland – float down the Atlantic coast past Canada's easternmost province. They usually arrive in April and May, peaking mid-May to June. You can stand onshore and watch these white titans drift by or board a boat for a closer look. Good spots include St Anthony, Twillingate, Bonavista and St John's/Cape Spear. Seabirds also start to show up in May, while by the end of the month the first whales appear.

Trip plan: From capital St John's follow the Atlantic coast north to the Bonavista Peninsula (home to pretty Trinity) and Twillingate ('Iceberg Capital of the World'). Veer west to the fjord-cut mountains of Gros Morne National Park, then north to northernmost Newfoundland, for St Anthony and the 1000-year-old Viking site of L'Anse aux Meadows.

Need to know: Newfoundland has its own time zone, which is 30 minutes ahead of Atlantic Standard Time.

Other months: Apr-May – mild, icebergs, whales arrive; Jun-Aug – warmest, peak whales; Sep-Oct – fall colours, cooling; Nov-Mar – cold, snow activities possible.

- Wildlife & nature
- Adventure
- Journey

RED CENTRE
AUSTRALIA

→ **Why now?** It's the right time to see the Rock.

Most visitors flock to Australia's Red Centre during the austral winter, to avoid the desert's scorching summers. However, in midwinter (June to July) temperatures can plunge below 0°C (32°F) after dark. May offers a happy compromise, and is less crowded. Days are dry, clear and manageably warm (mid-20°Cs; 70°Fs), while nights are cool, but not freezing. This makes the month a better choice for authentically 'Aussie' swag-sleeping, early starts to see sunrise, and late nights of gazing at star-filled skies. Warm-but-not-roasting days are comfortable for walks around the base of Uluru, Kata-Tjuta's Valley of the Winds, and Kings Canyon. Or consider sections of the Larapinta – May is the start of trekking season on this classic long-distance trail between Alice Springs and Mt Sonder.

Trip plan: Fly to Alice Springs. Hire a car to follow the Red Centre Way, a five-day loop through the West MacDonnell Ranges to Uluru-Kata Tjuta National Park, returning to Alice via Rainbow Valley.

Need to know: Alice Springs Airport is about 280 miles (450km) from Uluru; smaller Ayers Rock Airport at Yulara is a 20-minute drive from Uluru.

Other months: May-Sep – cool days (nights cold Jun-Jul); Dec-Feb – very hot; Mar-Apr & Oct-Nov – shoulder, still hot.

- Wildlife & nature
- Adventure
- Cultural

PRAGUE
CZECH REPUBLIC

→ **Why now?** To drink and be merry! May is the most intoxicating month to visit Prague. Never mind the lengthening, warming days (which are ideal for boat trips on the Vltava River and walking across Charles Bridge). No, it's Beer Festival time! More than 150 brews are showcased in a vast 10,000-seater tent in the city's Letná Park. Czech food – from spicy sausage to 'Moravian sparrow' (actually pork and dumplings) – is served up too. Away from the festival, there's more consuming to be done in the city's fin-de-siècle cafes and bars.

Trip plan: Allow a day for the Old Town and Jewish Quarter, a day for Prague castle and the Lesser Town, and a day for museums and shops. Get around by tram.

Need to know: The Prague Spring Music Festival, a celebration of classical, jazz and world music, is held in May.

Other months: Nov-Mar – cold (Dec: Christmas markets); Jul-Aug – hot, busy; Apr-Jun & Sep-Oct – warm, quieter.

© Matt Munro / Lonely Planet

May's longer (and warmer) days are ideal for boat trips and the Beer Festival

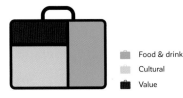

■ Food & drink
▢ Cultural
■ Value

© Jan Fidler / 500px

BEYOND PRAGUE

KUNTÁ HORA · 50 MILES (88KM) · Lovely Unesco-listed medieval town

KARLOVY VARY · 80 MILES (138KM) · Bohemian spa town with thermal fountains

BRNO · 110 MILES (177KM) · Czech second city and culture hub

BUDAPEST · 330 MILES (531KM) · Trains link to the Hungarian capital in under seven hours

SOUTHERN NAMIBIA

→ Why now? It's fresh, green and good for exploring.

Technically, May is the last month of the rainy season in Namibia. But it's all relative. In a country dominated by one of the world's driest deserts, May's five-or-so millimetres are sufficient to class it as a bit wet. In reality what this means is barely a shower but fresh, dust-free air, green landscapes and lots of warm sunshine while the curvaceous dunes of the Sossusvlei region might even be speckled with greenery; the vegetation of Etosha National Park is lush against the white salt pans. This is also the best month to tackle the Fish River Canyon Trek. This challenging multi-day hike, following the watercourse through the world's second-deepest gorge, is only open May to mid-September (October to April is too hot and prone to flash-flooding). In May, the river is more likely to be full and nights aren't so cold; the star-gazing is out of this world.

Trip plan: Namibia's good gravel roads are ideal for self-drive trips. Fish River Canyon is 249 miles (400km) south of capital Windhoek; combine with Lüderitz and the ghost-town of Kolmanskop on the Atlantic coast, and with the dunes and mountains of Namib-Naukluft National Park.

Need to know: English is the official language; German, Afrikaans, Oshiwambo and other tribal languages are also spoken.

Other months: Jun-Oct – dry, best wildlife-watching; Apr-May – mostly dry, green; Nov-Mar – wetter, hotter.

Wildlife & nature
Adventure

© Neil Emmerson / Getty Images

Etosha National Park is fairly green in May, but still full of wildlife

ROUTE 66 USA

→ **Why now?** To hit the empty, open road.

May is a fine time to be in Chicago. The city is warming, and there are many festivals. But it's also a fine time to leave the city – on the ultimate US road trip. Route 66, the famous 'Mother Road', was first designated in 1926 and ran from Chicago, Illinois, to Santa Monica, California, crossing eight states and measuring 2423 miles (3900km). The route, which changed over the years, is no longer officially signed, but about 80% can still be followed (with a guidebook), taking drivers through deserts, plains, mountains and many a small town's main street. It also passes old roadside diners and creaky-signed motels that hark back to the 1920s. The 66 'season' starts in May: earlier, and it'll be cold at the route's higher elevations; by July, the desert will be scorching and the roads busier.

Trip plan: For a Route 66 trip following the original as closely as possible, allow two to four weeks. Save time by using sections of faster Interstate. Or concentrate on one part – for example, drive Oklahoma to California to make a Steinbeck/*Grapes of Wrath* pilgrimage.

Need to know: Springfield, Missouri, is considered the official birthplace of Route 66.

Other months: May-Oct – best for road trip (Jun-Aug: busiest); Nov-Apr – cold, some attractions close.

INSIDE PASSAGE
USA & CANADA

→ **Why now?** Ride a world-beating ferry, before the masses.

The Alaska Marine Highway (AMH) is a local lifeline and a mind-blowing ride. Year-round, AMH ferries ply the Inside Passage, the route that sneaks along the island-sprinkled coast of northwest North America, from Bellingham (Washington State) to Skagway (Alaska). En route, these boats call at remote communities and unreel nautical mile upon mile of scenic treats. They inch through Canada's Gulf Islands, trace eastern Vancouver Island, pass the fathomless Great Bear Rainforest, then hit Alaska, where fjords carve, glaciers calve and Native American and gold-rush history abounds. There's prolific wildlife too, from orca and humpbacks to bald eagles and bears. The warmer months are best, but also busiest. Opt for the long days of May to preempt the crowds and the summer bugs. It's also when animals are at their most active.

Trip plan: Travel on the AMH, hopping on and off at ports en route to explore the wildlife-rich hinterland (though note, some ports are served by ferries daily, others only once a week). Cabins must be prebooked; alternatively, save money by camping out in the lounge or on deck.

Need to know: Bellingham is 68 miles (110km) north of Seattle.

Other months: May-Sep – main cruise season (Jun-Aug: busiest); Oct-Apr – AMH ferries still run, worse weather.

◾ Journey
◾ Cultural

◾ Journey
◾ Wildlife & nature

Pilgrims arriving at the
Cathedral of Santiago
de Compostela

GALICIA SPAIN

→ **Why now? For empty beaches or a perfect pilgrimage.**

Spain's far northwest province has a reputation for being wet. But this ensures it's gloriously green! In May to June especially, the Galician hills are bright with blossom and yellow broom. You'll probably get rain (though these are far from the dampest months), but you'll also get sun, warmth (low-20°Cs; 68-73°F) and empty countryside. Galicia's beaches are some of Spain's least developed (try dune-backed Playa de la Lanzada or the rock formations of Praia das Catedrais). And the walking is legendary: the Camino de Santiago, which starts in St Jean-Pied-a-Port in France, ends in Galician capital Santiago de Compostela. May to June is a prime time to make this pilgrimage – not too hot, not too busy, facilities all open and long days for those long miles.

Trip plan: The 485-mile (780km) Camino de Santiago takes around 30 days to walk. Alternatively, fly to Santiago to access north- and west-coast beaches and other towns (Pontevedra, A Coruña).

Need to know: Splurge on a night at the Parador de Santiago, the heritage hotel overlooking Santiago's cathedral.

Other months: Jul-Aug – hottest, busiest; Nov-Mar – cold, facilities close, wetter; Apr-Jun & Sep-Oct – warm, quieter.

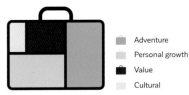

Adventure
Personal growth
Value
Cultural

Musicians playing traditional bluegrass tunes in Rosine, Kentucky

© Lottie Davies / Lonely Planet

SKYE SCOTLAND

→ **Why now? Long, bug-free days on the invigorating western isle.**

If you're blessed with good weather on Scotland's second-largest island, you're blessed indeed. Skye's lochs sparkle, the mountains blush, moors glow green. If you have bad weather, well, that's OK too – the Cuillin range in cloud or mist holds atmospheric allure. That said, May – statistically one of the driest months – is a good choice. This is when bluebells carpet the woods, lambs graze and seabirds return to the imposing cliffs. It also offers really long days (sunrise before 4am, sunset after 11pm), which leaves plenty of time for castles, crofting museums and the rock formations of the Trotternish peninsula. Come early in the month if you can – western Scotland is plagued by microscopic but maddening midges from mid-May to September (though they're worst July to August). Note, midges don't like wind, so a breezy ridge or coast hike should keep them away.

Trip plan: Skye is a five-hour drive from Glasgow (break the journey in Fort William). Stay as long as you can. Visit Portree and the Trotternish, hike the Cuillins, cruise to see sea eagles and sip a Talisker whisky.

Need to know: Skye is connected to mainland Scotland by road bridge and ferry.

Other months: Nov-Mar – dark, cold, aurora possible; Apr-Jun & Sep-Oct – quieter; Jul-Aug – peak season, midges.

- Wildlife & nature
- Relaxation
- Food & drink

DEEP SOUTH, USA

→ **Why now? For a musical, historical, gastronomical drive in five states.**

Deep South USA comprises Kentucky, Tennessee, Mississippi, Alabama and Louisiana. Perhaps as 'American' as America gets, it's a region of boundless hospitality, country, blues and jazz, cultural richness, barbecue and buttermilk biscuits. It has eccentricity, charm and spunk in spades. May is a good month for a regional road trip, when the sun is warm, the roads emptier and the flowers are in bloom. Start in Kentucky, where the bluegrass pastures and dogwoods look spectacular, and the riotous Kentucky Derby (Louisville, first Saturday in May) begins the month with a bang. South lie major musical treats: Nashville, Memphis, Tupelo (birthplace of Elvis) and Muscle Shoals ('Recording Capital of the World'). There are also plantation houses, Civil Rights sites, bourbon distilleries, Gulf-side fishing villages serving great gumbo and the irrepressible rhythms of New Orleans.

Trip plan: Plan a roadtrip suited to your available time. It's 715 miles (1150km) from Louisville to New Orleans, a huge distance even without any detours. If you're time poor, focus on a section, such as a week-long music pilgrimage from Nashville to New Orleans.

Need to know: In the USA, you must pay for gas before you fill your tank.

Other months: Mar-May & Sep-Oct – mild, pleasant; Jun-Aug – temperatures peak; Nov-Feb – cooler, wettest.

- Journey
- Cultural
- Food & drink

(L) Squirrel monkeys
and surf: reasons to
smile in Costa Rica
(R) A little bit of
Venice in Las Vegas

COSTA RICA

➜ Why now? To embrace the beginning of the 'green'.

Costa Rica feels like a natural theme park, Mother Earth at her most flamboyantly Disney. It's almost too perfect: varied yet conveniently compact; wild-seeming yet with outstanding infrastructure; laden with danger (raging rivers, active volcanoes) yet totally safe; visionary in its eco-ethos; unbelievable in its biodiversity. Oh, and jungle zip lining was invented here. Even its rainy season is given a positive spin. It's not 'wet', it's 'green', and the country looks even more alive. Waterfalls churn, and more rivers open for rafting. Also, in May (the beginning of the 'green'), there's still lots of sunshine, but accommodation prices can drop by 30% and the national parks are less busy. The surf is up too.

Trip plan: Fly to capital San José or Liberia. The latter is in Pacific-side Guanacaste province, the driest part of Costa Rica, which is often still dry in May – a good beach option. Also visit parks such as Monteverde Cloud Forest and Manuel Antonio to fully appreciate the greenness.

Need to know: Travel can be more difficult during rainy season – allow for delays.

Other months: Dec-Apr – drier, peak season; May-Jun & Nov – wet, cheaper; Jul-Aug – wetter, busy; Sep-Oct – wettest.

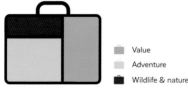

- Value
- Adventure
- Wildlife & nature

© Jonathan Gregson / Lonely Planet

LAS VEGAS USA

→ **Why now? To love and leave Sin City.**
Brash Las Vegas is a fantasyland, where you can do just about anything: glide in a Venetian gondola, gamble with Caesar, drive a full-sized bulldozer, ride the world's only indoor double-loop, double-corkscrew rollercoaster, fraternise with the Mob (at the Mob Museum) and get married by Elvis. But you can also do a whole lot just outside Sin City. While Vegas is the epitome of manmade mayhem, it sits within some of Mother Nature's most adventurous outdoors. The crimson hills of Red Rock National Conservation Area, 17 miles (27km) southwest, have world-class climbing, and hiking and biking trails. Deep-blue Lake Mead, 37 miles (60km) southeast, is good for kayaking, or paddle to nearby Hoover Dam. In Valley of Fire State Park, 56 miles (90km) north, you can walk amid Native American petroglyphs. Visit in spring, when the temperature is hot but manageable, whether you're exploring the desert or The Strip.

Trip plan: Spend a few days indulging in Vegas before hiring a car for a southern Nevada road trip.

Need to know: May is low-season for tourism, but check your visit doesn't coincide with any big conventions, which push up room prices.

Other months: Mar-May & Sep-Oct – warm not baking, quieter; Jun-Aug – very hot; Nov-Feb – cool, busy for Christmas.

© Mark Read / Lonely Planet

Adventure
Relaxation
Food & drink
Value

BEYOND LAS VEGAS

🚗 **DEATH VALLEY · 130 MILES (209KM) ·** Lowest, driest, hottest, weirdest North America

🚗 **ZION NATIONAL PARK · 165 MILES (266KM) ·** Utah's unique rock playground

✈ **GRAND CANYON · 200 MILES (320KM) ·** Flights skim over Arizona's endless, gorgeous gorge

🚌 **LAKE TAHOE · 490 MILES (787KM) ·** Super splotch of blue in the Sierra Nevadas

June
WHERE TO GO WHEN

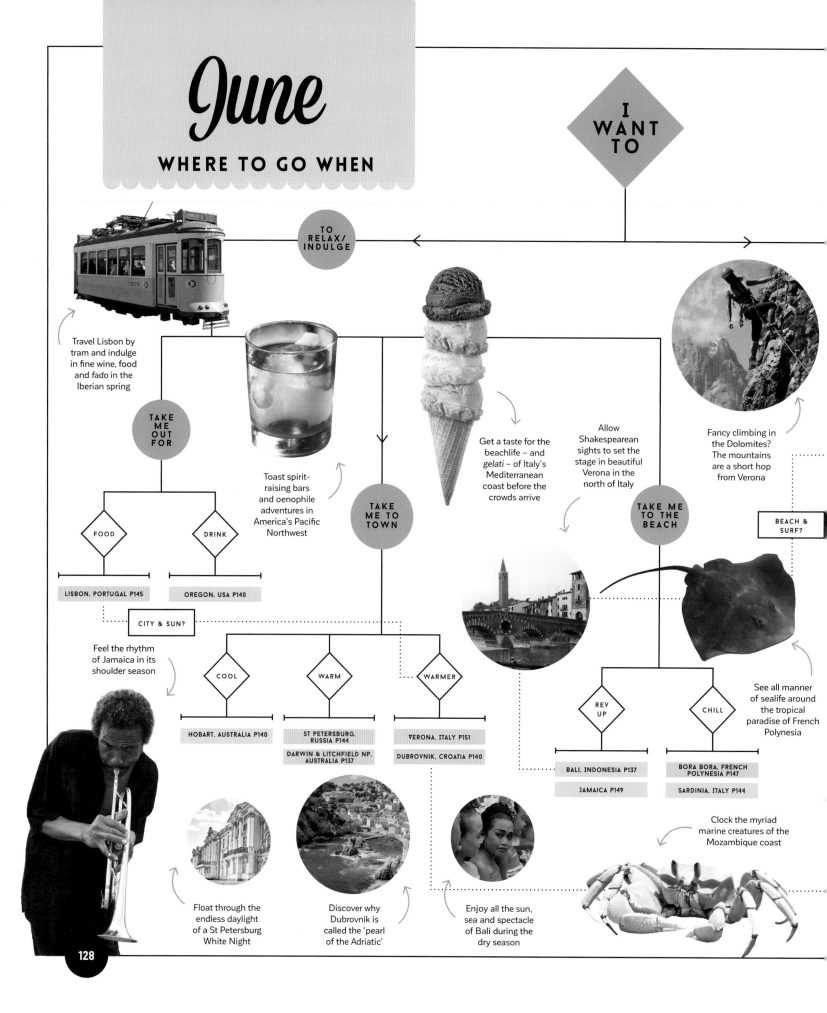

I WANT TO

TO RELAX/INDULGE

Travel Lisbon by tram and indulge in fine wine, food and *fado* in the Iberian spring

TAKE ME OUT FOR

Toast spirit-raising bars and oenophile adventures in America's Pacific Northwest

TAKE ME TO TOWN

Get a taste for the beachlife – and *gelati* – of Italy's Mediterranean coast before the crowds arrive

Allow Shakespearean sights to set the stage in beautiful Verona in the north of Italy

Fancy climbing in the Dolomites? The mountains are a short hop from Verona

TAKE ME TO THE BEACH

BEACH & SURF?

FOOD

DRINK

LISBON, PORTUGAL P145

OREGON, USA P140

CITY & SUN?

Feel the rhythm of Jamaica in its shoulder season

COOL

WARM

WARMER

REV UP

CHILL

See all manner of sealife around the tropical paradise of French Polynesia

HOBART, AUSTRALIA P140

ST PETERSBURG, RUSSIA P144

DARWIN & LITCHFIELD NP, AUSTRALIA P137

VERONA, ITALY P151

DUBROVNIK, CROATIA P140

BALI, INDONESIA P137

JAMAICA P149

BORA BORA, FRENCH POLYNESIA P147

SARDINIA, ITALY P144

Clock the myriad marine creatures of the Mozambique coast

Float through the endless daylight of a St Petersburg White Night

Discover why Dubrovnik is called the 'pearl of the Adriatic'

Enjoy all the sun, sea and spectacle of Bali during the dry season

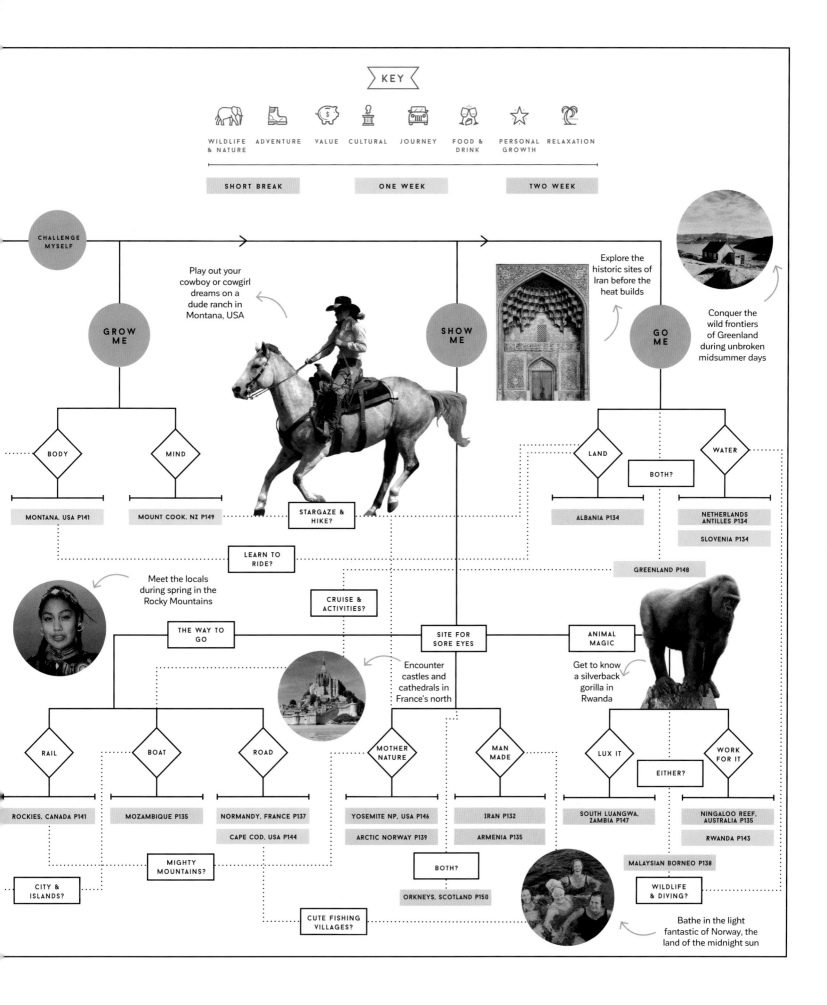

KEY

WILDLIFE & NATURE ADVENTURE VALUE CULTURAL JOURNEY FOOD & DRINK PERSONAL GROWTH RELAXATION

SHORT BREAK ONE WEEK TWO WEEK

CHALLENGE MYSELF

Play out your cowboy or cowgirl dreams on a dude ranch in Montana, USA

Explore the historic sites of Iran before the heat builds

Conquer the wild frontiers of Greenland during unbroken midsummer days

GROW ME

SHOW ME

GO ME

BODY

MIND

MONTANA, USA P141

MOUNT COOK, NZ P149

STARGAZE & HIKE?

LAND

WATER

BOTH?

ALBANIA P134

NETHERLANDS ANTILLES P134

SLOVENIA P134

LEARN TO RIDE?

GREENLAND P148

Meet the locals during spring in the Rocky Mountains

CRUISE & ACTIVITIES?

THE WAY TO GO

SITE FOR SORE EYES

ANIMAL MAGIC

Encounter castles and cathedrals in France's north

Get to know a silverback gorilla in Rwanda

RAIL

BOAT

ROAD

MOTHER NATURE

MAN MADE

LUX IT

WORK FOR IT

EITHER?

ROCKIES, CANADA P141

MOZAMBIQUE P135

NORMANDY, FRANCE P137

CAPE COD, USA P144

YOSEMITE NP, USA P146

ARCTIC NORWAY P139

IRAN P132

ARMENIA P135

SOUTH LUANGWA, ZAMBIA P147

NINGALOO REEF, AUSTRALIA P135

RWANDA P143

MIGHTY MOUNTAINS?

MALAYSIAN BORNEO P138

CITY & ISLANDS?

BOTH?

WILDLIFE & DIVING?

ORKNEYS, SCOTLAND P150

CUTE FISHING VILLAGES?

Bathe in the light fantastic of Norway, the land of the midnight sun

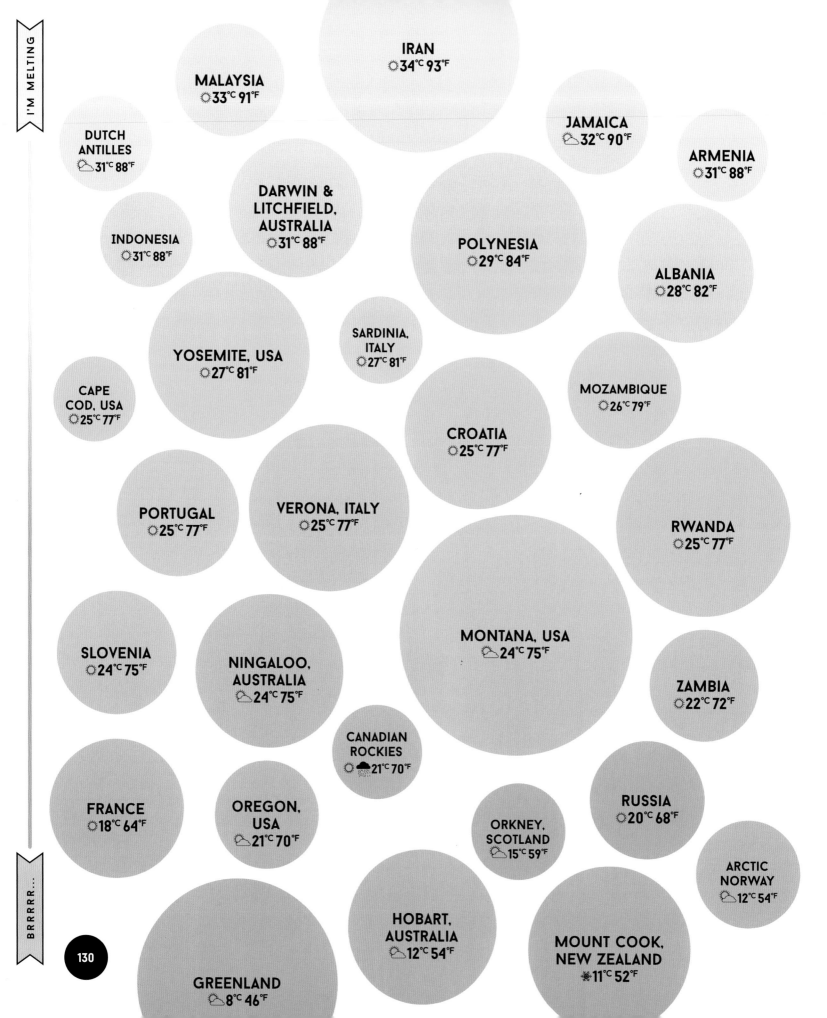

IRAN
☀ 34℃ 93°F

MALAYSIA
☀ 33℃ 91°F

JAMAICA
⛅ 32℃ 90°F

ARMENIA
☀ 31℃ 88°F

DUTCH ANTILLES
⛅ 31℃ 88°F

DARWIN & LITCHFIELD, AUSTRALIA
☀ 31℃ 88°F

INDONESIA
☀ 31℃ 88°F

POLYNESIA
☀ 29℃ 84°F

ALBANIA
☀ 28℃ 82°F

SARDINIA, ITALY
☀ 27℃ 81°F

YOSEMITE, USA
☀ 27℃ 81°F

MOZAMBIQUE
☀ 26℃ 79°F

CAPE COD, USA
☀ 25℃ 77°F

CROATIA
☀ 25℃ 77°F

PORTUGAL
☀ 25℃ 77°F

VERONA, ITALY
☀ 25℃ 77°F

RWANDA
☀ 25℃ 77°F

MONTANA, USA
⛅ 24℃ 75°F

SLOVENIA
☀ 24℃ 75°F

NINGALOO, AUSTRALIA
⛅ 24℃ 75°F

ZAMBIA
☀ 22℃ 72°F

CANADIAN ROCKIES
☀ 🌧 21℃ 70°F

FRANCE
☀ 18℃ 64°F

OREGON, USA
⛅ 21℃ 70°F

ORKNEY, SCOTLAND
⛅ 15℃ 59°F

RUSSIA
☀ 20℃ 68°F

ARCTIC NORWAY
⛅ 12℃ 54°F

HOBART, AUSTRALIA
⛅ 12℃ 54°F

MOUNT COOK, NEW ZEALAND
❄ 11℃ 52°F

GREENLAND
☁ 8℃ 46°F

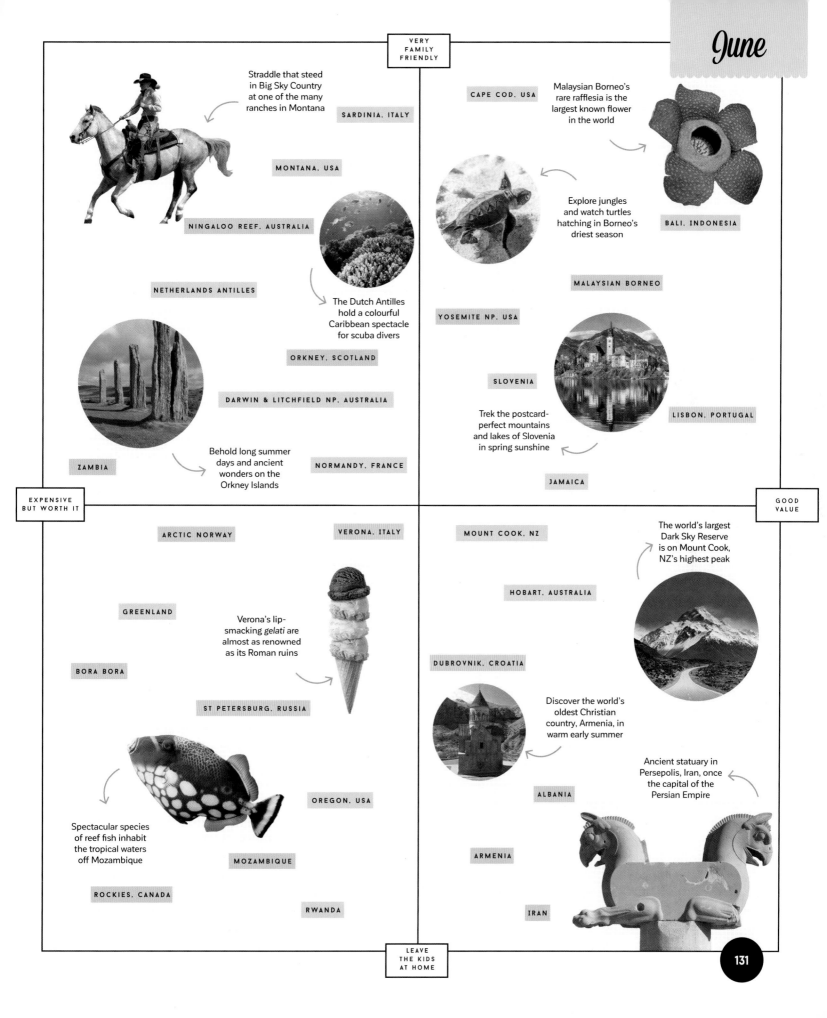

Straddle that steed in Big Sky Country at one of the many ranches in Montana

SARDINIA, ITALY

MONTANA, USA

NINGALOO REEF, AUSTRALIA

NETHERLANDS ANTILLES

The Dutch Antilles hold a colourful Caribbean spectacle for scuba divers

ORKNEY, SCOTLAND

DARWIN & LITCHFIELD NP, AUSTRALIA

ZAMBIA

Behold long summer days and ancient wonders on the Orkney Islands

NORMANDY, FRANCE

CAPE COD, USA

Malaysian Borneo's rare rafflesia is the largest known flower in the world

Explore jungles and watch turtles hatching in Borneo's driest season

BALI, INDONESIA

MALAYSIAN BORNEO

YOSEMITE NP, USA

SLOVENIA

LISBON, PORTUGAL

Trek the postcard-perfect mountains and lakes of Slovenia in spring sunshine

JAMAICA

ARCTIC NORWAY

VERONA, ITALY

MOUNT COOK, NZ

The world's largest Dark Sky Reserve is on Mount Cook, NZ's highest peak

HOBART, AUSTRALIA

GREENLAND

Verona's lip-smacking *gelati* are almost as renowned as its Roman ruins

BORA BORA

DUBROVNIK, CROATIA

Discover the world's oldest Christian country, Armenia, in warm early summer

ST PETERSBURG, RUSSIA

Ancient statuary in Persepolis, Iran, once the capital of the Persian Empire

ALBANIA

OREGON, USA

Spectacular species of reef fish inhabit the tropical waters off Mozambique

MOZAMBIQUE

ARMENIA

ROCKIES, CANADA

RWANDA

IRAN

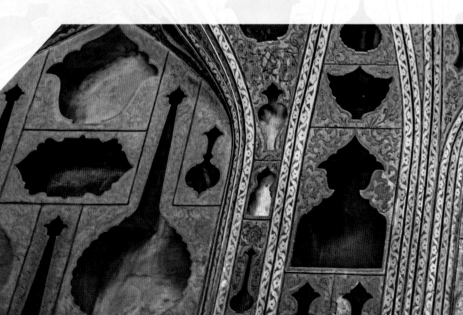

IRAN

→ **Why now? Explore ancient cities before the heat builds.**

The land once called Persia is where misconceptions come to die. Political posturing wins column inches, but there are so many treasures that really deserve the headlines: the extraordinary Islamic architecture of Esfahan, with its intricate blue patterned tiles; the huge, bustling bazaars of Tehran, Esfahan, Shiraz or Tabriz; the magnificent remains at Persepolis, dating back two-and-a-half millennia; the deserts; the poems; the food; and – most of all – the warm, welcoming people. By June the mercury is rising fast at lower altitudes, but prices and crowds are dropping. Summer is also the season for hiking in the Alborz Mountain, particularly the ascent of Mt Damavand, a true icon of Iran.

Trip plan: Fly to Tehran, head south to the desert city of Yazd, the ancient ruins at Persepolis, sophisticated Shiraz and majestic Esfahan, before scooting up to the Alborz Mountains to tackle Mt Damavand and roam among the Castles of the Assassins.

Need to know: Most visitors require a visa – apply well before you intend to travel. Females over the age of nine should wear a headscarf in visa application photos.

Other months: Mar-May – spring, cool, biggest crowds and highest prices; Jun-Aug – hot in lower regions, best for mountains; Sep-Oct – cooler, lower prices; Nov-Feb – cold.

- ■ Cultural
- ■ Adventure
- ■ Journey

The ornamental ceiling of Kakh-e Ali Qapu, Esfahan

ALBANIA

→ **Why now?** Hike the Accursed Mountains in blessed weather.

That traditional mountain lifestyle you feared had been swallowed by the modern world is still there – in the Albanian national park between Theth and Valbona, known as the Accursed Mountains. In June, warm days bring sunshine to the alpine meadows, and trekking through the peaks and forested valleys of this delightfully rural region will see you immersed in local culture. Stay in a homestay in Theth to experience everyday life in an Ottoman-era house, overlooked by the stone tower used as a lock-up when dealing with blood feuds. Elsewhere, look for thousands of mushroom-like bunkers (reminders of former dictator Enver Hoxha's communist regime) and more uplifting sites on the Mediterranean coast, including the ancient Greek/Roman site of Butrint.

Trip plan: From Tirana, head north via Shkodra to the 'Accursed Mountains' around Theth and Valbona (from where it's possible to pop into Kosovo), then double back south for walks in Llogora National Park and the Karaburun Peninsula, and beyond to Butrint.

Need to know: When asking a question, be aware that traditionally a shake of the head means yes, while a nod means no.

Other months: Apr-Oct – warm, dry; Nov-Mar – winter, good snowshoeing.

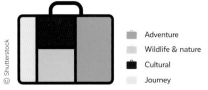

Adventure
Wildlife & nature
Cultural
Journey

NETHERLANDS ANTILLES

→ **Why now?** Soak up the Caribbean sun away from the hurricane belt.

It's the Caribbean, but not as you know it. The ABC islands, as Aruba, Bonaire and Curaçao are playfully known, sit just off the north coast of Venezuela. Although they're geographically part of South America, they've been governed by, and been part of, the Netherlands since the early 17th century. June is the sweet spot between the high season (which also happens to be the rainy season) in the northern winter, and the slightly hotter summer months. Since the islands are outside the hurricane belt (unlike most of the other Caribbean islands), they're a safe bet at this time of year, yet hotel rates are low and beaches less crowded. And what beaches: from gorgeous Eagle Beach on Aruba, beloved of honeymooners, to the resorts of Curaçao's southwest. Come to Aruba for nightlife, Bonaire for wonderful diving and snorkelling, and Curaçao for Dutch-influenced culture and cuisine, and to explore its colourful capital, Willemstad.

Trip plan: Direct flights from New York and Amsterdam serve Curaçao, Bonaire and Aruba, with flights from Miami to the first two.

Need to know: Corals spawn off Bonaire around September or October – a nocturnal spectacle for scuba divers.

Other months: Feb-Sep – consistently warm and dry; Oct-Jan – rainy season.

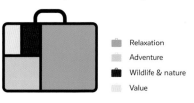

Relaxation
Adventure
Wildlife & nature
Value

SLOVENIA

→ **Why now?** Roam the Julian Alps in warm spring sunshine.

It's no coincidence that the people of Slovenia – one of Europe's most forested countries, a land of jaw-droppingly beautiful mountains, lakes and rivers – are so keen on outdoor activities. Whether it's hiking the Julian Alps, swimming in Lake Bled (warming up nicely in June), rafting the Soča River at Bovec or delving into the caverns of the Notranjska karst, you won't find Slovenians whiling away sunny June days just sitting and savouring the excellent cuisine and wines (though don't miss those). This magical month, after winter's chill has departed but before summer crowds descend, demands to be exploited to the max in this great outdoors, whether that means high-level climbing or simply heading to the (compact) coast and exploring Venetian-built towns such as Piran. Great value at any time, prices dip in this shoulder season.

Trip plan: If time's limited, concentrate on the west, looping from capital Ljubljana to the Adriatic Coast around the Venetian port of Piran via cave-plugging Predjama Castle, then north to the Julian Alps.

Need to know: Slovenia has only 29 miles (46km) of coastline – and that gets packed with Italian tourists in July and August.

Other months: Dec-Mar – good snowsports; Apr & Nov – variable weather; May-Jun – spring; Jul-Aug – high summer, crowds; Sep-Oct – warm, fine flowers and foliage.

Adventure
Wildlife & nature
Value

© Shutterstock

ARMENIA

Why now? Explore the world's oldest Christian country in summer. Armenia does ancient like almost nowhere else. This landlocked nation is packed with churches, monasteries and caravanserais dating from the first millennium AD, and with relics stretching back even further, including Karahunj (literally: 'stone henge'), reputedly constructed 7000 years ago. More than that, the dramatic backdrop of the Caucasus, with snow-capped Mt Ararat peering across the Turkish border, matches Armenia's turbulent history of invasion, oppression and aggression by neighbouring states. The weather is most clement in June, after the icy chill of winter and before the mercury soars into the high 30°Cs. From capital Yerevan's chilled cafe culture to the cave village of Khndzoresk and hilltop monasteries such as Tatev and Noravank, it's a mesmerising, diverse land that's not quite like anywhere else. The wine's not bad, either.

Trip plan: Fly to Yerevan and head south to Khor Virap, Noravank, Tatev and Karahunj, then skirt Lake Sevan (stopping to admire the field of Khachkars – engraved cross-stones) to explore the forested hills around Dilijan. Many add a visit to Georgia, just to the north.

Need to know: The non-country of Nagorno-Karabakh, an enclave of Armenian heritage surrounded by Azerbaijan, is a fascinating coda to Armenia – but check the current safety situation before travelling.

Other months: Mar-Jun – pleasant warmth, wildflowers; Jul-Aug – can top 40°C/104°F; Sep-Nov – cooler days; Dec-Feb – very cold.

- Cultural
- Journey
- Food & drink

BAZARUTO ARCHIPELAGO
MOZAMBIQUE

Why now? Dive and snorkel clear, warm, turquoise waters. Are these the most beautiful tropical islands on Earth? The Bazaruto Archipelago faces stiff competition from other Indian Ocean destinations (and Mozambique's own Quirimbas Archipelago) – but wriggle your toes into the silky sand on a glorious June morning (the start of the dry season), or gaze through your mask at impossibly colourful reef fish, and maybe a humpback whale migrating past, and they could stake a fair claim. Much of this chain of five islands off Mozambique's southeastern coast is protected as a national park, conserving dolphins, dugongs, sea turtles and around 2000 fish species. Oh, and Nile crocodiles – but perhaps you're not so keen to see those… This is a paradise for divers, but also for anyone seeking a truly barefoot beach holiday.

Trip plan: Several islands have airstrips, and access is usually by plane or helicopter, speedboat or *dhow* from the mainland port of Vilankulo. Day trips from Vilankulo are possible but most visitors arrive on a package to one of the luxury lodges with an upmarket tour operator, often incorporating South Africa's Kruger National Park.

Need to know: Humpback whales migrate past the archipelago from June or July to September or October.

Other months: Jun-Oct – dry; Apr-Jun & Sep-Nov – best diving; Nov-Mar – rains build.

- Relaxation
- Wildlife & nature
- Adventure

NINGALOO REEF AUSTRALIA

Why now? Dive with giants on Australia's other barrier reef. Now's the time to think Big. Visit Australia's largest state (area: around one million sq miles; 2.5 million sq km) in June to swim with the world's heftiest fish, the whale shark (length: up to 60ft; 18m) and manta rays (wing width: up to 18ft; 5.5m) as well as watching humpback whales (weight: up to 30 tonnes) on – OK – only Australia's second-largest reef, Ningaloo. Coral spawning from March prompts a zooplankton explosion, attracting the sharks until mid-August, while manta rays – present year-round at Coral Bay – tend to visit Exmouth May to November, and humpbacks migrate past June to November. The turquoise waters are beautifully clear for snorkelling and diving among dazzling reef fish, too.

Trip plan: Coral Bay and Exmouth are both good bases for visiting the reef. Learmonth airport near Exmouth is served by flights from Perth, an 800-mile (1300km) drive away. For a road-trip, stop off en route at the Pinnacles Desert near Cervantes, craggy Kalbarri National Park and the ancient stromatolites of Shark Bay.

Need to know: No more than 10 people are allowed in the water with a whale shark, and must not approach closer than 10ft (3m).

Other months: Apr-Jul – moderate heat, whale sharks; Oct-Apr – summer, high 30s°C/90s°F; Aug-Sep – warm.

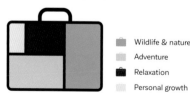

- Wildlife & nature
- Adventure
- Relaxation
- Personal growth

135

Balinese girls preparing for Pendat dance at Pura Samuan Tiga temple

(L) Find waterfalls in Litchfield National Park; (R) Normandy is the home of Camembert

© Hadi Zaher / Getty Images

DARWIN & LITCHFIELD NATIONAL PARK
AUSTRALIA

Why now? Get a taste of the Top End in the Dry.

You know the seasons are serious when they're divided simply into the Wet and the Dry. When planning a visit to the Northern Territory's tropical Top End, it pays to pick Dry – at least, if you want to get out and explore. June brings clear skies and dry days, so it's ideal for enjoying Darwin's largely outdoor attractions: amble through Bicentennial Park; browse the stalls at Mindil Beach Sunset Markets or pick up a souvenir at one of the other weekend bazaars; or catch a classic movie at the Deckchair Cinema. It's worth taking one of several easy escapes from the city for a day at least – cooling off under Wangi Falls in nearby Litchfield National Park, or discovering the unique Indigenous culture of the Tiwi Islands.

Trip plan: Fly to Darwin from most Australia cities plus Bali, Singapore and Kuala Lumpur, or ride the Ghan railway from Alice Springs and Adelaide. Day tours run to the Tiwi Islands and Litchfield National Park.

Need to know: Beware of box jellyfish when sea swimming – a bigger problem in the Wet, but check local information before diving in during the Dry.

Other months: May-Oct – the Dry (less rain, slightly cooler); Nov-Apr – the Wet (hot, wet).

Cultural
Adventure

NORMANDY
FRANCE

Why now? Encounter castles, cathedrals, cider, cheese, gardens and moving war cemeteries.

It's over a millennium since the Vikings ('Northmen', aka Normans) settled this part of northwest France. Over the intervening centuries, their descendants invaded England, perfected Camembert, cider and Calvados brandy, constructed magnificent castles, abbeys, châteaux and cathedrals, and finessed Impressionism. Explore this gorgeous region in June and you'll enjoy their legacy at its best, the garden of Claude Monet in Giverny blooming with poppies and roses, and the courageous soldiers of World War II commemorated at annual D-Day celebrations. Before the European holiday season really kicks in, popular destinations such as the rock-top abbey of Mont St Michel (actually just over the border in Brittany) and cutesy villages such as Beuvron-en-Auge are marginally less busy, while footpaths on the cliffs of Étretat and the Cotentin Peninsula beg to be hiked.

Trip plan: Normandy is most easily reached by ferry from England or train via Paris. Having your own transport is helpful – trains and buses are sparse in many areas.

Need to know: Normandy is well set-up for cyclists, with over 300 miles (483km) of cycle paths and seven long-distance waymarked routes.

Other months: May-Oct – late spring to autumn, most pleasant (Jul-Aug: high summer, roads, cities and hotels jammed); Nov-Apr – cooler, chance of poor weather.

Cultural
Food & drink
Adventure
Journey

BALI & LOMBOK
INDONESIA

Why now? Enjoy sun, sand, sea, surf and food in the dry season.

Indonesia is a bargain destination at any time, but in June the stars align for visitors to its twin tropical paradises, the islands of Bali and Lombok. The weather is dry and warm, but not too hot. Bali's west-coast surf breaks are at their best, yet it's before northern-hemisphere school holidays, so the crowds don't descend till July and prices are low. Whether you plan to climb a volcano (perhaps Agung on Bali, or Rinjani on Lombok), visit shore temples or Ubud's cultural highlights, dive or snorkel the Gili Islands or just get horizontal on the sand, this is the ideal time to come.

Trip plan: Denpasar receives direct flights from various Southeast Asian cities as well as several Australian cities and Auckland. Flights from most other regions usually involve a change in Southeast Asia or the Middle East.

Need to know: Though Bali is largely Hindu, across most of Indonesia Ramadan can affect travel, with possible delays during Ramadan and big crowds at the end.

Other months: May-Sep – dry season (busiest Jul-Aug, Christmas and New Year); Oct-Apr – rain sporadic.

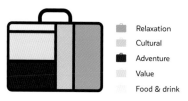

Relaxation
Cultural
Adventure
Value
Food & drink

Orangutans
at Semenggoh
Nature Reserve,
Malaysian Borneo

© Matt Munro / Lonely Planet

MALAYSIAN BORNEO

→ **Why now?** Explore jungles and see turtles hatching in the dry season. For some of us, Borneo seems a long way to travel for a beach. But if that beach is liable to erupt with hatching turtles and is backed by wildlife-rich rainforest, in which former head-hunters live largely traditional lifestyles – well, then the long journey seems entirely worthwhile. That's Borneo – or, more specifically, the Malaysian states of Sarawak and Sabah, at their best in the (relatively) dry month of June, when turtles hatch and orangutans thrive on plentiful fruit. Sarawak has the longhouse communities along the Batang (River) Rejang, the bat-thronged caves of Gunung Mulu National Park, the proboscis monkeys and enormous rafflesia flowers. Sabah has mighty Mt Kinabalu, Sepilok Orangutan Rehabilitation Centre, fine diving and those turtle-nesting beaches.

Both offer incredible wildlife and cultural experiences. And yes, both have beautiful stretches of sand on which to simply lie back and relax.

Trip planner: Fly to Kuching or Kota Kinabalu from Kuala Lumpur. There are regular flights between those two state capitals, and buses and boats serve other regional destinations.

Need to know: Some governments advise against travel to islands off the far eastern coast of Sabah. Check the latest advice before visiting those areas.

Other months: Apr-Sep – driest, but rain possible any time; Oct-Mar – wet, still hot.

■ Wildlife & nature
▫ Cultural
■ Adventure
▫ Relaxation

Stilted fisher's huts
on the seawater inlet
in Krystad, Norway

ARCTIC NORWAY

→ **Why now? Trip the light fantastic in the land of the midnight sun.**
In midsummer the corrugated coastline of far northern Norway is bathed in endless light – from mid-May to late July, the sun doesn't dip below the horizon. And you'll want every second of daylight for drinking in the scenery, driving between the colourful fishing villages and craggy ridges of the Lofoten Islands and Senja, roaming the vast pine and birch forests and trekking to the surf-crashed frontier at Knivskjelodden, the northernmost tip of Continental Europe. Be sure to spare time to discover the delights of Tromsø, the region's lively hub, with its profuse pubs and museums, the distinctive Toblerone shape of the Arctic Cathedral, and its annual midnight marathon.

Trip plan: Tromsø, far north Norway's main city, is served by direct flights from Oslo, Stockholm, London and other cities. Buses and the Hurtigruten ferry link towns in the region, but it's best to drive – from Tromsø, visit isolated fishing villages on Senja, the Sami centres of Kautokeino and Karasjok, and Europe's northernmost tip, near Nordkapp.

Need to know: June is peak season in Tromsø – book accommodation in advance.

Other months: Mid-May–late Jul – midnight sun; May-Oct – reliably above freezing; Nov-Apr – largely dark, cold.

© Matt Munro / Lonely Planet

■ Wildlife & nature
■ Journey
■ Cultural

139

HOBART
AUSTRALIA

Why now? To experience the arts maelstrom of Dark MoFo.

Embrace the austral midwinter in Hobart with the most varied, unpredictable event in the land: Dark MoFo (darkmofo.net. au). This melange of art installations and performances, dark music (classical or black metal equally likely), food, movies, a nude river swim and, well, undefinable happenings in the left-field Mona museum and around Hobart is a good reason for a mid-June break in the Tasmanian capital. Sure, it may be a bit chilly to be picnicking on the waterfront, but the museums, shops, restaurants and bars are as enticing as ever – warm the cockles with a sip of Tassie's own Sullivans Cove, recognised as the world's best single malt whisky in 2014. And if you feel the need to strap on a pair of skis or a board, Mt Mawson in Mount Field National Park is a 90-minute drive away.

Trip plan: Hobart has regular direct flights from Sydney, Melbourne and Brisbane.

Need to know: Hobart rarely gets really cold, but bring an umbrella or raincoat (at any time – there's less rain in June than October).

Other months: Dec-Feb – summer, long warm days; Mar-May – autumn, more consistent dry weather; Jun-Aug – winter, cool but not too cold; Sep-Nov – spring, expect rain.

Cultural
Food & drink

DUBROVNIK & DALMATIAN ISLANDS CROATIA

Why now? Discover the 'pearl of the Adriatic'.

A crescent of terracotta roofs curling round to embrace an azure coin of the Adriatic, Dubrovnik has been assaulted many times through the centuries – besieged by Saracens, overtaken by Venetians, devastated by earthquake in 1667, then by Napoleon and the war of 1991–92. Yet it's emerged more beguiling each time, and never more so than in June, the tipping point between spring's warmth and summer's somnolent heat, but before cruise passengers cram every alley. Once you've promenaded a circuit of the Old Town's walls and roamed the marbled streets (ideally very early in the morning), escape to a nearby island – perhaps Lokrum, Mljet or Šipan – to find a quiet beach, and a taverna serving fine seafood and local wines. Or head around the bay to peaceful Cavtat, founded by Greek settlers who fled Slavic attack to build the more famous Dubrovnik in AD 614.

Trip plan: Reasonably priced accommodation in the Old Town is limited; you'll find more in Lapad, a mile or so to the west, which also has a couple of beaches.

Need to know: The best spot from which to admire the city at sunset is the top of Mt Srd's cable car.

Other months: May-Oct – warm, clear days (Jun-Aug: busiest, priciest); Nov-Apr – cool, few tourists, many facilities closed.

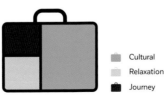

Cultural
Relaxation
Journey

PACIFIC NORTHWEST USA

Why now? For caffeinated outdoor adventures and grape encounters.

Think Oregon and Washington are all about dramatic coastlines, forests, volcanoes? Wake up and smell the coffee! And the hops. And the grapes… Sure, the region's natural wonders demand to be explored – climbing Mt Hood or Mt Rainier, hiking Crater Lake National Park, fishing the McKenzie River – but an adventure in the great outdoors starts indoors with a cup of joe. The proliferation of coffee micro-roasters means you're guaranteed a fine brew – and its provenance – anywhere. Then there's the beer: the draft brewing craze kicked off here, and today over 85% of US hops are grown in the northwest. Tour the brewpubs and bars of Seattle or Portland and you'll discover citrus tangs from close on 500 microbreweries. The bright, fresh, dry days of June are perfect for visiting the region's wineries: around Walla Walla for Cab Sauv and Merlot, Yakima for Chardonnay and Riesling, or down the Willamette Valley for Pinot Noirs.

Trip plan: A backroads trip tracing a triangle between Seattle, Portland and Walla Walla could traverse Mt Rainier and Mt Hood National Parks as well as the key winery regions.

Need to know: Climbing Mt Rainier is not an easy jaunt – book with an experienced guiding outfit for the multi-day ascent.

Other months: May-Sep – warmer, drier; Oct-Apr – cooler, rain peaking midwinter.

Food & drink
Journey
Adventure

CANADIAN ROCKIES

→ **Why now? Sit back and soak up springtime in the Rockies.**

Is there a more relaxing way to enjoy a mountain wilderness experience? Board a glass-roofed carriage, recline your comfy seat and watch the snow-capped peaks roll past. That's the idea of the Rocky Mountaineer, a luxurious train with glass-domed carriages that plies routes between Alberta's mountains and Vancouver, from Banff via Lake Louise and Kamloops, or from Jasper via Kamloops or Whistler and Quesnel. Ride the rails in June and you'll get the best of all worlds: spring flowers bloom yet peaks are still snow-capped, and Lake Louise is thawing to reveal that famed blue-green hue. June is the rainiest month in the Rockies – but you're snug inside, so why worry? VIA Rail's Canadian train between Toronto and Vancouver stops at Jasper, though it runs overnight through the best mountain scenery, between Kamloops

The Rocky Mountaineer passing through Banff National Park

and Vancouver. The Rocky Mountaineer service includes hotel accommodation in Kamloops or Quesnel and Whistler.

Trip plan: Rocky Mountaineer (www.rockymountaineer.com) offers three routes through the Rockies between Jasper or Banff and Vancouver. VIA Rail's train, the Canadian (www.viarail.ca), from Toronto to Vancouver via Jasper, is cheaper.

Need to know: Heading east, request a seat on the left for the best views (on the right if heading west).

Other months: Mid-Apr–mid-Oct – services operating; Mid-Oct–mid-Apr – no trains.

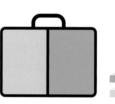

■ Journey
■ Wildlife & nature

MONTANA USA

→ **Why now? Time to play cowboy on a dude ranch.**

Saddle up, pardner! Most of us have dreamed of donning a pair of chaps and a stetson, mounting a horse and wielding a lasso, or just riding off into the sunset. Since the late 19th century, guest or 'dude' ranches have offered urbanites the chance to play out those fantasies, bedding down in log cabins and joining round-ups. Montana, straddling the majestic Rockies and with Yellowstone nestled in the crook of its central southern corner, is the archetypal

cowboy frontier destination, and June is the time to win your spurs, to beat the heat of high summer, and to spot the wobbly-legged calves of elk, deer and moose. Ranches offer a range of packages for riders of various levels, from horseriding novices to those with the experience to tackle the big cattle drive.

Trip plan: Montana's ranches are along the eastern Rockies, with the densest cluster south and east of Bozeman, which receives flights from several major US cities.

Need to know: The level of riding and involvement with cattle varies between

ranches and and time of year. The Dude Ranchers' Association website (www.duderanch.org) has details of member properties across the US and Canada.

Other months: Jun-Sep – most popular (Jul-Aug: high season); year-round – some ranches open with tailored activities.

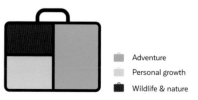

■ Adventure
■ Personal growth
■ Wildlife & nature

RWANDA

Why now? To see eye to eye with a silverback gorilla.

That something so huge (a male gorilla can top 180kg) can be so vulnerable is hard to understand. Yet only 700 or so endangered mountain gorillas survive in two isolated subpopulations. June, the start of Rwanda's dry season, is the time to venture to Volcanoes National Park to track one of its 10 habituated groups; prepare for muddy, steep trails, heady altitude (around 9850ft; 3000m) and the heart-melting sight of a precious primate family. A gorilla encounter is far from the only reason to come to Rwanda. The calm, neat capital, Kigali is a fine place to start, redolent with the aroma of Rwanda's great coffee; Nyungwe Forest harbours large populations of chimpanzees and Rwenzori colobus monkeys, while to the east Akagera National Park is a pretty mix of savannah, hills and valleys, with giraffe, zebra, elephant and some shy lions.

Trip plan: Fly to the capital, Kigali. Independent travel is fairly straightforward, with a good minibus service, though it's easiest to book a tour (including gorilla tracking) with an international operator.

Need to know: Book your gorilla-tracking permit (currently US$750) well in advance for this popular season.

Other months: Jun-Aug – driest season, gorilla-trekking easiest; Mar-May & Nov – heaviest rain; Sep-Oct & Dec-Feb – damp, possibly cheaper, better gorilla-permit availability.

- Wildlife & nature
- Journey
- Cultural

The steep slopes of Volcanoes National Park host hundreds of mountain gorillas

CAPE COD
USA

→ **Why now?** Celebrate sun, sea and sand (and seafood).

If you're fond of sand dunes and salty air, try New England's favourite seaside destination. The flexed arm of Cape Cod is lined with beaches, cutesy towns, oysters, clams and lobster rolls – no wonder millions flock here each year. Most, though, come in July and August; after Memorial Day the crowds thin, making June a delicious month to visit, with more chance of bagging accommodation and finding space on a beach. Not that it's too quiet: the month is peppered with events celebrating the arts (including Provincetown International Film Festival). Trace an arc around the Cape by car, pausing at the pretty harbours and heading out on a whalewatching cruise, or cycle the 25-mile Cape Cod Rail Trail between South Dennis and Wellfleet.

Trip plan: Cape Cod is easiet to access from Boston: flights serve Provincetown and Hyannis, fast ferries connect Boston and Provincetown several times daily in summer, and buses and a weekend train link Boston with Hyannis.

Need to know: Even in June, it pays to book accommodation well in advance.

Other months: Jun-Sep – summer; Oct-Nov & Apr-May – shoulder season; Dec-Mar – winter, cheaper, some facilities closed.

SARDINIA
ITALY

→ **Why now?** Soak in the sun and Mediterranean before the crowds.

Italy's second-largest island is, fair to say, famed mostly for one key asset: beaches. Nowhere else is the Mediterranean such an incredible shade of jade-turquoise-azure, lined with such perfect white-sand beaches. Best known is Costa Smeralda, the archetypal millionaire's playground, but there are plenty more for mere mortals to enjoy. And June's the time to enjoy them, with fine, clear weather but before the hordes of high summer descend. Which beach? South of capital Cagliari is Chia, with not one but five fine beaches; The Sinis Peninsula has good snorkelling and Greek ruins; Alghero has popular resorts; from Cala Gonone on the east coast boats depart for secluded beaches; and the Costa Rei further south is exquisitely beautiful. If you can stir from the sand, you'll find great hiking in the Gennargentu Mountains, historic old town centres – Cagliari included – and 3000-year-old *nuraghi* dwellings to discover.

Trip plan: International airports at Cagliari, Alghero and Olbia all receive low-cost flights.

Need to know: Many facilities close for a siesta in the early afternoon, particularly outside the main tourist resorts.

Other months: May-Jun – clear days; Jul-Aug – high season; Apr & Sep-Oct – shoulder, lower prices; Nov-Feb – colder.

ST PETERSBURG
RUSSIA

→ **Why now?** To float through the daylight of the White Nights.

The great city founded on the Neva River by Tsar Peter the Great in 1703 was always designed to impress. Its palaces, museums and theatres are as grand as its early masters (and mistresses) could imagine, and in midsummer, when the sun never sets and the city is bathed in a luminous glow 24/7, it looks that much more romantic. During the White Nights, roughly from the second week in June to the start of July, St Petersburg is a whirl of opera, ballet, music and general *zhizni radost* (joie de vivre). Stroll alongside the Neva or the Summer Garden, watch the bridges open and the ornate fountains of the Peterhof sprinkle.

Trip plan: You could spend a week wandering the riverbank, parks and streets, but make time for St Petersburg's grand palaces and churches, the incredible Hermitage Museum in the white, green and gold Winter Palace, and the monuments of the Peter and Paul Fortress, at least.

Need to know: Tourists must obtain a Russian visa, usually through a tour agency or invitation from a hotel, before arriving. Be prepared for high prices during White Nights.

Other months: Apr-Sep – warm, bright; Oct-Nov – cold, grey; Dec-Mar – dark, freezing, but magical.

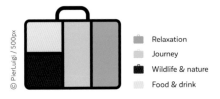

- Relaxation
- Journey
- Wildlife & nature
- Food & drink

© PierLuigi / 500px

- Relaxation
- Cultural
- Adventure
- Food & drink

- Cultural
- Wildlife & nature

LISBON
PORTUGAL

Why now? Indulge in fine wine, food and *fado* in the Iberian spring.
There are few European cities where you can plant yourself on a sunny terrace outside a hip cafe surrounded by historic architecture and be confident you won't get stung for an overpriced coffee or beer. Lisbon is the exception: probably the best-value major city outside the former Eastern Bloc, the Portuguese capital feels anything but cheap. Food and drink – sumptuous *presunto* (dried ham), port, *ginjinha* (cherry liqueur), seafood – all are delectable and keenly priced. The city's at its most enjoyable in June, when flowers bloom and festivals create a friendly buzz. The Feast of St Anthony sees Lisbon go sardine crazy, but at any time you're liable to smell someone grilling fish on an Alfama street corner. Take Tram 28 – touristy but fabulous – on a tour of the city, and be sure to catch Tram 15 to see the Torre de Belém and Jerónimos Monastery, and to try the finest *pasteis de nata* (custard tarts).
Trip plan: The Lisbon metro runs from the airport into the city centre. For convenience and character, pick accommodation in the Alfama, Baixa or Bairro Alto districts.

© Matt Munro / Lonely Planet

Eating a *pastel de nata* (custard tart) is a culinary right of passage

Need to know: Tram 28 is a favourite ride for pickpockets. No need for paranoia, just awareness and sensible precautions.
Other months: Apr-Sep – warm, dry; Oct-Mar – cooler, more rain.

- Cultural
- Food & drink
- Value

BEYOND LISBON

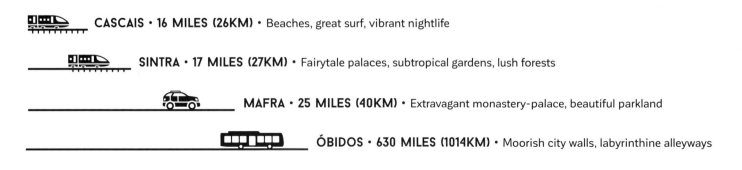

🚆 **CASCAIS · 16 MILES (26KM) ·** Beaches, great surf, vibrant nightlife

🚆 **SINTRA · 17 MILES (27KM) ·** Fairytale palaces, subtropical gardens, lush forests

🚗 **MAFRA · 25 MILES (40KM) ·** Extravagant monastery-palace, beautiful parkland

🚌 **ÓBIDOS · 630 MILES (1014KM) ·** Moorish city walls, labyrinthine alleyways

YOSEMITE NATIONAL PARK USA

→ **Why now?** For a classic hike amid nature resurgent.

Naturalist John Muir loved Yosemite; in 1869, he wrote that this slice of the Californian Sierra Nevada was 'by far the grandest of all the special temples of Nature I was ever permitted to enter'. It is truly special, a great glacier-gouged valley, with soaring domes and pinnacles, crashing waterfalls, meadows edged by oaks, cedars and firs, and wildlife in abundance. In late spring, the park is awakening. Wildflowers are rife, animals are stirring and the falls are at full throttle, thanks to snow melt. Also, by late May, it's usually possible to summit Half Dome, the national park's most iconic peak. The final push of this day-hike involves using cables to reach the top; the cables are removed every October but (depending on snow conditions) reinstalled in May.

Trip plan: Yosemite is a 3½-hour drive from San Francisco. Use shuttlebuses to access sites and trailheads. In a few days you could see Lower Yosemite Falls, Happy Isles, Vernal and Nevada Falls and the panorama from Glacier Point. Add more days for magnificent hiking.

Need to know: Be bear aware – store food in bear lockers at campsites.

Other months: Dec-Feb – cold, winter sports; Mar-May – spring flowers, quiet; Jun-Aug – hot, busy; Sep-Nov – quieter, cooling.

Adventure

Wildlife & nature

Yosemite Falls, as seen from the valley

© Mark Read / Lonely Planet

BORA BORA
FRENCH POLYNESIA

→ **Why now?** Relax in a tropical paradise in the balmiest season.

Blue, turquoise, azure, teal, indigo… there aren't enough words to describe the hues of the Pacific Ocean around French Polynesia on a clear, calm, sunny day. And there are plenty of those in June, the start of the driest season, when the main island of Bora Bora and its *motu* (ringing islands) bask around the high 20°Cs. This is the stuff of movies, with luxurious resorts perched over the crystal waters, shaded by swaying palms – and you need to be a film star to afford the prices at the very top hotels and resorts, though more modest accommodation can be found. As if the scenery wasn't paradisiacal enough, the snorkelling and diving, over coral gardens and with sharks and rays, is spectacular.

Trip plan: Bora Bora receives several flights daily from Tahiti, and a few from Huahine, Mo'orea, Maupiti and Ra'iatea. Try to get a seat on the left of the plane for the best views.

Need to know: Book well ahead if visiting in July (when the traditional Heiva i Bora Bora festival is held) and August, the most popular months.

Other months: Jun-Aug – driest, busiest; May & Sep-Oct – higher humidity, better availability, lower prices; Nov-Apr – wet season, high humidity.

■ Relaxation
■ Adventure

SOUTH LUANGWA NATIONAL PARK
ZAMBIA

→ **Why now?** Walk with the animals on a thrilling safari on foot.

The eyes of a lion give nothing away: not anger, not fear, not curiosity. That's something you notice when you encounter this majestic carnivore without the protection of a vehicle – on foot in the birthplace of the walking safari: Zambia's South Luangwa National Park. June's the ideal time to explore 'the valley' as it's the start of the dry season, before vegetation has withered. Amble alongside one of the continent's finest guides, spotting elephants, giraffes, dazzling birdlife and, if you're lucky, even wild dog. Seeing wildlife of any kind on foot is both electrifying and enlightening, bringing into focus not just the sights but also the sounds and smells of the bush. Leopards and various nocturnal species are often seen on night drives, too.

Trip plan: Fly via Zambia's capital, Lusaka, into the airstrip at Mfuwe, near the main park gate. It's easy to combine a few days in South Luangwa with Victoria Falls and other Zambian parks such as Lower Zambezi, Mana Pools in Zimbabwe or Lake Malawi.

Need to know: Though most visitors stay in luxurious accommodation in the park, budget safaris are possible staying at cheaper lodges or camps at Mfuwe.

Other months: Jun-Oct – dry season; Nov-May – 'emerald' season: trails may be washed out, fantastic for birders and photographers.

■ Wildlife & nature
■ Adventure

© Lottie Davies / Lonely Planet

Dog sledding is possible
in Greenland year round

GREENLAND

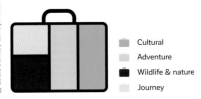

→ **Why now?** Explore a wild frontier in the endless midsummer days.

'When you've seen the world – well, then, there's always Greenland.' So goes the old traveller's bon mot – and after you've experienced the otherworldly light of June, when day never fades to night, you'll understand why. Austerely beautiful Greenland is the world's biggest island, rendered bigger still by transport logistics: with barely any roads, travel between the small, scattered communities usually involves a boat or helicopter ride – cheap, this isn't. But it also isn't like anywhere else. You can immerse yourself in the traditional lifestyles of Inuit communities, watch breaching whales in Disko Bay and browsing musk ox near Kangerlussuaq, and breathe the scent of pure Arctic ice as you hike or kayak isolated fjords such as Ilulissat or in the mountains of East Greenland.

Trip plan: Realistically, you'll want to plan a trip with a knowledgable tour operator who can book international flights (probably to the main settlement, Nuuk), accommodation and internal transport. Most itineraries focus on the (relatively) well-trodden west coast.

Need to know: Biting insects can become a pest later in summer (July and August). Bad weather can stymie any travel plans, so be flexible.

Other months: Jun-Sep – mildest weather, easiest travel; May & Oct – colder, less reliable weather; Nov-Apr – winter, husky sledding.

- Cultural
- Adventure
- Wildlife & nature
- Journey

A view across Canterbury Plains to Mt Cook and the Southern Alps

© Lottie Davies / Lonely Planet

JAMAICA

Why now? Soak up Caribbean culture in the shoulder season.

A steaming gumbo of bass rhythms, Rasta culture, craggy coasts, forested mountains and delicious beaches, Jamaica is a bewildering and bewitching destination. It's also highly seasonal: holidaymakers cram the resorts between mid-December and mid-April, bringing queues, high prices and sunbather jams on those beautiful beaches. June traditionally marks the start of the hurricane season, but since those tropical storms rarely get going for a while, this is a terrific month in which to enjoy all that makes Jamaica enticing – sun and sand, yes, but also hiking in the Blue Mountains, discovering the plants and animals of Cockpit Country, river rafting, rum tastings and of course the famous Kingston nightlife – without the crowds and with often massive discounts at hotels and resorts, and even on tours and airfares.

Trip plan: Check out the beaches and nightlife in Negril and Montego Bay, cool off in Dunn's River Falls near Ochos Rios (listen out for June's Jazz Festival), feast on jerk chicken at Boston Beach then hit the town in Kingston.

Need to know: Insect repellent is a must – occasional outbreaks of Chikungunya virus are spread by mosquitoes.

Other months: Mid-Dec–mid-Apr – high season, warm, dry, expensive; mid-Apr–Jul – shoulder season, rainier, but mostly dry; Aug-Nov – increased hurricane risk.

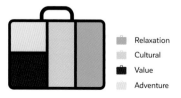

- Relaxation
- Cultural
- Value
- Adventure

MOUNT COOK NEW ZEALAND

Why now? Get star-struck in the world's largest Dark Sky Reserve.

Now's the time to discover the vast canvas and minute details of the night sky, and the place to do it is Aoraki Mackenzie Dark Sky Reserve – the world's largest, covering over 1660 sq miles (4300 sq km). Makes sense, really: Maori say that 12,218ft (3724m) Aoraki, whose name some translate as 'Sky Piercer', is the son of the Sky Father, Raki. During the crisp nights of winter, the constellations form a luminous veil across the firmament – visit one of the local observatories on a guided tour to learn about those countless distant suns. The clarity of the air is a dream for photographers, too, who capture glorious images of snow-capped Aoraki reflected in Lake Pukaki. And yes, you can ski – in fact, New Zealand's longest ice river, the Tasman Glacier, provides the country's longest ski

run of up to 7.5 miles (12km).

Trip plan: Aoraki Mount Cook Village is about 165 miles (266km) from Queenstown, or 205 miles (330km) from Christchurch; buses run daily from both. Accommodation options in the village range from a campground to the comfortable Hermitage lodge.

Need to know: Heavy snow and avalanches can block tracks and roads in winter – check local information before travelling.

Other months: Jun-Sep – winter, cold, crisp days; Nov-Feb – summer, temperatures can top 30°C (90°F); Mar-May, autumn, wildflowers bloom.

- Adventure
- Personal growth
- Wildlife & nature

The Ring of Brodgar
stone circle and the
Italian Chapel on
Lamb Holm

ORKNEY
SCOTLAND

© Justin Foulkes / Lonely Planet

→ Why now? Experience unending summer days among the island's ancient wonders.

Move over Stonehenge. For a more mystical summer solstice, on 20 June head to the Ring of Brodgar, a 341ft-wide (104m) stone circle on the Orkney isle Mainland. At this epicentre of a unique collection of neolithic sites, the longest day is celebrated with music, poetry and readings. Delve further into ancient Orcadian history at nearby Skara Brae, one of Europe's best-preserved Stone Age villages, and the rune-inscribed cairn and passage grave at Maes Howe. It's not all ancient history, though: June sees the cliffs bustling with breeding seabirds, notably comical puffins, while you'll probably see dolphins, porpoises and even orca off the coast, and seals along the shores. Legend has it some 'selkies' cast off their sealskins at midsummer to bewitch humans.

Trip plan: Flights from mainland Scotland serve Kirkwall, and ferries sail to several Orcadian ports. On the islands, buses provide local transport, though car hire or cycling allow more flexibility.

Need to know: Summer temperatures may average 15°C, but beware strong winds – come prepared with warm outer layers.

Other months: Jun-Aug – long, bright days, busier; May & Sep – also sunny; Oct-Apr – shorter days, rain frequent.

■ Cultural
■ Wildlife & nature
■ Journey

© Justin Foulkes / Lonely Planet

Ponte Pietra, a Roman arch bridge over the Adige River, Verona

VERONA ITALY

Why now? Absorb opera and history in cool early summer.
Shall I compare thee to a summer's day? To continue the Shakespearean quote, Verona in June is both lovely and temperate, after the rough winds have finished shaking the darling buds of May (*Sonnet 18*, if you're interested). Though overshadowed by its near neighbour Venice to the east, Verona is a terrific city to roam in early summer, relaxed and absorbing. Wander among its medieval *palazzi* and *loggias*, perhaps pausing to gaze longingly up at the balcony in the reputed Casa di Giulietta (Romeo and Juliet is largely set in Verona). Don't forget to explore its Roman remains – the Arena reverberates from late June with the sounds of the annual opera festival. Food and drink is an obsession in Verona, from some of Italy's best *gelati* (ice creams) to fine wines, pumpkin ravioli and thick *bigoli* pasta – this winsome city is nourishment for the body as well as the mind.
Trip plan: Verona receives low-cost flights from across Europe, and has a busy train station with widespread connections.
Need to know: Accommodation is at a premium during the Opera Festival (late June through August) – book well in advance, or earlier in the month.
Other months: May-Sep – average highs above 20°C (70°F); Apr & Oct – shoulder season, weather often pleasant; Nov-Mar – cool, less reliable weather.

Cultural

Food & drink

© Pete Seaward/ Lonely Planet

BEYOND VERONA

MANTUA · 28 MILES (45KM) · Palaces, domes, lakes, the 'most romantic city in the world'

LAKE GARDA · 30 MILES (48KM) · Water sports, Roman remains and gorgeous gardens

VENICE · 75 MILES (121KM) · Gondolas, canals, ducal palaces

TREVISO · 82 MILES (132KM) · Medieval gothic churches and amazing frescoes

July

WHERE TO GO WHEN

I WANT TO

Go on excursion to the Ionian islands and you'll settle into the gentle harbourside life

TO RELAX/INDULGE

Austria's Alpine region serves up delicious, hearty cuisine and cooler climes

TAKE ME OUT FOR

Austria's Alps will put a song in your heart and spring in your step

Make merry with the masses in the Danish capital of Copenhagen, where it's buzzing in July

EATING & ADVENTURE?

Now's the time to make that pilgrimage up Japan's favourite peak, Mt Fuji

FOOD

DRINK

TAKE ME TO TOWN

TAKE ME TO THE BEACH

| ALPS, AUSTRIA P173 |
| HUNTER VALLEY, AUSTRALIA P164 |

WILD DAYS

WILD NIGHTS

REV UP

CHILL

SAND & SNORKELLING?

| BOSNIA HERCEGOVINA P161 |
| PHILADELPHIA, USA P175 |

| COPENHAGEN, DENMARK P169 |

| ANTIGUA P168 |
| MICHIGAN, USA P159 |

| MARQUESAS, FRENCH POLYNESIA P168 |
| ZANZIBAR, TANZANIA P168 |
| IONIAN ISLANDS, GREECE P159 |

URBAN EATING?

Huddle up with warming local wines during winter in the Hunter Valley

Explore the sun-soaked, history-packed cities of Sarajevo and Mostar in Bosnia Herzegovina

Become enlightened as you travel the Great Lakes' gold coast in Michigan, USA

Dip your toes in the Indian Ocean under blue skies in Zanzibar

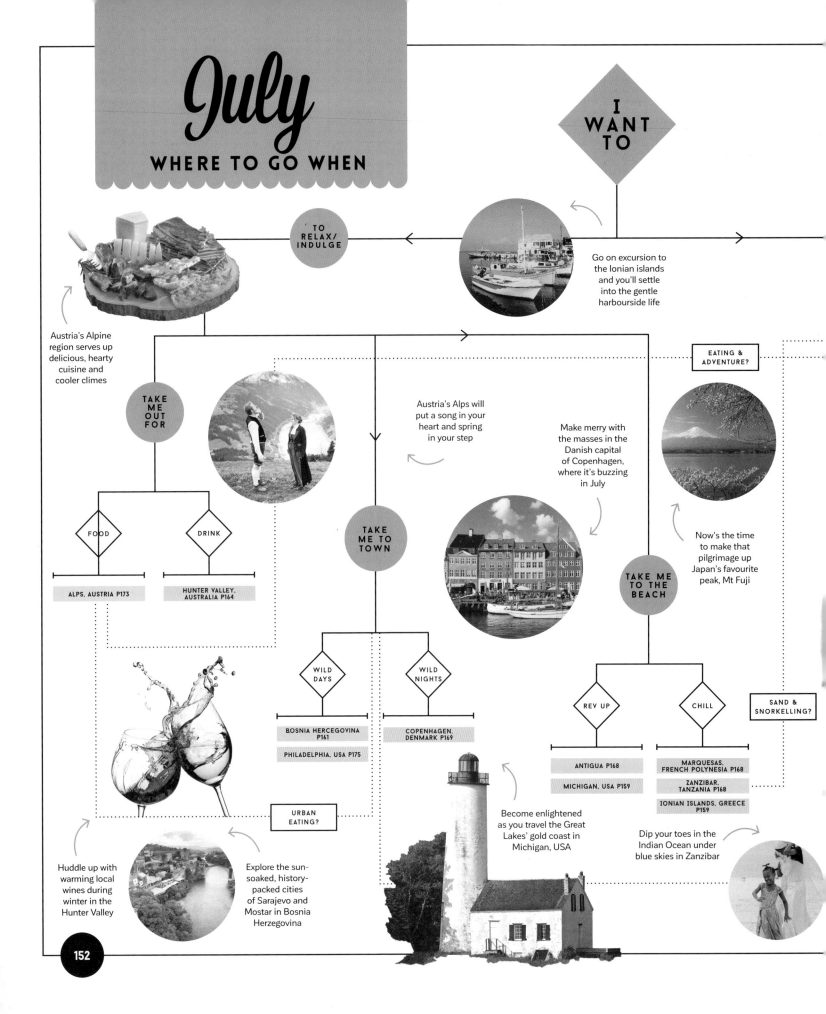

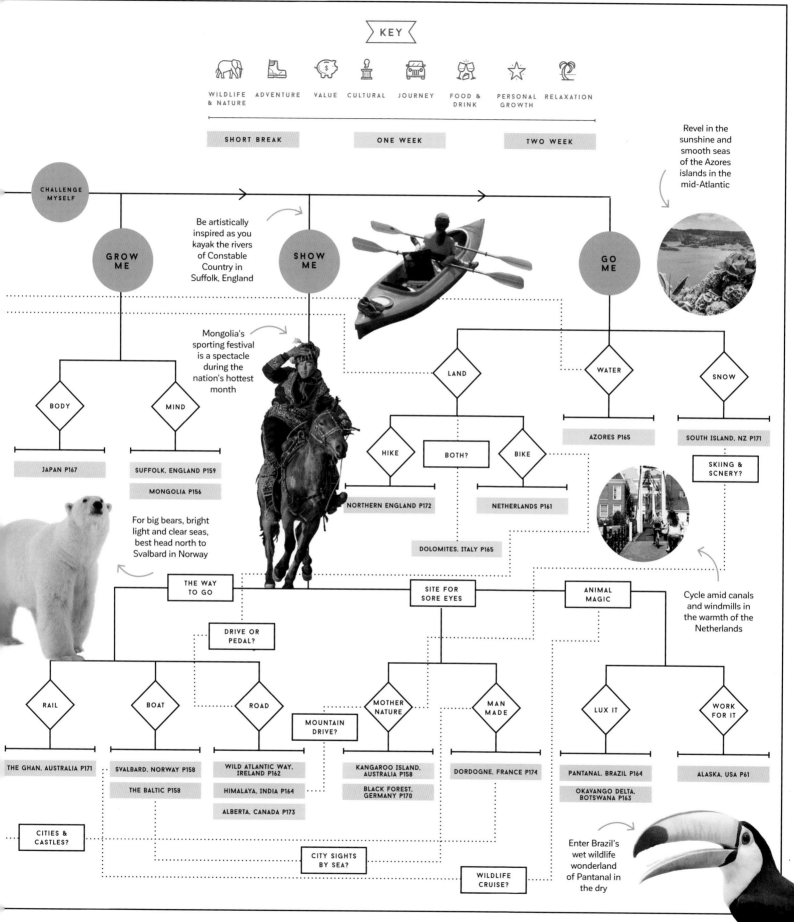

KEY

WILDLIFE & NATURE   ADVENTURE   VALUE   CULTURAL   JOURNEY   FOOD & DRINK   PERSONAL GROWTH   RELAXATION

SHORT BREAK   ONE WEEK   TWO WEEK

Revel in the sunshine and smooth seas of the Azores islands in the mid-Atlantic

CHALLENGE MYSELF

GROW ME

Be artistically inspired as you kayak the rivers of Constable Country in Suffolk, England

SHOW ME

GO ME

Mongolia's sporting festival is a spectacle during the nation's hottest month

LAND

WATER

SNOW

BODY

MIND

HIKE

BOTH?

BIKE

AZORES P165

SOUTH ISLAND, NZ P171

JAPAN P167

SUFFOLK, ENGLAND P159

MONGOLIA P156

NORTHERN ENGLAND P172

NETHERLANDS P161

SKIING & SCNERY?

For big bears, bright light and clear seas, best head north to Svalbard in Norway

DOLOMITES, ITALY P165

THE WAY TO GO

SITE FOR SORE EYES

ANIMAL MAGIC

Cycle amid canals and windmills in the warmth of the Netherlands

DRIVE OR PEDAL?

RAIL

BOAT

ROAD

MOUNTAIN DRIVE?

MOTHER NATURE

MAN MADE

LUX IT

WORK FOR IT

THE GHAN, AUSTRALIA P171

SVALBARD, NORWAY P158

THE BALTIC P158

WILD ATLANTIC WAY, IRELAND P162

HIMALAYA, INDIA P164

ALBERTA, CANADA P173

KANGAROO ISLAND, AUSTRALIA P158

BLACK FOREST, GERMANY P170

DORDOGNE, FRANCE P174

PANTANAL, BRAZIL P164

OKAVANGO DELTA, BOTSWANA P163

ALASKA, USA P61

CITIES & CASTLES?

CITY SIGHTS BY SEA?

WILDLIFE CRUISE?

Enter Brazil's wet wildlife wonderland of Pantanal in the dry

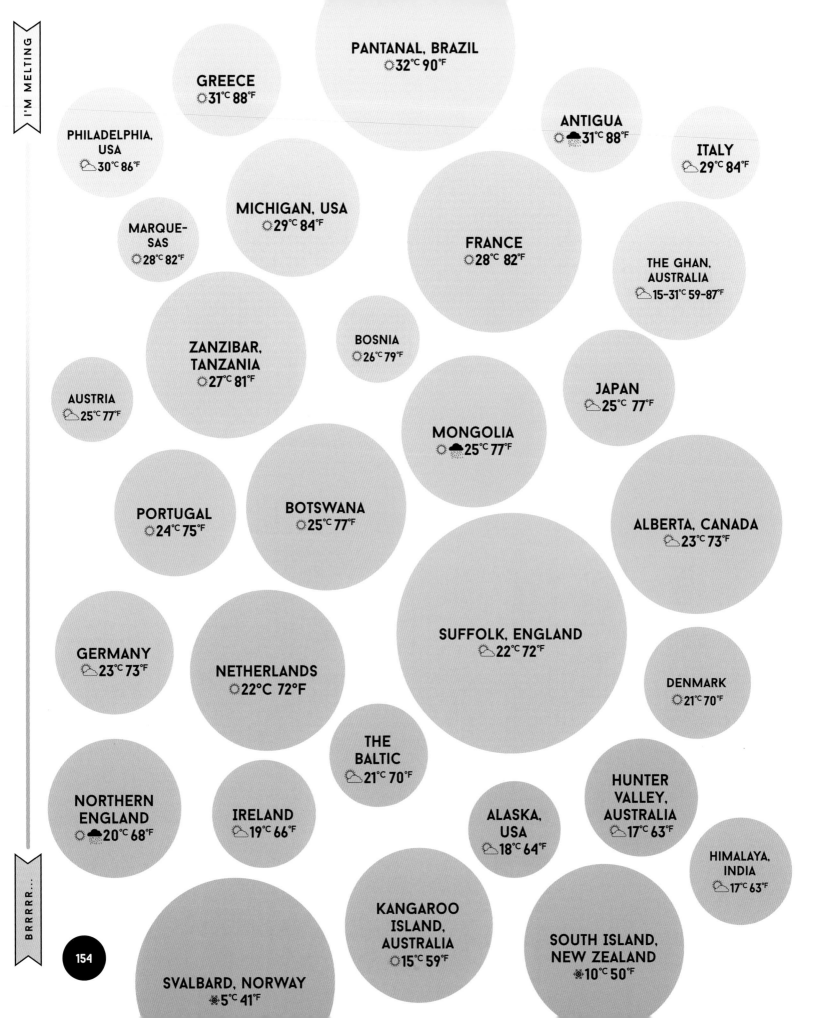

PANTANAL, BRAZIL
32°C 90°F

GREECE
31°C 88°F

ANTIGUA
31°C 88°F

ITALY
29°C 84°F

PHILADELPHIA,
USA
30°C 86°F

MICHIGAN, USA
29°C 84°F

FRANCE
28°C 82°F

MARQUE-
SAS
28°C 82°F

THE GHAN,
AUSTRALIA
15-31°C 59-87°F

ZANZIBAR,
TANZANIA
27°C 81°F

BOSNIA
26°C 79°F

JAPAN
25°C 77°F

AUSTRIA
25°C 77°F

MONGOLIA
25°C 77°F

PORTUGAL
24°C 75°F

BOTSWANA
25°C 77°F

ALBERTA, CANADA
23°C 73°F

GERMANY
23°C 73°F

NETHERLANDS
22°C 72°F

SUFFOLK, ENGLAND
22°C 72°F

DENMARK
21°C 70°F

THE
BALTIC
21°C 70°F

NORTHERN
ENGLAND
20°C 68°F

IRELAND
19°C 66°F

ALASKA,
USA
18°C 64°F

HUNTER
VALLEY,
AUSTRALIA
17°C 63°F

HIMALAYA,
INDIA
17°C 63°F

KANGAROO
ISLAND,
AUSTRALIA
15°C 59°F

SOUTH ISLAND,
NEW ZEALAND
10°C 50°F

SVALBARD, NORWAY
5°C 41°F

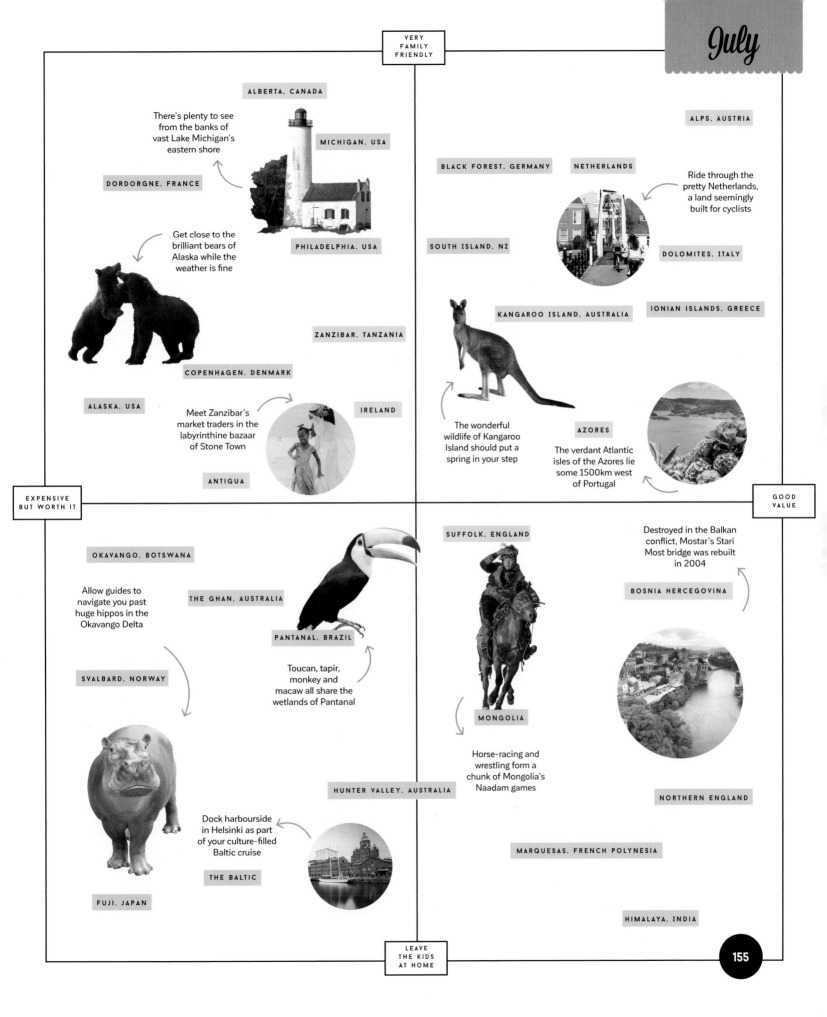

ALBERTA, CANADA

There's plenty to see from the banks of vast Lake Michigan's eastern shore

MICHIGAN, USA

ALPS, AUSTRIA

BLACK FOREST, GERMANY

NETHERLANDS

Ride through the pretty Netherlands, a land seemingly built for cyclists

DORDORGNE, FRANCE

SOUTH ISLAND, NZ

PHILADELPHIA, USA

DOLOMITES, ITALY

Get close to the brilliant bears of Alaska while the weather is fine

IONIAN ISLANDS, GREECE

KANGAROO ISLAND, AUSTRALIA

ZANZIBAR, TANZANIA

COPENHAGEN, DENMARK

ALASKA, USA

Meet Zanzibar's market traders in the labyrinthine bazaar of Stone Town

IRELAND

The wonderful wildlife of Kangaroo Island should put a spring in your step

AZORES

The verdant Atlantic isles of the Azores lie some 1500km west of Portugal

ANTIGUA

SUFFOLK, ENGLAND

Destroyed in the Balkan conflict, Mostar's Stari Most bridge was rebuilt in 2004

OKAVANGO, BOTSWANA

Allow guides to navigate you past huge hippos in the Okavango Delta

THE GHAN, AUSTRALIA

BOSNIA HERCEGOVINA

PANTANAL, BRAZIL

Toucan, tapir, monkey and macaw all share the wetlands of Pantanal

SVALBARD, NORWAY

MONGOLIA

Horse-racing and wrestling form a chunk of Mongolia's Naadam games

NORTHERN ENGLAND

HUNTER VALLEY, AUSTRALIA

Dock harbourside in Helsinki as part of your culture-filled Baltic cruise

MARQUESAS, FRENCH POLYNESIA

THE BALTIC

FUJI, JAPAN

HIMALAYA, INDIA

MONGOLIA

→ Why now? To see men wrestling in shiny pants.

Ulaanbataar is the world's coldest capital, so winter visits are not recommended. Even spring and autumn can be brisk across the Central Asian steppe. Not so July, Mongolia's hottest month – in a variety of ways. Temperatures can hit 30°C (86°F), higher in the Gobi Desert. But it's worth braving the heat to witness the country's hottest spectacle: Naadam. Held 11 to 13 July, this festival of 'manly arts' comprises horse-racing, archery and wrestling contests. Nomads converge on the capital, parades are held and locals play traditional games with *shagai* (the ankle bones of sheep). It's a fascinating insight into Mongolian culture. *Ger* camps in the southern Gobi are open for business at this time. If you don't fancy the extreme heat, focus instead on the Mongol ruins of Karakorum and cooler, northern Lake Khövsgöl, great for boating, hikes and encounters with reindeer herders.

Trip plan: Start in Ulaanbaatar. In two weeks, you could fly south to Dalanzadgad (Gobi) and travel north overland by 4WD to Lake Khövsgöl, via dunes, dinosaur fossils and ancient ruins. Fly back to Ulaanbaatar from Mörön.

Need to know: The Trans-Mongolian train between Moscow and Běijīng stops at Ulaanbaatar.

Other months: May-Oct – warm/hot (Jul-Aug: busiest); Nov-Apr – bitterly cold.

- Cultural
- Journey

Gripping action at Mongolia's Naadam festival

SVALBARD
NORWAY

Why now? Bright light, big bears, clear seas.

At Svalbard's lofty latitude, opportunities for cruising are limited. The northernmost shores of this high-Arctic archipelago are only free of ice for a month or two, which leaves a narrow window for sailing into the remotest fjords. But it's a window worth hitting. In July, the seas should have cleared, the temperature reaches a balmy 5°C (41°F) and the midnight sun shines, allowing 24-hour sightseeing. Expedition cruise vessels plough past the islands' mountains and creaking glaciers, and guides are on the lookout for wildlife: walrus colonies, herds of reindeer, Arctic foxes, seals, whales and, of course, polar bears. Around 2000 of the magnificent mammals stalk Svalbard; in summer, when the ice breaks up, the bears stay close to the coast. Inflatable Zodiac boats will take you to shore for a better look.

Trip plan: Fly to Longyearbyen on Spitsbergen (Svalbard's main island). Cruises from here last one to two weeks; itineraries and activities are dictated by weather conditions.

Need to know: Longyearbyen is a three-hour flight from Oslo; some cruises sail from mainland Norway to Svalbard.

Other months: Apr-Aug – midnight sun (May-Sep: boat trips); Sep-Mar – Northern Lights (Nov-Mar: very cold).

Journey
Wildlife & nature
Adventure

KANGAROO
ISLAND AUSTRALIA

Why now? Wonderful wildlife at wonderful prices.

Lying just 8 miles (13km) off the South Australian mainland, Kangaroo Island hasn't gone unnoticed. This sizeable outcrop (the country's third-largest island) is ruggedly handsome and renowned for wildlife – humans play second fiddle to koalas, echidnas, fur seals, sea lions, little penguins and, of course, kangaroos. Such a reputation attracts tourists and raises prices, especially in peak season. However, a visit in wintry July reduces both, so you can afford to spend longer exploring the beautiful beaches and bushland, with fewer other people. As an extra bonus, this is when you might spot newborn 'roos and wallabies emerging from their mother's pouches. It's not even that cold (8-15°C; 46-59°F) – chuck on a jacket and you'll be right.

Trip plan: You could do a day-trip, but take advantage of off-season prices to stay for longer. Wildlife hotspots include Seal Bay, Hanson Bay Sanctuary (koalas) and Flinders Chase National Park (kangaroos). Also visit Cape Willoughby's lighthouse, view the Remarkable Rocks and slurp oysters.

Need to know: Ferries from Cape Jervis (mainland) to Penneshaw take 45 minutes.

Other months: Jun-Sep – colder, cheaper, whales; Oct-Nov – spring, flowers; Dec-Feb – hottest, animals retreat into bush; Mar-May – warm, calm.

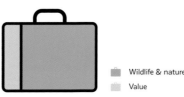

Wildlife & nature
Value

THE BALTIC

Why now? For a warm, culture-filled cruise.

The best way to travel between northern Europe's most magnificent cities is by boat. The Baltic Sea is lined with preeminent ports and, in the warmer summer months, cruise ships zip between them, showing the region to its best advantage, under the sunniest skies. Stockholm (Sweden) and Copenhagen (Denmark) are popular embarkation points, and glorious cities themselves – spend time island-hopping in the former, eating in the latter. Other stops might include Helsinki (Finland), with its lively waterfront; medieval Tallinn, Estonia's fairytale capital; Warnemunde (Germany) for inland excursions to Berlin; and the Unesco-listed Old Town of Riga (Latvia). For many, St Petersburg (Russia) is the highlight – boats dock here for multiple days to allow time for canal tours, the vast Hermitage gallery and visits to the countryside palaces of Peter the Great.

Trip plan: Itineraries vary, but usually include Scandinavian ports and St Petersburg as a minimum. Allow seven to 14 (or more) days. For a quick, cheap alternative, combine Helsinki and Tallinn by ferry.

Need to know: Multiple currencies are required: Norwegian krone, Swedish krona, Danish kroner, Russian rubles, euros for Finland, Estonia, Germany.

Other months: May-Sep – cruise season (Jun-Aug: warmest); Oct-Apr – cold, no cruises.

Journey
Cultural
Value

SUFFOLK
ENGLAND

Why now? To be artistically inspired.

Pack up your paintbrushes, it's time to head for 'Constable Country'. John Constable, born near Suffolk's Dedham Vale in 1776, became England's most beloved landscape artist. He was deeply inspired by his home – a place of big skies and sylvan meadows, threaded by the River Stour – just as visitors continue to be today. Book an artists' retreat here in July and August, when the weather is warmest for days at the easel. This is also the season in which Constable painted his famous *Hay Wain*; the view, of the Stour running past Willy Lott's Cottage, remains unchanged. Follow Constable's footsteps, strolling around pretty villages such as Flatford, Stratford St Mary and Stoke-by-Nayland, or explore at river-level – perhaps a two-day canoe trip from the market town of Sudbury towards the sea. Visit Dedham Vale Vineyard for a tasty drop too.

Trip planner: Art courses run at Willy Lott's Cottage, Flatford Mill and nearby villages. A week here could include boat trips, visits to medieval wool towns and beach time at arty Aldeburgh.

Need to know: Manningtree, near Dedham Vale, is one hour by rail from London Liverpool Street station.

Other months: Jun-Aug – warmest; Apr-May – flowers, quieter; Sep-Oct – mild; Nov-Mar – wintry.

- Wildlife & nature
- Personal growth
- Relaxation

IONIAN ISLANDS
GREECE

Why now? Brilliant beaches and sunny escapes.

To make the most of the Ionians' crystal-clear turquoise waters, you need to visit in summer, when every day is a beach day. This cluster of six islands, west of mainland Greece, has some of the country's best sands, and hot-blue skies make them even more inviting. July will be busy, but there are ways to avoid the crowds. For instance, there are many resorts on Corfu, but plenty of undeveloped countryside between them, especially in the north (where writer-naturalist Gerald Durrell lived) and in the herb-scented mountainous interior. Gorgeous Kefalonia balances mass tourism with authentic Greek towns; as the largest Ionian, it's better able to absorb visitors. The wine's good too. Or try largely undeveloped Lefkada – find untamed beaches on the west coast or join the windsurfers catching summer thermals in Vassiliki Bay.

Trip plan: Fly to Corfu and explore elegant Corfu Town, the interior and quiet northwest beaches. For a multi-Ionians trip, hop between Lefkada, Kefalonia and the pebbly coves of Ithaki, legendary home of Odysseus.

Need to know: Add on a sidetrip to Albania – Corfu Town to Saranda takes 30 minutes by hydrofoil.

Other months: Mar-May – warming, chilly swimming; Jun-Aug – hot, busy; Sep-Oct – sea still warm; Nov-Feb – facilities close.

- Relaxation
- Cultural

MICHIGAN USA

Why now? For fruity fun on the Great Lakes gold coast.

You could drive the 320 miles (515km) from Chicago to Traverse City in about a 5½ hours. But don't. You'd be whizzing past Lake Michigan's 'gold coast' – most golden in summer – which is dotted with cute towns, sandy beaches, lake cabins, lighthouses and holiday fun. This area will be busy in summer, but there's plenty of shoreline to go round. And, as a bonus, the bugs that can beleaguer Lake Michigan are traditionally gone by 4 July. Spots such as bohemian Saugatuck and Dutch-influenced Holland are at their most lively, while Traverse City, self-proclaimed 'Cherry Capital of the World', is particularly sweet. Its annual Cherry Festival is held in July, and the countryside is peppered with markets selling freshly picked fruit. Traverse is also the gateway to Sleeping Bear Dunes National Lakeshore, an area of rippling sand, shady forests and farmsteads that's been voted the USA's most beautiful spot.

Trip plan: Head east from Chicago to drive north up Lake Michigan's east shore. Allow seven to 10 days.

Need to know: From Mackinaw City (north of Traverse) catch a ferry to lovely, car-free Mackinac Island.

Other months: Jun-Aug – hottest, liveliest; Apr-May – chilly, rainy; Sep-Oct – warm, fall colours; Nov-Mar – very cold, snowy.

- Wildlife & nature
- Journey
- Relaxation
- Food & drink

Amus aut quo... volenis sum nis... Ihus doluptur re ent. Aliid quae plandisse

Historic Stari Most across the Neretva River, Moster, Bosnia and Hercegovina

Attention
Bears in Area

(R) Netherlands is a cyclists' haven; (L) July is great for bear watching in Alaska

ALASKA
USA

Why now? Best weather, brilliant bears.

They say the best things come in small packages, which is true of Alaska's summer season. The USA's northernmost state is only fully explorable for a few precious months; to see its unique highlights, you need to visit when the days are long and warm, and the region most accessible. This is especially true of Denali National Park's six million acres of wilderness – the one road here is only navigable from early June, and the shuttlebuses that open up the majestic backcountry stop running in September. Similarly, viewing the best bear action requires a July or September visit. For instance, July's a great month to be at Brooks Camp in Katmai National Park, when up to 100 grizzlies stand mid-river to fish for sockeye salmon.

Trip plan: A two-week trip could include the glaciers, icebergs and whales of Kenai Fjords National Park, wildlife watching and short hikes in Denali, close encounters with grizzlies in Katmai and a ride on the scenic Alaskan Railroad.

Need to know: Distances are vast. Consider floatplanes/scenic flights to reduce travel time (and get great views).

Other months: May & Sep-Oct – shoulder months, colder, quieter; Jun-Aug – warmest, busiest; Nov-Apr – snow pursuits, aurora.

NETHERLANDS

Why now? Cycle amid windmills in the warmth.

If you're huffing up steep hills then high summer isn't best for a bike ride. However, in the flat, mild Netherlands, it's ideal. The country has a maximum elevation of just 1056ft (322m), plus 20,000 miles (32,000km) of cycle paths and a culture geared towards two-wheeled travel – dedicated lanes, signposting and crossings for cyclists. It's safe, and ideal for families or beginners. There's plenty of variety, from dyke and polder landscapes to heathlands and woodlands, low-lying islands and historic cities chock-full of bikes. Opt for a cheesy ride from Edam to Gouda, via Amsterdam's canals. Or a circumnavigation of massive lake IJsselmeer, via Friesland towns and the 21-mile (34km) lake-crossing causeway. Or cycle trails around Kinderdijk on a July Saturday afternoon, when all 19 of the area's old windmills are set in motion.

Trip plan: Bike hire is widely available, often near train stations. Route options range from day trips to multi-day rides – allow a week or more. Other options include e-biking or combining biking with a barge holiday.

Need to know: There are no restrictions on taking bikes aboard trains in the Netherlands in July and August (in other months, bikes are not permitted aboard during peak hours).

Other months: Jun-Sep – mild, sunny; Apr-May – tulips; Oct – cooler; Nov-Mar – cold, rainy.

BOSNIA HERCEGOVINA

Why now? To explore two sun-soaked, history-packed cities.

Stari Most, the striking stone bridge over Mostar's Neretva River, is emblematic of Bosnia Hercegovina. Originally built by the Ottomans in the 16th century, the bridge speaks of the country's East-meets-West heritage. Destroyed in 1993, it's a poignant reminder of the bloody Balkan conflict. Rebuilt in 2004, it's a symbol of peace and unity. It's also the perch from which the brave dive 69ft (21m) into the water below. Bridge jumps happen all summer, but it's at the end of July that thousands gather for the Ikari, the longest-running high-dive competition. It's white-knuckle just watching. If you can't bear to, wander the delightfully higgledy-piggledy Old Town instead. Combine Mostar with Sarajevo, where Ottoman architecture and Arabian-style bazaars merge into communist blocks still scarred by 20th-century warfare – the city was under siege for almost four years. Ponder the recent tragedy, but be uplifted by Sarajevo's fun-loving people and hip, cheap underground bars.

Trip plan: Spend a few days in each city. Mostar to Sarajevo is a 2½-hour drive, via the formidable Neretva Canyon.

Need to know: Mostar is accessible by bus from Dubrovnik (three hours).

Other months: Jun-Sep – hot; Mar-May & Oct-Nov – quieter, cool, flowers/fall colours; Dec-Feb – snow, skiing.

Wildlife & nature
Journey

Journey
Cultural
Adventure

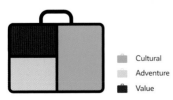

Cultural
Adventure
Value

© Pete Seaward / Lonely Planet

It's not just the setting of the Okavango Delta that is sublime – wildlife abounds in July

WILD ATLANTIC
WAY IRELAND

Derrynane Beach on southwest corner of the Ring of Kerry

→ **Why now? For lovely long days on the road.**

Irish weather is an unpredictable beast, especially along the Atlantic seaboard, where storms can roll in and out in a flash. However, in July – typically the country's warmest month – you can at least rely on the light: 18 hours of it a day, allowing you to sightsee (or pub-crawl) until 11pm. This makes it a great time to hit the Wild Atlantic Way, a 1490-mile (2400km) drive along the west coast, between Kinsale (County Cork) and the Inishowen Peninsula. The waymarked route unravels some of Ireland's finest scenery, including Mizen Head (the island's most southwesterly point), the massive Cliffs of Moher, fjord-side Killary Harbour and Malin Head (the most northerly point). Also along the way are 157 'Discovery Points', where you can learn

more. Stop in Cork for good eating and nearby Blarney Castle; trace the scenic Ring of Kerry and Dingle Peninsula; listen to live music in the bars of Galway; find surf in Sligo and Spanish Armada history in Grange.

Trip planner: Spend at least two weeks on the whole drive. Make time for diversions and absorbing the legendary *craic*.

Need to know: Drive south to north, so you're on the ocean side of the road.

Other months: Mar-May & Sep-Oct – mild; Jun-Aug – warmest, long days; Nov-Feb – wettest, bracing.

- Journey
- Wildlife & nature
- Food & drink
- Cultural

OKAVANGO DELTA
BOTSWANA

→ Why now? Great wildlife, growing waters.

Oddly, Botswana's vast Okavango is wettest when it's dry. The delta is fed by the Okavango River, which rises far away in Angola's highlands; the rain falls there at the start of the year and takes six months to trickle down to Botswana's 5800 sq miles (15,000 sq km) of floodplains, reed-beds, papyrus swamps and vein-like channels – by which time, skies here are cloudless blue. The waters usually arrive in June, so as July progresses, more of the fingery tributaries become navigable by *mokoro* (dugout canoe), enabling wonderful water-level wildlife viewing. Guides will punt you past crocs, hippos, waterlilies and birds; animals are drawn to the banks to drink, ensuring excellent sightings. This is peak season, but Botswana's focus on low-volume, high-value tourism means you'll still see few other people.

Trip plan: In the Okavango, consider staying on a private concession rather than Moremi Game Reserve; in the former, night drives and walking safaris are permitted. Combine the Okavango with Chobe National Park (renowned for elephants). Note, lodges can be exquisite, but commensurately expensive.

Need to know: Mornings can be chilly May to August – take warm clothes for sunrise game drives.

Other months: Nov-Apr – wet, hot, green season, low prices (Jan: wettest); May-Oct – dry, hot.

Wildlife & nature
Adventure
Journey

HIMALAYA INDIA

→ Why now? Snowless roads for a magnificent drive.

There are breathtaking road trips, and there are literally breath-taking road trips. The Khardung La is both. This 18,373ft (5600m) pass near Leh, amid the Indian Himalaya, was a key thoroughfare on the Silk Road and is now allegedly the world's highest motorable highway. Crossing it by bus is an adventure; crossing it astride a classic Enfield Bullet motorbike even more so. Either way, both mountain views and soaring altitudes will leave you gasping. The roads here are only open for a few months a year, so make the most of the warm, snow-free conditions. Bikers could zigzag up from Manali (Himachal Pradesh) to Leh (Ladakh) – one of the world's best mountain rides. Or fly from Delhi to Leh, visit the town's Tibetan-style palace and stupas before taking the Khardung La into the isolated Nubra Valley. The high road west into Kashmir, via Lamayuru Monastery and Zanskar, is an excellent add on; finish with a houseboat stay on the lake at Srinagar.

Trip planner: Fly from Delhi to Leh, explore the Indus and Nubra valleys, head west into Kashmir, fly back to Delhi from Srinagar.

Need to know: Most of India is hot and monsoonal at this time.

Other months: Jul-Sep – roads passable; Oct-Apr – cold/very cold, roads impassable; May-Jun – warming slowly.

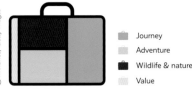

- Journey
- Adventure
- Wildlife & nature
- Value

PANTANAL BRAZIL

→ Why now? To enter a wet wildlife wonderland in the dry.

The Amazon steals all Brazil's biodiversity headlines, but it's actually in the country's Pantanal wetland (which lacks the Amazon's obstructive jungle) that you're more likely to spot wildlife. This is especially true during dry season, when foliage is even thinner and creatures gather at shrinking pockets of water. Animals are abundant here – species include giant otters, giant anteaters, howler monkeys, capybara, caiman, tapir, toucans and hyacinth macaws. Probably most sought is the jaguar. Supporting the world's highest density of these usually elusive cats, the Pantanal is the best place to spot one, especially June to August, when the deeper wilderness areas are easier to access. Travel at this time and spend a week making excursions from Porto Jofre, at the end of the Transpantaneira highway, and your chances of a jaguar sighting are high.

Trip plan: In two weeks, use internal flights to combine Rio with a visit to Iguaçu Falls, time at a lodge deep in the Pantanal (making forays by boat, kayak and on foot) and a cruise on the Amazon.

Need to know: Cuiaba, gateway city to the Northern Pantanal, has an airport.

Other months: May-Sep – dry; Oct-Apr – wet.

- Wildlife & nature
- Journey

HUNTER VALLEY AUSTRALIA

→ Why now? To huddle up with warming wines.

Crisp, dark skies; roaring log fires; a large glass of plummy shiraz, made from the vines outside... New South Wales' rolling, winery-striped Hunter Valley is budding in spring, warm in summer and golden in autumn, but cosiest and most invigorating in winter. Rainfall is low in July, providing blue-sky days that are ideal for walks amid the stark vines and lush grasses of Australia's oldest wine-growing region. With temperatures anywhere between 5°C (41°F) and 17°C (63°F), it might not even be that chilly. Cellar doors remain open for tastings, and there's plenty of fabulous food too, with winter putting dishes such as rhubarb crumble and pumpkin gnocchi on the menu. Book a class at one of the valley's cookery schools so you can take some local expertise home.

Trip plan: Most regional highlights are in the lower Hunter Valley, beneath the Brokenback Mountains. Cessnock is the largest settlement; Pokolbin, further north, is the main wine-tasting hub. There are more than 150 wineries, and some decadent hotels, ideal for romantic winter escapes.

Need to know: Hunter Valley is 93 miles (150km; two-hour drive) north of Sydney.

Other months: Jun-Aug – mild, cosy; Sep-Nov – green; Dec-Feb – hot, vibrant; Mar-May – golden, harvest.

- Food & drink
- Relaxation

THE DOLOMITES
ITALY

The Sassolungo is one of the Dolomites most spectacular massifs

© Matt Munro / Lonely Planet

Why now? To get up amid the marvellous mountains.

The Dolomites are arguably the Alps at their most magnificent. This 18-peak range in northern Italy is a jagged giant of deep valleys, high plateaux and piercing pinnacles. It also echoes with human history: between 1915 and 1918 Italian and Austro-Hungarian forces fought amid these unforgiving peaks, and remnants such as trenches and gun emplacements can still be seen. Cable cars and mountain huts open for summer from late June. There is hiking galore, plus opportunities for biking, e-biking, paragliding, trail-running and more. Try via ferrata (iron roads), a method of climbing via rungs and cables, first pioneered by those WWI soldiers. The food is fantastic too, from mountain cheeses to sweet strudel. Even huts serve meals devised by Michelin-starred chefs. Active efforts are well rewarded here.

Trip plan: The Dolomites fall within Trentino-Alto Adige province. Hub towns include Bolzano and Cortina d'Ampezzo. From here, strike into the valleys. For instance, base yourself in Corvara to explore Val Badia: kids will love the play parks and swimming lakes; history buffs can take the cable car to Lagazuoi's well-preserved WWI trenches.

Need to know: Alto Adige was formerly part of Austria. Locals speak German and Italian; places have both Italian and Germanic names.

Other months: Jun-Sep – hiking, warmest; Apr-May & Oct – quieter, less accessible; Dec-Mar – skiing.

- Adventure
- Food & drink
- Cultural
- Wildlife & nature

AZORES

Why now? Sunshine and smooth seas in the mid-Atlantic.

Remote indeed, the nine islands of the Azores are scattered 930 miles (1500km) west of their Portuguese motherland. The result of seabed volcanoes, this mid-Atlantic archipelago is a playground of gnarled rocks, black sands, lava tubes, crater lakes and soaring cones. July is the driest and warmest month. It's also when the ocean is calmest – best for boat trips to spot 20 cetacean species, including sperm whales. Landlubbers can watch from clifftop *vigias* instead – these old whale-hunters' lookout towers are now used by ecotourists. What else? Head to Pico island to bag Portugal's highest peak (7713ft; 2351m) and dive with manta rays (July to September). Find inland lakes, hike, birdwatch and gawk at flowers on Flores. Or plan a cycling adventure on Terceira, the 'lilac isle'.

Trip plan: Base yourself on one island – São Miguel is largest, with most tours. Or spend a week or two island-hopping: clustered Pico, Faial and São Jorge (The Triangle) are easy to travel between by ferries.

Need to know: São Miguel is home to Ponta Delgada International Airport.

Other months: Apr-Jun – sunny, flowers, whales; Jul-Aug – warmest, whales, diving; Sep-Oct – warm, whales; Nov-Mar – rainy.

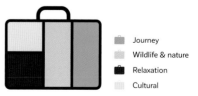

- Journey
- Wildlife & nature
- Relaxation
- Cultural

JAPAN

→ **Why now?** Make a pilgrimage up the nation's favourite peak.

Nothing looms larger in the Japanese psyche than Mt Fuji. The perfectly conical 12,388ft (3776m) volcano is considered sacred, and even features on the ¥1000 note. As such, during official climbing season – 1 July to 14 September, when trails are snow-free and facilities open – locals flock here in droves. Yes, trekking up Fuji now will be busy, but this is as much of a cultural experience as a physical one. Part of the allure is interacting with fellow climbers, not to mention buying fizzy pop from the path-side vending machines. Standing at the summit at dawn, watching the *goraiko* (arrival of the light) is moving, no matter how big the crowds. The weather is warm countrywide in July, a good time to visit another pleasingly packed site. The month-long Gion Matsuri (during which 10-tonne floats are hauled through the historic streets) sees Kyoto in full festive mode.

Trip plan: Explore Tokyo, head south to Hakone to access Fuji. Explore Kyoto, then catch the bullet train back to Tokyo.

Need to know: Public transport runs to trailheads part-way up Mt Fuji; there are four routes to the top.

Other months: Jul–mid-Sep – climbing season; Sep-Oct – fall colours; Nov-Mar – cold, snow; Mar-Apr – cherry blossom; May-Jun – warm.

■ Adventure
■ Personal growth
■ Cultural

(R) Chureito Pagoda, Fujiyoshida; (L) Fushimi Inari-Taisha, Kyoto

ZANZIBAR
TANZANIA

→ **Why now?** Delve into Stone Town and the Indian Ocean under blue skies.

The spice island Unguja – known to most as Zanzibar – is a scent sensation. Stroll the maze-like alleys of old Stone Town on a warm evening and you'll catch whiffs of nutmeg, clove and cinnamon in the Darajani bazaar, frying seafood at stalls in Forodhani Gardens, and the aroma of black coffee in Jaws Corner, where old men gather to watch TV and gossip. Zanzibar's historic heart, with its crumbling palaces and heartrending slave-trade relics, is just one gem of this treasure-trove island, at its best in July, in the middle of the dry season. Board a dhow to snorkel off the west coast, watching for dolphins; sniff the leaves and buds of a spice plantation; and find your own patch of coral-sand perfection on one of the wonderful beaches.

Trip plan: Spend at least a couple of days wandering the labyrinthine alleys of Stone Town and visiting a spice plantation before heading to a beach – Nungwi is a good base for dives off Tumbatu and Mnemba islands.

Need to know: Incidence of malaria has dropped in recent years, but consult a physician for the latest advice.

Other months: Jun-Oct – cool, dry; Nov-Dec & Mar-May – rainy; Jan-Feb – hot, dry.

MARQUESAS
FRENCH POLYNESIA

→ **Why now?** To sail the sunny south seas.

The Marquesas Islands are remote even by South Pacific standards. Despite this (or maybe because of it), they've long attracted artistic types, most notably Paul Gauguin, whose exotic, bountiful paintings have inspired many a visitor. The best way to get here is aboard the *Aranui*, which doubles as cargo ship and cruiser, delivering both people and supplies to this lush, culturally vibrant archipelago. The *Aranui* sails from Pape'ete (Tahiti), and calls at several of the Marquesas, including Nuku Hiva (where Herman 'Moby Dick' Melville jumped a whaling ship in 1842), Hiva Oa (where Gauguin lived) and dramatically lush Fatu Hiva, known for its hand-painted sarongs. Cliff hikes, village tours, breadfruit lunches and strolls amid frangipani trees fill each shore visit; a real highlight is the welcome the boat receives from local communities when it docks. The *Aranui* runs year-round, but dry July is a balmy, comfortable choice.

Trip plan: The *Aranui* takes 14 days to sail from Pape'ete to the Marquesas and back, via the Tuamotu Islands and Bora Bora.

Need to know: Lengths of shore visits are dictated by port and cargo operators; visits range from a few hours to a day or more.

Other months: May-Oct – dry, cooler; Nov-Apr – wet, hot, humid.

ANTIGUA

→ **Why now?** Carnival madness – and a bit of sunshine.

Hurricane season hits the Caribbean July to November. Or so they say. In reality, this is broad brushstrokes, and the worst storms are usually saved for the later months. So head to Antigua now for – with luck – some hot, sunny, largely dry weather. The island claims 365 beaches, which might be stretching the truth... but still, there's oodles of palm-swished loveliness to go round, as well as rum-serving beach bars. Fit in cultural stuff too, exploring the unique Georgian-era Nelson's Dockyard, where Admiral Nelson served for three years, and catch a game of cricket (the national sport). July also sees Antigua host its huge summer Carnival, with *soca* music, steel bands, high-energy parties and befeathered parades taking over the island. Order a Wadadli beer, pull on some comfy shoes and join in.

Trip plan: For a quieter stay, avoid the end of the month – the main Carnival period usually runs late July to early August. Stay a week, allowing time for snorkelling and a drive along the scenic Old Road into Antigua's volcanic hills.

Need to know: Turtle-nesting season is June to November.

Other months: Dec-Apr – dry, cool; May-Jun – hotter; Jul-Nov – hurricane season (worst Aug-Oct).

Relaxation
Adventure
Cultural

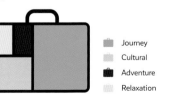

Journey
Cultural
Adventure
Relaxation

Relaxation
Cultural

COPENHAGEN
DENMARK

→ **Why now?** To make merry with the masses.

Wonderful, wonderful Copenhagen in July! Yes, this month is busy in the Danish capital, but it's also buzzing. It's when people fill the parks, spill out of the pavement cafes and spin gleefully on the rides at Tivoli Gardens. Visitor numbers are high, but so are temperatures (20°C; 68°F) and spirits. Copenhagen has garnered a great foodie reputation, and this is the ideal time to eat outside – try the street-food market at Paper Island or the funky verandahs of the Meatpacking District. This is also a good time to cool down with a traditional gammeldags ice-cream cone, complete with whipped cream, jam and *flødebolle* (choc-coated marshmallows). If it gets too hot, seek respite at Copenhagen's baths and beaches, such as family-friendly Amager Beach or the harbour pool at Brygge, where you can swim with city views.

Trip plan: Allow at least three days. Include sightseeing at Slotsholmen and Nyhavn harbour, shopping at Torvehallerne market and along pedestrianised Stroget, explorations of the hip Nørrebro and Vesterbro districts, and fun at Tivoli, the city's 19th-century amusement park.

© Sarah Coghill / Lonely Planet

Take a swing at Tivoli Gardens, Copenhagen

Need to know: Trains link Copenhagen airport to the city centre in 10 minutes.
Other months: Jun-Sep – sunny, lively, busy; Mar-May & Oct – quieter, cooler; Nov-Mar – chilly (Dec: Christmas market).

■ Food & drink
□ Cultural
■ Relaxation

BEYOND COPENHAGEN

🚄 **MALMÖ · 25 MILES ·** Øresund Strait bridge provides a speedy link to Sweden

🚄🚗 **ELSINORE · 28 MILES ·** Setting of Hamlet, home of Kronborg Castle

🚢 **OSLO · 317 MILES ·** Connect to the Norwegian capital with a 17-hour ferry trip, via scenic fjords

✈ **KANGERLUSSUAQ · 2200 MILES ·** Greenland, Denmark's distant Arctic territory, is a five-hour flight

BLACK FOREST
GERMANY

The church of Sankt Roman near Wolfach in the Black Forest

→ **Why now? For lakes, cakes and fairytales.**

Magical things lurk in the 'Schwarzwald'. Indeed, Germany's bucolic southwest corner inspired many a Brothers Grimm folktale: you can imagine princesses locked in the hilltop castles, pipers piping through the half-timbered towns and trolls lurking in the dark, dense woods. As such, it's a great place to take the kids on summer holiday, when it'll be busy but also pleasantly warm (23-26°C; 73-79°F). The region offers lovely hiking and cycling amid green hills, and is famed for its water, from the elegant spa town of Baden-Baden to the many pretty lakes, ideal for July dips. It's also very rural, and working farms offer homestays where you can pet the animals. The cherry on top? Cherries! These are harvested in summer. Perfect timing for a slice of *Schwarzwälder Kirschtorte* (Black Forest gateaux), a creamy sponge soaked in cherry liqueur.

Trip plan: Hire a car – there are wonderful scenic drives. Explore between Baden-Baden and lively Freiberg; many of the best spots occupy the triangle between Freiberg, Triberg (renowned for cuckoo clocks) and Sankt Blasien.

Need to know: A SchwarzwaldCard (valid for three days) grants free admission to more than 140 regional attractions.

Other months: Jun-Aug – warm, busiest; Mar-May & Sep-Oct – quieter, mild; Nov-Feb – cold, snowy.

- Adventure
- Wildlife nature
- Journey
- Food & drink

THE GHAN
AUSTRALIA

→ **Why now? For an epic outback rail ride.**

Named for the 19th-century Afghan cameleers who opened up Australia's hostile Red Centre, the Ghan is one of the world's greatest train journeys. It runs for 1864 miles (3000km) between Darwin (Northern Territory) and Adelaide (South Australia), bissecting the remote, rusty heart of the country to link the tropical Top End and the temperate Southern Ocean. En route lie miles and miles (and miles) of wallaby-hopped wilderness – but the view from the window doesn't get dull. The scale, beauty and infinity of stars remain mesmerising. Stop-offs provide time for quick excursions too – perhaps a cruise along lush Nitmiluk Gorge or a nature disocovery walk along dreaming trails in Simpsons Gap. July is a good time: the north is dry, the desert is cool, the south wintry but mild.

Trip plan: Darwin to Adelaide (or vice versa) in one go, takes the Ghan 54 hours, including two nights on board and short stops in Alice (for Uluru-Kata Tjuta) and Katherine.

Need to know: The Ghan has three classes: Red day-nighter seats, Gold cabins, Platinum deluxe cabins.

Other months: May-Oct – cooler; Nov-Apr – desert hot, Top End wet.

SOUTH ISLAND
NEW ZEALAND

→ **Why now? The snow is powdery perfection.**

By mid-June the South Island's Southern Alps are starting to call to powderhounds. By July, they're positively yelling. Fresh dumps mean the slopes are blanketed in fine, chalky snow and everywhere is open for business. There are resorts to suit all sorts. Spread across three bowls, Cardrona is excellent for beginners and families. Treble Cone, which receives the highest snowfall of any NZ ski locale, is better for advanced piste-heads, with 45 percent black runs and some steep drops. The delightfully named Remarkables, which rise above Lake Wakatipu, offer some of the most scenic skiing, as well as good learners' slopes and terrain parks for tricks. All three are near Queenstown, undisputed party town of the south, so lively après-ski is there if you want it.

Trip plan: Base yourself in Queenstown if you want to ski a range of different areas: the Remarkables are 15 miles (24km) southeast, Cardrona 36 miles (58km) northeast, Treble Cone 56 miles (90km) northeast; there are more resorts nearby. Some resorts are served by shuttles from Queenstown.

Need to know: NZ school holidays fall in July, so family-orientated resorts might be busier.

Other months: Jun-Oct – skiing, cold; Nov-Mar – warm, hiking; Apr-May – autumn, cool.

Journey
Wildlife & nature
Relaxation

Adventure
Wildlife & nature

One of the locals in Swaledale, Yorkshire Dales National Park

NORTHERN ENGLAND

Why now? Long days for a long hike. In 1973, legendary British fellwalker Arthur Wainwright described a 190-mile (305km) west-east route from St Bees (Cumbria) to Robin Hood's Bay (North Yorkshire) in his book, *A Coast to Coast Walk*. It's now one of the country's best-loved long-distance hikes. Many walkers see it as a personal challenge, or complete it for charity. Whatever the motivation, it doesn't disappoint. After dipping your toes in the Irish Sea, yomp through three national parks – the glittering Lake District, rolling Yorkshire Dales and heather-fluffed North York Moors – before dipping them in the North Sea. There's plenty of climbing up hill and down dale, and varied highlights: Grasmere (where Wordsworth lived), the dry-stone walls of Swaledale, castle-topped Richmond, wooded Eskdale. There are many excellent pubs too. July is the sunniest month, plus longer days give you more time to pack in the miles.

Trip plan: Most walkers take 12 to 14 days. Carry your own kit or arrange luggage transfers. You can camp or stay at B&Bs en route.

Need to know: Trains run from Carlisle to St Bees. From Robin Hood's Bay, buses run to Scarborough for trains to York.

Other months: May-Jun & Sep – quiet, mild; Jul-Aug – hottest; Apr & Oct – short days, possible snow; Nov-Mar – cold, sometimes snowy.

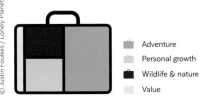

Adventure
Personal growth
Wildlife & nature
Value

© Justin Foulkes / Lonely Planet

The Calgary Stampede rolls into town each July

ALPS AUSTRIA

→ **Why now? Cool off amid mighty mountains.**

A European summer holiday doesn't have to mean a beach break by the Mediterranean. Look inland instead: right now, Austria's hills are alive! Amid the warm, sunny Alps, there are balmy lakes and pools to swim in, splendid mountains to climb (or ascend by cable car) and flowery, cow-grazed meadows to run through like Maria von Trapp. Activities such as rafting, climbing, canyoning and zip-lining will suit more adventurous types. There are vast amounts of speck, kaise and kuchen to be eaten too. It's even good value: Austria's ski resorts need to make money year-round, so deals can be found once the pistes have become hiking trails. They're less rowdy in summer too. Alternatively, stay in the Austrian Alpine Club's network of huts (usually open mid-June to September) to sleep right amid the mountains.

Trip plan: The Austrian Tyrol is a good choice – valleys filled with chocolate-box villages of geranium-draped chalets are the norm, and Salzburg and Innsbruck city breaks can be added. Allow one or two weeks.

Need to know: The Salzburg Festival is a high-calibre showcase of drama, opera and classical music that runs from mid-July to late August.

Other months: May-Jun, Oct – quiet, mild; Jul-Sep – hottest, hiking; Nov-Apr – snowy, skiing.

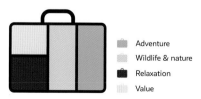

- Adventure
- Wildlife & nature
- Relaxation
- Value

ALBERTA CANADA

→ **Why now? Convene with cowboys, escape to the peaks.**

Pull on your blue jeans and ten-gallon hat: the world's greatest rodeo is rolling into town. The 10-day Calgary Stampede sees the Albertan city consumed by the spirit of the Wild West. Cowboys and cowgirls compete at steer wrestling, bronc riding and chuckwagon races; there are concerts, parades and First Nations festivals; barbecues sizzle. You'll either love it, or it'll send you running for the hills. Fortunately, there are excellent hills within easy reach. The Canadian Rockies are visible from Calgary, and in summer their turquoise-emerald lakes, snow peaks and forests of pine and spruce provide the prettiest playground for hikes, boat trips and canoe paddles. The Icefields Parkway, the magisterial road linking Banff (south) and Jasper (north) can get busy, but you'll want to take it slowly anyway, to detour down side-roads, walk on glaciers (possible at Athabasca), stop for photos and scan for bears.

Trip plan: Drive a square. Head west from Calgary to Banff and Lake Louise (hot springs, hikes, pioneer history). Drive north to Jasper (Moraine Lake, backcountry expeditions). Head east to lively Edmonton, then back south to Calgary.

Need to know: Be careful when driving, as animals often wander into the road.

Other months: Jun-Aug – sunny, hiking; Apr-May & Sep-Oct – changeable weather, quieter; Nov-Mar – skiing.

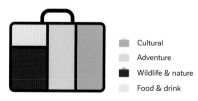

- Cultural
- Adventure
- Wildlife & nature
- Food & drink

173

DORDOGNE
FRANCE

→ **Why now?** It's lovely, despite the crowds.

A lazy, leafy river meandering between hill towns, turreted chateaux, ancient cave art and some of the country's most mouthwatering markets... This is why people adore the Dordogne, and why this inland region of southwest France will be busy right now – but is worth visiting anyway. Summers here are glorious: dry, warm (25-30°C; 77-86°F), and perfect for camping and canoeing. The aforementioned markets are bursting with goodies; medieval Sarlat even hosts a Thursday night market, June to September. There are ways to mitigate the crowds too. Come in early July, to beat French school holidays. Stay in a rural farmhouse, away from the hustle. Visit little villages off the tourist trail (many of which host small-scale summer festivals). For popular attractions, such as the world-class rock art of Lascaux and Font-de-Gaume, avoid queues by booking advance tickets online.

Trip plan: The Dordogne chunks into regions: Périgord Noir (southeast) has the most famous villages, castles and caves; Périgord Pourpre (southwest) is home to Bergerac and medieval bastide towns; Périgord Vert and Blanc (north) have fewer big sites and fewer visitors.

Need to know: The Dordogne's capital, Périgueux, is in Périgord Blanc.

Other months: Nov-Mar – cold, truffles; Apr-Jun – warm, quieter; Jul-Aug – hot, busy; Sep-Oct – mild, harvest.

- Food & drink
- Cultural
- Relaxation

Dordogne through the ages: prehistoric cave art at Lascaux II, and Périgueux's Cathedral and market

© Andrew Montgomery / Lonely Planet

PHILADELPHIA
USA

→ **Why now? Celebrate independence in the nation's birthplace.**

OK, Philly won't be peaceful this month, but if you're here to join the July 4th party, that's part of the fun. Celebrations start late June and include colonial reenactments and extended opening at the must-see Independence National Historical Park, home to the Liberty Bell and Independence Hall (where the Declaration of Independence was adopted). On the day itself, there's a flag-waving parade and fireworks galore, centred on Benjamin Franklin Parkway – bag a spot at the baseball fields at 22nd and Pkwy, or view the illuminations from a deckchair on Lemon Hill. Aside from Independence shenanigans, summer in Philadelphia is for making a Rocky Balboa run up the steps of the Museum of Art and hanging out by the Delaware River: catch alfresco music at lively Penn's Landing or relax on the urban beach at hip Spruce Street Harbor Park.

Trip plan: Allow at least three days, and book in advance if coinciding with Independence Day. Make time for the Constitutional, a 1.2-mile (2km) walking tour around 20 historic sites. Philly is easy to combine with other eastern US cities.

Need to know: Philly is very bike-friendly, with 435 miles (700km) of bike lanes and bikeshare available from 60 stations.

Other months: Mar-May – quieter, warming; Jun-Aug – hottest, busy; Sep-Oct – cooling; Nov-Feb – quiet, very cold.

© Bruce Yuanyue Bi / Getty Images

Musicians in Continental Army uniform perform on July 4th

Cultural
Food & drink

BEYOND PHILADELPHIA

🚲 **VALLEY FORGE HISTORIC PARK · 26 MILES (42KM)** · Schuylkill River Cycle Trail runs to a Revolutionary War camp

🚌 **ATLANTIC CITY · 62 MILES (100KM)** · Buzzing boardwalks, seaside kitsch, Vegas-lite

🚗 **THE POCONOS · 118 MILES (189KM)** · Active/chill-out mountain retreat from the city

🚆 **WASHINGTON DC · 137 MILES (220KM** · The nation's capital, museums a go-go

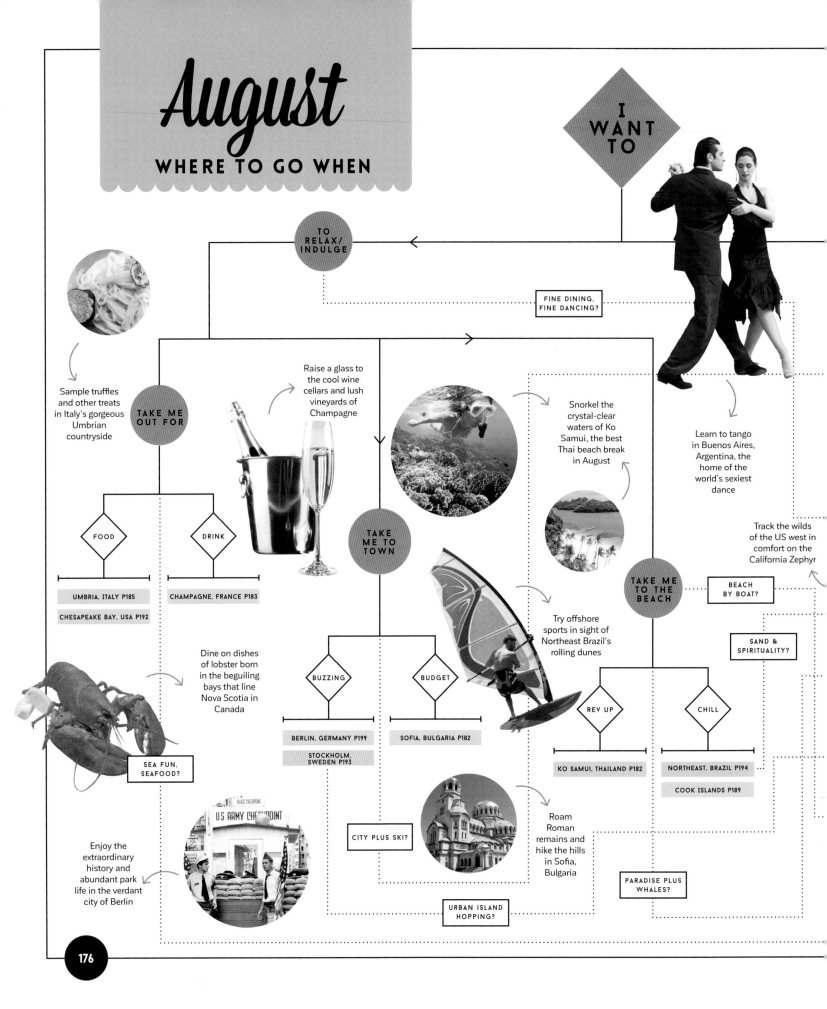

August
WHERE TO GO WHEN

I WANT TO

TO RELAX/ INDULGE

FINE DINING, FINE DANCING?

Sample truffles and other treats in Italy's gorgeous Umbrian countryside

TAKE ME OUT FOR

Raise a glass to the cool wine cellars and lush vineyards of Champagne

Snorkel the crystal-clear waters of Ko Samui, the best Thai beach break in August

Learn to tango in Buenos Aires, Argentina, the home of the world's sexiest dance

Track the wilds of the US west in comfort on the California Zephyr

FOOD

DRINK

TAKE ME TO TOWN

TAKE ME TO THE BEACH

BEACH BY BOAT?

UMBRIA, ITALY P185

CHAMPAGNE, FRANCE P183

SAND & SPIRITUALITY?

CHESAPEAKE BAY, USA P192

Try offshore sports in sight of Northeast Brazil's rolling dunes

Dine on dishes of lobster born in the beguiling bays that line Nova Scotia in Canada

BUZZING

BUDGET

REV UP

CHILL

BERLIN, GERMANY P199

SOFIA, BULGARIA P182

STOCKHOLM, SWEDEN P193

KO SAMUI, THAILAND P182

NORTHEAST, BRAZIL P194

SEA FUN, SEAFOOD?

COOK ISLANDS P189

CITY PLUS SKI?

Roam Roman remains and hike the hills in Sofia, Bulgaria

Enjoy the extraordinary history and abundant park life in the verdant city of Berlin

US ARMY CHECKPOINT

URBAN ISLAND HOPPING?

PARADISE PLUS WHALES?

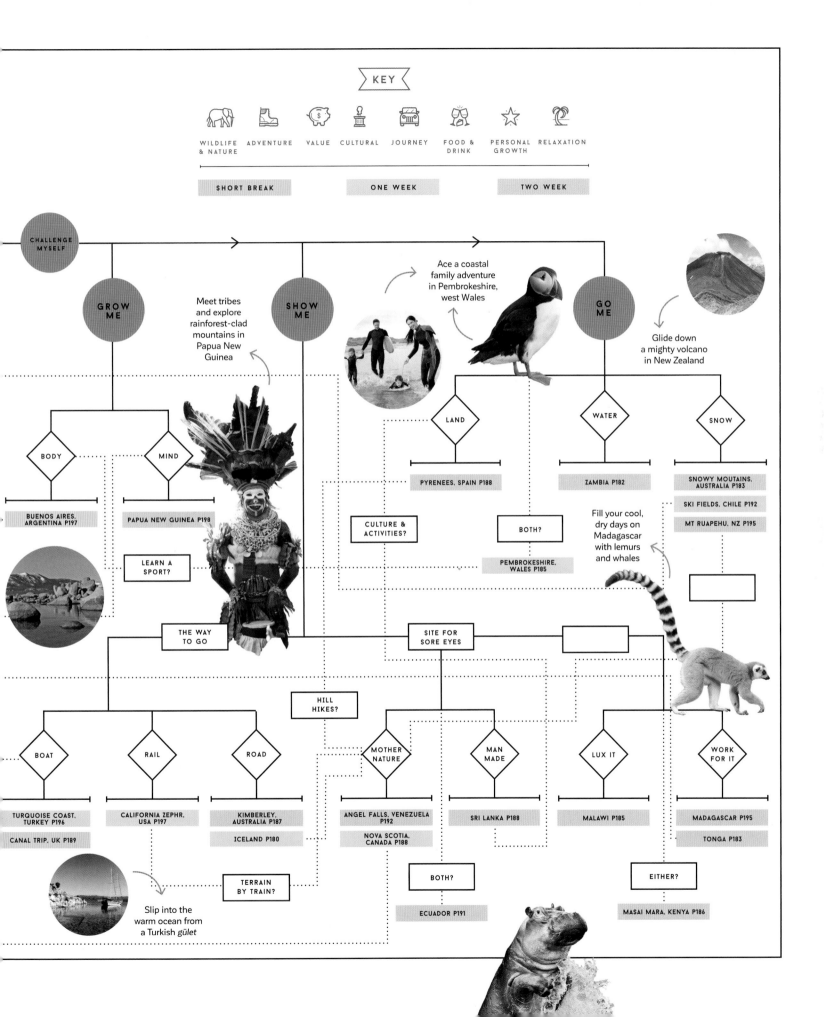

KEY

WILDLIFE & NATURE ADVENTURE VALUE CULTURAL JOURNEY FOOD & DRINK PERSONAL GROWTH RELAXATION

SHORT BREAK   ONE WEEK   TWO WEEK

CHALLENGE MYSELF

GROW ME

SHOW ME

GO ME

Meet tribes and explore rainforest-clad mountains in Papua New Guinea

Ace a coastal family adventure in Pembrokeshire, west Wales

Glide down a mighty volcano in New Zealand

BODY

MIND

LAND

WATER

SNOW

BUENOS AIRES, ARGENTINA P197

PAPUA NEW GUINEA P198

PYRENEES, SPAIN P188

ZAMBIA P182

SNOWY MOUTAINS, AUSTRALIA P183

SKI FIELDS, CHILE P192

MT RUAPEHU, NZ P195

LEARN A SPORT?

CULTURE & ACTIVITIES?

BOTH?

Fill your cool, dry days on Madagascar with lemurs and whales

PEMBROKESHIRE, WALES P185

THE WAY TO GO

SITE FOR SORE EYES

HILL HIKES?

BOAT

RAIL

ROAD

MOTHER NATURE

MAN MADE

LUX IT

WORK FOR IT

TURQUOISE COAST, TURKEY P196

CALIFORNIA ZEPHR, USA P197

KIMBERLEY, AUSTRALIA P187

ANGEL FALLS, VENEZUELA P192

SRI LANKA P188

MALAWI P185

MADAGASCAR P195

CANAL TRIP, UK P189

ICELAND P180

NOVA SCOTIA, CANADA P188

TONGA P183

TERRAIN BY TRAIN?

BOTH?

EITHER?

Slip into the warm ocean from a Turkish gület

ECUADOR P191

MASAI MARA, KENYA P186

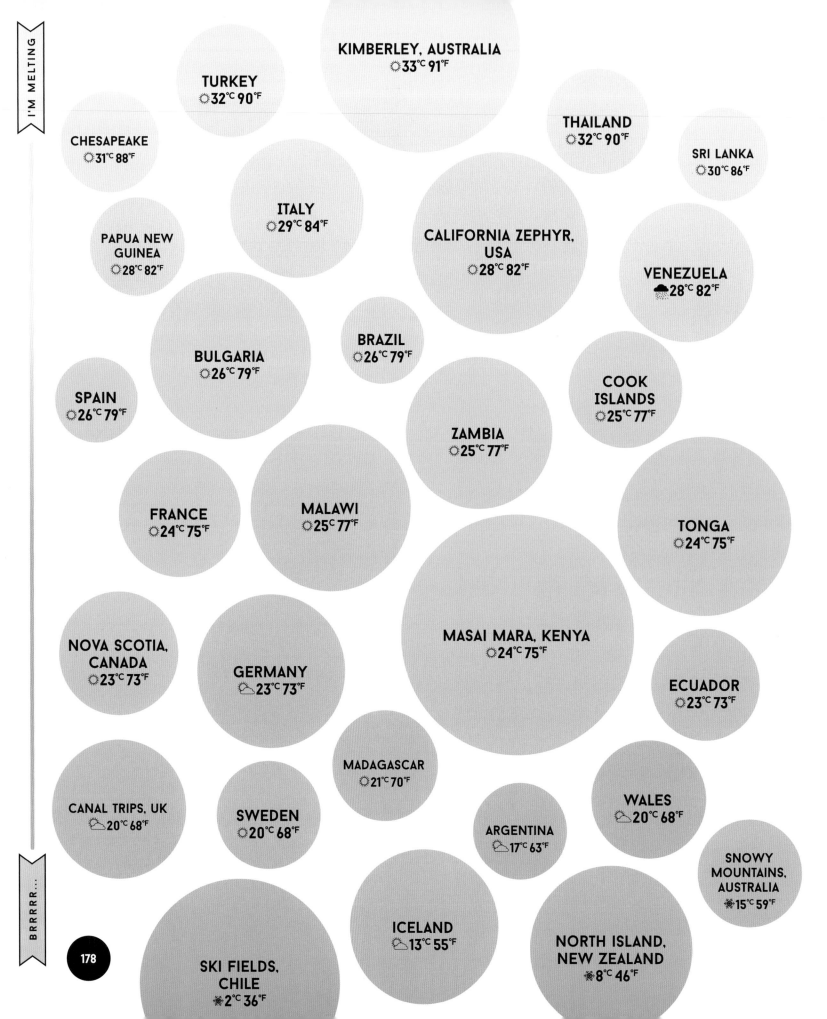

KIMBERLEY, AUSTRALIA
☼ 33℃ 91℉

TURKEY
☼ 32℃ 90℉

THAILAND
☼ 32℃ 90℉

CHESAPEAKE
☼ 31℃ 88℉

SRI LANKA
☼ 30℃ 86℉

ITALY
☼ 29℃ 84℉

CALIFORNIA ZEPHYR, USA
☼ 28℃ 82℉

PAPUA NEW GUINEA
☼ 28℃ 82℉

VENEZUELA
🌧 28℃ 82℉

BRAZIL
☼ 26℃ 79℉

BULGARIA
☼ 26℃ 79℉

COOK ISLANDS
☼ 25℃ 77℉

SPAIN
☼ 26℃ 79℉

ZAMBIA
☼ 25℃ 77℉

FRANCE
☼ 24℃ 75℉

MALAWI
☼ 25℃ 77℉

TONGA
☼ 24℃ 75℉

NOVA SCOTIA, CANADA
☼ 23℃ 73℉

GERMANY
⛅ 23℃ 73℉

MASAI MARA, KENYA
☼ 24℃ 75℉

ECUADOR
☼ 23℃ 73℉

MADAGASCAR
☼ 21℃ 70℉

CANAL TRIPS, UK
⛅ 20℃ 68℉

SWEDEN
☼ 20℃ 68℉

WALES
⛅ 20℃ 68℉

ARGENTINA
⛅ 17℃ 63℉

SNOWY MOUNTAINS, AUSTRALIA
❄ 15℃ 59℉

ICELAND
⛅ 13℃ 55℉

NORTH ISLAND, NEW ZEALAND
❄ 8℃ 46℉

SKI FIELDS, CHILE
❄ 2℃ 36℉

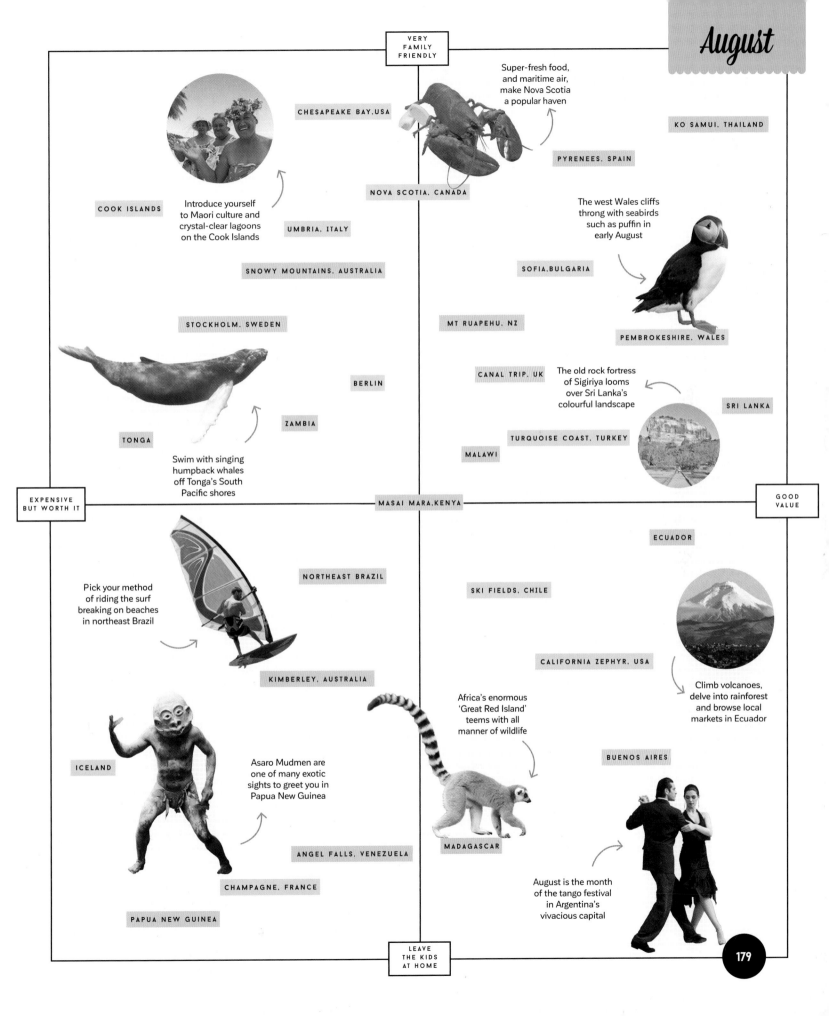

VERY FAMILY FRIENDLY

Super-fresh food, and maritime air, make Nova Scotia a popular haven

CHESAPEAKE BAY, USA

KO SAMUI, THAILAND

PYRENEES, SPAIN

NOVA SCOTIA, CANADA

Introduce yourself to Maori culture and crystal-clear lagoons on the Cook Islands

COOK ISLANDS

The west Wales cliffs throng with seabirds such as puffin in early August

UMBRIA, ITALY

SOFIA, BULGARIA

SNOWY MOUNTAINS, AUSTRALIA

STOCKHOLM, SWEDEN

MT RUAPEHU, NZ

PEMBROKESHIRE, WALES

The old rock fortress of Sigiriya looms over Sri Lanka's colourful landscape

CANAL TRIP, UK

SRI LANKA

BERLIN

TURQUOISE COAST, TURKEY

ZAMBIA

TONGA

MALAWI

Swim with singing humpback whales off Tonga's South Pacific shores

EXPENSIVE BUT WORTH IT

MASAI MARA, KENYA

GOOD VALUE

ECUADOR

Pick your method of riding the surf breaking on beaches in northeast Brazil

NORTHEAST BRAZIL

SKI FIELDS, CHILE

CALIFORNIA ZEPHYR, USA

KIMBERLEY, AUSTRALIA

Climb volcanoes, delve into rainforest and browse local markets in Ecuador

Africa's enormous 'Great Red Island' teems with all manner of wildlife

ICELAND

Asaro Mudmen are one of many exotic sights to greet you in Papua New Guinea

BUENOS AIRES

ANGEL FALLS, VENEZUELA

MADAGASCAR

CHAMPAGNE, FRANCE

August is the month of the tango festival in Argentina's vivacious capital

PAPUA NEW GUINEA

LEAVE THE KIDS AT HOME

ICELAND

→ **Why now?** Delve into Iceland's otherworldly interior.

When NASA wanted to train their astronauts for lunar conditions, they sent them to Iceland. A visit to the island's desolate interior reveals why. It's as barren and unforgiving as can be imagined, and experiences harsh conditions for much of the year; August is the optimum – indeed, almost the only – time you can penetrate its lava fields, volcanic craters and jagged rockscapes. A few historic routes wind through the inner highlands creating shortcuts between the north and south, with some sections only accessible to the toughest of 4WDs. The effort is rewarded with vistas of a muscular, fascinating, unique landscape, featuring turquoise hot-water lake Víti in vast Askja caldera; the mountain known as the 'Queen of the Desert', Herdubreid; and the weird formations of Kverkfjöll ice caves. There's fine hiking for the hardy, too.

Trip plan: Fly to Reykjavík, hire the toughest 4WD vehicle you can find, and stock up with plenty of supplies – there's not much in the interior! The least-challenging route is the Kjölur, crossing rivers over bridges rather than fords – it even carries a scheduled bus during the summer.

Need to know: Numerous huts offer accommodation across the interior, but they get booked up quickly over summer.

Other months: Jul-Aug – most routes only open during this brief window; May-Sep – other parts of Iceland pleasant; Oct-Apr – colder, dark, aurora may be visible.

▮ Journey
▮ Wildlife & nature
▮ Adventure

Icelandic horses crossing Svalaskard River in southern Iceland

ZAMBIA

→ **Why now?** Run the whitewaters of the Zambezi.

You might think the best time to raft some of the world's wildest whitewater is in the wet season. You'd think wrong. When the flow of Victoria Falls (Mosi-oa-Tunya – 'the smoke that thunders') starts to thunder more quietly, from August till the end of the year, falling water levels in the Batoka Gorge beneath the 354ft-high (108m) cascades provide the most thrilling rafting. Oblivion, Washing Machine, Gnashing Jaws of Death – these are just some of the rapids that flip adrenaline-pumped paddlers from their rafts. If you can catch your breath, gaze up at the cliffs, watching for birds including the rare Taita falcon. Once you've dried off, take a dip in the Devil's Pool on Livingstone Island at the very edge of the falls, before venturing on a wildlife drive in Mosi-oa-Tunya National Park to spot elephant, buffalo and giraffe.

Trip plan: Fly to Livingstone via Johannesburg or Lusaka. Rafting trips range from half a day to four days. Add on visits to the Livingstone's markets, viewing spots for Victoria Falls, a safari in the national park and perhaps a day kayaking above the falls.

Need to know: Rafting trips also run from Victoria Falls town in Zimbabwe.

Other months: May-Aug – cool, dry; Oct-Nov – hot, dry; Dec-Apr – wet (Aug-Dec: rafting best).

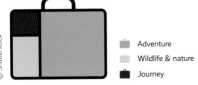
- Adventure
- Wildlife & nature
- Journey

© Shutterstock

SOFIA BULGARIA

→ **Why now?** Roam Roman remains and hike the hills.

The emperor Constantine loved the city then known as Ulpia Serdica, calling it: 'My Rome'. It's still lovable today, an intriguing blend of Roman basilicas, Ottoman mosques, onion-domed churches, art nouveau mansions and Soviet monoliths. It's also a cosmopolitan place with a vibrant bar and restaurant culture; visit in August to make the most of cafe terraces with views south to Mt Vitosha, the city's outdoor playground. Melding Turkish, Greece and Balkan influences, Sofia has that East-meets-West vibe; it's rapidly modernising but still terrific value, particularly for food, from hearty *banitsa* (cheese pastries) to more sophisticated traditional fare. Bulgarian red wines, particularly the mavruds, can be excellent.

Trip plan: Sofia Airport is southeast of the city. The metro line from Terminal 2 is the quickest way to the centre, which has a range of accommodation. After exploring the city, take a minibus out to Boyana to admire the 13th-century murals in its church, then continue to Aleko to hike on Mt Vitosha.

Need to know: For safety and standard metered fares, always use reputable official taxis – OK-Supertrans is a big, reliable firm.

Other months: Apr-Oct – spring, summer, autumn all pleasant; Jul-Aug – busiest; Nov-Mar – winter, cold, damp.

- Cultural
- Value
- Adventure

KO SAMUI
THAILAND

→ **Why now:** For the best Thai beach break in August.

The bad news for northern hemisphere travellers hoping to catch some sun and sand in Thailand in August: most of the country is being rained on. The good news: Ko Samui pretty much isn't. This beguiling isle in the Gulf of Thailand, fulfilling most fantasies of a tropical paradise – swaying palm trees fringing soft sand, fabulous food, a wide range of accommodation, heady nightlife if you want it, peaceful patches if you don't – enjoys relatively dry (though very hot) weather this month, making it ideal for a beach break. If you can wrest yourself from the wave-lapped sand, day trips to nearby Ang Thong National Marine Park offer spectacular snorkelling and kayaking among emerald-green specks rising from the tea-warm, jade-hued sea.

Trip plan: There are direct flights to Ko Samui from cities with intercontinental connections including Bangkok, Singapore, Kuala Lumpur and Hong Kong, and ferries from mainland ports including Don Sak. Then simply choose a coast and pick your beach.

Need to know: An admission fee for Ang Thong Marine National Park may be payable on top of tour costs. The marine park closes in November and December.

Other months: Dec-Feb – dry; Mar-Aug – hot, mostly dry; Sep-Nov – wet.

- Relaxation
- Adventure
- Wildlife & nature
- Food & drink

CHAMPAGNE
FRANCE

→ **Why now?** Explore cool wine cellars and grape-laden vineyards.

'I am drinking the stars!' No, oenophile monk Dom Pérignon probably didn't say that; nor did he invent the process for making the sparkling wine we now call champagne. No matter: the region that's now the byword for fizz remains the heartland of sparkles, and August – when all France is on holiday and the countryside sizzles – is a great month in which to delve into cool cellars and enjoy a *dégustation*. Most great champagne houses and caves are split between historic Reims, with its magnificent cathedral and basilica, and the 'Avenue de Champagne' in Épernay, nestled into vine-clad hillsides to the south. Here you'll find big international brands such as Veuve-Cliquot, Pommery, Krug, Taittinger and Pol Roger, as well as smaller boutique winemakers and cellars.

Trip planner: Reims is 80 miles (129km) east of Paris, about 45 minutes by the fastest train, and Épernay is another 15 miles (24km) to the south. Clearly, driving between wineries isn't ideal, but there are plenty of guided tours, and cycling is a great way to explore the countryside. Find route ideas at www.champagne.fr/en.

Need to know: Cellar tours at the big champagne houses ought to be booked in advance.

Other months: Apr-Oct – warm, driest (Oct: grapes harvested); Nov-Mar – cooler, rainier.

- Wildlife & nature
- Relaxation
- Cultural

SNOWY MOUNTAINS
AUSTRALIA

→ **Why now?** Combine carving the slopes with cosy inns.

Australia's liveliest ski resorts sit in the Snowy Mountains straddling the New South Wales/Victoria border, notably those in Kosciuszko National Park, around the eponymous 7310ft (2228m) peak. There are pretty alpine villages, great aprés-ski, and – in August particularly – snow. Lots of snow. Perisher, the biggest resort, has 47 lifts serving five square miles, with a couple of hundred snow guns in case the dumps ease up. Thredbo is an attractive village with a European vibe and the 2.3-mile (3.7km) Supertrail run, while Charlotte Pass – at 5791ft (1765m) Australia's highest resort – is accessible only by snow cat, and is great for ski-touring. There are slopes for boarders and skiers of all levels, plus tree-skiing, snowshoeing, cross-country and a packed program of events.

Trip plan: The nearest airport is at Canberra, 130 miles away (209km; about a three-hour drive); regular buses serve Thredbo from Sydney and Canberra. Driving is the best way to arrive and get around.

Need to know: The entry fee for Kosciuszko National Park is A$29 daily per car or A$11.45/3.60 per adult/child.

Other months: Early Jun-early Oct – ski season; Oct-Dec – good bushwalking; Dec-Feb – wildflowers; Mar-May – good for mountain biking and fishing.

- Adventure
- Wildlife & nature

TONGA

→ **Why now?** Swim with singing humpback whales.

Tonga welcomes various visitors regular as clockwork. There are surfers, who come here to ride 10ft (3m) swells and offshore reef breaks. There are game fishers, who come to reel in blue marlin. There are sun- and beach-lovers, who seek out their own untouched piece of paradise among the 170-plus islands. But the biggest fans of this gorgeous South Pacific archipelago are the humpback whales who migrate here from Antarctica between July and September each year to calve. This is one of the few places in the world where it's possible to swim with these melodic behemoths – select a responsible operator and be sure not to disturb the new families. With manta rays, dolphins, sea turtles and a host of dazzling marine life joining the underwater party, Tonga is a spectacular place to snorkel and dive, while kayaking is a great way to explore the atolls and islands. There's ancient history in the form of huge trilithons and the royal stone tombs around Mu'a, while getting to know today's laidback community is a treat.

Trip plan: Tonga's airport at Nuku'alofa is served by direct flights from Auckland, Fiji and Sydney, with lots of connections.

Need to know: Humpback whales gather around Tonga to calve from July to September.

Other months: Dec-Mar – wettest; Apr-Nov – drier.

- Wildlife & nature
- Relaxation
- Cultural

Rocca Maggiore standing above the pilgrimage town of Assisi, Umbria

Standing on Marloes Sands in Pembrokeshire, west Wales

With vegetation at a minimum, wildlife spotting in Malawi is great in August

UMBRIA
ITALY

Why now? Find your private rural retreat amid central Italy's gorgeous countryside.

Let's not pretend: Italy in August is hardly a secret retreat – least of all with Italians, who holiday en masse this month. But pick the right spot and it's a splendid time to visit. And that spot might well be Umbria: Tuscany's quieter neighbour has the rolling hillsides, the medieval-walled hill towns, the artistic gems and the food (oh my, the food) and wine, but far fewer visitors. Quintessentially Italian *agriturismos* – mostly self-catering accommodation in rooms or apartments within working farms, many with pools – provide wonderful rural bases for couples, friends or families. From your cool hilltop lair, you can explore the Roman amphitheatres, frescoes, palaces and basilicas of Spoleto, lovely Gubbio and Assisi (of St Francis fame), and sample Norcian truffles, white Orvieto wine and Perugian chocolates.

Trip plan: Perugia, Umbria's provincial capital, receives international flights, as do Rome, Florence and Ancona, all a short drive or train journey away. Car hire is essential for exploring. Various websites list details of *agriturismos*; try www.agriturismo.it.

Need to know: In early August in particular, popular towns such as Assisi, Spoleto and Orvieto will be busy with Italian tourists, and some restaurants may be closed.

Other months: Jul-Aug – peak season, sights busy; Apr-Jun & Sep-Oct – pleasant weather, towns uncrowded; Nov-Mar – chilly.

- Relaxation
- Cultural
- Food & drink

MALAWI

Why now? For fine weather in the 'Warm Heart of Africa'.

Malawi seeps under your skin. Its wildlife parks aren't the biggest (though there's lots of animals to see); its mountains aren't the highest (though Mt Mulanje is magnificent); and it has no sea coast (though Lake Malawi has lovely, calm beaches). But there's something about the place, a warmth exuded from its peaceful countryside and ever-smiling people, that will have you hooked. It's amazing more people don't visit. August is one of the loveliest months, with warm days, cool nights and clear, dry skies – ideal for lazing on the sandy lakeshore or kayaking amid leafy islands. Also, the vegetation has died back a little, allowing good wildlife-watching. Liwonde National Park is good for elephants, sable antelopes and boat trips on the hippo-filled Shire River; restocked Majete Wildlife Reserve now boasts the Big Five.

Trip plan: Malawi is long and thin, with capital Lilongwe roughly central, and is dominated by its titular lake. Head south to combine Liwonde and Majete, backtracking to Lake Malawi for relaxation by the water – perhaps Mumbo Island, just off Cape Maclear.

Need to know: Malaria is present in Malawi – take precautions.

Other months: Dec-Apr – wet; May-Aug – dry, cool; Sep-Nov – dry, hot.

- Wildlife & nature
- Adventure
- Relaxation

PEMBROKESHIRE
WALES

Why now? Get the adrenaline pumping on a coastal family adventure in the far west of Britain.

The broad beaches, pretty fishing villages and seabird-bustling cliffs of the Pembrokeshire coast rival perennial British holiday favourites such as Cornwall, yet draw a fraction of the crowds. Bring the family in August and you won't be alone, sure – but it's easy to find a patch of shoreline to call your own. There's a full roster of activities, too: hiking, coasteering, climbing, cycling, surfing and kayaking, for starters. Add imposing castles at Pembroke, Carew and Manorbier, the hidden cathedral at St Davids, porpoise-spotting cruises, and boat trips to the puffin-and-seal havens of Skomer, Skokholm and Ramsey Islands, and you have a heady brew for family adventures.

Trip plan: Base yourself at an appealing seaside town or village – Tenby or Manorbier in the east, Lower Solva or Porthgain to the west, Fishguard or Newport on the north coast – or historic St David's, Britain's smallest cathedral city. A reasonably comprehensive bus service runs in summer.

Need to know: Access to Skomer, Skokholm and Ramsey Islands is limited – book the few beds in advance and arrive early for boat trips. Puffins depart Skomer during August, so come earlier for larger numbers.

Other months: Mid-Jun–mid-Sep – warm, larger crowds; Apr–mid-Jun & mid-Sep–Oct – shoulder seasons, quieter; Nov-Mar – winter, good walking from Feb.

- Adventure
- Wildlife & nature
- Cultural
- Relaxation

(Below)Wildebeest on the move during the 'Great Migration'(R) Bell Gorge on the Gibb River Road, Kimberley, Western Australia

©Nigel Pavitt / Getty Images

MASAI MARA KENYA

Why now? Watch hordes of wildebeest brave a river crossing. When hundreds of thousands of trundling wildebeest hit a river, you get a huge bottleneck – the gnu-jam to end them all. And when they wade in to cross en masse, frantically splashing and dodging hungry crocodiles, it's the highest drama imaginable. The circular migration of some 1.5 million blue wildebeest, plus attendant zebras and Thomson's gazelles, usually reaches the Mara River flowing through Kenya's Masai Mara National Reserve around August, which is the time to watch the spectacle of mass crossings (and feastings by crocs and lions).

Trip planner: Most safarigoers fly into one of the airstrips in the Mara, though driving from Kenya's capital, Nairobi, is straightforward. The lodges and camps in the west and northwest of the reserve, near the confluence of the Mara and Talek rivers, are convenient for witnessing crossings.

Need to know: Staying in a private conservancy to the north or east of the Mara can provide more intimate wildlife watching. An alternative is to stay in the northern Serengeti in Tanzania near the Grumeti River, usually crossed in June. Crossings are never entirely predictable, though.

Other months: Jul-Sep – wildebeest move into Masai Mara; Oct – grazing in Mara; Nov-Mar – return to graze and calve in southern Serengeti; Apr-Jun – migrate northwest.

Wildlife & nature

Journey

KIMBERLEY
AUSTRALIA

→ **Why now?** Undertake an epic outback odyssey.

Look at a map of Hwy 1 across the Kimberley and you'll see what appears to be a shortcut. Don't be fooled: the Gibb River Road between Derby and Kununurra may cover fewer miles, but it's a much, much longer, tougher journey. Also much, much more thrilling. This 410-mile (660km) track, all corrugated red dirt and river fords, is one of the great overland expeditions, possible only in the middle of the dry season – August being the most popular month. Bushwalk into remote gorges and cool off beneath waterfalls, camp out in a swag beneath a canopy of stars, and learn what it means to be one with the outback.

Trip plan: If you're confident at handling a 4WD in wilderness conditions, you can self-drive between Derby (east of Broome) and Kununurra; alternatively, join an eight-day guided tour. Detour south to Lake Argyle and Purnululu National Park to wander among the giant red beehives of the Bungle Bungles, or north to the Mitchell Plateau, for its dramatic waterfalls.

Need to know: Crocodiles are common in Kimberley waterways; along the Gibb they tend to be the less-dangerous freshwater variety, but check local advice about salties, particularly near the coast.

Other months: May-Sep – dry, cooler, road navigable; Oct-Apr – wet season (Jan-Feb: heat and rain peaking).

■ Journey
■ Wildlife & nature

NORTHEAST SRI LANKA

→ **Why now?** Loll or surf at Indian Ocean beaches under the sun.

There's a triple whammy of good news about Sri Lanka's northeast in August: the weather is great, prices are low, and beaches are quiet. Unlike the southwest, which catches the rain now, the northeast coast this month has blue skies, warm waters and – at Arugam Bay particularly – fine surf. Civil war ensured this region was largely off limits till recently, so the coast is little developed – you can still find an empty patch of sand at spots such as Nilaveli, Uppuveli and Passikudah. The centre is also pretty dry in August, good for visiting the rock fortress of Sigiriya and spiritual hub Kandy, which bursts into noisy, colourful life during the Esala Perahera celebrations honouring the sacred tooth relic of Buddha each summer. Be warned: spicy Sri Lankan food is addictive.

Trip plan: International flights serve Colombo; internal flights access Batticaloa, but Trincomalee and the northeastern beaches are reached by train or bus and taxi.

Need to know: Dates for the 10-day Esala Perahera festival vary across July and August depending on how the month of Esala falls.

Other months: Oct-Jan – northeast and centre wet; Feb-Sep – dry, warm; Dec-Mar – southwest dry.

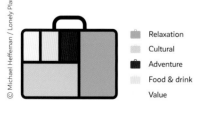

Relaxation
Cultural
Adventure
Food & drink
Value

SPANISH PYRENEES

→ **Why now?** Hike, bike, kayak, abseil and raft this mountain playground.

If the Alps are Europe's mountain model, the tall, leggy pin-up, the Pyrenees are the pretty girl next door. Some Alps resorts have been made over for tourism, but in general that's not true of the Spanish Pyrenees. Here, towns and stone-built villages perched amid glorious mountain scenery provide bases for outdoor activities with a family bent: hiking and cycling trails, canyoning gorges, abseiling, kayaking, rafting – with guesthouses and restaurants providing boltholes in which to rest and feed before the next day's adventures. In August, the weather is most consistent, high paths free from snow, and outdoor facilities ready for action. Popular bases include Vielha and Sort (great for river rafting) near Aigüestortes i Estany de Sant Maurici National Park in northern Catalonia, and Berdún in neighbouring Aragón province.

Trip plan: Depending on which part of the Pyrenees, Bilbao, Toulouse or Barcelona (Girona) airports might be most convenient. Tour operators offer family adventure holidays in northern Catalonia and Aragón.

Need to know: Though activities may be tailored to kids, be sure yours are comfortable cycling and swimming outdoors.

Other months: Jul-Sep – summer; Oct-Nov – weather variable; Dec-Feb – winter, skiing; Mar-Jun – snow on passes.

Adventure
Wildlife & nature
Food & drink

NOVA SCOTIA
CANADA

→ **Why now?** For buskers, blueberries and beguiling bays.

The quintessential Nova Scotian experience? Strolling a salt-scented seashore, listening to waves swish and masts clank while chewing a lobster roll. This experience is loveliest in August, when it's warm, dry and ideal for being outside. Start on the waterfront of the capital Halifax, with its food shacks, excellent museums and infectious Busker Festival (late July/early August). Move on to the postcard-perfect coasts at Unesco-listed Lunenberg and Peggy's Cove. On the Bay of Fundy, expect an influx of other seaside visitors – finback, minke and humpback whales hang out here June to September. Fundy is also home to the world's biggest tides, best appreciated on kayak trips or, uniquely, eating a chef-cooked dinner on the sandy seabed. For more food fun, embrace wild blueberries. Only harvested in August, they're now fresh and delicious.

Trip plan: In one week, drive from Halifax along the pretty South Shore (Lunenberg), then north to the Bay of Fundy and east along the Annapolis Valley. With two weeks, continue east to spectacular Cape Breton.

Need to know: Ferries link Nova Scotia to ports in Newfoundland, New Brunswick, Prince Edward Island and Maine, USA.

Other months: Nov-Feb – snowshoeing and cross-country skiing; Mar-Apr – warming, slushy; May-Aug – warm, whales; Sep-Oct – cooler, quieter.

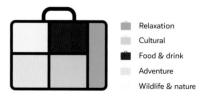

Relaxation
Cultural
Food & drink
Adventure
Wildlife & nature

COOK ISLANDS

Why now? Snorkel crystal-clear lagoons and dazzling coral reefs.

These Pacific paradise isles are at their best in August, when rain is at a minimum and the cobalt-blue lagoons are clear and warm. Rarotonga, the largest of the Cook Islands, is the most popular destination – no wonder: its lushly clad volcanic pinnacle rises from the azure ocean, with a natural infinity pool enclosed by its circling reef off the south and east coast. Coconut palms sway, flowers scent the air and fine white sand sifts through the toes; no wonder many struggle to wrest themselves from the beach. But do: there's fabulous snorkelling and diving – particularly off Muri on the east coast, where dazzling reef fish flit past your mask – and rewarding hikes into the hilly interior. The islands' intriguing Maori culture is experienced most entertainingly at an 'island night' – a bonanza of song, dance and local *kai* (food). For an even more laidback ambience, take the short

The water within the Cook Islands' lagoons is crystal clear in August

© Pete Seaward / Lonely Planet

flight to Aitutaki, a desert-island idyll with a spectacular lagoon and fine diving.

Trip plan: Direct flights from Pape'ete, Auckland and LA serve Rarotonga; Aitutaki is 50 minutes from Rarotonga by air.

Need to know: Malaria isn't a problem on the islands, but dengue fever outbreaks occur, and mosquitoes can be pestilential – use insect repellent.

Other months: Apr-Oct – drier, cooler; Nov-Mar – wetter, hotter.

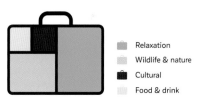

- Relaxation
- Wildlife & nature
- Cultural
- Food & drink

UK'S CANALS

Why now? Set your own pace afloat on Britain's waterways.

The earliest canals in Britain were built by the Romans nearly two millennia ago, and for substantial chunks of the intervening centuries they've been the arteries of industry and commerce and the home of lively communities of boat people. The past few decades have seen the restoration and revival of many waterways, now thriving again and best explored during the long, sunny days and balmy evenings of August.

The slowest of slow travel, a canal-boat holiday might see you chugging through spectacular scenery and past sights such as the potteries of Staffordshire; across Thomas Telford's masterwork, the Pontcysyllte Aqueduct in north Wales; or – our pick – along the Kennet and Avon Canal past glorious Georgian Bath, sleepy villages (and great pubs), honey-hued mill town Bradford on Avon and the engineering marvel of the Caen Hill Locks.

Trip planner: The Canal and River Trust manages 2000 miles (3219km) of waterways in England and Wales; its website (https://canalrivertrust.org.uk) has plenty of useful planning information for a break from a day to a couple of weeks.

Need to know: Speed limit on most canals is 4mph (6km/h), and locks can slow progress down significantly.

Other months: Jun-Sep – warm, driest; Apr-May & Oct – quiet; Nov-Mar – wetter, colder.

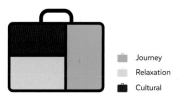

- Journey
- Relaxation
- Cultural

ECUADOR

→ Why now? Climb volcanoes, delve into rainforest and browse markets. Little Ecuador packs the best of South America into one handy-sized package. It has colonial architecture in Quito and Cuenca; Inca remains at Ingapirca; indigenous markets at Otavalo, Saquisilí and Zumbahua; magnificent cones (including picture-perfect Cotopaxi) along the 'Avenue of the Volcanoes'; and profuse wildlife in the Amazon, the Galápagos and the northern cloud forests. Both highlands and rainforest are driest in August, so it's prime time for absorbing the cultural highlights and getting active on volcanoes and rafting whitewater rivers. Ecuador's a bargain, to boot, with great-value accommodation.

Trip plan: From capital Quito, head north to spot iridescent hummingbirds in Mindo cloud forest and on to the bustling market at Otavalo (pausing en route to hop back and forth across the equator). Then dip back south to hike on Cotopaxi or Chimborazo, soak in the thermal waters at Baños, explore the Inca remains at Ingapirca and admire historic Cuenca. It's worth spending time and money flying deep into the Amazon along the Napo River to stay in one of the wonderful community-run eco-lodges.

Need to know: A Galápagos cruise is less appealing in August, with rough seas and more cloud.

Other months: Jan-May – cool, wet in highlands and Amazon; Jun-Sep – driest months in highlands and Amazon; Oct-Dec – wet in Amazon, dry in highlands.

- Wildlife & nature
- Cultural
- Adventure
- Journey
- Value

Cloud forest reserves host incredible scenes, such as Purple-bibbed whitetip hummingbirds' courtship dances

SKI FIELDS CHILE

→ **Why now?** Luxuriate in deep powder snow.

The powder lies deep on Chile's Andean slopes in August, when lucky Santiaguiños enjoy two terrific nearby ski zones: the 'three valleys' of Valle Nevado, La Parva and El Colorado just to the east, and exclusive Portillo a little further north. Valle Nevado is a modern, European-style resort with plenty of wide, groomed runs and ample off-piste opportunities; add budget options in neighbouring El Colorado and family-friendly El Parva and it's a great all-round package. Portillo, conversely, is a one-hotel resort. But what a hotel: the iconic, family-run yellow property overlooking the Laguna del Inca, in the shadow of Mt Aconcagua (22,841ft; 6962m), offers some of the best and least-crowded skiing in the southern hemisphere – many national teams train here during the northern summer.

Trip plan: Valle Nevado is 37 miles (60km; about an hour's drive) east of Santiago; Portillo is 87 miles (140km) and two hours from Santiago. Both have good ski-in-ski-out accommodation.

Need to know: The road to Valle Nevado operates a one-way system at weekends and holidays – mornings up, afternoons down.

Other months: Late Jun-Oct – ski season; Nov-May – ski resorts mostly closed; Sep-Apr – pleasant weather in Santiago.

Adventure
Cultural

CHESAPEAKE BAY USA

→ **Why now?** Relax on family-friendly beaches and savour seafood.

It's over four centuries since European settlers recognised the bounty of what's now called Chesapeake Bay, John Smith writing how oysters 'lay as thick as stones', as his crew feasted on fish and shellfish. Though the landscape has changed a little since those early explorations, one thing's still true: this is a seafood-lover's paradise, with oysters, rockfish and Maryland's famed blue crabs topping the menu. In August – middle of the crab season – a journey around the bay makes a great family getaway. Bolster beach time with varied attractions: historic towns such as Annapolis and old-time fishing villages; marshland reserves hosting otters, cranes and feral Chincoteague ponies; and, of course, eateries steaming those delectable crabs.

Trip plan: Start in Washington DC and move clockwise, visiting Annapolis and fishing settlements such as Tilghman Island, skirting east to the Atlantic shore of Delaware, Maryland and Virginia to explore beaches at Lewes, Assateague Island and Chincoteague Island, returning up the west coast to DC.

Need to know: August is a popular month, so accommodation gets booked up fast.

Other months: Apr-Jun – breezy, blossoms; Jul-Sep – balmy, busiest; Oct-Nov – fall colours; Dec-Mar – cold.

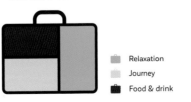

Relaxation
Journey
Food & drink

ANGEL FALLS VENEZUELA

→ **Why now?** See the world's highest waterfall in full torrential flow.

To burst the bubble up front: this loftiest of cascades in Venezuela's southeast wasn't named for some celestial being, but for Jimmie Angel, the aviator who crashed his plane on top of the flat-topped mountain Auyantepui in 1937. Still, it's an apt epithet for the diaphanous cataract that plummets 3212ft (979m) into the Cañon del Diablo (Devil's Canyon) – nearly 20 times the height of Niagara Falls. August is prime waterfall-watching time: the middle of Venezuela's rainy season, when the falls thunder in their most fulsome flow, and when rivers are swollen and navigable by boat.

Trip plan: Light aircraft offer aerial views, but overflights may be cancelled during the wet season if the top of Auyantepui is clad in clouds. The most rewarding way to see the falls is aboard a motorised canoe from Canaima, the nearest airstrip. The two- or three-day boat trip along the Carrao and Churún rivers, traversing lush jungle, passing other falls and rapids and camping in hammocks, is an unforgettable experience in itself.

Need to know: Angel Falls face east, and so is in direct sunlight during the morning – important information for photographers.

Other months: Nov-Apr – dry season, travel comfortable; May-Oct – wet season, falls most impressive.

Wildlife & nature
Journey

STOCKHOLM
SWEDEN

→ **Why now?** Island-hop the coastal capital on long summer days.

Less a city, more a wooded archipelago that happens to host some important buildings, Sweden's capital is, like much of the country and its inhabitants, unreasonably attractive. Never more so than in sunny August, when the sun glints on the water and the city's many parks beckon. Stockholm has enough cultural attractions to pack several days, from the cobbled alleys of Gamla Stan (old town) and open-air museum Skansen to its exceptional museums and contemporary galleries, and the sleek modern shopping district of Norrmalm, with ample welcoming cafes and restaurants for the all-important *fika* (coffee and cake break). It's easy to roam the city's 14 main islands on foot or by bike or metro, but the tens of thousands more islands and rocks in the archipelago are best explored by ferry, on a boat cruise or – better yet – by kayak.

Trip plan: Arlanda airport is only 20 minutes from the city by express train, twice that by bus. With ample bike lanes, cycling is a great way to get around.

Need to know: Even in high summer, bring warm layers for evenings when temperatures can drop 10°C (18°F).

Stockholm Royal Opera: one of the city's many cultural offerings

© Andrey Omelyanchuk / 500px

Other months: Nov-Feb – winter, holiday markets; Mar-May – cool, cheaper; Jun-Aug – warm, busiest; Sep-Oct – cooler, autumn colours.

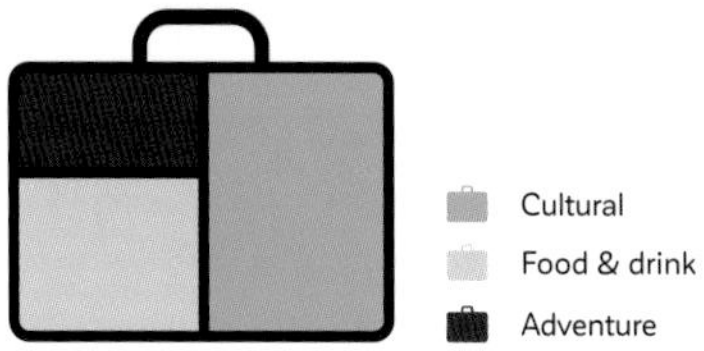

- Cultural
- Food & drink
- Adventure

BEYOND STOCKHOLM

DROTTNINGHOLM PALACE · 9 MILES (14KM) · Grand palace on the 'Queen's Islet', still the royal residence

SIGTUNA · 29 MILES (46KM) · Sweden's first town, historic wooden buildings, nearby Skokloster Castle

MARIEFRED · 31 MILES (50KM) · Picturesque town, Gripsholm castle, steamboat journey from Stockholm

UPPSALA · 40 MILES (64KM) · Charming city, Bronze-Age burial mounds, huge cathedral

NORTHEAST BRAZIL

Why now? Dive into crystal-clear waters among rolling dunes.

Word got out about Jericoacoara a while ago, so this travellers' beach paradise, with its water sports, capoeira classes and laidback vibe, is now everyone's favourite secret. Yet the stretch of Brazil's north coast between São Luís and Fortaleza is still something special. There are dozens of places, including regional capital Fortaleza, at which to enjoy sea, sun, sand, and sports such as surfing, windsurfing and kitesurfing. Then there's the remarkable Lençóis Maranhenses National Park, a vast expanse of folded dunes interspersed with limpid pools (full in August) just begging to be plunged into, plus mangroves, lagoons and turtles.

Trip plan: Explore the coast on a road trip between São Luís, with its pastel-hued colonial mansions, and Fortaleza, both accessible on flights from Rio de Janeiro and other Brazilian cities, pausing at Lençóis Maranhenses National Park and Jeri en route.

Need to know: The Pôr do Sol (sunset dune) at Jeri is reputedly one of the few places you can see the 'emerald flash' – a green spark as the sun dips into the ocean.

Other months: Jul-Feb – sunny, dry, best windsurfing (Dec-Feb: national holidays, beaches busy); Mar-Jun – rainy season.

Relaxation

Adventure

Wildlife & nature

Perched on paradise, Lagoa Paraiso, near Jericoacoara

MADAGASCAR

→ **Why now?** Meet lemurs, chameleons and whales on cool, dry days.

The 'Great Red Island' is one of the planet's great wildlife pageants, populated by mischievous lemurs, dancing sifakas, dazzling birds, mysterious aye-ayes, bug-eyed chameleons, cat-like fossas, giraffe-necked weevils… the animal cast list is vast and dizzyingly varied. Dry and cool August is prime time to witness this natural diversity, and to explore the spiny forests, jagged tsingy rock formations and fine beaches. It's also the season for whale watching, when humpbacks pass Île Sainte Marie off the east coast, and perhaps for witnessing *famadihana* (turning of the bones) ceremonies, honouring and remembering the dead.

Trip plan: Madagascar is big – about the size of France – and roads are often poor, so flying makes sense, as does a visit of at least a fortnight. A typical trip starting at the capital, Antananarivo (Tana), might visit Andasibe-Mantadia National Park, Berenty Reserve, the beach at Ifaty and Isalo National Park in the south before heading back north to Tana via the rainforest at Ranomafana National Park.

Need to know: The highlands can be cold in August, which is also peak season – book well in advance.

Other months: Apr-Oct – generally cool, dry; Nov-Mar – wet.

- Wildlife & nature
- Journey
- Cultural

MT RUAPEHU
NEW ZEALAND

→ **Why now?** Glide down the flanks of a mighty volcano.

New Zealand's biggest ski zone lies in Tongoriro National Park, right on the flanks of mighty Mt Ruapehu. It's true: you get to carve your way down a huge, and distinctly active, volcano – one that receives its biggest snow dumps in August. Whakapapa Ski Area, on the giant massif's northwestern slopes, is the country's largest, with a generous area dedicated to beginners, plus plenty of groomed slopes for intermediate and expert skiers, and the lift-accessed Black Magic backcountry area. Turoa, to the southwest, is slightly smaller but boasts Australasia's longest vertical descent (2369ft; 722m) and highest chairlift. There's more than just skiing here, though: the Tongariro Alpine Crossing is particularly thrilling in winter, offering a hike among craters and cones caked with snow.

Trip plan: Choice of ski area may dictate where you stay: Whakapapa Village or within the national park for the Whakapapa Ski Area, Ohakune for Turoa. The nearest airport is at Taupo, about an hour's drive from the park, a little further from Ohakune. Auckland and Wellington are both a four-hour drive away.

Need to know: Hiking trails in the national park, notably the Tongariro Alpine Crossing, are not to be taken lightly in winter – an experienced guide is essential.

Other months: Jul-Oct (sometimes Nov) – ski season; Nov-Dec – spring; Jan-Mar – summer, peak trekking season; Apr–mid-June – shorter days but trekking can be good.

- Adventure
- Wildlife & nature

Explore and enjoy the alluring waters of the Turquoise Coast by *gület*

© Mark Read / Lonely Planet

TURQUOISE COAST TURKEY

→ **Why now?** Slip into the bath-warm Aegean or Med from the deck of a traditional *gület.*

If diving off the wooden deck of a twin-masted sailboat (*gület*) into the impossible blue of the Mediterranean is your idea of heaven on a hot August day, you're not alone. Back in the 1920s, renowned Turkish writer Cevat Şakir Kabaağaçlı took to hiring local sponge-divers' boats to cruise along the so-called Turquoise Coast from Bodrum on what he called 'Blue Voyages'. In the intervening decades increasing numbers of Turkish and foreign tourists recognised the appeal, and today a plethora of vessels – some more traditional, some built specifically for the cruises – ply the waters along the Aegean and Mediterranean Coast from Bodrum, Marmaris and Fethiye, stopping to visit ancient sites such as Letoön and Patara, to swim, lounge on a beach, eat and drink. It's a perfect holiday for families, too.

Trip plan: Dalaman is the nearest international airport to both Marmaris and Fethiye; Bodrum has its own airport. Plan ahead for an August departure, to ensure a place on a quality boat. International tour operators offer one-week or longer packages.

Need to know: Not all *gülets* use their sails. Check in advance whether your chosen vessel will be sailing or using a diesel motor.

Other months: May-Oct – dry, warm; Nov-Apr, cooler, more rain.

Journey
Relaxation
Adventure

CALIFORNIA ZEPHYR USA

→ Why now? Discover the wild landscapes of the west by rail in air-con comfort.

You could fly from Chicago to San Francisco in under five hours. Or you could experience one of the world's great journeys, an epic rail odyssey covering 2438 miles (3924km) – two thirds of the breadth of the US – crossing the mighty Mississippi River and the vast plains of Nebraska, visiting mile-high city Denver, traversing the Rockies (watch out for deer and elk trackside) and Colorado's canyons, passing Utah's buttes and mesas, crossing the Sierra Nevada and reaching the Pacific at San Francisco Bay. In toasty August the California Zephyr offers a comfortable, air-conditioned ride through these diverse landscapes (and climates), its Sightseer observation lounge with wraparound windows providing widescreen vistas. It's a bargain, to boot: specials bring one-way fares for the 51-hour ride to well under US$200 in a spacious seat, a little over twice that in a roomette. Not bad for arguably North America's most scenic ride.

Trip plan: The California Zephyr runs daily in each direction between Chicago and Emeryville, CA, with bus transfers to Oakland and San Francisco. Book seats or berths with Amtrack (www.amtrak.com).

Need to know: Travel the route east-to-west to best enjoy the sunsets and cross the mountains in daylight.

Other months: Jul-Sep – summer, fine mountain views; year-round – train runs.

■ Journey
■ Value
■ Cultural
■ Wildlife & nature

Buenos Aires is home to the tango, the world's sexiest dance

© Matt Munro / Lonely Planet

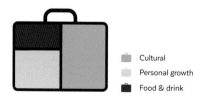

BUENOS AIRES ARGENTINA

→ Why now? Learn to tango in the home of the world's sexiest dance.

Nowhere else are a city and a dance so inextricably linked. Tango is, simply, the heartbeat of Buenos Aires, and the Argentine capital's passion for both the music – exemplified by the songs of Carlos Gardel, which still waft out of many a window – and the dance never seems to diminish. The cool month of August isn't just a wonderful time to visit BA, it also sees the city fling itself into its annual Tango Buenos Aires festival, with performances and concerts by the finest exponents. At other times you can enjoy more or less touristy (but usually high-calibre) tango shows at various clubs and theatres, or simply watch the weekly Sunday sessions in Plaza Dorrego. But to really feel the spirit of the dance join a lesson at a San Telmo *milonga* (dancehall) and stay for the late-night free-for-all with expert Porteños afterwards, fuelled by fine Argentine red wine.

Trip plan: The city centre and Recoleta, Palermo and San Telmo districts offer the best accommodation options.

Need to know: The action starts late in Buenos Aires – don't expect dances to get started before midnight.

Other months: Dec-Mar – hot, humid; Apr-May & Sep-Nov – pleasant temperatures, more rain; Jun-Aug – cool but drier.

■ Cultural
■ Personal growth
■ Food & drink

(L) Woman near Mount Hagen wearing ceremonial costume; (R) *Badeschiff* (bathing ship) on River Spree, Berlin

PAPUA NEW GUINEA

→ Why now? Meet tribes and explore rainforest-clad mountains.

PNG is no place for the faint of heart, but for intrepid travellers it's one of the final frontiers, where wild-eyed tribesmen sporting garish painted faces and feathered headdresses engage in a mass sing-and-dance-off. August is the ideal month to explore this lush, rugged land, when rain is at its lowest ebb and when two major 'sing-sings' are held: the Sepik River Crocodile Festival in Ambunti, and the famed Mount Hagen Cultural Show, both gathering dozens of tribes for a colourful bonanza of music and dance. This is also a good time for hardened trekkers to tackle the 60-mile Kokoda Track, and to spot the courtship displays of flamboyant male birds of paradise (August to February).Or you could just hit the beach…

Trip plan: Independent travel can be challenging – infrastructure is poor, and many areas are only accessible by plane or boat, so joining a guided tour is sensible. Fly into capital Port Moresby, head to Mt Hagen to meet tribespeople and search for birds of paradise, boat up the Sepik River and explore the jagged peaks and valleys around the Tari Gap.

Need to know: Malaria is a problem in lower regions across the country – pack insect repellent and take precautions.

Other months: May-Oct – driest, busiest season; Apr & Nov – shoulder months, humid and hot; Dec-Mar – wet.

Cultural
Wildlife & nature
Adventure

© Matt Munro / Lonely Planet

BERLIN
GERMANY

Why now? Enjoy park life in this verdant city.

Just over a quarter of a century ago, Germany's capital was split by the infamous wall between West Berlin and the communist east. Today, the reunified city is probably the coolest and friendliest European capital, with hip bars galore. It's also very green, with more than 2500 parks and gardens. Explore the cultural highlights in sunny August: the heritage of Museumsinsel (Museum Island), the more recent history of Checkpoint Charlie, the Jewish Museum and Holocaust Memorial, the magnificent rebuilt Reichstag. But spare time for parklife, too. Tiergarten is the biggie, stretching from Brandenburg Gate west to the zoo. At weekends head to Mauerpark (literally, 'Wall Park') in funky Prenzlauer Berg, buzzing with buskers, flea-market stalls and open-air karaoke. Or go southwest past Charlottenburg to Grunewald ('Green Forest') and landscaped Pfaueninsel (Peacock Island).

Trip plan: Berlin has two airports. Schönefeld is a half-hour train journey south of the centre, while regular buses make the 30-minute ride from Tegel.

Need to know: The view from the dome of the Reichstag is spectacular but advance booking is essential.

Other months: Jun-Sep – pleasantly warm; Oct-Nov – cooler, colourful foliage; Dec-Feb – very cold, Christmas markets; Mar-May – warming, can be wet.

© Mark Read / Lonely Planet

- Cultural
- Food & drink
- Relaxation

BEYOND BERLIN

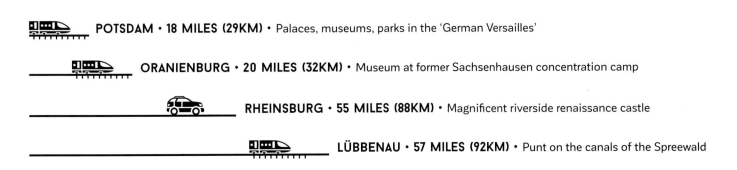

POTSDAM · 18 MILES (29KM) · Palaces, museums, parks in the 'German Versailles'

ORANIENBURG · 20 MILES (32KM) · Museum at former Sachsenhausen concentration camp

RHEINSBURG · 55 MILES (88KM) · Magnificent riverside renaissance castle

LÜBBENAU · 57 MILES (92KM) · Punt on the canals of the Spreewald

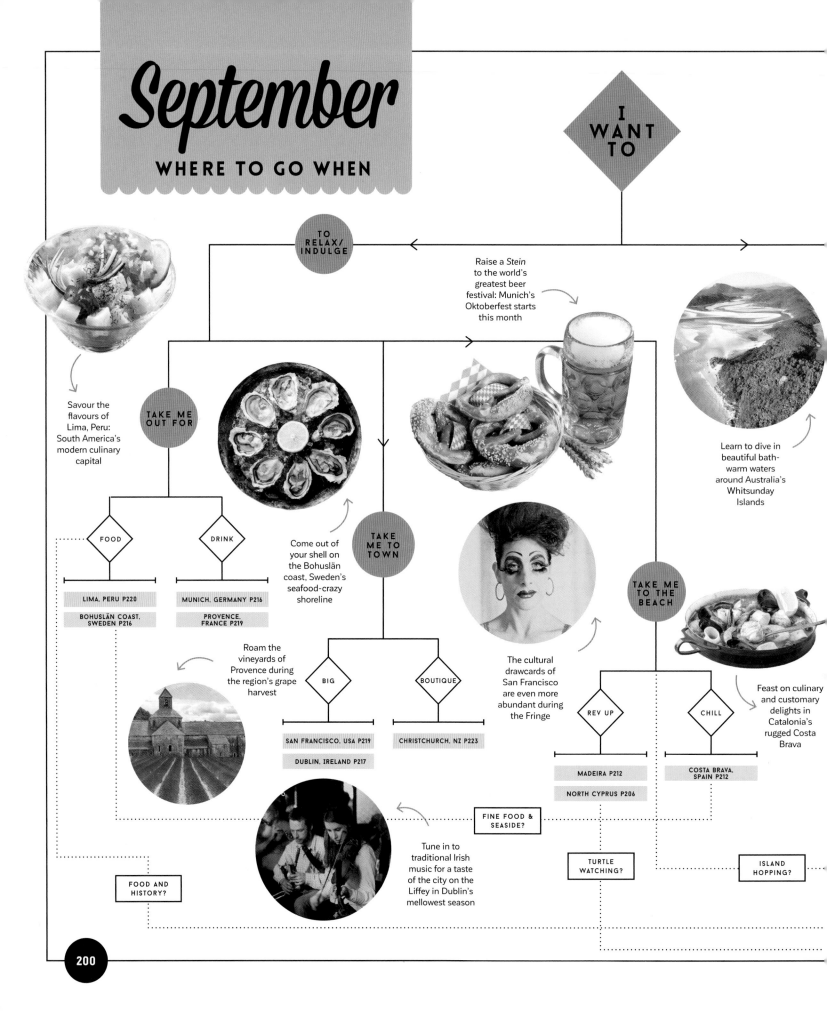

September

WHERE TO GO WHEN

I WANT TO

TO RELAX/ INDULGE

Raise a *Stein* to the world's greatest beer festival: Munich's Oktoberfest starts this month

Savour the flavours of Lima, Peru: South America's modern culinary capital

Learn to dive in beautiful bath-warm waters around Australia's Whitsunday Islands

TAKE ME OUT FOR

TAKE ME TO TOWN

TAKE ME TO THE BEACH

Come out of your shell on the Bohuslän coast, Sweden's seafood-crazy shoreline

FOOD

DRINK

LIMA, PERU P220

BOHUSLÄN COAST, SWEDEN P216

MUNICH, GERMANY P216

PROVENCE, FRANCE P219

The cultural drawcards of San Francisco are even more abundant during the Fringe

Feast on culinary and customary delights in Catalonia's rugged Costa Brava

Roam the vineyards of Provence during the region's grape harvest

BIG

BOUTIQUE

REV UP

CHILL

SAN FRANCISCO, USA P219

DUBLIN, IRELAND P217

CHRISTCHURCH, NZ P223

MADEIRA P212

NORTH CYPRUS P206

COSTA BRAVA, SPAIN P212

FINE FOOD & SEASIDE?

Tune in to traditional Irish music for a taste of the city on the Liffey in Dublin's mellowest season

TURTLE WATCHING?

ISLAND HOPPING?

FOOD AND HISTORY?

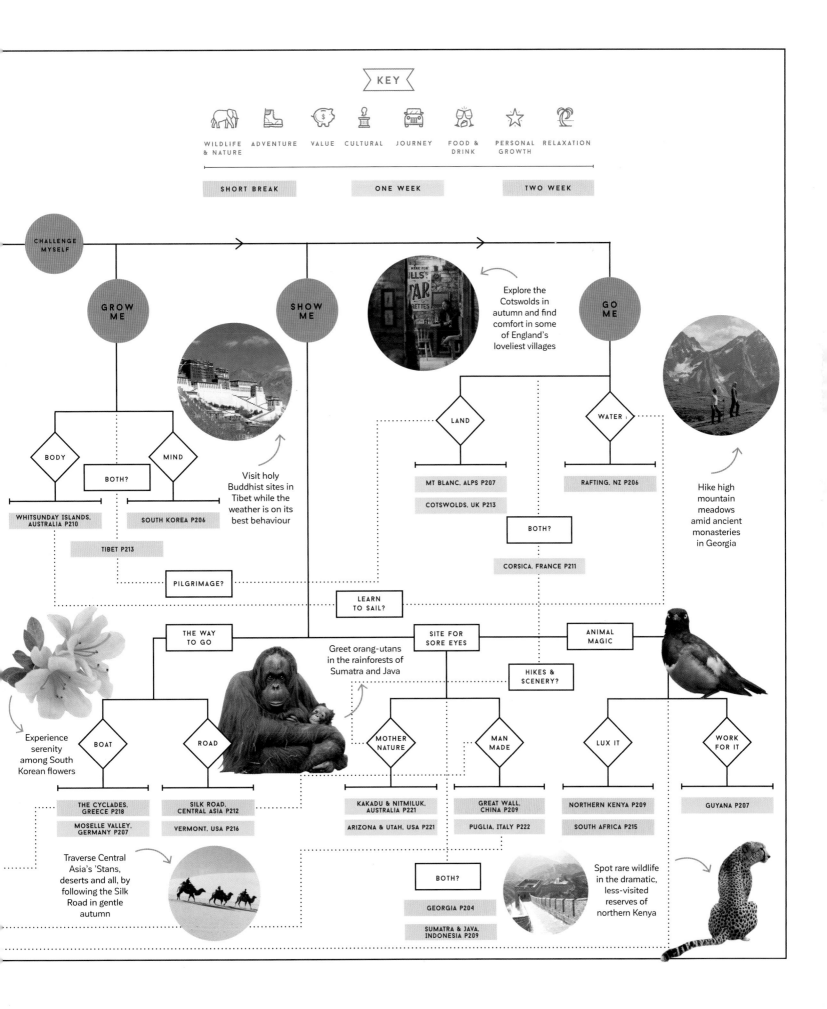

KEY

WILDLIFE & NATURE | ADVENTURE | VALUE | CULTURAL | JOURNEY | FOOD & DRINK | PERSONAL GROWTH | RELAXATION

SHORT BREAK | ONE WEEK | TWO WEEK

CHALLENGE MYSELF

GROW ME

SHOW ME

GO ME

Explore the Cotswolds in autumn and find comfort in some of England's loveliest villages

BODY

BOTH?

MIND

Visit holy Buddhist sites in Tibet while the weather is on its best behaviour

WHITSUNDAY ISLANDS, AUSTRALIA P210

SOUTH KOREA P206

TIBET P213

PILGRIMAGE?

LAND

WATER

MT BLANC, ALPS P207

COTSWOLDS, UK P213

RAFTING, NZ P206

Hike high mountain meadows amid ancient monasteries in Georgia

BOTH?

CORSICA, FRANCE P211

LEARN TO SAIL?

THE WAY TO GO

SITE FOR SORE EYES

ANIMAL MAGIC

Greet orang-utans in the rainforests of Sumatra and Java

HIKES & SCENERY?

Experience serenity among South Korean flowers

BOAT

ROAD

MOTHER NATURE

MAN MADE

LUX IT

WORK FOR IT

THE CYCLADES, GREECE P218

SILK ROAD, CENTRAL ASIA P212

KAKADU & NITMILUK, AUSTRALIA P221

GREAT WALL, CHINA P209

NORTHERN KENYA P209

GUYANA P207

MOSELLE VALLEY, GERMANY P207

VERMONT, USA P216

ARIZONA & UTAH, USA P221

PUGLIA, ITALY P222

SOUTH AFRICA P215

Traverse Central Asia's 'Stans, deserts and all, by following the Silk Road in gentle autumn

BOTH?

GEORGIA P204

SUMATRA & JAVA, INDONESIA P209

Spot rare wildlife in the dramatic, less-visited reserves of northern Kenya

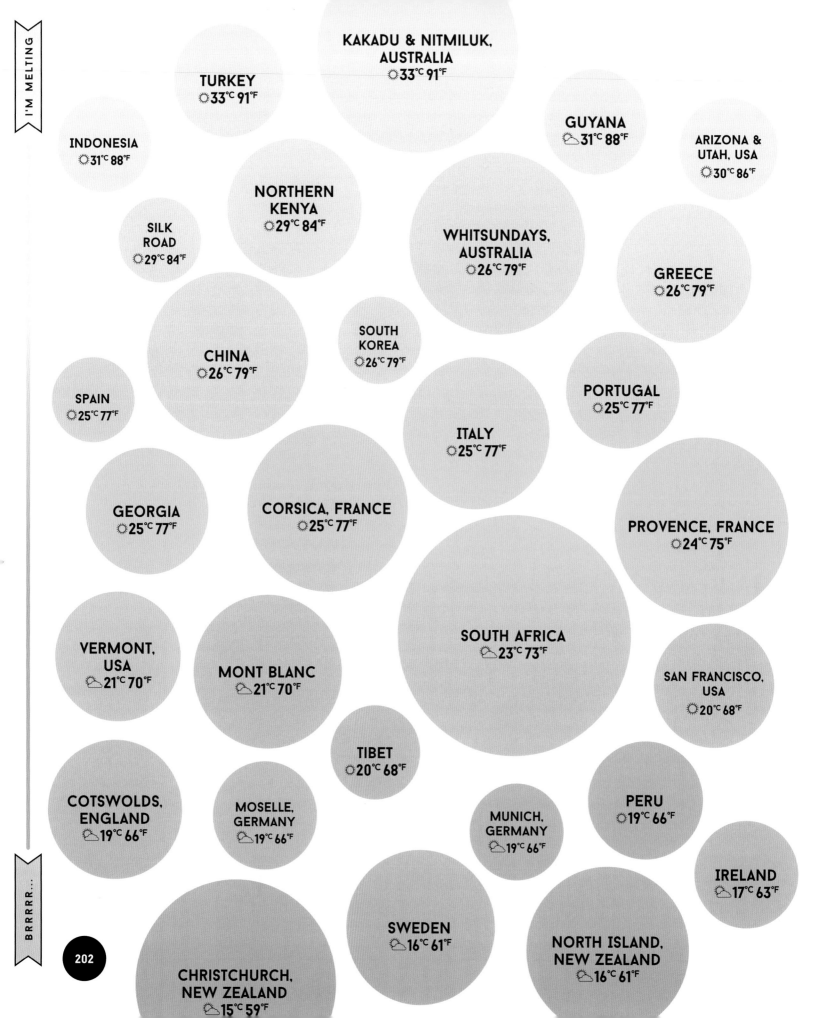

KAKADU & NITMILUK, AUSTRALIA
☀33°C 91°F

TURKEY
☀33°C 91°F

GUYANA
⛅31°C 88°F

INDONESIA
☀31°C 88°F

ARIZONA & UTAH, USA
☀30°C 86°F

NORTHERN KENYA
☀29°C 84°F

SILK ROAD
☀29°C 84°F

WHITSUNDAYS, AUSTRALIA
☀26°C 79°F

GREECE
☀26°C 79°F

CHINA
☀26°C 79°F

SOUTH KOREA
☀26°C 79°F

PORTUGAL
☀25°C 77°F

SPAIN
☀25°C 77°F

ITALY
☀25°C 77°F

GEORGIA
☀25°C 77°F

CORSICA, FRANCE
☀25°C 77°F

PROVENCE, FRANCE
☀24°C 75°F

SOUTH AFRICA
⛅23°C 73°F

VERMONT, USA
⛅21°C 70°F

MONT BLANC
⛅21°C 70°F

SAN FRANCISCO, USA
☀20°C 68°F

TIBET
☀20°C 68°F

COTSWOLDS, ENGLAND
⛅19°C 66°F

MOSELLE, GERMANY
⛅19°C 66°F

MUNICH, GERMANY
⛅19°C 66°F

PERU
☀19°C 66°F

IRELAND
⛅17°C 63°F

SWEDEN
⛅16°C 61°F

NORTH ISLAND, NEW ZEALAND
⛅16°C 61°F

CHRISTCHURCH, NEW ZEALAND
⛅15°C 59°F

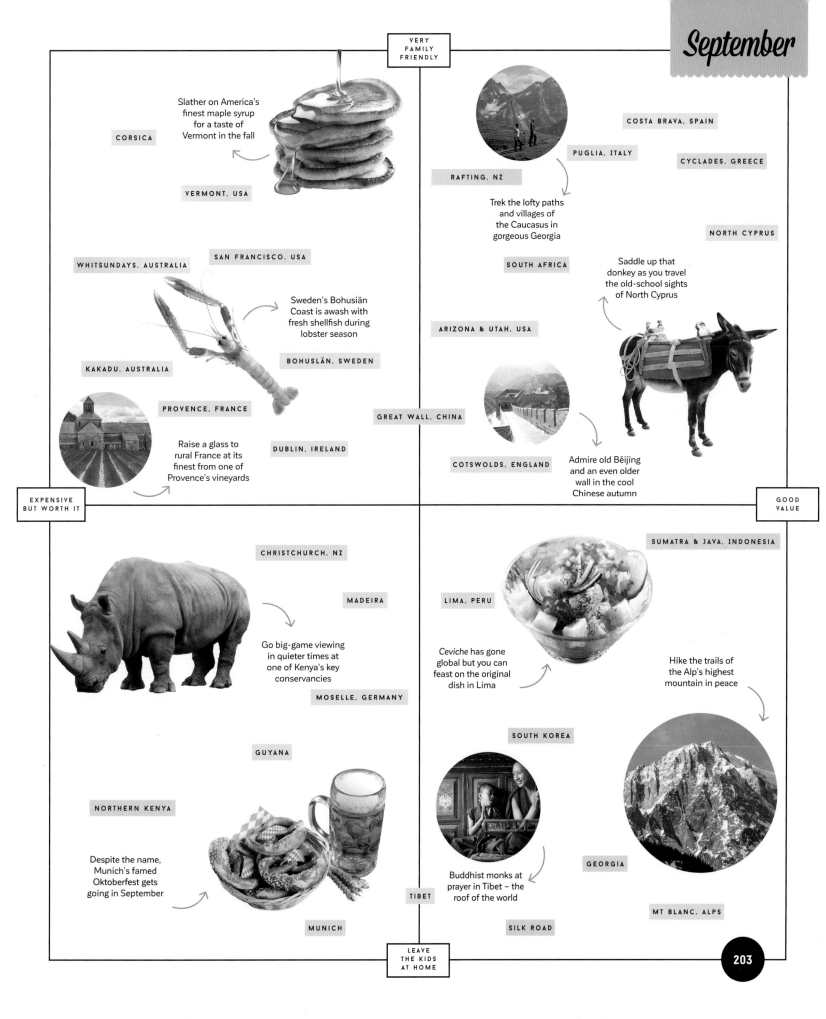

VERY FAMILY FRIENDLY

Slather on America's finest maple syrup for a taste of Vermont in the fall

CORSICA

VERMONT, USA

COSTA BRAVA, SPAIN

PUGLIA, ITALY

CYCLADES, GREECE

RAFTING, NZ

Trek the lofty paths and villages of the Caucasus in gorgeous Georgia

NORTH CYPRUS

WHITSUNDAYS, AUSTRALIA

SAN FRANCISCO, USA

SOUTH AFRICA

Saddle up that donkey as you travel the old-school sights of North Cyprus

Sweden's Bohusiän Coast is awash with fresh shellfish during lobster season

ARIZONA & UTAH, USA

BOHUSLÄN, SWEDEN

KAKADU, AUSTRALIA

PROVENCE, FRANCE

GREAT WALL, CHINA

Raise a glass to rural France at its finest from one of Provence's vineyards

DUBLIN, IRELAND

COTSWOLDS, ENGLAND

Admire old Běijing and an even older wall in the cool Chinese autumn

EXPENSIVE BUT WORTH IT

GOOD VALUE

CHRISTCHURCH, NZ

SUMATRA & JAVA, INDONESIA

MADEIRA

LIMA, PERU

Go big-game viewing in quieter times at one of Kenya's key conservancies

Ceviche has gone global but you can feast on the original dish in Lima

Hike the trails of the Alp's highest mountain in peace

MOSELLE, GERMANY

GUYANA

SOUTH KOREA

NORTHERN KENYA

Despite the name, Munich's famed Oktoberfest gets going in September

Buddhist monks at prayer in Tibet – the roof of the world

GEORGIA

TIBET

MUNICH

SILK ROAD

MT BLANC, ALPS

LEAVE THE KIDS AT HOME

GEORGIA

→ **Why now?** Hike mountain meadows amid ancient monasteries then enjoy great local wine.

Tucked away between the Black Sea and the high Caucasus, south of Russia, north of Turkey, Georgia is a land where stone watchtowers guard verdant valleys, ancient churches nestle beneath lofty peaks, and – so legend says – wine was first created 7000 years ago. The soft shades of September signal the welcome start of autumn in Georgia; in the lowlands the punishing heat of summer has subsided, fall hues are beginning to spread, and the grape harvest in the eastern region of Kakheti is a siren call to sample some of the country's finest vintages.

Trip plan: Start in capital Tbilisi, its traditional balconied houses guarded by ancient Narikala Fortress. Head east into Kakheti for some wine-tasting, then into the peaks of the Caucasus around Kazbegi to discover remote churches, and west into the Svaneti region to trek the high paths among villages guarded by medieval *koshkebi* (defensive stone towers). Descend to ancient Colchis, where according to Greek myth Jason found the golden fleece, and return to Tbilisi via the vast cave monastery of Vardzia.

Need to know: Check your government's travel advice before visiting the regions of Abhkazia and South Ossetia, which have declared independence.

Other months: May-Jun & Sep-Oct – warm, sunny; Jul-Aug – hot and humid in lowlands; Nov-Apr – highlands cold.

- Cultural
- Adventure
- Food & drink
- Journey

Vineyard and Alaverdi Cathedral, backed by the Caucasus Mountains

NORTH CYPRUS

→ **Why now?** Sun, sand, turtles, time travel.

Visiting the northern half of divided Cyprus is a bit like holidaying in the 1970s. It might lack a certain slickness, but there's also a pleasing lack of development. Some of the Med's most unspoilt sands are here, especially along the wild Karpaz Peninsula, where you're more likely to see donkeys and turtles than other people. Indeed, turtles visit North Cyprus regularly, and from June to late September, the Society for the Protection of Turtles runs guided, eco-sensitive night tours to view them from its base at Alagadi Beach, just east of Kyrenia's harbour. September is a fine time to visit: the crowds have gone but weather and waters are warm. It's ideal for hiking between ruined Crusader castles in the Kyrenia range or strolling the well-preserved ancient city of Salamis. Don't miss Lefkoşa, the world's only divided capital. Amble the minaret-speared streets before passing a checkpoint for a weird wander into the bullet-scarred no man's land that separates Turkish north and Greek south.

Trip plan: Spend a week mixing beaches, ruins, castles and traditional villages.

Need to know: Fly to Ercan Airport (North Cyprus) via mainland Turkey.

Other months: Apr-May & Sep-Oct – warm, quieter; Jun-Aug – hottest, busy; Nov-Mar – cool, wettest.

▦	Relaxation
▦	Cultural
■	Value

SOUTH KOREA

→ **Why now?** Experience serenity with a temple stay among fall foliage.

'Live Like the Wind and Water, then Leave Your Body!' That's the promise of a temple-stay at Haeinsa. This 1200-year-old Unesco-listed Buddhist complex is famed for the Tripitaka Koreana, an incredible collection of 81,258 wooden printing blocks bearing the Buddhist sutra, carved in the 13th century. A short stay makes an unforgettable centrepiece to a visit to the Republic of Korea – especially in warm, dry September, when tourist numbers thin, prices fall and amber leaves presage the arrival of autumn. Be dizzied by hyper-modern cities, including capital Seoul, and indulge in *kimchi* and other Korean cuisine, but also spend a few days in a mountain temple to glimpse the country's ancient soul.

Trip plan: From Incheon international airport, visit Changdeokgung Palace and the bustling Namdaemun and Dongdaemun markets in Seoul, peer across the Demilitarised Zone, see Gyeongju's historic sites and Busan's beaches, explore volcanic Jeju-do island and enjoy the peace of a templestay at Haeinsa.

Need to know: For an insight into traditional life, time your visit for Chuseok, the Korean thanksgiving festival honouring ancestors.

Other months: Jun-Aug – hot, wet; Sep-Nov – warm, dry; Dec-Feb – cold, skiing; Mar-May – warm, cherry and azalea blooms.

▦	Cultural
▦	Personal growth
■	Wildlife & nature
▦	Food and drink

RAFTING
NEW ZEALAND

→ **Why now?** Raft the wildest whitewater.

Don your lifejacket and grab your paddle in September to raft New Zealand's surging rivers, as spring rainfall and mountain meltwater set some of the country's most thrilling whitewater surging. On the South Island, the Shotover near Queenstown and the Rangitata southwest of Christchurch run high and strong in spring, as snow melts in the Southern Alps. For an accessible high, try the Kaituna River, which plunges 23ft (7m) down Tutea Falls – reputedly the world's highest commercially raftable waterfall. In September the Kaituna is engorged by heavy spring rains around Rotorua, and being among the country's warmest rivers, it's a comfortable temperature to raft now, when the native rainforest in the gorge is lush and green. If you do feel the post-thrill chill after a day of rafting, warm up afterwards in a steaming thermal pool in Rotorua.

Trip plan: Several rafting operators run day trips from Rotorua.

Need to know: Bear in mind that some rapids are best at low water, when more rocks are exposed, and others have limited periods of whitewater: the Wairoa – a Grade V ride between Matamata and Tauranga – runs on only 26 days each year when the hydro dam is opened.

Other months: Sep-Apr – most commercial rafting trips operate; May-Aug – cold, few rafting trips.

▦	Adventure
▦	Wildlife & nature

GUYANA

→ **Why now?** Admire roaring waterfalls and rainforest wildlife.

Guyana is an extraordinary land, where turtles nest on shell beaches, jaguars stalk the rainforest, giant otters frolic and huge harpy eagles soar over thundering waterfalls. Its climate is also extraordinary, with multiple rainy seasons hitting coast and interior at different times. September is a junction month, when most of the country is dry after the heavy rains, making road travel easier and life more comfortable in general, but with jungles at their lushest. The big-ticket attraction is Kaieteur Falls, which plummets 741ft (226m) in a single drop into the depths of the rainforest. Add to that the canopy walkway and wildlife of Iwokrama, ecolodges offering encounters with Makushi indigenous peoples, the otters of the Rupununi and the cowboys of vast Dadanawa Ranch, and you have an epic adventure in the making.

Trip planner: Booking an organised tour – with a group or tailor-made – is the way to go. A typical two-week itinerary visits coastal capital Georgetown, Kaieteur Falls, the rainforest at Iwokrama, the Amerindian village at Surama, and a chance to meet the giant otters at Karanambu.

Need to know: Malaria is a problem, and mosquitoes are pesky in any case – cover up and use insect repellent.

Other months: Feb-Apr & Sep-Nov – mostly dry, hot; May-Aug & Dec-Jan – wet (Apr-Aug: interior wet).

- ■ Wildlife & nature
- ▨ Journey
- ■ Cultural

© Rostislav Sedlacek / Shutterstock

MONT BLANC
SWITZERLAND, FRANCE & ITALY

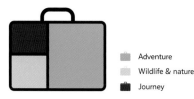

→ **Why now?** Hike the trails in sunshine and peace.

The highest mountain in the Alps looks spectacular from any angle – so why not view it from them all? The idea of hiking a circuit around Mont Blanc isn't a new one – it's 250 years since Horace Bénédict de Saussure set out with friends to trace the loop in 1767. And since Victorian times it's become the benchmark for Alps trails, attracting hordes of hikers. Most, though, come in July and August, so by September the paths are quiet and refuges and other accommodation are no longer bulging at the seams, yet the weather is settled and warm. Typically trekkers start from Les Houches (France) and walk in an anticlockwise direction, heading through France, Italy and then Switzerland to cover the most popular 105-mile (169km) route over 10 to 12 days.

Trip plan: Geneva is the most convenient airport, with buses to Les Houches running several times a day. Trains run from Paris and Geneva to St-Gervais-Les-Bains, from where local trains serve Les Houches.

Need to know: If walking the route clockwise rather than anti-clockwise, it's advisable to begin at Champex (Switzerland) rather than Les Houches to avoid starting with a daunting ascent.

Other months: Nov-May – snow on the trails; Jun & Oct – may be possible; Jul-Sep – paths likely to be snow free (mid-Jul–Aug: busiest).

- ■ Adventure
- ▨ Wildlife & nature
- ■ Journey

MOSELLE VALLEY
GERMANY

→ **Why now?** Cruise or hike one of Germany's most beautiful rivers.

A gorgeous ribbon of water snakes through Germany, its banks striped with vineyards and ridges topped with fairytale castles. No, not the Rhine – rather, its pretty tributary, the Moselle, which enjoys most of the former's attributes but without the cargo ships and tourist traffic. Emerging from Luxembourg near the ancient city of Trier (blessed with impressive Roman remains), the Moselle winds between medieval towns such as Bernkastel-Kues, Traben-Trarbach, Beilstein and Cochem before meeting the Rhine at Koblenz. September is the ideal time to trace its meanders: the grape harvest is celebrated with wall-to-wall festivals and tasting opportunities. Both visitor numbers and rainfall are lower this month, too. Fancy offsetting your wine with walking? Try a section of the recently waymarked Moselsteig footpath alongside the river.

Trip plan: Many cruises combine the Rhine and Moselle rivers. From May to October scheduled boats link towns along the Moselle several times daily; it's easy to plot your own oenophile odyssey.

Need to know: Canoeing the Moselle is a popular option, with dozens of canoe-hire outfits, campsites and spots to climb out and taste local wines.

Other months: Jul-Aug – summer, busy; Sep-Oct – also popular; Nov-Mar – many facilities closed; Apr-Jun, warmer.

- ■ Food & drink
- ▨ Journey
- ■ Cultural
- ▨ Adventure

White rhino on the
Laikipia Plateau, Kenya

The Jiankou section
of the Great Wall
of China

Java's Borobudur,
monument looms
large, and looks out
to Merapi volcano

NORTHERN KENYA

→ **Why now?** Spot rare wildlife in dramatic, less-visited reserves.

North of Mt Kenya stretch the Laikipia Plateau and eventually the Samburu National Reserve. Never heard of them? Exactly – that's why this area of kopje-studded plains and acacia-clad hills is a dream. Whereas in the Masai Mara at peak times each lion might be ringed by a dozen mini-buses, in the reserves and community-run conservancies of northern Kenya you'll probably be alone with the wildlife (and local Maasai and Samburu peoples). That's especially true in September, after the height of the season when safarigoers flock to Kenya to see the Great Migration, but before the rains. Prices fall with tourist numbers, which is good for the wallet as well as for wildlife watching. But this is no second-rate experience: as well as the biggies – lions, cheetahs, elephants, rhinos black and white – you might spot endangered species such as wild dog and Grevy's zebra.

Trip plan: Domestic airlines fly to Lewa Downs and Samburu from Wilson Airport, Nairobi. Rates at safari lodges usually include most wildlife-watching activities, meals and drinks, but not airstrip transfers.

Need to know: Daily conservation fees are payable at most reserves and community conservancies – when booking, check whether these are included in accommodation rates.

Other months: Jun-Oct – warm, dry; Nov-Dec – 'short rains'; Jan-Mar – hot, fairly dry; Apr-May – 'long rains'.

BĚIJĪNG & THE GREAT WALL
CHINA

→ **Why now?** Admire old Běijīng and an even older wall in the autumn.

The people of Běijīng have an epithet describing this season: *tian gao qi shuang* – 'The sky is high and the air is fresh'. After the steamy heat of summer, September brings relief with mellowing temperatures and falling humidity, a window of calm between summer and the national holiday in the first week of October. So get out now to wander its traditional *hútòng* (alleys), perhaps watching old men crouched around a table battling it out with mah-jong or cards, and to explore the city's treasures: the Forbidden City's gates, halls and museums, Tiān'ānmén Sq, the Summer Palace, and the many temples and parks. Autumn is the perfect time to visit the Great Wall, too, when maples are in their fiery fall finery; busy Bādálǐng is picturesque, but other wall sections at Mùtiányù, Sīmǎtái and Huánghuā are quieter and also rewarding.

Trip plan: Beijing's varied sights – old and startlingly modern – merit several days. Regular departures to various wall sections run from Dongzhimen Bus Station.

Need to know: To avoid crowds, visit the wall on a weekday. Mid-Autumn Festival (late September) is also busy with mooncake-munching holidaymakers.

Other months: Jun-Aug – hot, humid; Sep-Oct – cooler, dry; Nov-Feb – very cold; Mar-May – windy, sandstorms.

SUMATRA & JAVA
INDONESIA

→ **Why now?** Meet orangutans and explore rainforest, volcanoes and ancient temples.

Indonesia is part of the world's largest archipelago, and is packed with wonders as you'd imagine. Visit the westernmost islands of Sumatra and Java for a relatively compact taster. September offers the best overall conditions: mostly dry, with great surf off the west coast but lower visitor numbers and even cheaper prices. In the north of rainforest-clad Sumatra, meet the 'man of the forest' at Bohorok Orangutan Centre and tube the Bohorok river at Bukit Lawang. Berastagi is the base for ascents of Sibayak volcano, while at Danau Toba you can swim in the world's largest volcanic crater lake and admire traditional sheer-roofed Batak architecture. Across on Java, admire ancient Prambanan and Borobudur, reputedly the world's largest Buddhist temple, and hike among the smoking triple craters-within-a-supercrater of Mt Bromo.

Trip plan: Fly (or ferry from Penang) to Medan, then overland to Bukit Lawang and south to Berastagi, Danau Toba and Bukittinggi before flying from Padang to Jakarta. Take another flight or train to cultural capital Yogyakarta for the temples, and on to Bromo.

Need to know: The far north of Sumatra catches more rain in September – take a raincoat to Medan and Bukit Lawang.

Other months: May-Sep – dry; Oct-Apr – wet, regional variations.

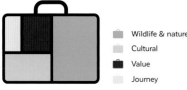

- Wildlife & nature
- Cultural
- Value
- Journey

- Cultural
- Food & drink

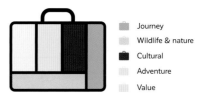

- Journey
- Wildlife & nature
- Cultural
- Adventure
- Value

The clifftop town of Bonifacio, Corsica

WHITSUNDAY ISLANDS
AUSTRALIA

All smiles, a dive instructor waiting to take the plunge in the Whitsundays

Why now? Learn to dive in bath-warm, translucent waters.

Some places are easy sells for tourist boards. Exhibit A: the Whitsundays, a string of 74 emeralds ringed with white gold, afloat in warm turquoise seas sheltered by the Great Barrier Reef. See? September, with rain-free days and clear seas, is prime time to explore. Many visitors simply loll on the deck of a yacht or find a patch of pristine sand – perhaps Whitehaven, which regularly tops world's-best-beach polls – but this is also a great place to learn to dive or develop your sub-aqua skills with short courses and liveaboard dive vessels cruising among the islands and out to the Great Barrier Reef. As well as seeing countless dazzling reef fish, you could observe sea turtles, sharks, dolphins and manta rays, which feed around the fringing reefs from May to September.

Trip plan: Airlie Beach and nearby Shute Harbour are hopping-off points for day trips, cruises, dive boats and island transfers. Hamilton Island and Whitsunday Coast Airport at Proserpine have flights from various Australian cities.

Need to know: The Great Barrier Reef proper is about 50 nautical miles (93km) – a two-hour boat journey – east of the Whitsunday Islands.

Other months: Dec-Mar – hot, humid; Apr-May – warm, showers; Jun-Sep – mild, dry (Jul-Aug: busy); Oct-Nov – hotter, some showers.

- Relaxation
- Adventure
- Wildlife & nature

CORSICA
FRANCE

→ **Why now?** The Île de Beauté is beautifully un-busy.

There's barely a straight road on the wildly rumpled Mediterranean isle of Corsica. Tarmac has to twist around mountains and through the herby maquis shrubland that blankets the interior. As such, you don't want to tackle these roads in high summer, when the whole of France decamps to Corsica's gorgeous shores. Instead, wait until September, when the air and sea are still warm, and the beaches – arguably Europe's best – are empty again. Also amble the precipitous, cliff-perched town of Bonifacio; feel the introspective vibe in hilltop Sartène; hit the Napoleon trail in lively Ajaccio, birthplace of Napoleon Bonaparte; or tour the tiny fishing ports of offbeat Cap Corse. The seemingly impenetrable interior is laced with hiking trails, including the tough but epic GR20. Tackle it all, or just a section, or book a villa in the hills, crack a Pietra beer, nibble brocciu cheese and simply contemplate the wilderness instead.

Trip plan: With one week, concentrate on one area: the north (Calvi, Île-Rousse, Bastia) or south (Propriano, Bonifacio, Porto-Vecchio). The 112-mile (180km) GR20 takes 15 days.

Need to know: Ferries sail to Corsica from France and Italy; journey time is from four to six hours.

Other months: Jul-Aug – hottest, busiest; Apr-Jun & Sep-Oct – warm, quieter; Nov-Mar – cool, some facilities close.

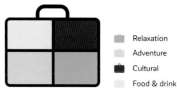

- Relaxation
- Adventure
- Cultural
- Food & drink

MADEIRA
PORTUGAL

→ **Why now?** Chill out or climb the levadas in warm autumn sunshine.

It's Portugal, but it's Africa. Madeira, a rugged speck adrift in the Atlantic, is closer to Morocco than to its motherland, as the year-round sunshine attests. This subtropical beauty is best known for its eponymous wine (celebrated with a festival in early September), but is also renowned as a paradise for hikers. Early autumn offers ideal weather for stepping out along the network of *levadas* – old irrigation channels – leading into the wild mountains and vertiginous valleys: cool enough at lower levels, warm enough at altitudes of 5900ft (1800m) or more. If you prefer to keep your shoes off, big Atlantic swells provide surf for experienced board-riders at spots such as Jardim do Mar, though beginners can find a gentler introduction at Fajã da Areia.

Trip planner: The main town, Funchal, deserves a few days – ride the toboggan down from Monte, and nose around the fishing harbour of Câmara de Lobos. Then branch out to explore the island's paths, historic villages and surf breaks.

Need to know: Madeira's beaches are mostly stony or black volcanic affairs; for a 5-mile (8km) stretch of sand, head to sister island Porto Santo, 2¼ hours by ferry or a 25-minute flight away.

Other months: Year-round – though cooler and wetter Oct-Mar.

- Relaxation
- Adventure
- Cultural
- Food & drink

SILK ROAD
CENTRAL ASIA

→ **Why now?** Traverse the 'Stans in mellow autumn.

Traders had been criss-crossing Asia for over 1200 years before Marco Polo's 13th-century odyssey to the court of Kublai Khan in Běijīng. The allure of the Silk Road hasn't waned, especially Central Asia between the Caspian Sea and the ancient trading city of Kashgar in west China, where conditions are best in September – not meltingly hot in Turkmenistan's deserts of or the fabled cities of Uzbekistan, not too snowy in the mountains and turquoise lakes of Kyrgyzstan and remote western China.

Trip plan: Popular overland routes run from İstanbul through Turkey and via Iran or Georgia and Azerbaijan to Turkmenistan. Visit the Darvaza gas crater and quirky Ashgabat in Turkmenistan, the tiled medressas and minarets of Samarkand and Khiva in Uzbekistan, the mountain meadows and Song-Köl lake in Kyrgyzstan, and Kashgar's Sunday Market en route to Xī'ān and Běijīng in China. Can't spare three months? Two weeks could take you from Ashgabat to Tashkent (Uzbekistan), or Tashkent to Bishkek (Kyrgyzstan).

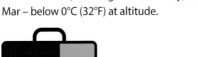

Need to know: You'll need a visa and/or letter of invitation to enter Turkey, Iran, Turkmenistan and China.

Other months: Apr-May & Sep-Nov – moderate heat; Jun-Aug – deserts fiery; Dec-Mar – below 0°C (32°F) at altitude.

- Journey
- Cultural
- Wildlife & nature

COSTA BRAVA
SPAIN

→ **Why now?** Discover the culinary and cultural delights of Catalonia.

While stretches of Spain's southern coast have surrendered to the fly-and-flop brigade, the dramatic shoreline northeast of Barcelona retains its Catalan soul – not to mention palate: it's lauded for its cuisine, including delectable *zarzuela de mariscos* (seafood stew). Sure, there are large resorts towards the south, but at smaller spots such as Llafranc and Tamariu sheltered beaches slope down to the turquoise Mediterranean, particularly appealing in balmy September after the peak of the summer season. There's more to this 'rugged coast' than beaches, though. Explore ancient Greco-Roman remains at Empúries; medieval, castle-capped Begur; and the surreal legacy of Salvador Dalí in his museum at Figueres, castle at Púbol, and house-museum at Portlligat on far-flung Cap de Creus.

Trip plan: Girona receives international flights, and merits exploring before heading to the coast.

Need to know: It would be criminal not to visit Barcelona while on the Costa Brava; if possible, time your stay for the Festes de la Mercè around 24 September, when the streets buzz with crowds cheering *gegants* (giants), *capgrossos* ('big heads') and precarious-looking human castles.

Other months: Jul-Aug – summer, hot, busy; May-Jun & Sep – warm, quieter; Feb-Apr & Oct-Nov – brief rainy periods; Dec-Jan – cooler, wetter.

- Relaxation
- Food & drink
- Cultural

COTSWOLDS
ENGLAND

→ **Why now?** Walk between some of England's loveliest villages in autumn sunshine.

In the golden autumn light of September the Cotswolds seem to simply ooze honey. This land of rolling hills – 'wolds' – hiding wool towns and stone hamlets in their clefts and valleys has long attracted urbanites seeking an idealised English idyll. Visit in September not just to miss the heaviest onslaughts of coach parties, but also to enjoy the countryside at its finest, and to admire the flaming hues at the wonderful arboreta at Westonbirt and Batsford.

True, this is hardly an undiscovered gem; chocolate-box favourites such as Castle Combe and Bourton-on-the-Water can be thronged with tourists. But it's not hard to find peace, especially if you're prepared to stretch your legs: a comprehensive network of footpaths laces the region, while the 102-mile (164km) Cotswold Way runs along the escarpment, linking charming sites between Chipping Campden and Bath.

Trip plan: If you're not hiking, choose a base from which to explore: Broadway in the north, perhaps, for quirky Snowshill Manor, Batsford Arboretum and peaceful, stunning Stanway; or Tetbury in the south, for antiques, historic Malmesbury and Westonbirt.

Need to know: Many attractions, particularly those managed by the National Trust, close or have reduced opening hours November to April.

Other months: Nov-Mar – colder (some facilities closed, villages pretty and quiet in winter); Apr-Oct – mostly warm.

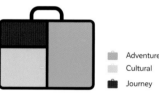

Adventure
Cultural
Journey

© Tom Robinson / Lonely Planet

A well-earned view of the Cotswolds

TIBET

→ Visit holy Buddhist sites in the best weather.

The roof of the world, a land of soaring snow-capped peaks, remote valleys, turquoise lakes and monasteries echoing with Buddhist chants – no wonder Tibet captures the imagination of so many adventurers. It's not the easiest place to travel, physically or politically – special permits may be required on top of a Chinese visa, and journeys can be long and arduous – but the rewards are spectacular, from the imposing bulk of Lhasa's Potala Palace and Jokhang temple complex to remote stupas and jaw-dropping Himalayan vistas. Travel in September to enjoy warm days after the summer rains have eased, prime time for trekking – perhaps the kora (pilgrimage circuit) of holy Mt Kailash, 'navel of the world' – before snow arrives in October.

Trip plan: The classic overland journey from Lhasa to Kathmandu runs via the ancient monasteries of Sera, Gyantse, Ganden, Samye, Tashilhunpo and Rongphu, with its mesmerising views of the north face of Everest. The drive should take about a week, though the Nepal–China border is prone to closure.

Need to know: On first arriving, take time to acclimatise to the high altitude (over 11,500ft; 3500m), and bring warm clothes – temperatures can plummet during a single day.

Other months: Jun-Aug – warm, increasing rain; Sep-Oct – sunny, dry; Nov-Mar – cold, wind rising; Apr-May – warmer, dry.

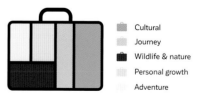

Cultural
Journey
Wildlife & nature
Personal growth
Adventure

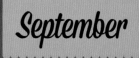

SOUTH AFRICA

→ **Why now? Admire wildlife and wildflowers in spring bloom.**

Visit South Africa in September and it seems as if the whole country has put on a show: the west is festooned with wildflowers; southern right whales gather off Cape Agulhas, southeast of Cape Town, which is warming up nicely; big swells keep rolling in to thrill surfers thanks to the 'Roaring Forties'; and in reserves such as Kruger National Park wildlife gathers around shrinking waterholes. Outside the summer peak, visitor numbers are fairly low and you can enjoy good deals, too.

Trip plan: Time's the limiting factor, but a big circuit might head north from Cape Town through the flower-strewn expanses of Namakwa and the Kalahari to Johannesburg, perhaps via the family-friendly Madikwe Game Reserve. The wildlife of Kruger, iSimangaliso Wetland Park and Big Five-hosting Hluhluwe-Imfolozi Park come next, then turn southwest back towards the Cape – via a hike in the Drakensbergs or along the surf-crashed Wild Coast.

Need to know: The Hermanus Whale Festival, usually held over five days in late September, is a cetacean celebration with boat tours, music, performances, food and drink.

Other months: Sep-Mar – dry around Cape, northeast wetter; Apr-May – largely warm and dry; Jun-Aug – cool and wetter around Cape, northeast dry.

■ Wildlife & nature
□ Journey
■ Cultural

Surf's up on the Wild Coast and wildflowers bloom in Namakwa

BOHUSLÄN
COAST SWEDEN

Why now? Think pink along Sweden's seafood-crazy shore.

Love shellfish? The world's your oyster on West Sweden's Bohuslän coast north of Göteborg (Gothenburg). This tessellated shoreline, noted for its pink granite rocks, produces Sweden's finest seafood. September marks the start of lobster season, the perfect time to explore the 8000 or so islands and rocky islets along the coast, sampling the local langoustine, prawn, mussel, oyster and, of course, those big-clawed crustaceans. Join a 'seafood safari' with fishermen from Smögen to catch and cook your own, or – even better – hire a canoe and paddle among colourful fishing villages such as Gullholmen, Käringön and Fiskebäckskil, stopping off to taste test the area's welcoming eateries: try Salt och Sill in charming Klädesholmen.

Trip plan: Göteborg, Sweden's second city, is the gateway to the Bohuslän coast and has international flights. Travel is easiest with a vehicle, though cycling around local centres is a great idea. Islands are linked to the mainland by bridges or short ferry rides.

Need to know: Don't be alarmed if someone proposes *fika* – Swedes are partial to these regular pauses for coffee and cake.

Other months: Jun-Aug – sunny, busy; May & Sep-Oct – pleasant, quiet; Nov-Apr – cold.

Food & drink
Cultural
Adventure

VERMONT USA

Why now? Be dazzled by fiery autumn colours.

There's gold in them thar hills – plus russet, scarlet, amber and countless other hues. By late September Vermont's hillsides are donning their fiery fall foliage, maples and ashes and aspens and red oaks flaming yellows and reds. Over the course of about six weeks, the whole state becomes awash with colour, starting on the ridges of the Green Mountains and gradually seeping down into the valleys. Driving tours are incredibly popular, but better still saddle up and pedal between the winsome towns and villages of the lower Champlain Valley. Scoot between artsy Brandon, college town Middlebury and Lake Champlain, fuelling up on craft beers, artisan cheeses, and – naturally – America's finest maple syrup.

Trip plan: Rutland airport, convenient for the lower Champlain Valley, has flights from Boston, 150 miles (241km) to the southeast. A good 100-mile (161km), three-day triangular cycle route links historic inns in Brandon, Middlebury and Shoreham.

Need to know: There are long stretches without supplies – if cycling, plan ahead to ensure you have enough food and water.

Other months: Dec-Mar – skiing; Apr & Nov – shoulder, facilities closed; May-Sep – warm; mid-Sep–late Oct – autumn foliage.

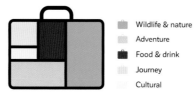

Wildlife & nature
Adventure
Food & drink
Journey
Cultural

MUNICH
GERMANY

Why now? Raise a stein to toast the world's greatest beer festival.

In Bavaria, an alternative holy trinity has been revered for 500 years: water, barley and hops – the only ingredients permitted in beer, according to the purity law (Reinheitsgebot) adopted by the south German state in 1516. In September, aficionados make a pilgrimage to the tent city on Munich's Theresienwiese meadow to drink, sing, drink, dance, drink and… well, you get the idea: over seven million litres of beer are swilled each year. Oktoberfest actually runs for 16 days from mid-September, finishing on the first Sunday in October. Colourfully bedecked horse-drawn brewery carriages brighten up the opening ceremony, followed by an evening concert showcasing traditional folk music and a big procession. There's plenty of Bavarian cuisine on hand to soak up the suds, plus activities to keep the family happy. Don your *dirndl* or *lederhosen*, raise a Maß (one-litre glass) and get glugging.

Trip plan: As you'd imagine, Munich during Oktoberfest gets busy – it pays to book transport, accommodation and a place in a beer tent well in advance.

Need to know: Munich's beer halls are a delight at all times, but particularly during Starkbierzeit in February and March, celebrating the eponymous strong beer.

Other months: Mar-Apr & Sep-Oct – cool; Nov-Feb – very cold, Christmas markets; May-Aug – warm, frequent rain.

Food & drink
Cultural

© Matt Munro / Lonely Planet

The Long Room at Trinity College Library, Dublin

© Andrew Montgomery / Lonely Planet

DUBLIN IRELAND

Why now? Get a taste of the city on the Liffey in the mellowest season.

Dublin in September, often the sunniest month, sees a diminishing numbers of tourists, after the crowds of July and August have dispersed. This city is many things to many people. Yes, you'll find lively pubs (and they deserve detailed examination), historic marvels, humour and national pride, but Dublin is also a cultural powerhouse, boasting magnificent galleries and museums, notably the Chester Beatty Library in Dublin Castle, one of Europe's finest. During September, too, the Irish capital welcomes hundreds of arts performances during the fortnight-long Tiger Dublin Fringe festival.

Trip plan: Wander the genteel streets of the Georgian Southside, admiring the ancient illuminated *Book of Kells* (and the spectacular library in which it's displayed) in Trinity College, mighty Dublin Castle and the arts-and-bars hub of Temple Bar, then sample the Guinness in one (or more) of the famed music-filled bars to experience a night of legendary Irish bonhomie. Repeat till you're out of time, money or stamina…

Need to know: The All-Ireland championship finals of Gaelic football and hurling – reputedly the world's oldest sport – are contested in September at Croke Park.

Other months: Jun-Aug – warmest, dry; Sep-Oct – cooler, fairly dry; Nov-Feb – cold; Mar-May – rainy.

■ Cultural
■ Food & drink

BEYOND DUBLIN

POWERSCOURT ESTATE · 11 MILES (17KM) · Grand Palladian mansion, magnificent formal gardens

GLENDALOUGH · 30 MILES (48KM) · Medieval monastic settlement in Wicklow Mountains

BRÚ NA BÓINNE · 35 MILES (56KM) · Huge neolithic passage graves at Newgrange, Dowth and Knowth

KIKENNY · 81 MILES (130KM) · Medieval city, imposing castle

THE CYCLADES
GREECE

The town of Plaka on the island of Milos, the Cyclades

➔ Why now? Island-hop between whitewashed fishing villages and gorgeous beaches.

In the 1970s Aegean island-hopping was a backpacker's rite of passage; today, with flights and fast ferries, it's easier – and more popular – than ever. But despite the numbers of tourists, Greek and foreign, thronging the best-known islands in high season, there's still magic to be found – particularly if you arrive in September, when the weather is still balmy and the seas calm, but prices and visitor numbers fall. You might not have the picture-postcard views across whitewashed, blue-roofed Oia on Santorini to yourself, but on many islands you can find an empty beach, a traditional taverna, and a working harbour with fishing boats bobbing at anchor.

Trip plan: There are international airports on Mykonos and Santorini. A busy ferry network links the islands with each other and to mainland ports including Piraeus for Athens. A tempting itinerary might include Mykonos for nightlife (plus a trip to ancient Delos), Paros for hillside villages, beaches and windsurfing, Naxos for hiking and diving, Santorini for those views from Oia across the crater, and one of the Little Cyclades to step off-grid.

Need to know: Hotels, tavernas and other services on most islands close from mid-October to Orthodox Easter.

Other months: May-Sep – hot (Jul-Aug: busiest); Apr & Oct – mild; Nov-Mar – cool, sleepy.

Relaxation

Journey

Cultural

SAN FRANCISCO
USA

→ **Why now?** Enjoy an Indian summer of love.

You really need a special reason to visit SF at any time? OK, here's one: September is the warmest month – officially. After the midsummer fogs have subsided, the city is also more welcoming, weird, wacky and wonderful than ever, and with crowds subsiding prices slip, too. This is the harvest season, when those multiplying food trucks are laden with fresh fruit and veggies. It's also the season of inspiring events, with the annual Fringe, Chocolate, Blues, Comedy, and Architecture and the City festivals, plus street fairs, and classical and opera galas. Not to mention the season of wandering the steep hills, riding the streetcars and cable cars, roaming the parks, marvelling at the Mission murals, discovering the artsy treats of Fort Mason and generally enjoying the city in the Indian summer.

Trip plan: If you're making a plan for your trip, you're doing it wrong…

Need to know: …unless you want to visit Alcatraz, for which you'll need to book your place on the ferry to the prison island in advance (www.alcatrazcruises.com).

Other months: Mar-May – spring, mild; Jun-Aug – summer, foggy; Sep-Nov – warm, sunny; Dec-Feb – chilly, rainy.

PROVENCE
FRANCE

→ **Why now?** Roam the vineyards during the grape harvest.

France isn't short of vineyards. With more than 300 appellations producing 4.5 billion litres each year, you don't have to go far to find a hillside clad with neat rows of vines. Come September, the pickers are out in force harvesting the grapes in the annual *vendange* – and with fine weather blessing the Provençal countryside, and the masses departed back to the cities, this is a dream month for exploring the region. Villages are bustling, market stalls are laden with autumn produce, and communities celebrate the harvest with festivities. The trickiest challenge is picking where to explore: coastal Cassis or Côtes de Provence, the rocky hills of the Vaucluse or famed Châteauneuf-du-Pape along the Rhône between Orange and former papal seat Avignon?

Trip plan: Make a multiday loop from Avignon, first heading northeast into the Vaucluse to the vineyards and charming hilltop villages beneath mighty Mont Ventoux, before heading west to admire the monumental Roman theatre at Orange and meandering down the Rhône Valley through Châteauneuf-du-Pape.

Need to know: Look out for menus featuring another less-known but delicious Provençal product being harvested in September: *riz rouge* – Camargue red rice.

Other months: Jul-Aug – summer, very busy; Sep-Oct – warm, beautiful light; Nov-Mar – cooler, wetter; Apr-Jun – warm, spring blooms.

Cultural
Food & drink

Food & drink
Cultural
Journey

September is a great month to discover the culinary treats of Lima

LIMA PERU

Why now? Savour the flavours of South America's culinary capital.
Peru's capital is a huge, ancient, chaotic, modern, vibrant contradiction, where Spanish colonial architecture meets pre-Columbian remains and gleaming high-rises. It's also the continent's gastronomic hotspot, with a host of renowned chefs such as Gastón Acurio producing both long-time favourites such as *ceviche* (lime-marinated fish) or *carapulcra* (pork and potato stew) and innovative creations. As Peruvian cuisine makes waves overseas, so its proponents continue to push the envelope in Lima. In September you can discover the latest taste trends at the annual Mistura food festival, with cooking demos, samples of new products and restaurant awards. This is a fine month to explore further afield, too, offering great weather but lower numbers on Inca Trail treks (book well ahead anyway) and at other key sites.

Trip plan: Explore the colonial gems and museums of Centro, including the cathedral and the catacombs of the Monasterio de San Francisco, and visit the pre-Columbian ruins at Pachacamac, 20 miles (32km) to the southeast. Many of the finest restaurants are clustered in the Mirafores and San Isidro districts.

Need to know: Half- and full-day food tours usually include a market visit and a cooking class, learning to prepare *ceviche* and other typical dishes.

Other months: Year round – hottest and driest Apr-Oct.

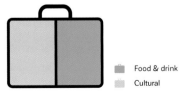

Food & drink
Cultural

KAKADU & NITMILUK
AUSTRALIA

→ **Why now?** Watch profuse birdlife and cool off under waterfalls.

To the indigenous people of Kakadu and Nitmiluk, this hot, dry season (one of six) has a special name: *Gurrung*. September marks a turning point in the calendar – the end of the Dry, but before the humidity cranks up and the Wet begins in earnest. The waters of the Katherine River are warming up, so it's perfect for kayaking the spectacular gorges of Nitmiluk National Park, while the billabongs of adjacent Kakadu National Park are thronged with magpie geese and some 280 other bird species. Visitor numbers are falling, too, so camping grounds and Kakadu's incredible Aboriginal rock-art sites at Nourlangie and Ubirr are quieter, and a dip under Twin Falls that much more special.

Trip plan: With a week to spare, you can explore Kakadu's falls and gorges, wetlands and rock art in depth, and add a day or two kayaking or cruising Nitmiluk. It's 160 miles (257km; about three hours' drive) from Darwin to Kakadu's main service centre at Jabiru; from there, the road south through the park leads towards Hwy 1 to Katherine and the entrance to Nitmiluk. Return to Darwin via Litchfield Natinoal Park.

Need to know: Take local advice before diving into Kakadu's inviting pools – saltwater crocs often lurk.

Other months: May-Oct – dry, cooler; Nov-Apr – wet, humid.

- Wildlife & nature
- Cultural
- Adventure
- Journey

The view while hiking into the Indian Garden, Grand Canyon

© Mark Read / Lonely Planet

ARIZONA & UTAH USA

→ **Why now?** Drive, raft or hike the grandest canyons.

Everything's big about the Grand Canyon: the length (277 miles; 446km), the width (up to 18 miles; 29km), the depth (a mile; 1.6km) – and the crowds, if you visit in high summer. But arrive later in September and not only have the families and summer-vacationers departed, but temperatures are more sensible for tackling one of the walks along the rim or down into the canyon. It's also a great time to raft the Colorado, particularly since motorised launches aren't permitted after 15 September, making for a more peaceful, intimate experience. Similarly, the other big rock stars in northern Arizona and southern Utah – Zion and Bryce Canyons, Canyonlands national parks, Monument Valley – are quieter in September; the later, the better.

Trip plan: A standard loop from Las Vegas via Zion and Bryce Canyons, Arches and Canyonlands national parks, Monument Valley and the Grand Canyon takes one or two weeks, depending on time spent exploring; add several days for whitewater rafting on the Colorado River.

Need to know: For nostalgists, it's possible to drive sections of the old Route 66 bypassed by Interstate 40 in Arizona, notably between Crookton and Topock (http://azrt66.com).

Other months: Dec-Feb – snow closes much of national park; Mar-May & Sep-Nov – cooler, thinner crowds; Apr-Oct – Grand Canyon rafting tours.

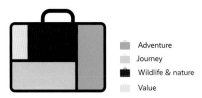

- Adventure
- Journey
- Wildlife & nature
- Value

PUGLIA ITALY

→ **Why now?** For a *trulli* tasty break. Down at heel? Yes and no. Largely agricultural Puglia, the stiletto of the Italian boot, is one of the country's least wealthy regions; traditional Pugliese cuisine is even known as *cucina povera* (poor kitchen). However, it's also a richly satisfying destination – the 'poor' food is delicious, and historic little towns, baroque piazzas, olive groves and sandy shores are abundant. In September, Puglia is the place to lose the crowds, still enjoy warm sunshine and indulge in both autumnal bounty and year-round local specialities, such as Burrata cheese, oricchiette pasta, seafood, endless breads (the Salento region alone has over 100 types). Hunker down in a converted *masserie* (fortified farmhouse) or, better, one of Puglia's *trulli* – mysterious conical limestone dwellings that pepper the peaceful countryside. Explore from your atmospheric base.

Trip plan: Allow one to two weeks, taking in the baroque beauty of Lecce ('Florence of the south'), 13th-century Castel del Monte, the Grotte di Castellana cave network, the unspoilt beaches and forests of the Gargano promontory, the white city of Ostuni and the 400-odd *trulli* of Alberobello, an Unesco World Heritage Site.

Need to know: Bari and Brindisi both have international airports.

Other months: Nov-Apr – cool/cold, wettest; May & Sep-Oct – warm, quieter; Jun-Aug – hottest, busiest.

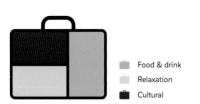

- Food & drink
- Relaxation
- Cultural

(Below) A street lined with traditional *trulli* dwelllings, Puglia; (R) Punting on the River Avon, Hagley Park

© Michael Heffernan / Lonely Planet

CHRISTCHURCH
NEW ZEALAND

Why now? Roam the garden city in spring bloom.

Christchurch was long known as the most English of Kiwi cities, with its punts and elegant architecture. Though the 2010/11 earthquakes flattened swaths of the CBD, today buds of growth are burgeoning: literally, in the daffodils, bluebells and cherry blossoms of Hagley Park and the Botanic Gardens in spring, and metaphorically, as the city centre evolves anew. The punts and blossoms still charm, but delve into the centre, among the building sites and road diversions, to find innovative new bars, pop-up container restaurants and shops, street art, the inspiring 'cardboard cathedral', and quirky Gap Filler projects: bring your mates and an MP3 player, pop two dollars in the Dance-O-Mat and get jiving!

Trip plan: Cycling is a convenient way to explore, with ample bike-sharing and hire opportunities; the new bus interchange offers secure bike storage. Hot areas for interesting bars, eateries and shops include Strange's Lane and southeast High St, Victoria St, Colombo St in Sydenham and the Tannery development.

Need to know: Get terrific views over the city and the Banks Peninsula from the

© Doug Pearson / Getty Images

Christchurch Gondola; regular shuttles depart from Canterbury Museum.

Other months: Dec-Feb – summer; Mar-May & Sep-Nov – cool but pleasant; Jun-Aug – winter; Year-round – rain minimal.

Cultural
Food & drink

BEYOND CHRISTCHURCH

AKAROA • 51 MILES (82KM) • 'French village', good restaurants, dolphin watching

HANMER SPRINGS • 84 MILES (135KM) • Thermal pools, spa village, adventure activities

KAIKOURA • 113 MILES (181KM) • Whale watching, snorkelling with seals, seafood

GREYMOUTH • 144 MILES (231KM) • Journey over Southern Alps via Arthur's Pass

223

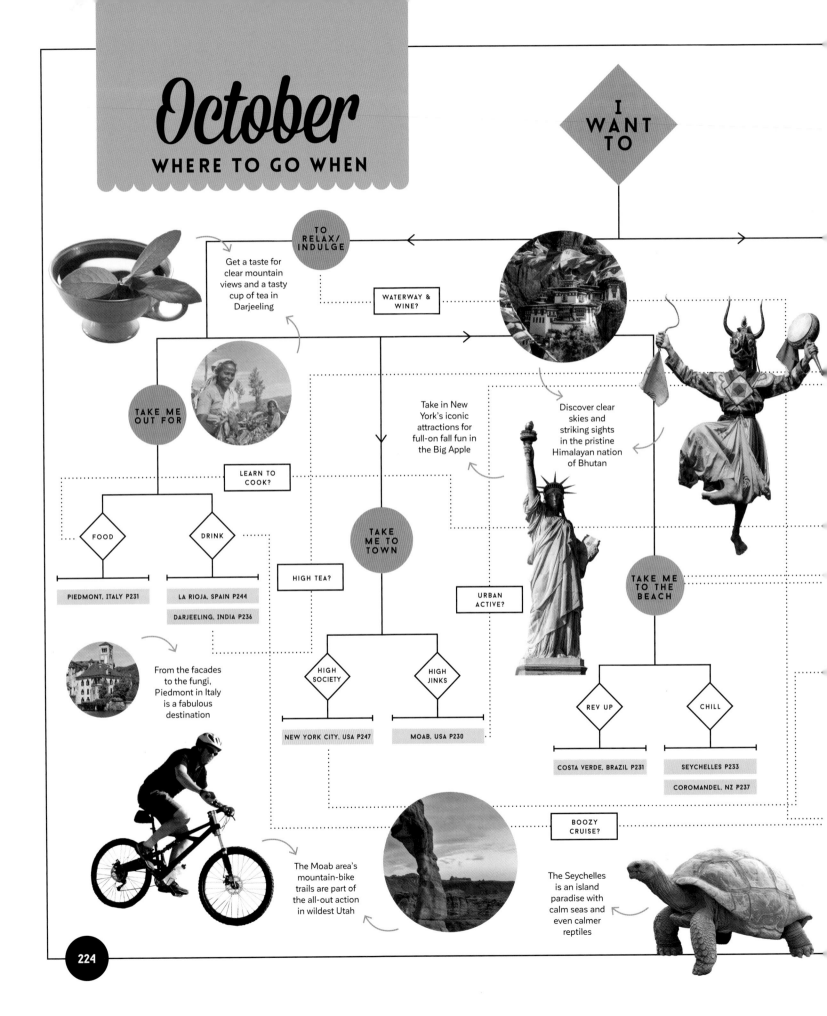

October
WHERE TO GO WHEN

I WANT TO

TO RELAX/ INDULGE

Get a taste for clear mountain views and a tasty cup of tea in Darjeeling

WATERWAY & WINE?

TAKE ME OUT FOR

Take in New York's iconic attractions for full-on fall fun in the Big Apple

Discover clear skies and striking sights in the pristine Himalayan nation of Bhutan

LEARN TO COOK?

FOOD

DRINK

TAKE ME TO TOWN

PIEDMONT, ITALY P231

LA RIOJA, SPAIN P244

DARJEELING, INDIA P236

HIGH TEA?

URBAN ACTIVE?

TAKE ME TO THE BEACH

From the facades to the fungi, Piedmont in Italy is a fabulous destination

HIGH SOCIETY

HIGH JINKS

REV UP

CHILL

NEW YORK CITY, USA P247

MOAB, USA P230

COSTA VERDE, BRAZIL P231

SEYCHELLES P233

COROMANDEL, NZ P237

BOOZY CRUISE?

The Moab area's mountain-bike trails are part of the all-out action in wildest Utah

The Seychelles is an island paradise with calm seas and even calmer reptiles

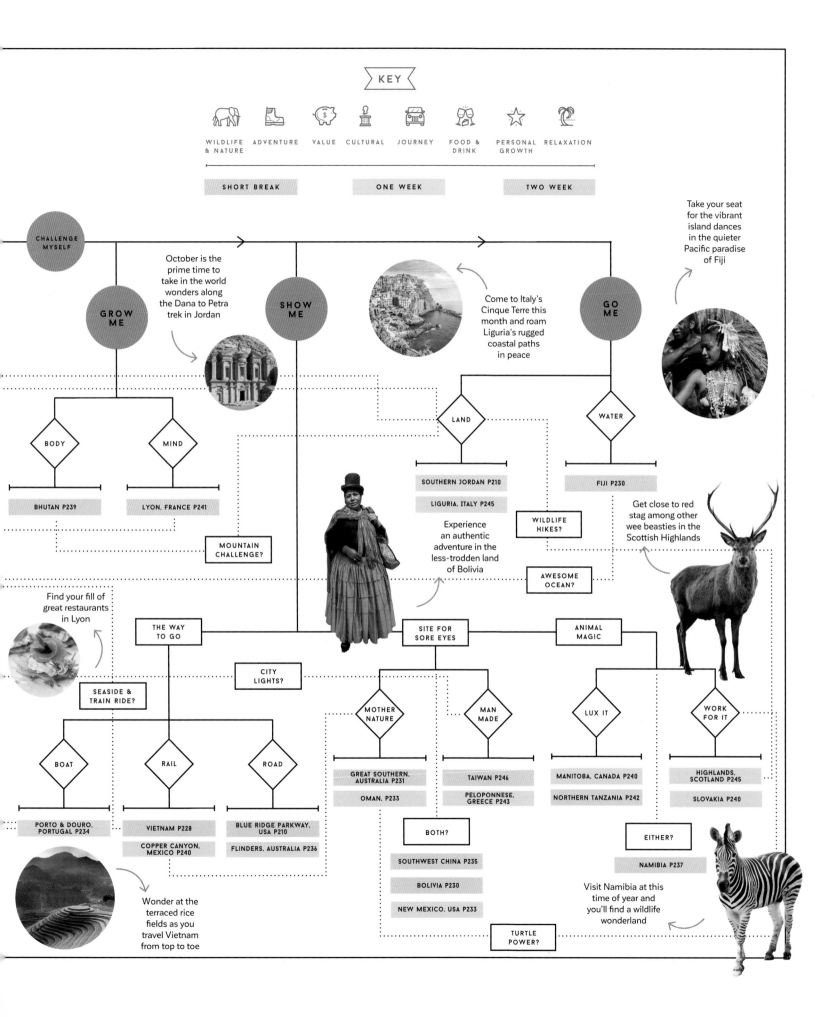

KEY

WILDLIFE & NATURE · ADVENTURE · VALUE · CULTURAL · JOURNEY · FOOD & DRINK · PERSONAL GROWTH · RELAXATION

SHORT BREAK · ONE WEEK · TWO WEEK

CHALLENGE MYSELF

GROW ME

October is the prime time to take in the world wonders along the Dana to Petra trek in Jordan

SHOW ME

Come to Italy's Cinque Terre this month and roam Liguria's rugged coastal paths in peace

GO ME

Take your seat for the vibrant island dances in the quieter Pacific paradise of Fiji

LAND

WATER

BODY

MIND

BHUTAN P239

LYON, FRANCE P241

MOUNTAIN CHALLENGE?

SOUTHERN JORDAN P210

LIGURIA, ITALY P245

Experience an authentic adventure in the less-trodden land of Bolivia

WILDLIFE HIKES?

FIJI P230

Get close to red stag among other wee beasties in the Scottish Highlands

AWESOME OCEAN?

Find your fill of great restaurants in Lyon

THE WAY TO GO

SITE FOR SORE EYES

ANIMAL MAGIC

CITY LIGHTS?

SEASIDE & TRAIN RIDE?

BOAT

RAIL

ROAD

MOTHER NATURE

MAN MADE

LUX IT

WORK FOR IT

PORTO & DOURO, PORTUGAL P234

VIETNAM P228

COPPER CANYON, MEXICO P240

BLUE RIDGE PARKWAY, USA P210

FLINDERS, AUSTRALIA P236

GREAT SOUTHERN, AUSTRALIA P231

OMAN, P233

TAIWAN P246

PELOPONNESE, GREECE P243

MANITOBA, CANADA P240

NORTHERN TANZANIA P242

HIGHLANDS, SCOTLAND P245

SLOVAKIA P240

BOTH?

SOUTHWEST CHINA P235

BOLIVIA P230

NEW MEXICO, USA P233

EITHER?

NAMIBIA P237

Visit Namibia at this time of year and you'll find a wildlife wonderland

Wonder at the terraced rice fields as you travel Vietnam from top to toe

TURTLE POWER?

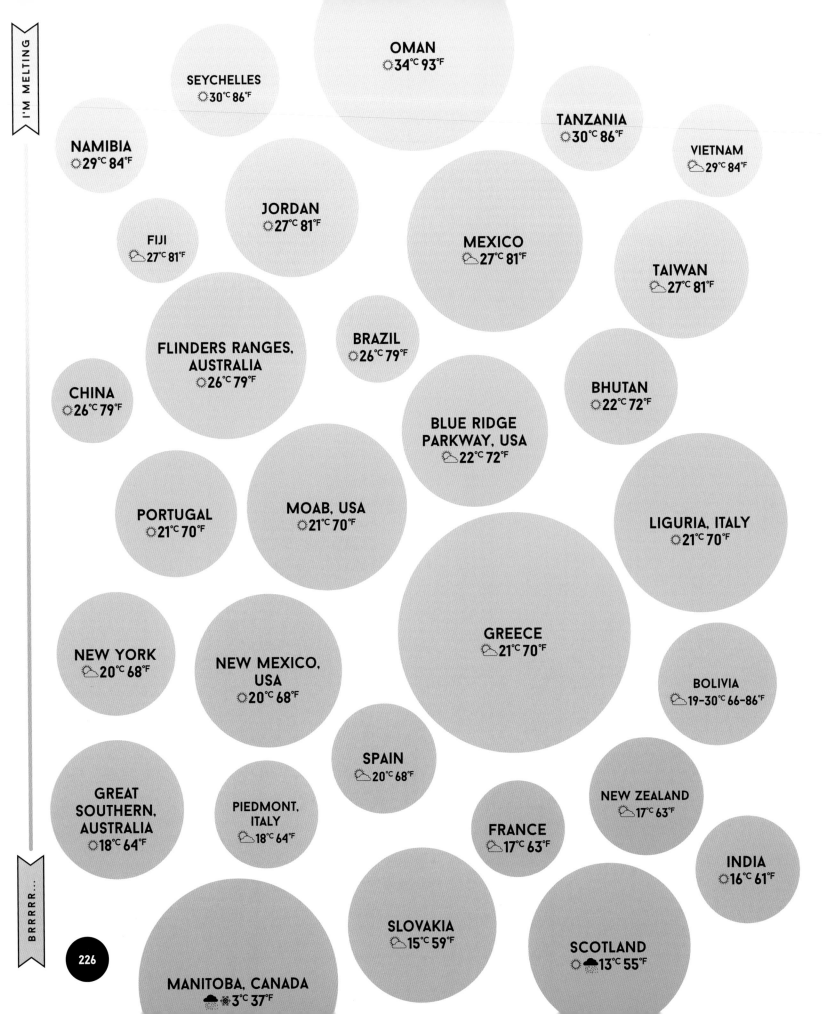

OMAN
☀ 34°C 93°F

SEYCHELLES
☀ 30°C 86°F

TANZANIA
☀ 30°C 86°F

VIETNAM
⛅ 29°C 84°F

NAMIBIA
☀ 29°C 84°F

JORDAN
☀ 27°C 81°F

FIJI
⛅ 27°C 81°F

MEXICO
⛅ 27°C 81°F

TAIWAN
⛅ 27°C 81°F

BRAZIL
☀ 26°C 79°F

FLINDERS RANGES,
AUSTRALIA
☀ 26°C 79°F

BHUTAN
☀ 22°C 72°F

CHINA
☀ 26°C 79°F

BLUE RIDGE
PARKWAY, USA
⛅ 22°C 72°F

PORTUGAL
☀ 21°C 70°F

MOAB, USA
☀ 21°C 70°F

LIGURIA, ITALY
☀ 21°C 70°F

GREECE
⛅ 21°C 70°F

NEW YORK
⛅ 20°C 68°F

NEW MEXICO,
USA
☀ 20°C 68°F

BOLIVIA
⛅ 19–30°C 66–86°F

SPAIN
⛅ 20°C 68°F

GREAT
SOUTHERN,
AUSTRALIA
☀ 18°C 64°F

PIEDMONT,
ITALY
⛅ 18°C 64°F

NEW ZEALAND
⛅ 17°C 63°F

FRANCE
⛅ 17°C 63°F

INDIA
☀ 16°C 61°F

SLOVAKIA
⛅ 15°C 59°F

SCOTLAND
☀🌧 13°C 55°F

MANITOBA, CANADA
☁❄ 3°C 37°F

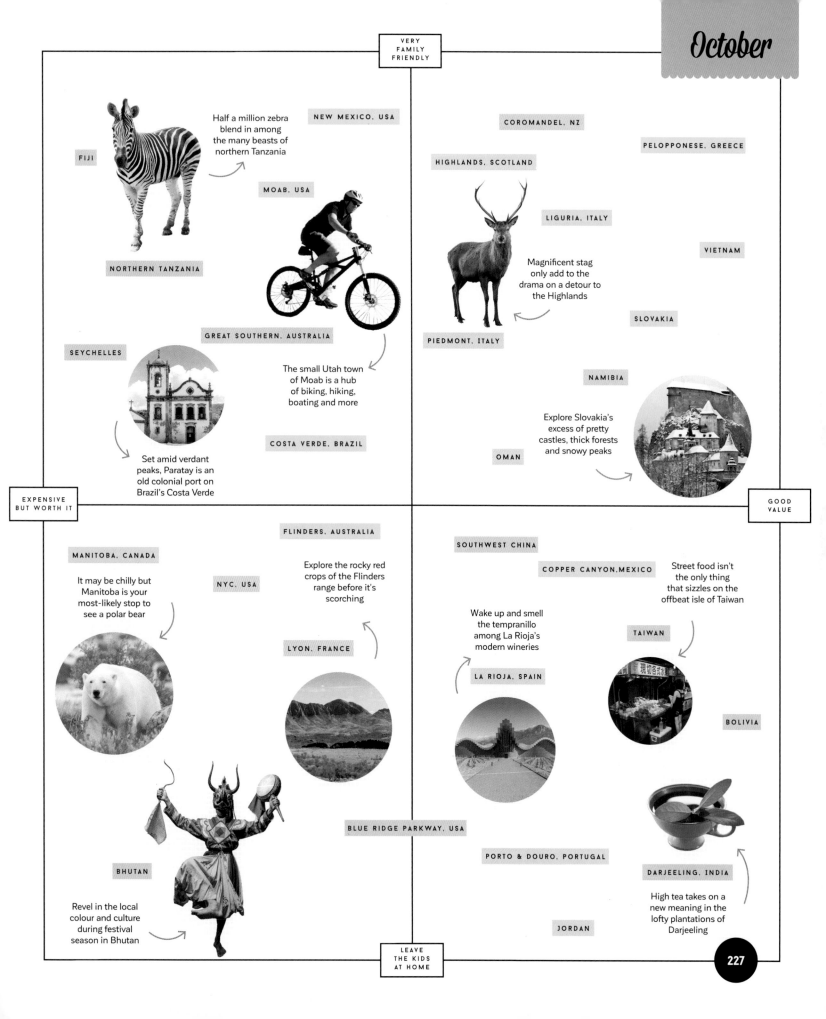

VERY FAMILY FRIENDLY

EXPENSIVE BUT WORTH IT

GOOD VALUE

LEAVE THE KIDS AT HOME

FIJI

NORTHERN TANZANIA

Half a million zebra blend in among the many beasts of northern Tanzania

NEW MEXICO, USA

MOAB, USA

GREAT SOUTHERN, AUSTRALIA

The small Utah town of Moab is a hub of biking, hiking, boating and more

SEYCHELLES

Set amid verdant peaks, Paratay is an old colonial port on Brazil's Costa Verde

COSTA VERDE, BRAZIL

COROMANDEL, NZ

PELOPPONESE, GREECE

HIGHLANDS, SCOTLAND

LIGURIA, ITALY

Magnificent stag only add to the drama on a detour to the Highlands

VIETNAM

SLOVAKIA

PIEDMONT, ITALY

NAMIBIA

Explore Slovakia's excess of pretty castles, thick forests and snowy peaks

OMAN

MANITOBA, CANADA

It may be chilly but Manitoba is your most-likely stop to see a polar bear

FLINDERS, AUSTRALIA

Explore the rocky red crops of the Flinders range before it's scorching

NYC, USA

LYON, FRANCE

BHUTAN

Revel in the local colour and culture during festival season in Bhutan

SOUTHWEST CHINA

COPPER CANYON, MEXICO

Street food isn't the only thing that sizzles on the offbeat isle of Taiwan

Wake up and smell the tempranillo among La Rioja's modern wineries

TAIWAN

LA RIOJA, SPAIN

BOLIVIA

BLUE RIDGE PARKWAY, USA

PORTO & DOURO, PORTUGAL

DARJEELING, INDIA

High tea takes on a new meaning in the lofty plantations of Darjeeling

JORDAN

VIETNAM

→ **Why now: Explore 'Nam from top to bottom.**

Vietnam's quirky climate, with two monsoons in winter and summer, means it's tricky to find the balance between hot, cold, dry and wet. October ticks most boxes: fairly clear weather in the north for Hanoi and Halong Bay, warm enough for trekking around Sapa, drying off around Saigon and the Mekong Delta. It's also low season for tourism: prices dip and hotel availability climbs, so an October visit can be great value – leaving more cash to spend on Vietnam's lip-smacking cuisine; be sure to try a streetside *pho* on your trip.

Trip plan: To make the best of the weather, fly into Hanoi and start with a trek among the hill tribes of the Sapa region and a cruise on Halong Bay or Bai Tu Long Bay. Then head south by train through the historic sites of Hue and Hoi An (carry an umbrella for this bit) to roam seething Saigon, visit the Cu Chi Tunnels and explore the Mekong Delta before hitting the beach at Phu Quoc.

Need to know: To visit Cambodia or Laos on the same trip, be sure to apply for a multi-entry visa.

Other months: South – dry Dec-Apr, rains May-Nov; central coast around Hue – dry Mar-Aug, rains Sep-Feb; north – cold Dec-Mar, wet Apr-Sep, dry and cool Oct-Nov.

■ Journey
■ Cultural
■ Value
■ Food & drink

Cruise ships dot the waters of Halong Bay

229

FIJI

→ **Why now? For a quieter Pacific paradise.**

Fiji is paradise made easy. The most accessible and tourism-attuned outpost of the South Pacific, Fiji has an idyll to suit everyone across its 333 islands. That makes it popular, which is why October is perfect: it's after peak season but still pleasantly cool and dry; you may find cheaper deals, and you will find fewer people. There's white-sand-blue-sea magnificence across the archipelago – the dreamy Yasawa and Mamanuca groups are the most 'developed', but even here no buildings are taller than a coconut palm. You could happily swim, surf, snorkel and loll about at a lively or low-key resort here for weeks. Viti Levu, Fiji's largest island, offers the greatest variety. Make a circuit: drive the coastal Queens Rd and highlands Kings Rd, hike at Sigatoka sand dunes and taste colonial architecture and Fijian-Indian cuisine in capital Suva.

Trip plan: Fly to Nadi (Viti Levu). Boats run from here to various ports on the Yasawas and Mamanucas – pick a base or hop between spots. Allow a week to explore Viti Levu. Divers should head for Astrolabe Reef or Taveuni's waters.

Need to know: English is the official language; 'Bula!' means 'Hello!' in Fijian.

Other months: Jul-Sep – dry, busy; May-Jun & Oct – dry, shoulder seasons, quieter; Nov-Apr – wet, cyclones possible.

- Relaxation
- Adventure
- Cultural
- Value

MOAB USA

→ **Why now? For all-out action in wildest Utah.**

Couch potatoes, take note: Moab is not for you. The main reason to come to this little Utah town (especially in pleasantly mild October) is to leave it – by bike, boot, raft, 4WD or whatever else takes your fancy. First established by Mormon pioneers in the 1850s, Moab is now adventure HQ for a whole lot of world-class wilderness. The town itself is likeable and lively if aesthetically unlovely, but the area around it is lovely indeed. The outdoor playgrounds of Arches and Canyonlands national parks are right on the doorstep: the former is an untouched immensity of crimson sandstone, artfully carved by Mother Nature; the latter a crumple of chasms, cracks, buttes and plateaus. Both are jaw-dropping. The Moab area is also home to countless mountain-bike trails, not least the Slickrock, a tough, twisty 9-mile (15km) loop across the Sand Flats' Navajo sandstone. Prefer water? Rafting trips along the Colorado River run April to October.

Trip plan: Spend four or five action-packed days, mixing up hikes, bikes and more.

Need to know: Salt Lake City to Moab is a four-hour drive.

Other months: Apr-May & Sep-Oct – mild; Jun-Aug – hot; Nov-Mar – cool/cold.

- Adventure
- Wildlife & nature

BOLIVIA

→ **Why now? For a proper adventure.**

Many travellers on a grand tour of South America expect to be wowed by Peru or Brazil, but come away loving understated Bolivia the most. Diverse, dramatic, even verging on the inaccessible, the country remains unspoilt; some say it's the continent at its most authentic. Certainly it's the continent in microcosm: snowy Andean highs, steamy Amazon lows, surreal lakes, salt flats, colonial treasures and remnants of ancient civilisations are all found here. The dry, winter season is the most comfortable time to travel. In October, the end of the dry, all roads should be mud-free and passable, while skies are brilliant blue, temperatures are warming and peak-season crowds have gone. Negotiating the mountains and raw, breath-stealing altiplano can still be arduous, but you're guaranteed a true adventure.

Trip plan: A trip of two to three weeks might include lofty La Paz, an Amazon eco-stay, Lake Titicaca, the pre-Columbian ruins of Tiwanaku, colonial Sucre, Potosi's silver mine, the shimmering Salar de Uyuni salt flats and the multi-coloured altiplano lakes. Consider adding the Che Guevara sites around La Higuera and the Jesuit missions of Chiquitos.

Need to know: Bolivia is cheap; budget travellers could get by on US$15 a day.

Other months: May-Oct – dry, cooler, busy (busiest Jun-Sep); Nov-Apr – wet, hotter, humid.

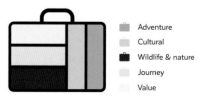

- Adventure
- Cultural
- Wildlife & nature
- Journey
- Value

GREAT SOUTHERN
AUSTRALIA

Why now? It's blooming marvellous. The great thing about the 'Great Southern' is that it's a bit too far away. Encompassing a hunk of the southwest coast and hinterland from Denmark to Esperance, it's not really doable in a weekend from Perth, leaving its vineyards, mountains and squeaky-white beaches mostly tourist-free outside peak season. October is a good choice: winter rains have finished and the countryside is alive with wildflowers; from vanilla lilies to pixie mops, more than 4000 flowering species grow hereabouts, 80 percent of which are endemic. See them in the Porongurup Range and Fitzgerald River National Park. Whales are also gliding by – take a boat trip from Albany, or watch from land at Bremer Bay. The further east you go, the wilder things get. Forge towards Esperance, where flaming outback meets cerulean Southern Ocean; nearby is Lucky Bay, Australia's whitest beach.

Trip plan: Time poor? Focus on the Rainbow Coast (Walpole–Denmark–Albany). Climb huge karri trees, slurp at Denmark's wineries and visit Albany's National Anzac Centre (the first Anzac troops departed for WWI from here). More time? Continue to Esperance and the Recherche Archipelago.

Need to know: Perth to Albany is 261 miles (420km; 4½-hour drive); Perth to Esperance is 472 miles (760km; 9½ hour).

Other months: Sep-Nov – flowers (whales Jul-Nov); Dec-Feb – hot, busy; Mar-May – autumn, harvest; Jun-Aug – dry, cooler.

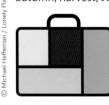

- Wildlife & nature
- Journey
- Relaxation
- Food & drink

COSTA VERDE
BRAZIL

Why now? To go green. Rio de Janeiro gets called the Cidade Maravilhosa (Marvellous City), but really, it's the Marvellous State – the namesake province around the metropolis is equally good-looking. Indeed, just west lies the Costa Verde, where jungly hills and waterfalls tumble to a sparkling blue-green sea. Make a beeline for Paraty (186 miles, or 300km, from Rio), an elegant 18th-century colonial port set against mountains, where the cobbled streets are traffic free, bright-painted boats zip about the bay, and cafes serve up succulent seafood. Then make a break for Ilha Grande – formerly a leper colony and prison, now a Mother Nature–ruled chill-out retreat. There are no cars, and just a few settlements. Book into a *pousada* and spend days hiking trails into the island's Atlantic rainforest and hopping between its 102 beaches. October, when spring temperatures rise (27°C; 81°F) but peak season has yet to start, is a good choice.

Trip plan: Spend a few days in Rio, then head along the Emerald Coast. Combine time on Paraty's beaches with forays into Serra da Bocaina National Park before taking the ferry to Ilha Grande.

Need to know: Buses depart Rio for Angra dos Reis (for Ilha Grande ferries) and Paraty.

Other months: Nov-Mar – hottest, busiest, rainier; Apr-Oct – cooler, drier.

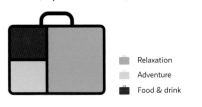

- Relaxation
- Adventure
- Food & drink

PIEDMONT
ITALY

Why now? The fungi are fabulous. Bordered by France and Switzerland, the northwestern region of Piedmont sits beneath the Alps and a little apart from the rest of Italy. It doesn't draw the same crowds as Tuscany, yet has similarly sylvan countryside, hilltop towns and foodie-ness. This is especially true in autumn when Piedmont's wild mushrooms abound, its red nebbiolo grapes are harvested and its white truffles – the world's most expensive fungi – come into season. Other specialities include excellent beef, Arborio rice and cheeses (try crumbly Castelmagno). Head to Alba, a cluster of medieval towers and baroque and Renaissance palaces. It has splendid restaurants and is fun in October: it has a truffle festival and a donkey version of nearby Asti's high-brow Palio horse race. Also venture into the forested Langhe hills to join a truffle hunt and visit tiny cantinas to taste the region's Barbaresco and Barolo wines.

Trip planner: Fly to Turin, visit the city's museums and churches, then head to rural Piedmont. A hire car is handy for reaching smaller villages. Allow a week.

Need to know: Alba is 39 miles (65km) south of Turin; Asti and Alba have train stations.

Other months: Dec-Mar – cold, skiing; Apr-May – warming, quiet; Jun-Aug – very hot; Sep-Nov – warm, harvest.

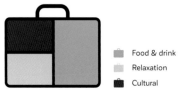

- Food & drink
- Relaxation
- Cultural

231

Cruise (and swim) the waters along the Musandam Peninsula, Oman

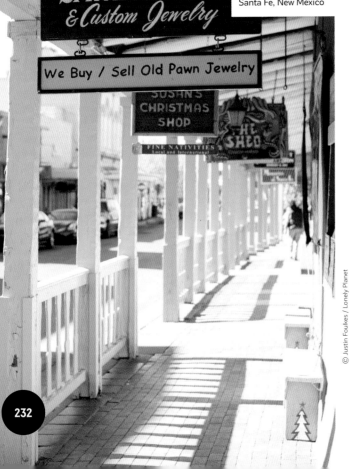

SANTA FE ARTS & Custom Jewelry

We Buy / Sell Old Pawn Jewelry

SUSAN'S CHRISTMAS SHOP

Quiet streets and quaint storefronts in Santa Fe, New Mexico

Surreal rock formations and sand at Anse Source d'Argent, La Digue, Seychelles

OMAN

→ **Why now? Mellow fruitfulness, mellow weather.**

Wonderfully warm climes (30°C; 86°F); markets overflowing with fresh-harvested walnuts and pomegranates; 20,000 turtles laying their eggs... October is an amazing time to visit Oman, the spectacular Gulf state that offers a taste of old Arabia. There is modern development, but mainly it's a land of raw canyons and rippled desert, date plantations, palm-fringed sands, adobe villages and spicy souks. Most trips begin in capital Muscat, where the old port area of Muttrah mixes with urban sprawl and glitzy beach resorts. Southeast lies Ras al Jinz where thousands of green turtles haul ashore to nest (best seen August to November); take a guided night tour. Inland is Sharqiya Sands, a perfect sea of dunes where camel rides, sandboarding and 4WD dune-bashing can be arranged from desert camps. Further west still, the Hajar Mountains rise in craggy splendour, cut by caves and canyons, and speckled with sites such as ancient Nizwa – the spot to explore a fort, buy a goat and strike out into the hills.

Trip plan: Allow nine days to loop northern Oman. Add extra to sail around the inlet-notched Musandam Peninsula.

Need to know: Muscat's massive Sultan Qaboos Grand Mosque is Oman's only mosque open to non-Muslims.

Other months: Dec-Feb – coolest; Mar-Apr – warming, quiet; May-Sep – very hot, humid (monsoon in south); Oct-Nov – hot, harvest.

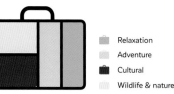

- Relaxation
- Adventure
- Cultural
- Wildlife & nature

SEYCHELLES

→ **Why now? Calm seas in paradise.**

The Seychelles is probably how Pixar would draw paradise: swaying palms, supernaturally blue seas, bling-white sand, artfully smoothed and scattered boulders, plus a few cute turtles wriggling ashore. Fantasy made real. Given these high levels of loveliness, and the balmy 25°C to 30°C (77-86°F) year-round temperatures, there's no awful time to visit this Indian Ocean archipelago. However, October, the period between the brisker southeasterly trade winds switching to the lighter northwesterlies, brings especially calm conditions, so is excellent for swimming, snorkelling and diving. The water can be 29°C (84°F), visibility is around 30m and migrating whale sharks have arrived. It's also cheaper than the peak of June to August.

Trip plan: The Seychelles has over 100 islands. Use ferries to hop between mountainous, arty Mahé (the main island), car-free La Digue and Praslin, home to the Vallee de Mai's raunchy coco de mer palms. Elsewhere, Bird Island is brilliant for, er, birds. North Island is the world's most exclusive resort. The remote Aldabra Group, 715 miles (1150km) from Mahé and only accessible by boat, is the Indian Ocean's Galápagos, home to over 100,000 giant tortoises.

Need to know: Festival Kreol, the Seychelles' biggest cultural event, is held across Mahé in late October.

Other months: Nov-Mar – rainier season; Apr & Oct – between trade winds, calm, warm, cheaper; May-Sep – dry, warm, windy

- Relaxation
- Cultural
- Wildlife & nature

NEW MEXICO USA

→ **Why now? For cool weather and hot air.**

New Mexico, officially the 'Land of Enchantment', is especially enchanting in sunny, mild October – the 20°C (68°F) days are ideal for discovering the historical riches and extraordinary outdoors of this foreign-feeling United State. Sites such as 1000-year-old Taos Pueblo nod to the region's Native American roots, while capital Santa Fe (founded by Spanish missionaries in 1610) combines old adobe houses, Romanesque architecture and a slew of modern-art galleries. Then there's the plentiful wilderness, from the Sangre de Cristos mountains of the north to the blinding-white dunes of the south. Scenic drives cut through these badlands, while there are opportunities for activities and ranch stays aplenty.

Trip plan: With one week, loop the north. From Albuquerque, drive the Turquoise Trail to Santa Fe; browse the galleries of Canyon Rd and bird-watch at the Audubon Center. Trek among ancient ruins at Bandelier National Monument then head to boho Taos for margaritas and hikes or horse-rides around Taos Pueblo. Climb Wheeler Peak, New Mexico's highest, then return to Albuquerque on the High Rd, via the arty villages of Cordova and Chimayo.

Need to know: Albuquerque International Balloon Fiesta is held in early October.

Other months: Mar-May – mild, windy; Jun-Aug – hot, wettest; Sep-Nov – warm; Dec-Feb – mild (cold at altitude).

- Adventure
- Cultural
- Food & drink
- Journey

A bread baker in Porto, and the steeply terraced vineyards rising from the banks of the Rio Douro

PORTO & THE DOURO PORTUGAL

→ **Why now?** To float down the river at its most intoxicating.

The Douro Valley is the godfather of wine production. This heady region, now listed by Unesco, is the world's oldest *appellation contrôlée*: the Portuguese started authenticating the provenance of their produce 200 years before the French. Take a boat trip down the Douro River and you're assured a fine drop, as well as unrolling pastoral scenes – particularly delightful in autumn, when the sun is still warm and the grape-heavy vines turn golden. Also cruise past traditional *rabelos* (cargo boats), tiny towns plastered with azulejo tiles and numerous *quintas* (wineries) where you can stop for tastings. Tumbling down hills at the river's mouth is historic Porto, first settled by the Romans and now Portugal's second-largest city.

The old, narrow-streeted Ribeira district is a must, as is Vila Nova de Gaia, on the opposite bank, brimful of venerable port-wine houses.

Trip planner: Spend a few days in Porto, before a week-long river cruise to Vega de Terron, on the Spanish border (two hours by road from Salamanca).

Need to know: The Douro's best sites are not right by the river; road transfers from boat docks are required.

Other months: Nov-Mar – cool, barren; Apr-Jun – warming, blossom; Jul-Aug – hottest; Sep-Oct – warm, harvest.

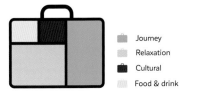

- Journey
- Relaxation
- Cultural
- Food & drink

Winding between the old buildings of Lìjiāng are many cobbled alleys to explore

SOUTHWEST CHINA

Why now? Fine climes in two picture-perfect provinces.

Guǎngxī and Yúnnán are China at its most poetic. The rice terraces, karst hills, plunging gorges and snowy peaks of these diverse southwest provinces evoke an ancient land far removed from the nation's forward-thrusting cities. October, with its mild, dry weather and golden colours is a particularly good time to get out into the countryside here, which ranges from the mountainous Tibetan Plateau to tropical lowlands where colourful minority cultures thrive. Guìlín is at the heart of Guǎngxī's karst country, and is the place to arrange scenic cruises down the Li River to laidback Yángshuò and visits to the Miao, Yao, Dong and Zhuang villages around Lóngshèng. In Yúnnán, find heat, jungle hikes and a more Southeast Asian vibe in the Xīshuāngbǎnnà region, or head north for Lìjiāng's cobbled alleys, treks along the sheer sides of Tiger Leaping Gorge and the utopian snow-capped highs around Zhōngdiàn, officially renamed Shangri-La.

Trip plan: Allow two to four weeks to visit both Yúnnán and Guǎngxī, or focus on one. Handy trains and flights link Guìlín, Kūnmíng (Yúnnán's capital) and Lìjiāng.

Need to know: There is a national holiday 1–7 Oct – transport/sites will be heaving. Avoid if possible.

Other months: Apr-Sep – hot, humid (Jul-Sep: typhoons); Oct-Nov – warm, dry; Dec-Mar – cooler, cold at altitude.

© Mark Read / Lonely Planet

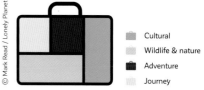

Cultural
Wildlife & nature
Adventure
Journey

BLUE RIDGE PARKWAY USA

Why now? Follow a classic road trip through flaming fall foliage.

Forget Appalachian spring – autumn is the season to be snaking through the forested highlands of Virginia and North Carolina, along the 470-mile (755km) Blue Ridge Parkway, winding from Shenandoah National Park to Great Smoky Mountains National Park. The road took over half a century to construct, such is the testing terrain – and it's that rugged landscape that makes it such a rewarding journey. That, and the foliage fireworks that set the hillsides ablaze in October: the deep reds of dogwoods and blackgums, orange sassafras, crimson maples and maroon oaks.

Trip planner: You could drive the parkway in a couple of days, but better to take a week or more, stopping to camp (watch for bears), pick apples and hike to viewpoints en route. Start from the northern end: autumn colours get more vivid and views more spectacular as you head into the southern reaches topping 6000ft (1800m) south of Mt Pisgah, North Carolina.

Need to know: Maximum speed limit on the parkway is 45 mph (72km/h) – lower in places, especially when leaf-peepers are dawdling on the road. There are no fuel stations on the parkway itself.

Other months: May-Oct – parkway reliably open; Nov-Apr – snow can cause closures.

Journey
Wildlife & nature
Cultural

DARJEELING INDIA

Why now? Clear mountain views and a tasty cup of tea.

In the early 19th century, Darjeeling was the health-boosting hill station of choice for the Raj-era elite. It remains a refreshing escape from the hot plains of West Bengal, and can still be reached by the narrow-gauge Toy Train that's been puffing up to the town since the 1880s. People flock to Darjeeling to eat scones in colonial-throwback hotels and take tours of the leafy tea plantations before sipping a cuppa – said to be the 'champagne of tea'. Mainly, though, people come for the views: a sweep of high Himalaya, including Kanchenjunga (the planet's third-highest peak). A crisp, clear October day is a good time to ensure perfect panoramas, or to hit the trails. Hiking along the Singalila Ridge offers even more heart-soaring vistas: from the summit of Sandakphu, you can gaze at four of the world's loftiest mountains, including Mt Everest itself.

Trip plan: Fly from Kolkata to northern Bagdogra. Visit the Buddhist monasteries at Rumtek and Pemayangtse, as well as Darjeeling. Singalila Ridge hikes begin at Manebhanjan, 31 miles (50km) from Darjeeling.

Need to know: Overnight sleeper trains run from Kolkata to New Jalpaiguri, departure station for the Toy Train.

Other months: Mar-Apr & Sep-Nov – cool, clear; Dec-Feb – cold; May-Aug – wet.

Relaxation
Adventure
Cultural
Wildlife & nature

FLINDERS RANGES AUSTRALIA

Why now? Explore the outback before its scorching.

Winding amid the red-orange-purple creases of the Flinders Range is like time travelling. These mountains, which begin 124 miles (200km) north of Adelaide and stretch for over 249 miles (400km) into deepest South Australia, were formed 540 million years ago. It's an ancient landscape of gorges and escarpments that oozes quintessential outback Oz. It gets awfully hot in summer, so come in October (late spring), just before the mercury shoots prohibitively high; this is also when wildflowers are in beautiful bloom. From Adelaide, drive north to Mt Remarkable National Park; embark on day hikes along streams and lofty ridges, or up the 3150ft (960m) namesake peak. In Quorn pause to ride the Pichi Richi steam railway before reaching the range itself. Continue to Wilpena Pound, the Flinders' headline act. This vast rock amphitheatre has rich Aboriginal associations, as does nearby Arkaroo Rock, where there's a gallery of ancient art. Further north still, atmospheric towns sit amid the hills. Stop off at Blinman and Parachilna for a good feed and a cold beer.

Trip plan: With 10 days, drive north from Adelaide to Parachilna via Mt Remarkable and Wilpena Pound.

Need to know: For excellent views of Wilpena Pound, do the Wangara Lookout Hike (3½ hours).

Other months: May-Aug – coolest, wettest; Sep-Oct – hot, bearable; Nov-Apr – searingly hot.

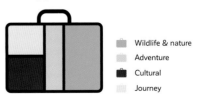

Wildlife & nature
Adventure
Cultural
Journey

© Matt Munro / Lonely Planet

COROMANDEL PENINSULA
NEW ZEALAND

→ **Why now? Spring sun with the beaches to yourself.**

Kiwis love the Coromandel. This peninsula jutting into the Pacific has some of New Zealand's best weather and is only a 90-minute drive from Auckland. Prime summer holiday territory. However, in October you'll find warm temperatures but fewer people. (If it does turn chilly, warm up at the Lost Spring natural spa or by digging your own thermal bath at Hot Water Beach). The lack of crowds and general vibe makes the Coromandel perfect for an unhurried spring break. It has lots of browsable, gallery-filled towns (the legacy of an influx of arty types in the 1960s). And the glorious topography – a lush, mountainous spine, fringed by cliffs and golden shores – lends itself to leisurely scenic drives. Active pursuits are readily available – the Hauraki Rail Trail cycleway, hikes up the Pinnacles, kayaking into Cathedral Cove. But you could just hole up in a coastal cafe and watch the world go by.

Trip plan: Allow three or four days to amble around the peninsula. Thames (west coast) and Whitianga (east) are the main hubs.

Need to know: September/October is the start of scallop season; try them at the restaurants along Whitianga's Esplanade.

Other months: Dec-Feb – warmest, busiest; Mar-May – cool/mild; Jun-Aug – coldest; Sep-Nov – warm, quieter.

© Nick Twyford Photography / Getty Images

Waves flow into Cathedral Cove, a great location for kayaking

■ Relaxation
■ Food & drink
■ Wildlife & nature

NAMIBIA

→ **Why now? A wildlife wonderland.**

By the end of the dry season, Namibia is looking parched. Temperatures are rising, rains are a distant memory, the skies are cloudless blue – and wildlife is visible everywhere. The bush has died right back, and animals gather in great numbers at ever-shrinking waterholes. Etosha National Park is Namibia's headline reserve; during the dry, you might see elephants, giraffes, zebra, rhinos and big cats parading across the shimmering salt pans. The excellent road network makes a self-driving simple: just park next to a waterhole and wait for the wildlife. For chances to spot black rhino and desert-adapted elephants (plus San rock art) head to Damaraland. Walvis Bay on the wild Atlantic coast, is the place for humpbacks, which migrate past from July to November.

Trip plan: Drive west from capital Windhoek into the Namib Desert to see the dunes at Sossusvlei. Head north to Swakopmund, then northeast to Etosha, via Damaraland. Return to Windhoek via a farmstay in the central highlands. Allow two weeks.

Need to know: Windhoek's beer-filled Oktoberfest is in late October.

Other months: Dec-Mar – rainier, hottest; Apr-May – dry, green; Jun-Oct – dry, warm/hot; Nov – unpredictable.

■ Wildlife & nature
■ Journey

BHUTAN

→ **Why now? Clear skies, sights and trails in the pristine Himalaya.**

For the happiest holiday, visit Bhutan. This Himalayan Shangri-La measures success in terms of Gross National Happiness rather than material wealth, and most Bhutanese people live guided by traditional values and spirituality. It's as refreshing as the mountain air on a crisp October day. Yes, October – the most beautiful month. Delightful temperatures and dry, blue skies are perfect for hiking and sightseeing; rare black-necked cranes arrive in the Phobjikha Valley too (they stay until February). Cultural journeys involve dramatic drives to *dzongs* (fortresses), many of which – including Thimphu and Gangtey – host colourful *tsechus* (festivals) this month. More active trips head into the mountains. There are hikes to suit all levels, from the essential half-day climb to cliff-perched Tiger's Nest Monastery to the Jhomolhari, a seven-day trek into one of the most pristine parts of the Himalaya.

Trip plan: A seven- to 10-day trip could include Paro, Thimphu and Punakha, taking in *dzongs*, views, short walks and traditional activities (archery, hot-stone baths). Allow longer to include multi-day hikes.

Need to know: Visitors must pay a minimum fee of US$250 a day (US$200 Dec-Feb, Jun-Aug).

Other months: Dec-Feb – cold, clear; Mar-May – flowers, warm; Jun-Sep – wet; Sep-Nov – cooler, clear, dry.

- ▨ Cultural
- ▨ Adventure
- 🧳 Wildlife & nature

Monks walk, flags flutter and prayer bells ring at Tango Goemba monastery

© Jonathan Gregson / Lonely Planet

MANITOBA
CANADA

→ **Why now?** To play with polar bears.
With temperatures averaging -2°C (28°F), there needs to be a very good reason to brave the remote Manitoba outpost of Churchill in October. And there is – about 900 of them. Churchill is the self-proclaimed 'Polar Bear Capital of the World', with almost 1000 of the magnificent mammals living in the area. In October and November, the bears move from their summer home on the tundra to their seal-hunting grounds on Hudson Bay, passing near Churchill in the process. Tours leave town in tundra buggies, fat-wheeled trucks that enable super-close safe encounters. It's also possible to stay at remote, fly-in lodges to track the bears on foot – with an expert armed guide. Arctic fox, ptarmigan and caribou might also be spotted. October's dark skies at this northerly latitude make aurora sightings a possibility too.

Trip plan: October trips to Churchill must be booked well in advance. Allow a week, to include buggy tours and other activities.

Need to know: Trains (45 hours) and planes (four hours) connect Winnipeg, Manitoba's capital, and northern outpost Churchill.

Other months: Oct-Nov – cold, polar bears; Dec-Mar – very cold, aurora, dog-sledding; Apr-May – cold; Jun-Sep – warmest, belugas, birds.

© Chris Kolaczan / Shutterstock

Wildlife & nature
Adventure

COPPER CANYON
MEXICO

→ **Why now?** Explore a gorge rich in history and activities.
The Mexican north is a sparsely inhabited wild frontier redolent of a Hollywood western. Its compelling star is the Tarahumara range, sliced by the Copper Canyon – and one of the world's best train rides. Aided by 36 bridges and 87 tunnels, the Copper Canyon Railway masters high plains and ravines for 407 miles (655km) between Pacific coast Los Mochis and Chihuahua. It takes 13 hours non-stop, but the canyon deserves more time: stay in towns such as Creel and Divisadero. Organise horse-rides and drive to canyon-floor Urique to hike to 17th-century silver-mining hub, Batopilas. And visit indigenous Tarahumara villages to run with the legendary Rarámuri. Summers are roasting, winters chilly; come in October, when landscapes are freshly watered.

Trip plan: Head to Chihuahua, ride the train, then fly to Baja for beaches. Or linger in the canyon area – there are hikes, horse trails and villages enough to fill a week.

Need to know: Chihuahua is 230 miles (370km) south of El Paso (USA), 907 miles (1460km) north of Mexico City (two-hour flight).

Other months: Nov-Feb – cool, dry, busy; Apr-Jun – driest, blossoms; Jul-Sep – hot, wet (waterfalls full); Oct – warm, green, quiet.

Adventure
Cultural
Wildlife & nature
Journey

SLOVAKIA

→ **Why now?** Golden, glorious, growl-filled exploration.
Only an independent country since 1993, and landlocked by Austria, the Czech Republic, Poland, Ukraine and Hungary, tiny Slovakia can be tough to quickly characterise. Why go? What's there? Well, plenty, including an excess of castles, many medieval towns, rampant forests, High Tatras peaks – and around 800 brown bears. Autumn, when the animals are drawn to open slopes to eat grasses and berries, is a good time to see them. Spend three days in the mountains with a good guide and it's reckoned your chances of a sighting are 90%-plus. You'll certainly see magnificent fall colours. If the temperature does cool, the underground bars of capital Bratislava, the medicinal mud and mineral waters of Piešťany, and a shot of *slivovica* (plum brandy) will warm you up. The country is so compact, you can flit between wild and urban in a flash.

Trip plan: In a week visit Bratislava, Piešťany's spas, Trenčín castle, the 16th-century time-warp mining town of Banská Štiavnica and the Tatras – though longer is better for bear-watching.

Need to know: Arrange bear-watching with Slovak Wildlife Society guides, to maximise chances of sightings.

Other months: Nov-Mar – cold, Tatras skiing; Apr-Jun – mild, blossom; Jul-Aug – hottest, busiest; Sep-Oct – warm, settled, fall colours.

Cultural
Wildlife & nature
Value

The Saône River meets the Rhône River near Lyon

LYON FRANCE

Why now? C'est délicieux!

Lyon might be France's second city, but it's the world's first when it comes to food – it has more restaurants per square metre than anywhere else on the planet. These range from Michelin-starred spots creating nouvelle cuisine (a cooking style invented here) to traditional Lyonnais *bouchons* (family bistros) serving calves' feet and tripe sausage. Elite chefs are tripping over each other down the ancient *traboules* (passages built to shelter silk-weavers). There are markets overflowing with Bresse chickens, Saint-Bonnet-le-Froid mushrooms, world-class cheeses and all sorts of offal. And there are traditional charcuteries, fromageries, chocolatiers, boulangeries... Plus, the Rhône Valley vineyards are on the doorstep. October is a great time for autumn produce and wine touring. Its cooler temperatures (10-18°C; 50-64°F) aren't a problem if you're inside eating, or taking a class at one of Lyon's cookery schools. Movie buffs should also visit the Institut Lumière, which honors the local brothers who invented cinematography; the Lumière Festival is held in October.

Trip plan: Allow three to four days for sightseeing (Old Town, Saone River cruise, galleries) and eating.

© Frederic Prochasson / 500px

Need to know: Many markets, including Les Halles, are closed on Mondays.

Other months: Nov-Mar – chilly; Apr-May – warming, blooming; Jun-Aug – warmest, busiest; Sep-Oct – cooling, harvest.

■ Food & drink
■ Cultural
■ Personal growth

BEYOND LYON

FLEURIE & MORGON • 34 MILES (54KM) • Heart of Beaujolais wine country

GENEVA • 90 MILES (144KM) • Short hop to genteel lakeside Switzerland

ARLES • 165 MILES (265KM) • South to Provence via River Rhone cruise

PARIS • 200 MILES (321KM) • Just two hours by TGV from the capital

NORTHERN TANZANIA

→ **Why now?** Incredible wildlife is at its greatest.

Safaris don't get more superabundant than this. The amount of wildlife that flows around Tanzania's 'northern circuit' is bewildering: wildebeest and zebra herds numbering in the millions, hundreds of thousands of assorted antelopes, and healthy numbers of predators waiting to pick them all off... The end of the dry season, when the plains are unobstructed by vegetation, is when animals are easiest to see. Also, the skies are clear and immense. By now, the herds of the Great Migration are usually grazing in the Serengeti's far north, making this a good choice. Ngorongoro Crater, a big, beautiful bowl of wildlife, is also ideal – animals are visible, and it's a little less busy than July to September. Complement these with Lake Manyara (for tree-climbing lions) and lesser-visited Tarangire National Park, where wildlife clusters at the riverine swamps.

Trip plan: From Kilimanjaro Airport, make a northern circuit. Highlights include panoramic camps on the lip of Ngorongoro and seeking out parts of the Serengeti where walking safaris are permitted (in many areas, they're not). Allow 10 to 14 days.

Need to know: The Great Migration isn't an exact science; herd movements vary year to year.

Other months: Mar-May – long rains; Jun-Oct – dry; Nov-Dec – lighter rains; Jan-Feb – dry.

■ Wildlife & nature
■ Journey

The Cape buffalo is one of the most formidable animals on the African plains

PELOPONNESE
GREECE

→ **Why now? Cool ruins, warm seas.**
You don't have to visit the Peloponnese in the off season. Inexplicably, though this hand-shaped peninsula has some of Greece's least-developed beaches, best-preserved sites, most appealing mountains and even the original Arcadia, it sees only a fraction of the tourists that besiege other corners of the country. October offers even smaller crowds as well as clement temperatures (around 22°C; 72°F) for walking amid both hills and ruins. Must-sees include Olympia, where the Olympic Games was held for 1000 years; the citadel of Mycenae, swirled by Homeric legends; Epidaurus's 14,000-seater amphitheatre; and the Byzantine port of Monemvasia, huddled on a battleship-like islet. The wild Mani peninsula offers fine hiking, particularly around Výros Gorge, while the west coast has some of Greece's best sand – head to curvaceous, unspoilt Voidhokilia.
Trip plan: From Athens, cross onto the Peloponnese via ancient Corinth, and visit nearby Mycenae, Epidaurus and the pretty Venetian town of Nafplio – doable in a few days. With more time, head south to Monemvasia and the Mani, then back north via the west coast and Olympia.
Need to know: Athens to Corinth is 53 miles (85km; 55-minute drive); buses, trains and ferries run from near Athens to the Peloponnese.
Other months: Nov-Mar – cold; Apr-May – warming, flowers; Jun-Aug – hot, busy; Sep-Oct – warm, quieter.

- Relaxation
- Cultural
- Adventure

SOUTHERN JORDAN

→ **Why now? Prime climes for world wonders.**
With scorching summer cooling to balmy autumn (27°C; 81°F), and a few drops of rain greening the countryside, October is a refreshing time to explore two Jordanian gems. Petra, the rock-hewn city carved by secretive Nabateans 2000 years ago, is a manmade wonder to rival any in the world; inching down its Indiana Jones–trodden Siq to reach the Treasury is a bucket-list moment. Then, a little north, sits Dana Nature Reserve, a wilderness of 1500m sandstone highs and below-sea-level wadis (dry river valleys). Here, there is millennia of human history and rampant nature – junipers and date palms, pistachios and pomegranates, ibex and mountain gazelle. This pretty pair combine easily by road, but best on foot. The 28-mile (45km) Dana to Petra trek – the 'Middle East Inca Trail' – follows old Bedouin paths and mule tracks across the rocky desert from Dana's wadis to Petra's mighty facades. Nights camped under the stars add extra magic.
Trip plan: Travel south from Amman, via Madaba's mosaics and the salty Dead Sea, to Dana. Spend four or more days trekking to Petra. Return to Amman. Allow eight to 10 days.
Need to know: Amman to Petra direct is 130 miles (210km; drive of 2½ to three hours).
Other months: Mar-Apr & Oct-Nov – warm, greener; Dec-Feb – coldest; May-Sep – hot.

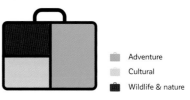

- Adventure
- Cultural
- Wildlife & nature

Base yourself in
medieval, fortified
Laguardia to explore
La Rioja's wineries

LA RIOJA SPAN

Why now? To wake up and smell the tempranillo.

The northern Spanish region of La Rioja somehow crams around 1200 wineries into its small proportions. Vineyards stripe the craggy Ebro River Valley, flourishing amid traces of past settlers – from neolithic to Moorish to medieval sites. It's a slow-paced, history-rich place to get a drink. Come in autumn and La Rioja will be in the festive flurry of harvest, the air thick with fermenting fruit, the vines crisping to golden umber. Tastings are a must. There are venerable chateau-style wineries clustered around Haro, in the Rioja Alta; Rioja Alavesa is more contemporary – architects such as Gehry and Calatrava have designed wineries here. Logroño, La Rioja's capital, is packed with bars serving cheap, tasty pinchos (tapas), making it the ideal place to soak up the booze.

Trip plan: Loop La Rioja. Visit Haro's bodegas, head east to Briones' castle and do a *pinchos* crawl along Logroño's Calle del Laurel. On the return, stop at medieval Laguardia, below the Sierra de Cantabria; Calatrava's wave-like Ysios winery is nearby.

Need to know: The nearest airport to Haro is Bilbao, 81 miles (130km) north.

Other months: Nov-Mar – cold, stark, crisp; Apr-May – green; Jun – warm, Haro's 'wine war'; Jul-Aug – hot; Sep-Oct – warm, harvest.

Food & drink

Relaxation

Cultural

It's rutting season for wild red deer in the highlands of Scotland

© Craig Easton / Lonely Planet

LIGURIA ITALY

→ **Why now? Roam rugged coastal paths in peace.**

You've admired the photos of pastel-hued fishing villages tumbling down a precipitous hillside to the Ligurian Sea. So, too, have hundreds of thousands of day-trippers and cruise-ship passengers who throng the Cinque Terre, along the coast east of Genoa, each summer. The five villages of Monterosso, Vernazza, Corniglia, Manarola and Riomaggiore attract hordes of visitors in high season, and even the spectacular walking trails linking the ports can get busy. Come in October, though, and the pressure eases, along with prices; you can explore these gorgeous villages, nearby beaches and the dramatic coastline in peace, and even nearby jetset hangouts like Portofino become almost accessible to mere mortals. Beyond those honeypots, less busy spots such as Portovénere, Sestri Levante and Tellaro are similarly charming.

Trip plan: The less-touristed towns of Lévanto and La Spezia offer down-to-earth stopovers; just along the coast, Genoa is a historic port with train links to the Cinque Terre.

Need to know: To access footpaths around Cinque Terre you'll need to buy a trekking card. Paths are susceptible to landslips and floods, and can be closed at short notice.

Other months: May-Sep – warm, very busy; Apr & Oct – quiet; Nov-Mar – cool, pleasant for walking.

⬛ Relaxation
⬜ Cultural
⬛ Adventure
⬜ Food & drink

HIGHLANDS SCOTLAND

🐘 ⛩ 🍷 🚙

→ **Why now? Get stuck in a rut.**

A swirl of mist, moorland glowing red-gold in the dawn light, the anguished bellow of a stag angling for a fight... October mornings in the Scottish Highlands are an atmospheric affair. This is the month that red deer males rut, jousting with their impressive antlers to secure control over the does. Whether you explore by 4WD or on foot, it certainly adds an extra frisson to the already breathtaking lochs, glens and moors. Tourist (and midge) season is winding down now too, making it a good time to combine stags with quieter sightseeing: Stirling, Eilean Donan Castle, Glen Coe, Fort William. Warm up with a wee dram at the end of the day, and tuck into fantastic October food: Scottish lobster and langoustines; plentiful pheasant, grouse and game.

Trip plan: Fly to Inverness to loop northern Scotland, taking in dramatic landscapes, lochs and castles. Add on wildlife safaris – for instance, to the hidden glens of Lochaber (near Fort William) or the hills around Loch Torridon.

Need to know: Deer are most active just after dawn and at dusk; watch with a guide and keep a safe distance.

Other months: Apr-May – quieter, blooming; Jun-Aug – warmest, long days, midges; Sep-Oct – fall colours, deer rut; Nov-Mar – cold, snow possible.

⬛ Cultural
⬜ Wildlife & nature
⬛ Food & drink
⬜ Journey

TAIWAN

→ **Why now? The best weather for exploring an offbeat isle.**

Taiwan surprises people. Dubbed Ilha Formosa ('Beautiful Isle') by 16th-century sailors, this East Asian stunner has more latterly become famed for manufacturing cheap stuff. But while its economy has developed apace, the country has also managed both to preserve more Chinese traditions than mainland China and to forge a cosmopolitan culture that's distinctly Taiwanese. The food – Chinese and Japanese dishes, Hakka specialities, sizzling street food – is sensational too. Autumn is the best time to visit. It's cooler and less humid (meaning locals start leaping into the hot springs), and maple leaves are starting to turn. Start in capital Taipei, to visit the National Palace Museum (a matchless repository of Chinese art); add on Sun Moon Lake, Taroko Gorge, old Lugang and Foguangshan (a huge Buddhist monastery where you can stay overnight). The water is still warm enough for snorkelling in coastal Kenting National Park, while the mountains of Alishan offer good hiking.

Trip plan: Allow two weeks and explore Taiwan by train – the rail network connects cities and national parks; include the Forest Train, which rumbles into Alishan.

Need to know: Ferries run between mainland China and Taiwan.

Other months: Jan-Feb – coldest, drier; Apr-May – unpredictable, rainy; Jun-Aug – hot, humid, typhoons; Sep-Nov – cooler, dry (Oct: typhoon season ends).

Tour a historic site, such as Matsu Temple in Tainan, or browse a street market in Taipei

© Lottie Davies / Lonely Planet

© Michael Hermanto / 500px

Cultural
Food & drink
Journey

NEW YORK CITY USA

Forage the shops and markets of Brooklyn for a picnic's ingredients

Why now? Fall fun in the Big Apple. Given that New York never sleeps, there's no really bad time to visit. The Big Apple will always be expensive, exciting, busy and brilliant, its shops and museums enticing whatever the weather. However, autumn offers respite from the stickiness of summer, while retaining the chance of some lovely warm days (10-20°C; 50-68°F). The trees are on the turn too. You can see flaming hues in Central Park, Fort Tyron Park and Staten Island's Greenbelt. Or venture into upstate New York for a full-on fiery feast – try the Adirondack Mountains or the Finger Lakes region (which is also in delicious grape-harvest mode right now). October is an especially comfortable time for a guided NYC walking tour. Themed options on offer are eclectic, from foraging in Brooklyn and food heritage in Harlem to the gargoyles of Manhattan and the ghosts of the Upper West Side.

Trip plan: Allow at least five days for NYC. Add an extra five to head upstate – NYC to Syracuse (for the Finger Lakes) is 5½ hours by train.

Need to know: New York Open House Weekend is held in October – a good chance to peek behind some of the city's usually closed doors.

Other months: Nov-Feb – cold, snow possible; Mar-May – warming, showery; Jun-Aug – hot, humid; Sep-Oct – cool.

© Sivan Askayo / Lonely Planet

Cultural
Food & drink
Wildlife & nature

BEYOND NEW YORK

HOBOKEN • 1 MILE (1.6KM) • Eight-minute Hudson River ferry crossing to hippest New Jersey

MONTAUK • 120 MILES (193KM) • Laidback Hamptons village at the end of Long Island

NIAGARA FALLS • 465 MILES (748KM) • Nine hours via Amtrak's scenic Empire Services

LA • 3000-ISH MILES (4830KM) • Epic coast-to-coast road trip

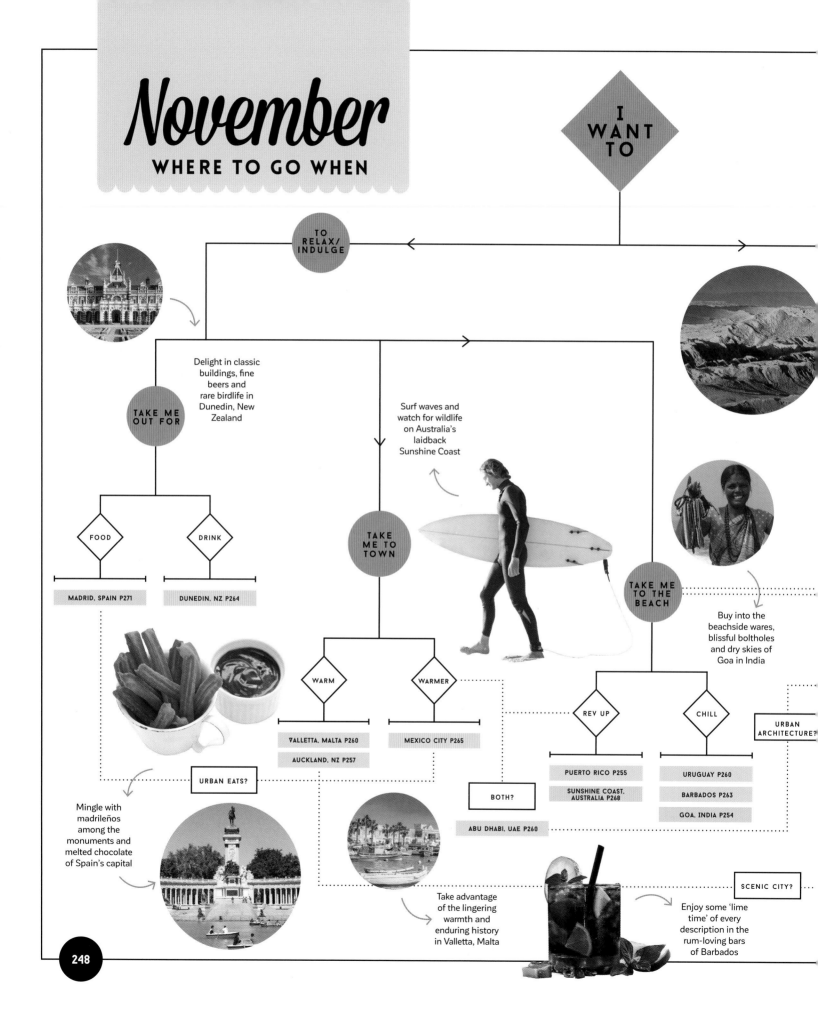

November
WHERE TO GO WHEN

I WANT TO

TO RELAX/ INDULGE

TAKE ME OUT FOR

Delight in classic buildings, fine beers and rare birdlife in Dunedin, New Zealand

Surf waves and watch for wildlife on Australia's laidback Sunshine Coast

TAKE ME TO TOWN

TAKE ME TO THE BEACH

Buy into the beachside wares, blissful boltholes and dry skies of Goa in India

FOOD

DRINK

MADRID, SPAIN P271

DUNEDIN, NZ P264

WARM

WARMER

VALLETTA, MALTA P260

AUCKLAND, NZ P257

MEXICO CITY P265

REV UP

CHILL

URBAN ARCHITECTURE?

PUERTO RICO P255

SUNSHINE COAST, AUSTRALIA P268

URUGUAY P260

BARBADOS P263

GOA, INDIA P254

URBAN EATS?

Mingle with madrileños among the monuments and melted chocolate of Spain's capital

BOTH?

ABU DHABI, UAE P260

Take advantage of the lingering warmth and enduring history in Valletta, Malta

SCENIC CITY?

Enjoy some 'lime time' of every description in the rum-loving bars of Barbados

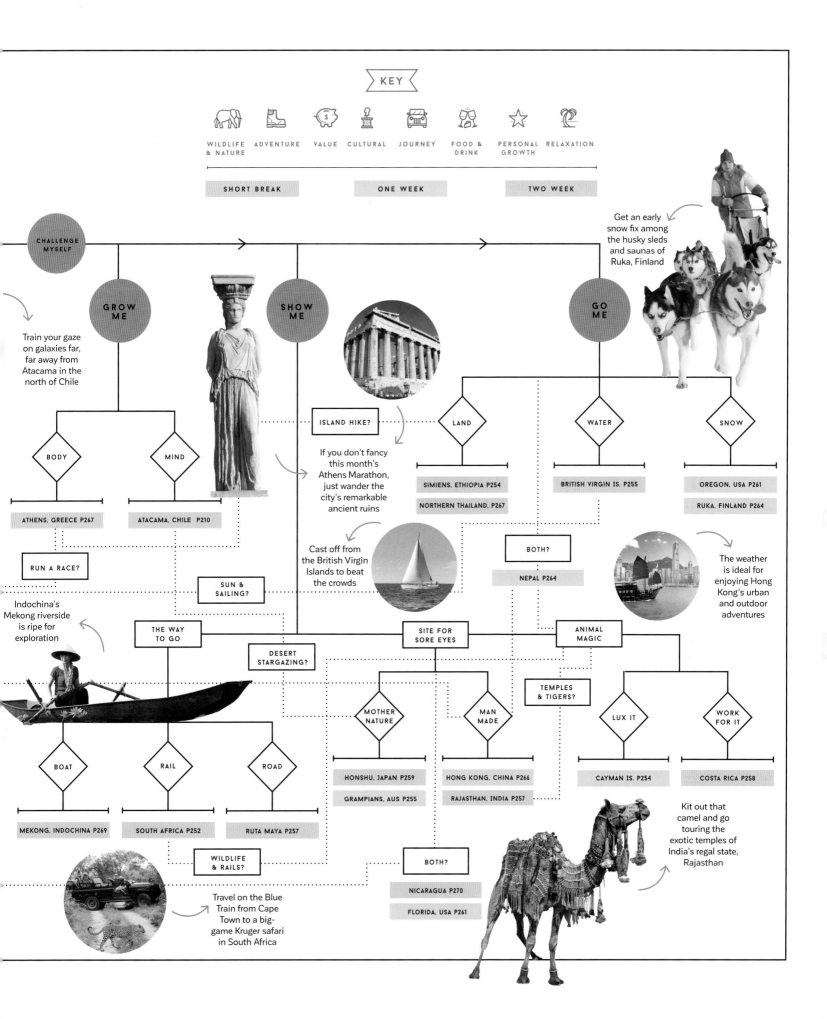

KEY

WILDLIFE & NATURE | ADVENTURE | VALUE | CULTURAL | JOURNEY | FOOD & DRINK | PERSONAL GROWTH | RELAXATION

SHORT BREAK   ONE WEEK   TWO WEEK

CHALLENGE MYSELF

GROW ME

SHOW ME

GO ME

Get an early snow fix among the husky sleds and saunas of Ruka, Finland

Train your gaze on galaxies far, far away from Atacama in the north of Chile

ISLAND HIKE?

If you don't fancy this month's Athens Marathon, just wander the city's remarkable ancient ruins

LAND

WATER

SNOW

BODY

MIND

ATHENS, GREECE P267

ATACAMA, CHILE P210

SIMIENS, ETHIOPIA P254

NORTHERN THAILAND, P267

BRITISH VIRGIN IS. P255

OREGON, USA P261

RUKA, FINLAND P264

RUN A RACE?

Cast off from the British Virgin Islands to beat the crowds

BOTH?

NEPAL P264

The weather is ideal for enjoying Hong Kong's urban and outdoor adventures

Indochina's Mekong riverside is ripe for exploration

SUN & SAILING?

THE WAY TO GO

SITE FOR SORE EYES

ANIMAL MAGIC

DESERT STARGAZING?

TEMPLES & TIGERS?

MOTHER NATURE

MAN MADE

LUX IT

WORK FOR IT

BOAT

RAIL

ROAD

HONSHU, JAPAN P259

GRAMPIANS, AUS P255

HONG KONG, CHINA P266

RAJASTHAN, INDIA P257

CAYMAN IS. P254

COSTA RICA P258

MEKONG, INDOCHINA P269

SOUTH AFRICA P252

RUTA MAYA P257

Kit out that camel and go touring the exotic temples of India's regal state, Rajasthan

WILDLIFE & RAILS?

BOTH?

NICARAGUA P270

FLORIDA, USA P261

Travel on the Blue Train from Cape Town to a big-game Kruger safari in South Africa

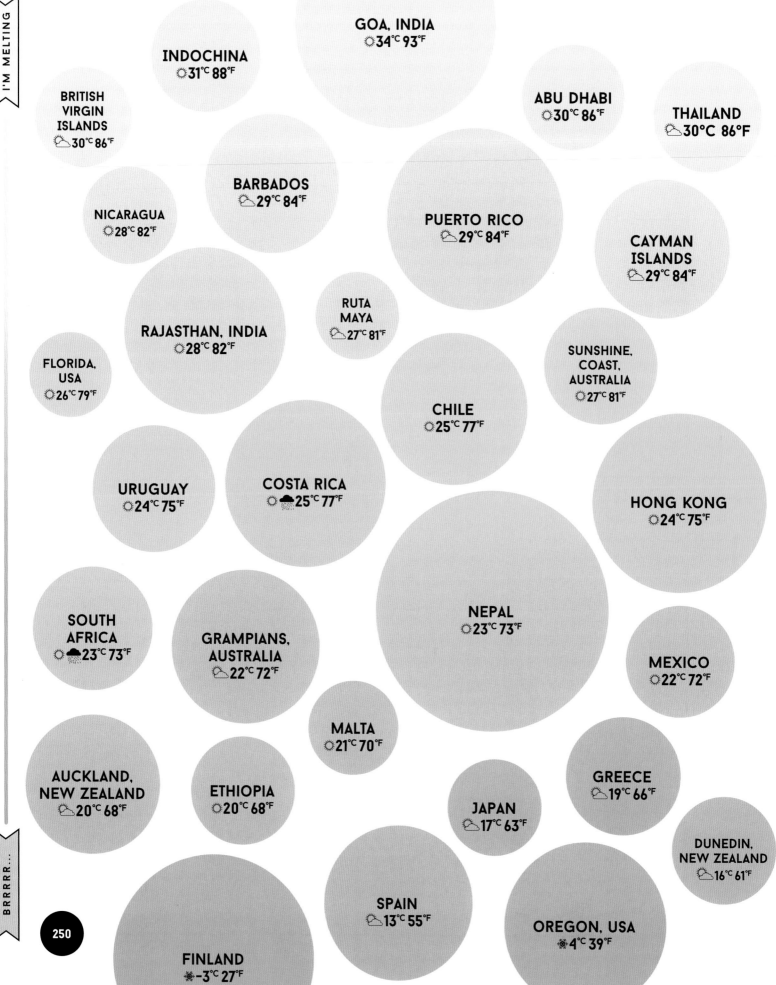

GOA, INDIA
☀ 34℃ 93℉

INDOCHINA
☀ 31℃ 88℉

ABU DHABI
☀ 30℃ 86℉

THAILAND
⛅ 30℃ 86℉

BRITISH
VIRGIN
ISLANDS
⛅ 30℃ 86℉

BARBADOS
⛅ 29℃ 84℉

PUERTO RICO
⛅ 29℃ 84℉

CAYMAN
ISLANDS
⛅ 29℃ 84℉

NICARAGUA
☀ 28℃ 82℉

RUTA
MAYA
⛅ 27℃ 81℉

SUNSHINE,
COAST,
AUSTRALIA
☀ 27℃ 81℉

RAJASTHAN, INDIA
☀ 28℃ 82℉

FLORIDA,
USA
☀ 26℃ 79℉

CHILE
☀ 25℃ 77℉

URUGUAY
☀ 24℃ 75℉

COSTA RICA
☀🌧 25℃ 77℉

HONG KONG
☀ 24℃ 75℉

SOUTH
AFRICA
☀🌧 23℃ 73℉

GRAMPIANS,
AUSTRALIA
⛅ 22℃ 72℉

NEPAL
☀ 23℃ 73℉

MEXICO
☀ 22℃ 72℉

MALTA
☀ 21℃ 70℉

AUCKLAND,
NEW ZEALAND
⛅ 20℃ 68℉

ETHIOPIA
☀ 20℃ 68℉

JAPAN
⛅ 17℃ 63℉

GREECE
⛅ 19℃ 66℉

DUNEDIN,
NEW ZEALAND
⛅ 16℃ 61℉

SPAIN
⛅ 13℃ 55℉

OREGON, USA
❄ 4℃ 39℉

FINLAND
❄ -3℃ 27℉

VERY
FAMILY
FRIENDLY

FLORIDA, USA

SUNSHINE COAST, AUSTRALIA

NICARAGUA

RUKA, FINLAND

PUERTO RICO

GRAMPIANS, AUSTRALIA

OREGON, USA

Book a cookery
course then head to
the hilly rice fields of
north Thailand

AUCKLAND, NZ

BARBADOS

Sup on Bajan rum
by turquoise seas in
wonderfully laidback
Caribbean style

NORTHERN THAILAND

CAYMAN IS.

HONG KONG, CHINA

RAJASTHAN, INDIA

NEPAL

November is when
the skies are clearest
over the world's
highest mountain

VALLETTA, MALTA

ABU DHABI, UAE

Make the most of
Malta's mild climes
and holiday in a
Unesco-listed city

BRITISH VIRGIN IS.

ATHENS & EVIA, GREECE

GOA, INDIA

EXPENSIVE
BUT WORTH IT

GOOD
VALUE

MADRID, SPAIN

MEKONG, INDOCHINA

HONSHU, JAPAN

RUTA MAYA

During autumn
on Honshu, the
countryside is
aflame with colour

DUNEDIN, NZ

COSTA RICA

Hone your predatory
instincts for spotting
animals on a South
African safari

SOUTH AFRICA

A trip along the
Mekong will take you
through Cambodia,
Vietnam and Laos

MEXICO CITY

URUGUAY

South America's
smallest country
serves super steaks
and a great coastline

ATACAMA, CHILE

With its mountains
and elevated castles,
Ethiopia offers a
unique high

SIMIENS, ETHIOPIA

LEAVE
THE KIDS
AT HOME

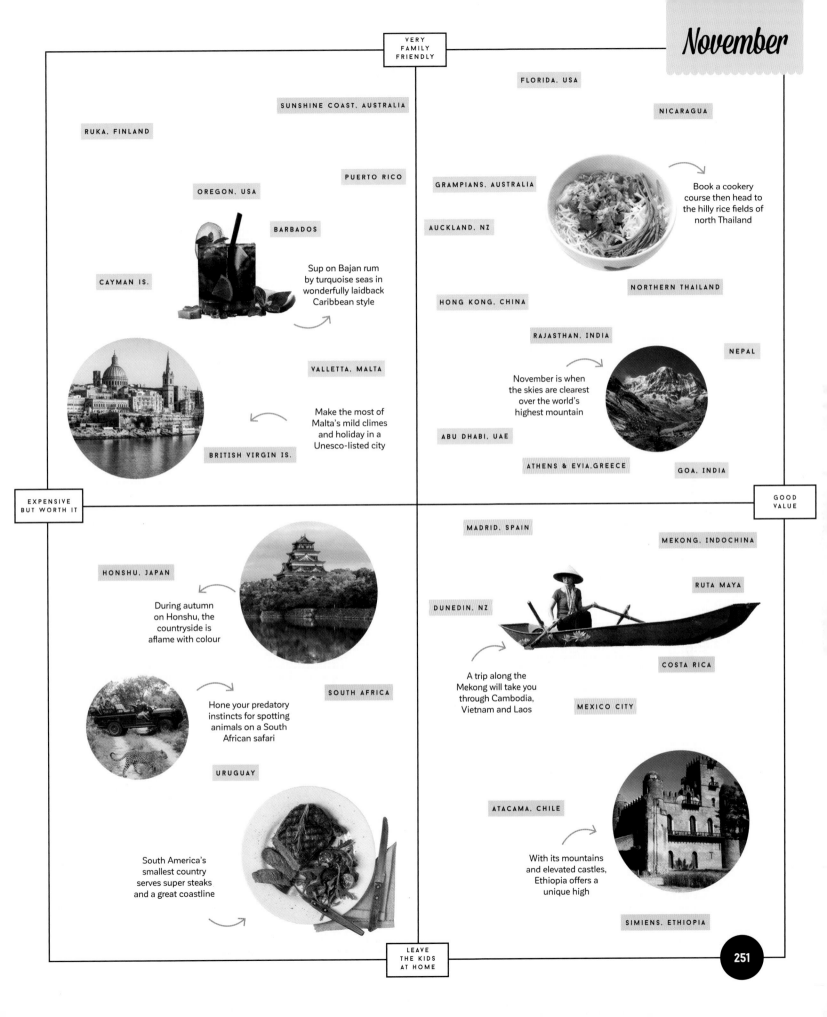

SOUTH AFRICA

→ **Why now? Take a great train and view some wonderful wildlife.**

Cape Town in late spring is lovely – buzzy, dry and warm (23°C; 73°F). Further northeast, around Kruger National Park, things are more dramatic – the beginning of the rains heralds electrifying thunderstorms and greening landscapes (thrilling for photographers) as well as exciting wildlife-viewing as a glut of cute newborns arouses the predators. It's an interesting time to combine two classic South Africa experiences: the luxurious Blue Train and a Kruger safari. The Blue Train rolls between Cape Town and Pretoria (near Johannesburg), via neat vineyards and the wild Karoo. Complete with butler service and fancy trimmings, it's one of the world's great rail journeys (though note: no-frills Shosholoza Meyl trains run the same route for a fraction of the price). Kruger is one of Africa's premier parks, chock-full of animals – including the Big Five – plus ancient rock art.

Trip plan: Spend several days in Cape Town before riding the train north (27 hours). Flights link Johannesburg to Kruger; choose a self-drive safari (good value, good for families) or a stay at an adjoining private game reserve (more expensive, more activities possible).

Need to know: Kruger is in a malaria-risk area – seek advice on prevention.

Other months: Nov-Apr – warm/hot, Kruger wet (Jan-Feb: rains peak); May-Oct – cooler, Kruger dry.

■ Wildlife & nature
■ Cultural
■ Value
■ Journey

Silver service, the dining car aboard the Blue Train, South Africa

GOA
INDIA

Why now? Dry skies and blissful boltholes.

Goa is no longer the hippy enclave it once was. The boho beaches of Anjuna and Vagator are increasingly commercialised – though still fun for fleamarket browsing and a party vibe. However, Goa has plenty of other peaceful, palm-wafted enclaves. Seek them out in November (average 28°C; 82°F), when the landscape is lush from the recent monsoon but barely a raindrop falls. The state's south tends to be quieter – there are fishing villages and scenic sands around Canacona where you can chill in coastal bungalows or heritage homestays. Try Agonda Beach or Galgibag. In the north, head for the area around Morjim and Mandrem, home to funky bars and boutique hotels, as well as an inventive Goan-fusion foodie scene.

Trip plan: Fly to Goa's Dabolim Airport and choose the bolthole that best suits. There are backpacker cabins, converted Portuguese mansions and a proliferation of yoga retreats (especially in the north). Allow time for a spice plantation tour, the ruins of Old Goa and a houseboat cruise along the Siolim River's backwaters.

Need to know: The scenic Mumbai–Mangalore Konkan Railway crosses Goa.

Other months: Oct-Mar – dry, cool; Apr-May – hot; Jun-Sep – monsoon, wet.

CAYMAN ISLANDS

Why now? Beaches, bargains and buccaneers.

Comprising the three islands of Cayman Brac, Grand Cayman and Little Cayman, this British Overseas Territory is the world's fifth-largest banking centre. But Cayman isn't only a haven for wealth – it's also a wildlife haven. It has more flora species than the Galápagos; a 20,000-strong colony of red-footed boobies; and some remarkable endemics, from the Cayman Brac parrot to the blue iguana. The beaches are beautiful: Grand Cayman's Seven Mile Beach is great for families and water sports. Head elsewhere, especially to the two smaller isles, and you'll find white sands without another soul. In November, the rains have largely abated, the temperature is glorious (25-30°C; 77-86°F) and the mid-month Pirate Week adds a dash of swashbuckling. Also, prices are lower before peak season – the money men would approve.

Trip plan: Island-hop by plane. Visit Grand Cayman for shopping and boat trips to Stingray City sandbar; Cayman Brac for limestone bat caves and wreck diving; Little Cayman for nesting turtles, beaches and dives at Bloody Bay Wall.

Need to know: Cayman is 480 miles (770km) south of Miami (70-minute flight).

Other months: Dec-Apr – dry, cool, busy; May-Jul – hot, quieter; Aug-Oct – wettest; Nov – cheaper, drier.

SIMIEN MOUNTAINS
ETHIOPIA

Why now? For a unique high.

Ethiopia is known as the 'Roof of Africa' – it has more mountains than any other country on the continent. Its highest peak, 15,157ft (4620m) Ras Dashen, sits within Ethiopia's most striking landscape, the Simien range. Geologically speaking, there's nowhere else like this extraordinary swath of basaltic peaks, pinnacles, gullies and escarpments, which have been eroded over millions of years. It's prime trekking terrain, with options ranging from day hikes along ancient paths to a two-week traverse. All routes reveal jaw-dropping views, tiny time-warp villages and, with luck, endemic wildlife – from walia ibex to gelada monkeys. Dry November, when the countryside is still lush from the rains, is an ideal month.

Trip plan: From capital Addis Ababa, travel north via Gondar's castles and the rock-hewn churches of Lalibela to Debark (the Simiens' hub). Here, arrange a multi-day hike; for example, spend five to 10 days hiking from Sankaber to Ras Dashen via the Geech Abyss and the breathtaking Imet Gogo lookout.

Need to know: Altitude sickness is common in Ethiopia – even Addis Ababa is at 7726ft (2355m). Stay well-hydrated and acclimatise before strenuous activity.

Other months: Nov-Feb – dry, cool; Mar-Apr – warming; May-Jun – warmer, some rain; Jul-Oct – rainy (Jul-Aug: wettest).

- Relaxation
- Cultural
- Food & drink
- Value

- Relaxation
- Value
- Wildlife & nature

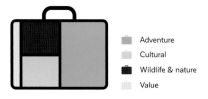

- Adventure
- Cultural
- Wildlife & nature
- Value

© Wil Bignal / 500px

PUERTO RICO

Why now? To feel thankful.
A US 'unincorporated territory' and proudly Latino, Puerto Rico brings a unique cultural mix to Caribbean paradise. It has incredible sands – notably on the islands of Vieques and Culebra, where former US navy occupation kept developers away. But there are also Spanish colonial towns, a cave-riddled countryside and swaths of mountainous jungle (viewable via some of the world's longest zip lines). Deals can be found in pre-peak-season November. While there's a chance of rain, more likely are lovely 30°C (86°F) days, plus a festive vibe as Puerto Rico readies for its own take on Thanksgiving – here, turkeys get stuffed with mashed plantain.

Trip plan: Explore the alleys of Old San Juan (founded 1521) then head into El Yunque rainforest for hikes. Sail to Vieques to kayak with glowing plankton in Bioluminescent Bay. Take another ferry to offbeat Culebra to explore the wildlife refuge. Return to the main island, travelling to lively second city, Ponce. Veer into the mountains (stay at a highland retreat), then surf at Rincón. Return to San Juan via the caves of Karst Country. Intersperse beach time. Allow two weeks.

Need to know: Kayak in Bioluminescent Bay around new moon, when skies are darkest.

Other months: Dec-Apr – dry, busy; May-Jun – quieter, hottest; Jul-Oct – wettest; Nov – warm, cheaper.

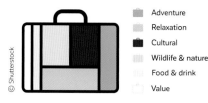

Adventure
Relaxation
Cultural
Wildlife & nature
Food & drink
Value

BRITISH VIRGIN ISLANDS

Why now? Set sail before the crowds.
BVI is probably the best place on the planet to hoist the mainsail and float off into the blue. Conditions are just about perfect for sailors of all levels: the BVI's 60-or-so islands are closely huddled, so navigation by line-of-sight is possible; trade winds are consistent and warm; waters are safe and sheltered; tidal currents are minimal; the marinas are splendid. Sailing makes it easy to hop between the four main islands: Tortola, the most developed; laidback Virgin Gorda, home to blissful granite pools called the Baths; party island Jost Van Dyke; and reef-fringed Anegada. Experienced sailors will be in heaven. Beginners can learn with the Royal BVI Yacht Club or hire a crewed boat to enjoy the benefits of sailing – such as private coves and deck-top sundowners – without the effort. November (25-30°C; 77-86°F) is still hurricane season, but is rarely stormy and offers the yachtie lifestyle at cheaper prices.

Trip plan: Join a flotilla holiday, suitable for sailors and novices. A week's itinerary might include the Baths, Norman Island's caves, the Dogs (three clustered islets) and Jost Van Dyke's lively Great Harbour.

Need to know: There are no direct flights to BVI from airports outside the Caribbean.

Other months: Dec-Mar – dry, busy; Apr-May – hotter; Jun-Oct – wetter, hurricanes possible; Nov – cheaper.

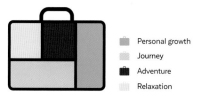

Personal growth
Journey
Adventure
Relaxation

GRAMPIANS
AUSTRALIA

Why now? For the start of summer in the marvellous mountains.
As far as the traditional owners of the Gariwerd (Grampians) are concerned, November is when Petyan, a season of regrowth and wildflowers, turns into butterfly-filled Ballambar, the onset of summer. It's a lovely time to explore the escarpments and forests of these sandstone ranges. Waterfalls are full, bushfire risk is low and temperatures ideal (23°C; 73°F). Halls Gap is the main hub, and home to the Brambuk Cultural Centre, where you can learn dreamtime stories and plan excursions into Grampians National Park. Hiking routes abound, including sections of the Grampians Peaks Trail; on completion in 2019, this will be a 89-mile (144km) epic. Near Halls Gap there are also spectacular viewpoints: stroll through stringybark forest to the Balconies for a sweeping panorama.

Trip plan: Drive the Grampians Way, linking Halls Gap, Wartook Valley (for horseriding and quadbiking), Stapylton (olive oil tasting), Billimina Shelter's rock art, and fine-dining in Dunkeld.

Need to know: Melbourne to Halls Gap is a three-hour drive. Stop on the way at wineries in the Pyrenees to buy peppery shiraz.

Other months: Dec-Feb – hottest, bushfire risk; Mar-May – mild; Jun-Aug – cold; Sep-Nov – wildflowers, warming.

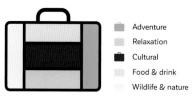

Adventure
Relaxation
Cultural
Food & drink
Wildlife & nature

© Shutterstock

© BlueOrange Studio / Shutterstock

Overview of Cape
Reinga, New
Zealand's most
northerly point

El Palacio, one of the
key Mayan ruins at
Tulum, Mexico

The Peacock
Gate inside City
Palace, Jaipur

© Matt Munro / Lonely Planet

256

AUCKLAND & NORTHLAND
NEW ZEALAND

Why now? Sneak in some pre-season city and wilderness fun.

Quick! Kiwi schools kick out mid-December, so choose quieter, warming November to explore Auckland and the north. Late spring brings mild weather (20°C; 68°F) to NZ's biggest city – good for climbing 643ft Mt Eden (196m; Auckland's highest volcano), braving the Harbour Bridge Climb or helming an America's Cup yacht in Waitemata Harbour – well, this is the City of Sails. If it rains, admire Auckland Museum's Māori art. Nearby lie wineries and wild surf beaches, but if you have time, head into Northland, NZ's only subtropical region, for outdoor thrills and historical punch. The beautiful Bay of Islands will please walkers, kayakers, cruisers and history buffs – visit Waitangi, where New Zealand's founding treaty was signed. Keep going north to drive on Ninety Mile Beach and reach land's end at Cape Reinga, where the spirits of deceased Māori are said leave this world.

Trip plan: From Auckland, allow a week to loop Northland. Include a night walk amid Waipoua's massive kauri trees and go dune-surfing at Hokianga (fun for families). Stop in Tutukaka for world-class diving off the Poor Knights Islands.

Need to know: Hire cars aren't insured for beach driving – join a tour of Ninety Mile Beach.

Other months: Dec-Feb – warm, busy; Mar-May – cooler, changeable; Jun-Aug – cold, wetter; Sep-Nov – warming, quieter.

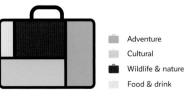

- Adventure
- Cultural
- Wildlife & nature
- Food & drink

RUTA MAYA
GUATEMALA, BELIZE & MEXICO

Why now? Cool climes for ancient ruins.

The Mayan civilisation, which flourished from 2000 BC until the 17th century, left quite a mark on Central America. The remains of their mighty cities are scattered across the region, notably around Mexico's cave-riddled Yucatán Peninsula, jungly northern Guatemala and tiny Belize. Follow the unofficial Ruta Maya to fully appreciate their architectural skills. Start in Cancún – this busy resort is a handy gateway for accessing the Yucatán's cool cenotes (sinkholes) plus vast Chichén Itzá (one of the biggest Mayan centres), the seaside ruins of Tulum and astronomically aligned Uxmal. Further southwest, visit forest-shrouded Palenque before crossing into Guatemala's Petén region to see monkeys bounding amid Tikal's pyramids. There are also remoter ruins here (such as half-excavated El Mirador) that can only be reached via multi-day trek. From Petén, hop into Belize for the huge temples of Caracol. Finish by the Caribbean at Caye Caulker. November, before peak season starts, and when it's largely dry and cool (20-27°C; 68-81°F), is a good month.

Trip plan: Allow two weeks to travel from Cancún to Belize; with more time, add on Honduras to visit the ruins of Copán.

Need to know: Drives between sites can be slow and bumpy; allow for delays at borders.

Other months: Nov-Apr – warm, dry; May-Oct – hotter, wet.

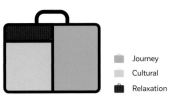

- Journey
- Cultural
- Relaxation

RAJASTHAN & THE GOLDEN TRIANGLE INDIA

Why now? Temperate touring around the regal state.

Rajasthan is the India of your imagination: colourful, chaotic, pulsating, exotic; full of tigers, temples, palaces and bazaars. It's the ideal choice for India first-timers, and is ideal in November, when days are dry and sunny but not oppressively hot (29°C; 84°F). Begin in sense-assaulting Delhi, then head to Rajasthan's three major cities: bustling pink-painted Jaipur; cobalt-blue Jodhpur, with its clifftop fort; and whitewashed Udaipur, which sits by Lake Pichola. En route lies Ranthambore National Park, where tigers stalk amid jungle and medieval ruins. Further west lies Jaisalmer, a desert citadel in the Thar Desert. Near Delhi, but just outside Rajasthan, is Agra, home to the unmissable Taj Mahal.

Trip plan: With one week, combine Delhi, Jaipur and Agra by train or private car, with a quick stop at the abandoned city of Fatehpur Sikri. With 10 days, add Ranthambore. With two weeks, include Udaipur and Jodhpur. Ideally allow three.

Need to know: November sees thousands of decorated dromedaries gather at the Pushkar Camel Fair; Diwali sometimes falls this month too.

Other months: Oct-Mar – warm, dry, sunny; Apr-Jun – very hot, humid; Jul-Sep – hot, wet, monsoon.

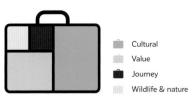

- Cultural
- Value
- Journey
- Wildlife & nature

Playa Sámara makes
a great add-on
to turtle-saving
expeditions

Kyoto's Kinkaku-ji
(Golden Pavilion),
a great place to
take in *koyo*

© Jonathan Gregson / Lonely Planet

COSTA RICA

→ **Why now? To save turtles.**
Marino Las Baulas National Park, in Costa Rica's northwestern Guanacaste province, is one of the world's most important nesting sites for leatherback turtles. These huge reptiles, which can weigh up to 1100lb (500kg), have probably been hauling ashore to lay their eggs on these dazzling Pacific beaches for millions of years; the park was created in 1995 to protect them. The leatherbacks usually visit from November to February, and it's possible to join a guided night tour to try to see them. Alternatively, sign up for a volunteer program to help protect these ancient creatures. Tasks might include beach patrols, attaching tracking devices to the turtles and relocating eggs to a hatchery. As a bonus, arid Guanacaste is

prettiest in November – it's the end of the rainy season, so the land looks fresh and green.

Trip planner: Volunteer placements usually last a week or more. Add on trips to the volcanic landscapes of nearby Rincón de la Vieja National Park and the fine beach of Playa Sámara.

Need to know: Guanacaste's Liberia Airport is 56 miles (90km) from the park.

Other months: Jan-Apr – driest, busiest; May-Aug – green season; Sep-Oct – wettest; Nov-Dec – variable, green, drying.

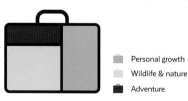

■ Personal growth
■ Wildlife & nature
■ Adventure

TOKYO & HONSHU

JAPAN

→ **Why now? The country is aflame with autumn hues.**

Japan in November? Come for *koyo* – the autumnal turn of the trees, which sets cities and countryside on fire. November is peak month for leaf-peeping on Honshu, Japan's main island; fewer tourists, mild temperatures (16°C; 61°F) and relatively low rainfall add to the appeal. In Tokyo, head for the landscaped garden of Rikugien, which does nighttime illuminations during peak leaf season. Outside the city, see autumn enliven the Fuji Five Lake region – Lake Kawaguchiko offers especially scenic views of fall colours and Mt Fuji. Kyoto is a *koyo* hotspot: stroll beneath the crimson maples at Tōfuku-ji temple or admire the burning hillsides behind Arashiyama's temples, which usually turn in mid-November. In Kurobe Gorge, a tree-cloaked ravine in the Japanese Alps, a scenic train runs amid the autumn splendour.

Trip plan: Start in Tokyo: admire the bright-yellow ginkgo trees (a symbol of the city) and eat well (November is especially good for seafood). Then view the colours in the countryside around Nikkō or Hakone before heading to a traditional *ryokan* (inn) in Kyoto.

Need to know: During the season, a daily *koyo* forecast is issued, predicting when colours will peak.

Other months: Mar-May – blossom; Jun-Aug – warmest; Sep-Nov – fall colours; Dec-Feb – snow, coldest.

Wildlife & nature
Cultural
Food & drink

259

ABU DHABI
UNITED ARAB EMIRATES

Why now? Manageable heat and artistic masterpieces.

A few decades ago, this spot on the Persian Gulf was no more than a fishing village. Now UAE capital Abu Dhabi is a metropolis of glass and steel, dripping in oil money and six-star hotels. If you want a luxe stay with guaranteed sun (30°C; 86°F), unlikely rain and well-groomed sandy beaches, a November visit to this Emirate might be just the thing. The overpowering summer heat has subsided, but the winter peak hasn't yet begun, so cheaper deals are possible. You can enjoy Abu Dhabi's expanding cultural side too. See Islamic worship at its most opulent at the vast Sheikh Zayed Mosque, which has 80 domes and the world's largest hand-loomed carpet. Also, the new Jean Nouvel–designed Abu Dhabi Louvre and the Frank Gehry–designed Guggenheim (open in 2017) add significant architectural and artistic heft. Works by the likes of Andy Warhol and Leonardo da Vinci will be on display.

Trip plan: Combine a luxury hotel stay with activities: walk the Corniche, visit the mosque and museums, venture inland for camel rides and dune-bashing.

Need to know: Sheikh Zayed Mosque is open to non-Muslims in conservative dress.

Other months: Apr & Nov – hot, quieter; May-Sep – roasting; Dec-Mar – mildest, busy, wettest (though still dry).

Relaxation
Cultural

VALLETTA MALTA

Why now? Lingering warmth, enduring history.

Tiny Malta has a marvellous Mediterranean climate – it's still toasty warm in November, when much of Europe shivers. Indeed, with temperatures around 21°C (70°F) and seas holding on to the last of the summer's heat, hitting the beautiful beaches of sister-isle Gozo remains viable. However, the mild climes are especially suited to a Valletta city break. Malta's harbour-hugging capital looks much as it has for 400 years, when it was founded by the Knights of Malta. The baroque palaces, churches, narrow lanes and beefy fortifications are so well-preserved that the city is Unesco-listed in its entirety, and will be European Capital of Culture in 2018. For the best overview, head to the Upper Barrakka Gardens. To see Valletta from water-level, sail across the Grand Harbour in a traditional *dghajsa* (open boat).

Trip plan: Allow a week. Stay in Valletta (perhaps in a converted palazzo) and hire a car. Visit St Paul's Bay, the Blue Grotto, Marsaxlokk (for great seafood), medieval Mdina and the Dingli Cliffs. Take the ferry over to Gozo for a peaceful farmstay.

Need to know: The Malta–Gozo ferry takes 25 minutes.

Other months: Dec-Apr – chilly; May-Jun & Oct-Nov – warm, uncrowded; Jun-Sep – hot, dry, busy.

Cultural
Relaxation
Food & drink

URUGUAY

Why now? Warm, offbeat sands and super steaks.

Tiny Uruguay, South America's smallest country, isn't the continent's most obvious holiday destination. But with *asado* (barbecue) to rival Argentina and gorgeous white sands to match Brazil, it deserves more attention. November is lovely (24°C; 75°F), and the beaches are quieter than peak-season December. There's also still the chance to spot southern right whales from the shore (they pass by July to November). In capital Montevideo you can stroll leafy boulevards and eat amazing meat at the wrought-iron Mercado del Puerto; more atmospheric is cobbled, Unesco-listed Colonia del Sacramento, Uruguay's oldest town. Along the country's 410-mile (660km) coast, find glamour at Punta del Este, boutiquey glitz at José Ignacio, laidback cabañas in La Pedrera or splendid isolation at Cabo Polonio (only accessible on foot or by horse). Inland, where cowboy culture rules supreme, stay at a working *estancia* amid the rolling plains to combine days in the saddle with great steaks and fine wines.

Trip plan: Visit Colonia, Montevideo, the golden coast and gaucho country. Tag on time in Buenos Aires. Allow two weeks.

Need to know: Ferries across the River Plate link Buenos Aires and Colonia (one hour).

Other months: Dec-Feb – hot, busiest; Mar-May – cooler, still-warm seas; Jun-Aug – coldest (Jul-Nov: whales); Oct-Nov – warming, quieter, whales.

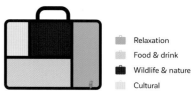

Relaxation
Food & drink
Wildlife & nature
Cultural

© Shutterstock

Art Deco-era hotel
on Ocean Drive,
South Beach, Miami

© Kris Davidson / Lonely Planet

FLORIDA USA

Why now? For parks and recreation.
Whether you're interested in real animals or cartoon ones, November is a fine time to visit the Sunshine State. It's the start of the dry season, so it's ideal for biking, air-boating and canoeing in the wildlife-filled Everglades without the nuisance of bugs. However, if you'd rather see Goofy than alligators, November is good for that too. Orlando's hotels tend to be cheaper and theme parks quieter this month (aside from the period around Thanksgiving). That means potential financial savings and less time spent queuing at Disney World, Universal Studios and the like – you might also see the Christmas decorations and shows, without the December crowds. And although winter is approaching, the temperature is still a delight (26°C; 79°F), so Florida's beaches remain tempting too.
Trip plan: Spend a week indulging your

inner child at Orlando's theme parks and a week elsewhere: the Gulf of Mexico coast for white beaches and Cape Canaveral; southern Florida for Miami and the Everglades; or a drive from Miami down through the Florida Keys.
Need to know: Miami to Orlando is a one-hour flight, four-hour drive or seven-hour train ride.

Other months: May-Sep – hot, busy, wet; Oct-Nov – dry, warm, uncrowded; Dec – dry, cool, busy; Jan-Apr – cool/warm, quieter.

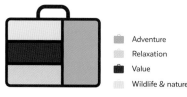

- Adventure
- Relaxation
- Value
- Wildlife & nature

OREGON USA

Why now? Early ski fun, with a macabre edge.
Mt Hood, a 11,250ft (3429m) stratovolcano amid the Cascade Range, has North America's longest ski season. You can swoosh down the glaciers here in mid-June. However, the winter season usually starts early November, as the snow begins to dump and the full range of pistes becomes runnable. Mt Hood's Timberline ski area has 41 runs (25% beginner, 50% intermediate, 25% advanced), plus the Pacific Northwest's longest vertical drop. It

also has characterful old Timberline Lodge, built in 1937 as part of a public works program during the Great Depression, and now designated a National Historic Landmark. It's the state's only ski-in hotel, and even played a role in The Shining movie. It's an atmospheric place to stay whether you're a powderhound or not.
Trip plan: Bar-hop in Portland before heading to Timberline. Group and private ski/snowboard lessons are available. The lodge has a sauna, hot tub and heated outdoor pool (open year-round).

Need to know: Timberline is 62 miles (100km) east of Portland; Mount Hood Express buses run from Sandy (east of Portland) to the lodge.
Other months: Nov-May – snow; Jun-Aug – summer skiing; Sep-Oct – possible skiing, dependent on conditions.

- Adventure
- Wildlife & nature
- Relaxation

BARBADOS

→ **Why now? For some lime time on the island.**

'Liming' is the Caribbean word for relaxing while sharing good food, drink and company. If that sounds appealing, then balmy, boozy Barbados is just the ticket. There's a beach for everyone: sands are golden yellow, bright white and rosy pink, lapped by calm seas or pounded by world-class surf. There are glamorous hotels, cliff-top yoga retreats and family-run guesthouses, accoladed eateries and late-night fish frys. And there's rum, lots of rum. The sugar cane liquor is thought to have originated on Bajan slave plantations in the 17th century, and continues to be the local drink of choice. Sipping a shot while watching the sun slide into the turquoise waves is quintessential Barbados. That said, there's more to the island. Capital Bridgetown's historic Garrison area is a fascinating detour, while the fertile, undulating interior is flecked with botanic gardens, plantation houses, caves and ravines. Visit in November, when storms are unlikely but peak season hasn't begun, to get a cheaper deal.

Trip plan: Pick your spot. The west coast has the calmest waters and most luxurious hotels; the south is more developed; the wild Atlantic-facing east is unspoiled, but rougher. Include excursions into the interior.

Need to know: Topless sunbathing is against the law.

Other months: Dec-Apr – dry, busy; May-Jun – quieter, stickier; Jul-Oct – wettest, hurricanes possible; Nov – shoulder month.

Relaxation
Cultural
Value
Food & drink

Sunny inside and out, Mullins Beach Bar, Barbados

DUNEDIN
NEW ZEALAND

→ **Why now?** Beer, buildings and birds.
Dunedin is one of those places that you visit for a weekend and end up not wanting to leave. Immensely liveable, the South Island town is home to New Zealand's oldest university. This gives it a cultural edge (it's even a Unesco City of Literature), while the large student population ensures an abundance of coffee shops, craft-brew bars, indie music and arts events. Dunedin wears its heritage well too and, since earthquakes devastated Christchurch, now has the country's highest density of historic buildings. If you need further convincing to take a late-spring break here (when highs average 16°C; 61°F), know that Cadbury's chocolate and Speight's beer are produced in the city; you can tour both sites. Dunedin is also gateway to the Otago Peninsula. In less than an hour, you can be at Taiaroa Head, gazing at the world's only mainland albatross colony, plus penguins, fur seals and cliffs rife with birds.
Trip plan: Take a long weekend. Visit Otago Farmers' Market (Saturdays), follow the Street Art Trail and take a guided heritage walk, then drive to Taiaroa.
Need to know: Dunedin is 221 miles (356km) south of Christchurch.
Other months: Dec-Feb – hottest, busiest; Mar-May – cooler; Jun-Aug – cold; Sep-Nov – warming.

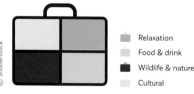

Relaxation
Food & drink
Wildlife & nature
Cultural

RUKA FINLAND

→ **Why now?** An early snow fix.
Do you really, really need to ski? Then get thee to Ruka! On account of its northerly location and usually reliable dumps of snow, this Finnish resort boasts the longest non-glacier ski season in Europe. Its slopes usually open in October (though are best from November) and don't close until May. Cute, car-free Ruka village is an especially good base for families: it has the biggest beginner area in the country and offers a range of other activities, from sleigh rides and husky-sledding to ice-fishing and traditional Finnish saunas. The downhill slopes, 34 in all, are never that crowded; most of them are floodlit, so you can ski during the 24-hour darkness of polar night. Keep an eye out for the aurora borealis too.
Trip plan: Book a week in a cosy log cabin in Ruka, mixing downhill skiing with excellent cross-country trails and other snow activities.
Need to know: Ruka is 500 miles (800km) from Helsinki. It is a one-hour flight from Helsinki to Kuusamo Airport, 15 miles (25km) from Ruka.
Other months: Oct-Apr – winter, snow activities; May – thawing; Jun-Sep – warmer, midnight sun.

Adventure
Wildlife & nature

NEPAL

→ **Why now?** The clearest skies over the highest Himalaya.
Crisp, cloud-free, warm, dry – a delight. November is perfect for exploring all of Nepal, from its mountain highs to its jungly lows and the culture-rich ripples in between. In the Kathmandu Valley, 22°C (72°F) days are comfortable for temple touring in Patan and Bhaktapur. Down on the steamy *terai* (plain), it's 27°C (81°F) and mud-free, so it's easier to search for rhinos, tigers and other creatures that lurk therein. Rivers are full countrywide, and offer great rafting for all levels – from the serene Seti to the raging Kali Gandaki. And then there are the mountains: 26,000ft (8000m) peaks soaring into clear blue skies; myriad hiking trails open for business. The main routes, such as the Annapurna Sanctuary, will be busy – good for trekker camaraderie. But choose one of Nepal's more offbeat routes (Kanchenjunga Base Camp, Upper Dolpo) if you'd prefer to hike away from the crowds.
Trip plan: In two weeks, link the Kathmandu Valley, Chitwan and lakeside Pokhara, incorporating short walks. Multi-day treks, which can be remote, may require longer stays.
Need to know: Practise the traditional Nepali greeting: hold your palms together, say 'Namaste' (I salute the god within you).
Other months: Oct-Nov – clear, dry; Dec-Feb – dry, colder; Mar-May – warm, flowers; Jun-Sep – hot, monsoon (Jul-Aug: wettest).

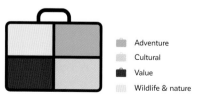

Adventure
Cultural
Value
Wildlife & nature

MEXICO CITY
MEXICO

→ Why now? A ghoulishly good time. This month starts with a bang in Mexico. Día de Muertos (Day of the Dead; 1–2 November) sees families honour their dearly departed by building altars and adorning them with marigolds, candles, sugar skulls and tequila. In Mexico City, skeleton outfits are de rigueur and an enormous altar is erected in the main Zócalo square. It's the quirkiest, most colourful of occasions. But mountain-ringed Mexico City – one of the world's largest metropolitan areas – is fun to visit throughout the month. The rains have ended and temperatures are cool (10-22°C; 50-72°F), good for exploring the sites of the Centro Histórico: the Palacio Nacional's Diego Rivera murals, the remains of the Aztec Templo Mayor, and the massive Metropolitan Cathedral. Mexico City is also fabulously foodie. Take a guided culinary tour through Merced Market, where you can buy almost anything, from candy to *chapulines* (grasshoppers). Or graze in the neighbourhoods of Cuauhtémoc and Zona Rosa, hopping between stalls selling steamed tamales, tacos filled with *frijoles* (beans), *carnitas* ('little meats') and fresh tortilla flatbreads.

Trip plan: Tag a few days in the city onto a

© High Gamma / 500px

Caribbean-coast beach break.
Need to know: Benito Juárez airport is 7 miles (11km) east of the city centre.
Other months: Nov-Feb – cool, dry; Mar-May – hottest, dry; Jun-Oct – wet.

The grand facade of Palacio de Bellas Artes

■ Culture
■ Food & drink

BEYOND MEXICO CITY

TEOTIHUACÁN · 30 MILES (48KM) · Remains of a gargantuan pre-Colombian city

PUEBLA · 80 MILES (128KM) · Colonial gem, with fantastic food and volcano views

MONARCH BUTTERFLY BIOSPHERE RESERVE · 115 MILES (185KM) · Billions of butterflies fill the forests

MÉRIDA · 800 MILES (1287KM) · Fly 1¾ hours to the Yucatán's Mayan sites and Caribbean beaches

HONG KONG
CHINA

→ **Why now?** Ideal weather for urban and outdoor adventures.

This is the best month to make the most of multifaceted Hong Kong. The Special Administrative Region of China is renowned for its skyscrapers, which look especially shiny under November's sunny skies (admire them from the deck of the famed Star Ferry). But Hong Kong also has a wilder side: less than 25% of this mountainous territory is developed; much is protected within country parks where ridges, bird-filled lagoons and sandy bays offer stark contrast to the 21st-century mega-glitz. The comfortably warm, dry days of November are ideal for hiking. Hit peaceful Lantau Island or sections of the 62-mile (100km) MacLehose Trail to uncover fishing villages, indigenous Hakka heritage and views of both tree-cloaked peaks and glittering towers.

Trip plan: See the highlights in 48 hours or stay a week to explore the city and countryside. Allow time for eclectic eating: this cosmopolitan foodie hub serves everything from dim sum and hotpot to Indian curries and high tea.

Need to know: Hong Kong Airport is 15 miles (24km) west of the city; Airport Express trains connect to the centre in 25 minutes.

Other months: Oct-Dec – warm, dry, sunny; Jan-Mar – cool, dry, cloudy; Apr-May – hotter, wetter; Jun-Sep – wettest, typhoons possible.

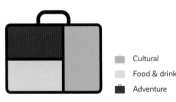

Cultural
Food & drink
Adventure

Although famous for its skyline, Hong Kong has plenty of nature to explore

ATHENS & EVIA
GREECE

→ **Why now?** To run or rest amid ancient ruins.

Ever wanted to run a marathon? Then do it here, in its spiritual home. In 490 BC, Pheidippides dashed from Marathonas to Athens to announce the Greek army's victory over the Persians (then promptly died). Today's Athens Marathon, held along the same route in early November, is a great way to combine a personal challenge with a warm city-and-beach break. However, you don't have to run 26.2 miles to enjoy Athens in autumn. The temperatures (10-18°C; 50-64°F) are ideal for wandering the sites, from the Acropolis to panoramic Lykavitós Hill. Most fun is exploring Athens' neighbourhoods – Pláka, Monastiráki, Psyrrí – and hopping between bars and tavernas until the small hours. Then, do as the Athenians do and escape to Evia, Greece's second-largest island, but one largely overlooked by foreign tourists. It has glittering Aegean beaches, a mountainous interior, ancient sites and great food – perfect for recovering from a marathon, or modern life in general.

Trip plan: Allow three days in Athens before decamping to Evia. Chalkida, Evia's ancient capital, is halfway down the west coast; explore from here.

Need to know: Evia is linked to the mainland by two bridges plus ferry services.

Other months: Mar-May & Oct-Nov – warm, cheaper; Jun-Sep – sweltering; Dec-Feb – cool, wet.

NORTHERN THAILAND

→ **Why now?** To escape to the hills.

They call north Thailand Lanna – 'the land of a million rice fields'. Indeed, this cool, mountainous realm is terraced with paddies, abundant in fruit trees and filled-in with rampant jungle. It's an ideal retreat in November: the rains have just ended, leaving everything green, yet temperatures are still warm (23-26°C; 73-79°F); from December to February, nights are pretty chilly. Laidback Chiang Mai is the main hub – book a cookery course, haggle at the markets and arrange forays into the hills. Head to Mae Sariang (near the Burmese border) or the Golden Triangle (north of Chiang Rai) to trek among waterfalls and hill tribes. Staying with families in their bamboo stilthouses gives greater insight; witness their distinctive dress, and help with cooking or tea picking. While in the north, you can also cycle amid paddies and ruins, and admire the old teak houses of Lampang and Phrae.

Trip plan: Fly (70 minutes) or take the train (13 hours) from Bangkok to Chiang Mai. Allow three/four days for hill-tribe treks; allow seven/10 days for more exploration. Phuket is lovely in November, if you want to add on beach time.

Need to know: Loi Krathong festival, when candlelit baskets are floated downriver, usually falls in November. It's best seen in the north.

Other months: Nov-Feb – cool, dry; Mar-May – hot; Jun-Oct – wet

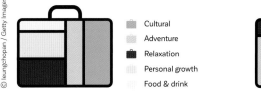

- Cultural
- Adventure
- Relaxation
- Personal growth
- Food & drink

- Adventure
- Cultural
- Food & drink

Surfers walking
along the shore
of Noosa Heads

SUNSHINE COAST
AUSTRALIA

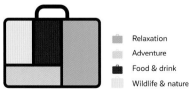

→ **Why now? Laidback shores, with waves and wildlife.**

The clue is in the name: Queensland's Sunshine Coast – stretching from Caloundra to Noosa – enjoys warm weather year-round; even winter days can top 20°C (68°F). It's also less brash and blingy than the Gold Coast, further south. In November (late spring), temperatures are around 27°C (81°F), and the beaches are emptier and inviting. Nestled alongside a headland at the mouth of a river, gorgeous Noosa is the pick of the shoreline. Vintage shops and cheap cafes mingle with chic boutiques and restaurants – part surf-grunge, part Côte d'Azure. Alternatively, Mooloolaba and Maroochydore are less fancy, but offer great waves, surf schools and cool bars. The best base for families is Caloundra, with its watersports, boardwalks and soft sands. For something different, head into the hinterland for hikes in the Glass House Mountains, fine arts and fresh produce in Mapleton and Maleny, and a visit to Steve Irwin's Australia Zoo.

Trip plan: With four/five days, mix beach time with a zoo visit, surf lessons and a river cruise.

Need to know: The Sunshine Coast is around 60 miles (97km; two hours' drive) north of Brisbane.

Other months: Dec-Feb – hot, busy; Mar-May – warm; Jun-Aug – mild; Sep-Nov – warm, cheaper.

Relaxation
Adventure
Food & drink
Wildlife & nature

MEKONG
INDOCHINA

© Philip Lee Harvey / Lonely Planet

When not stargazing, sip South American coffee in San Pedro de Atacama

→ **Why now? The riverside is ripe for exploring.**

The climates of Cambodia, Vietnam and Laos do vary. But, in general, November is a great month for a multi-country adventure, using the Mekong River as a guide. The rains have stopped, landscapes are vibrant and temperatures pleasantly hot (25-30°C; 77-86°F). In Laos, you could take a slow boat from the Thai border to charismatic Luang Prabang, pick up the Mekong in Laotian capital Vientiane, or navigate the 4000 Islands area from Pakse, looking for river dolphins. Travel into Cambodia to visit Angkor's matchless temples, then rejoin the Mekong: it's possible to cruise from Siem Reap right to Vietnam's Ho Chi Minh City, via Chnok Tru stilt village, Cambodian capital Phnom Penh, Chau Doc and Cai Be. Alternatively, from Chau Doc veer into the Mekong Delta, a labyrinth of channels, islets, pagodas and rice paddies where you can sink into traditional river life.

Trip plan: A cruise from Siem Reap to Ho Chi Minh, including time at Angkor, takes 10 days. To combine all three countries, by flights and river journeys, allow three weeks.

Need to know: You need a visa in advance if arriving in Vietnam by boat – visa-on-arrival is only available at airports.

Other months: Nov-Feb – dry, cool; Mar-Jun – hot, humid; Jul-Oct – wet.

Journey
Cultural
Relaxation

NORTH CHILE

→ **Why now? To gaze at galaxies far, far away.**

November isn't quite the driest month in northern Chile's Atacama. But it's all relative when you're talking about the world's driest desert. So, expect 3mm of rain if you're unlucky, but also fewer tourists, warm daytime temperatures (25°C; 77°F) and lovely clear skies – all the better for stargazing. Indeed, the high-altitude, unpolluted Atacama is one of the world's best places for astronomy. Several top-flight observatories are located here; some open to the public, including world-beating ALMA (which captures constellations that are billions of light years away). There are opportunities to join tours with expert astronomers. The Atacama is equally alluring during the day. Base yourself at the dusty little town of San Pedro de Atacama to visit the Valley of the Moon, where salt mountains have been eroded into fantastical shapes. Also, see the El Tatio Geysers fizz at dawn, and scour the salt flats for ancient geoglyphs, flamingos and intensely hued lagoons.

Trip plan: Fly to Santiago, stroll the historic centre and day trip to Maipo Valley's vineyards. Fly north to Calama, 62 miles (100km) from San Pedro, to access the Atacama. Allow a week.

Need to know: ALMA, 31 miles (50km) from San Pedro, is open Saturday and Sunday mornings (book in advance).

Other months: Dec-Mar – hottest, wettest; Apr-May & Oct-Nov – warm, quieter; Jun-Sep – sunny, cold, dry.

Wildlife & nature
Personal growth
Adventure

Swim in the natural water hole of Ojo de Agua, or swing in a hammock on the Caribbean coast

NICARAGUA

➜ **Why now? Active volcanoes and activities galore.**

Things are a-bubbling in Nicaragua – and we're not talking about its many active volcanoes. There's a sense that this previously troubled nation is on the cusp of becoming Central America's Next Big Thing. It has all the attractions – colonial towns, beaches, wildlife, adventures – but few tourists. It's a particularly good choice for families, thanks to a wealth of available activities (zip lining, river kayaking, volcano boarding), a relaxed vibe and a population that adores children. November is a great month, with the countryside fresh from recent rains yet the weather dry and warm (20-28°C; 68-82°F). You might even see olive ridley turtles nesting at Isla Juan Venado (they visit August to December).

Trip plan: From capital Managua head to colonial León. From here, visit Isla Juan Venado and climb the active slopes of Cerro Negro volcano. Veer south for surf lessons at Pacific-coast Playa los Cardones. Stop at a cacao plantation en route to Lake Nicaragua and volcanic Ometepe Island. Then delve into cloudforest for zip lining and monkeys, take carriage rides around elegant Granada and take a short flight to the Corn Islands, for Caribbean snorkelling and relaxation.

Need to know: Nicaraguan currency is the córdoba; many places accept US dollars.

Other months: Nov-Apr – dry, warm; May-Jun – hot, rains start; Jul-Oct – wettest (Sep-Oct: worst).

- ■ Adventure
- ■ Wildlife nature
- ■ Cultural
- ▦ Relaxation

© Philip Lee Harvey / Lonely Planet

© Philip Lee Harvey / Lonely Planet

Plaza de San Andrés, one of Madrid's grand plazas

MADRID SPAIN

Why now? To mingle with the madrileños.

The main reason to visit Madrid is not its monuments or museums – though there are some good ones. The Spanish capital's chief draw is the lifestyle of the madrileños themselves, whose infectious energy flows from tapas bars and terraces all night long. Consequently, for a more local atmosphere, visit Madrid when it's largely free of tourists – such as off-season November. Weather can be variable – some sunny T-shirt days, some wet ones – but the latter don't dampen the *marcha* (action). When it's warm, stroll the grand plazas and medieval alleys, and browse the massive Rastro fleamarket (Sundays, year-round). If the weather turns, shelter in the Prado, Reina Sofía and Thyssen-Bornemisza museums, home to world-class art, including paintings by Goya, Velázquez, Dalí and Picasso. Allow lots of time to eat, too. Foodie Madrid has everything from gastronomic hotspots to traditional tapas bars. Do try *churros con chocolate* (fried pastries and melted chocolate), just the thing to warm up a November night.

Trip plan: Madrid warrants at least three days. Try to catch a football match at the Bernabéu (advance booking required).

Need to know: Lunch is the main meal; dinner is usually eaten late (9pm to 10pm).

Other months: Dec-Feb – cold; Mar-May & Sep-Nov – warm/cool; Jun-Aug – hot.

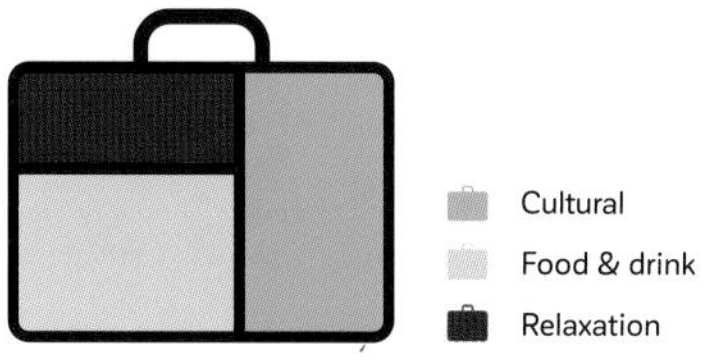

© Mark Read / Lonely Planet

Cultural
Food & drink
Relaxation

BEYOND MADRID

MANZANARES EL REAL · 34 MILES (55KM) · Mountain village with cool castle and great hiking

TOLEDO · 45 MILES (72KM) · Marvellous medieval hub, once home of El Greco

SEVILLE · 310 MILES (499KM) · Moorish Andalucía, 2½ hours by high-speed rail

BUENOS AIRES · 6200 MILES (9900KM) · Barajas Airport is the key gateway between Europe and South America

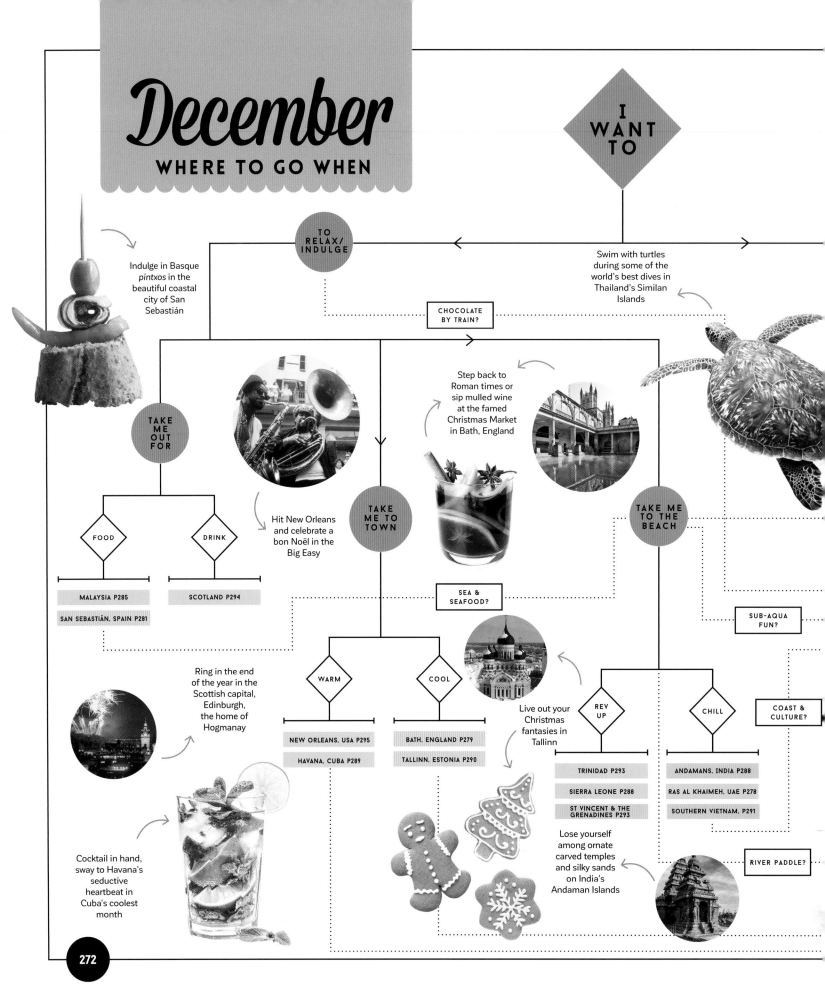

December
WHERE TO GO WHEN

I WANT TO

TO RELAX / INDULGE

Indulge in Basque *pintxos* in the beautiful coastal city of San Sebastián

Swim with turtles during some of the world's best dives in Thailand's Similan Islands

CHOCOLATE BY TRAIN?

Step back to Roman times or sip mulled wine at the famed Christmas Market in Bath, England

TAKE ME OUT FOR

Hit New Orleans and celebrate a bon Noël in the Big Easy

TAKE ME TO TOWN

TAKE ME TO THE BEACH

FOOD

DRINK

| MALAYSIA P285 |
| SAN SEBASTIÁN, SPAIN P281 |

| SCOTLAND P294 |

SEA & SEAFOOD?

SUB-AQUA FUN?

Ring in the end of the year in the Scottish capital, Edinburgh, the home of Hogmanay

WARM

COOL

Live out your Christmas fantasies in Tallinn

REV UP

CHILL

COAST & CULTURE?

| NEW ORLEANS, USA P295 |
| HAVANA, CUBA P289 |

| BATH, ENGLAND P279 |
| TALLINN, ESTONIA P290 |

| TRINIDAD P293 |
| SIERRA LEONE P288 |
| ST VINCENT & THE GRENADINES P293 |

| ANDAMANS, INDIA P288 |
| RAS AL KHAIMEH, UAE P278 |
| SOUTHERN VIETNAM, P291 |

RIVER PADDLE?

Cocktail in hand, sway to Havana's seductive heartbeat in Cuba's coolest month

Lose yourself among ornate carved temples and silky sands on India's Andaman Islands

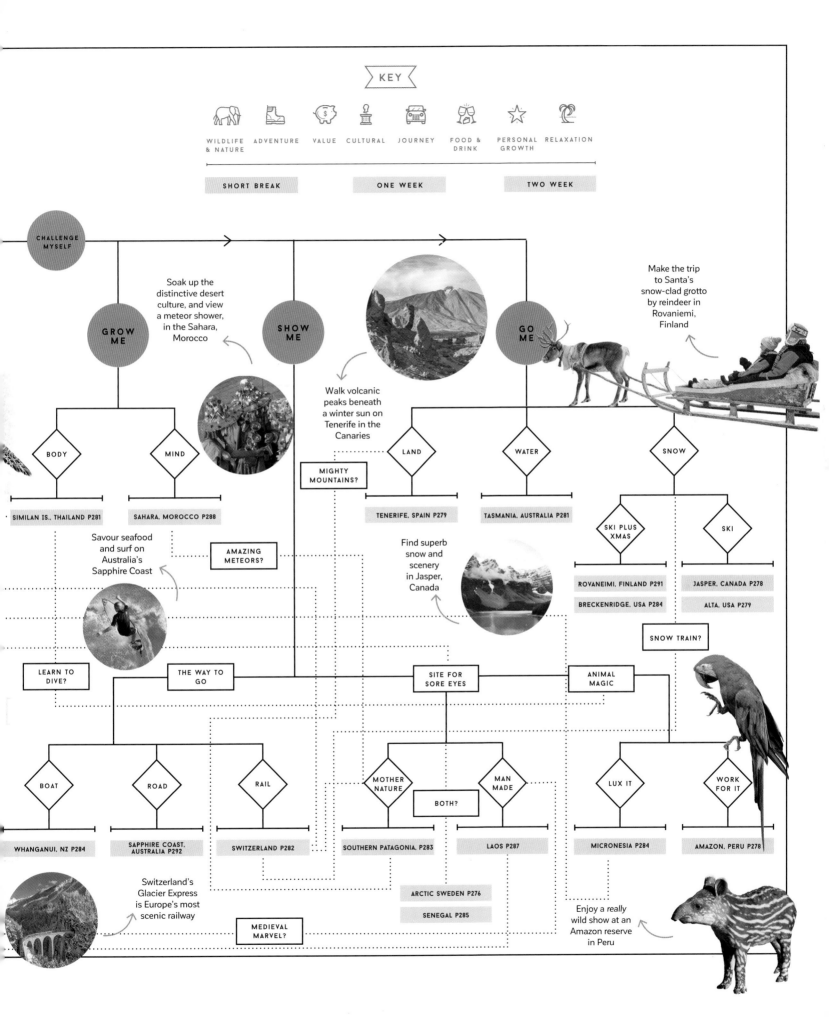

KEY

WILDLIFE & NATURE ADVENTURE VALUE CULTURAL JOURNEY FOOD & DRINK PERSONAL GROWTH RELAXATION

SHORT BREAK   ONE WEEK   TWO WEEK

CHALLENGE MYSELF

GROW ME

SHOW ME

GO ME

Soak up the distinctive desert culture, and view a meteor shower, in the Sahara, Morocco

Make the trip to Santa's snow-clad grotto by reindeer in Rovaniemi, Finland

Walk volcanic peaks beneath a winter sun on Tenerife in the Canaries

BODY

MIND

LAND

WATER

SNOW

MIGHTY MOUNTAINS?

SIMILAN IS., THAILAND P281

SAHARA, MOROCCO P288

TENERIFE, SPAIN P279

TASMANIA, AUSTRALIA P281

SKI PLUS XMAS

SKI

Savour seafood and surf on Australia's Sapphire Coast

AMAZING METEORS?

Find superb snow and scenery in Jasper, Canada

ROVANEIMI, FINLAND P291

JASPER, CANADA P278

BRECKENRIDGE, USA P284

ALTA, USA P279

SNOW TRAIN?

LEARN TO DIVE?

THE WAY TO GO

SITE FOR SORE EYES

ANIMAL MAGIC

BOAT

ROAD

RAIL

MOTHER NATURE

MAN MADE

LUX IT

WORK FOR IT

BOTH?

WHANGANUI, NZ P284

SAPPHIRE COAST, AUSTRALIA P292

SWITZERLAND P282

SOUTHERN PATAGONIA, P283

LAOS P287

MICRONESIA P284

AMAZON, PERU P278

Switzerland's Glacier Express is Europe's most scenic railway

ARCTIC SWEDEN P276

SENEGAL P285

Enjoy a really wild show at an Amazon reserve in Peru

MEDIEVAL MARVEL?

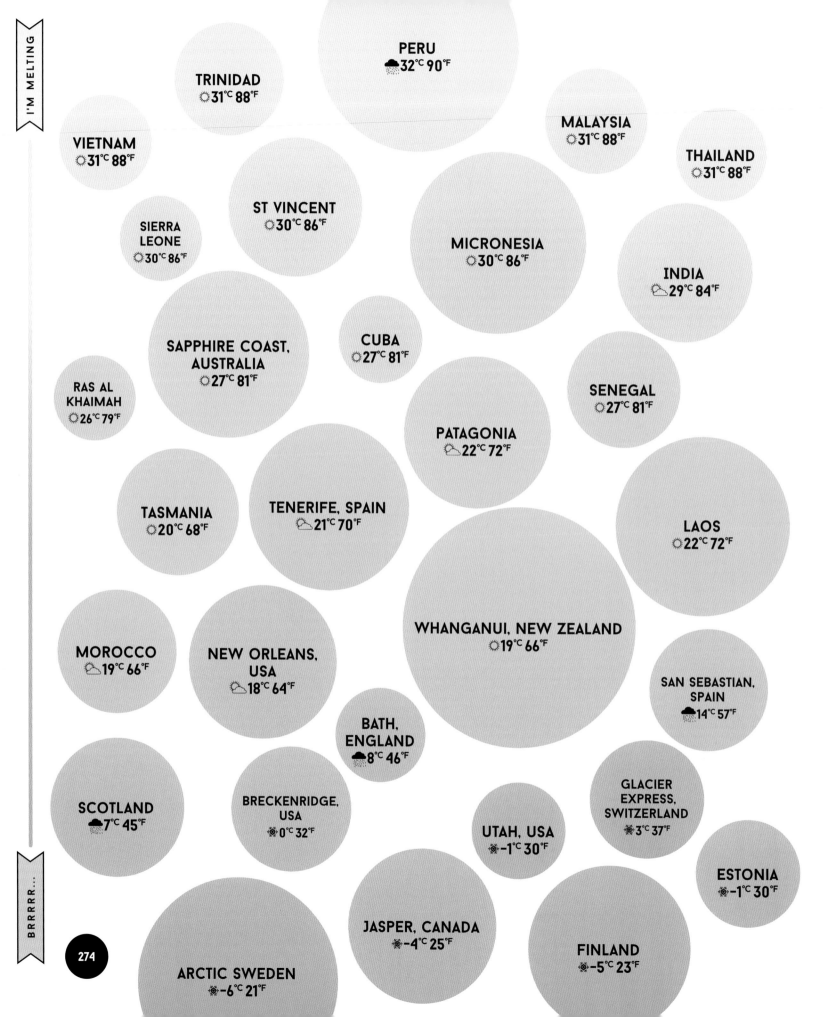

PERU
☔32°C 90°F

TRINIDAD
☀31°C 88°F

MALAYSIA
☀31°C 88°F

THAILAND
☀31°C 88°F

VIETNAM
☀31°C 88°F

ST VINCENT
☀30°C 86°F

MICRONESIA
☀30°C 86°F

INDIA
⛅29°C 84°F

SIERRA
LEONE
☀30°C 86°F

CUBA
☀27°C 81°F

SAPPHIRE COAST,
AUSTRALIA
☀27°C 81°F

SENEGAL
☀27°C 81°F

RAS AL
KHAIMAH
☀26°C 79°F

PATAGONIA
⛅22°C 72°F

LAOS
☀22°C 72°F

TASMANIA
☀20°C 68°F

TENERIFE, SPAIN
⛅21°C 70°F

WHANGANUI, NEW ZEALAND
☀19°C 66°F

MOROCCO
⛅19°C 66°F

NEW ORLEANS,
USA
⛅18°C 64°F

SAN SEBASTIAN,
SPAIN
☔14°C 57°F

BATH,
ENGLAND
☁8°C 46°F

SCOTLAND
☔7°C 45°F

BRECKENRIDGE,
USA
❄0°C 32°F

GLACIER
EXPRESS,
SWITZERLAND
❄3°C 37°F

UTAH, USA
❄-1°C 30°F

ESTONIA
❄-1°C 30°F

JASPER, CANADA
❄-4°C 25°F

FINLAND
❄-5°C 23°F

ARCTIC SWEDEN
❄-6°C 21°F

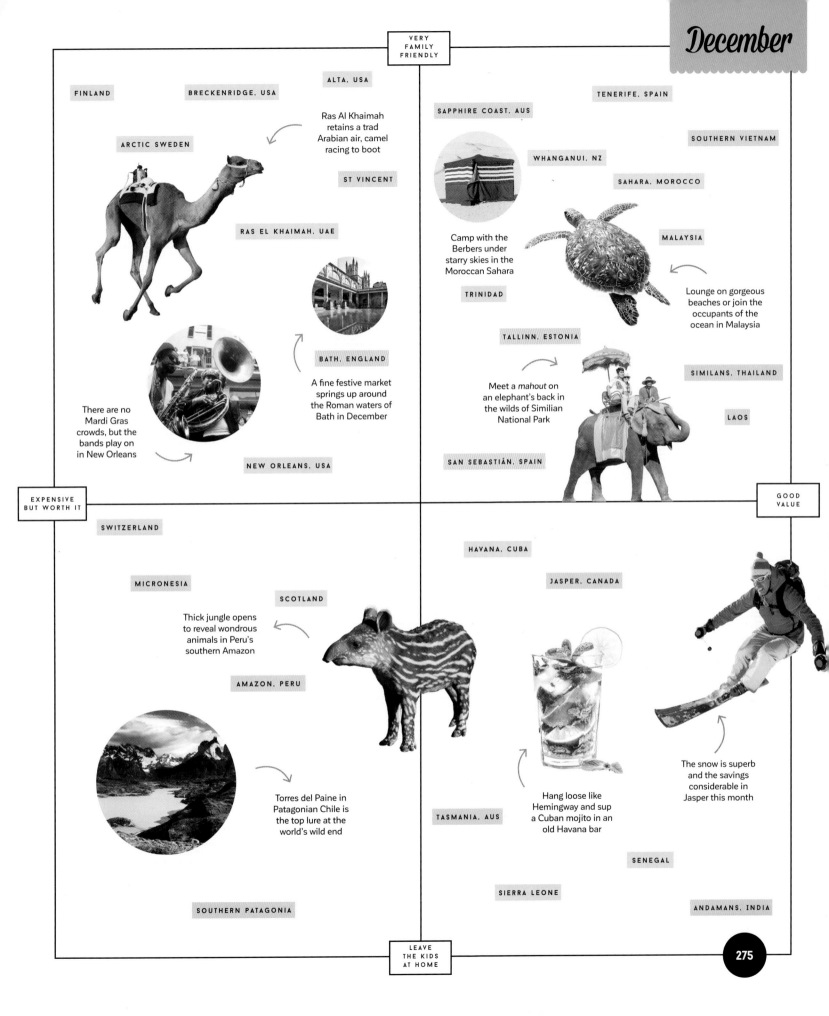

VERY FAMILY FRIENDLY

EXPENSIVE BUT WORTH IT

GOOD VALUE

LEAVE THE KIDS AT HOME

ALTA, USA

FINLAND

BRECKENRIDGE, USA

TENERIFE, SPAIN

SAPPHIRE COAST, AUS

ARCTIC SWEDEN

SOUTHERN VIETNAM

Ras Al Khaimah retains a trad Arabian air, camel racing to boot

WHANGANUI, NZ

ST VINCENT

SAHARA, MOROCCO

MALAYSIA

RAS EL KHAIMAH, UAE

Camp with the Berbers under starry skies in the Moroccan Sahara

TRINIDAD

Lounge on gorgeous beaches or join the occupants of the ocean in Malaysia

TALLINN, ESTONIA

SIMILANS, THAILAND

BATH, ENGLAND

Meet a *mahout* on an elephant's back in the wilds of Similian National Park

LAOS

A fine festive market springs up around the Roman waters of Bath in December

There are no Mardi Gras crowds, but the bands play on in New Orleans

SAN SEBASTIÁN, SPAIN

NEW ORLEANS, USA

SWITZERLAND

HAVANA, CUBA

MICRONESIA

JASPER, CANADA

SCOTLAND

Thick jungle opens to reveal wondrous animals in Peru's southern Amazon

AMAZON, PERU

The snow is superb and the savings considerable in Jasper this month

Torres del Paine in Patagonian Chile is the top lure at the world's wild end

Hang loose like Hemingway and sup a Cuban mojito in an old Havana bar

TASMANIA, AUS

SENEGAL

SIERRA LEONE

SOUTHERN PATAGONIA

ANDAMANS, INDIA

Encounter migrating reindeer in Arctic Sweden

ARCTIC SWEDEN

Why now? Bed down amid ice sculptures beneath the enthralling Northern Lights

At the Swedish village of Jukkasjärvi, one degree of latitude north of the Arctic Circle, in the last three weeks of the year the sun never rises. In December, darkness is the dominant state – perfect for watching the swirling lightshow of the aurora borealis in sable skies. Jukkasjärvi is the home of the original Icehotel, carved anew each year from the pristine waters of the Torne River, and a base for cross-country skiing, husky sledding, snowmobiling, meeting reindeer and learning about traditional Sámi culture – magical for kids and grown-ups alike. Some 60 miles (97km) to the northwest, Abisko National Park is even further removed from the light, an otherworldly landscape offering arguably the world's best aurora-watching – head to the top of 2953ft (900m) Mt Nuolja for spectacular views of light and land.

Trip plan: Kiruna, 10 miles (16km; 20-minute drive) west of Jukkasjärvi, has flights from Stockholm and international cities. Trains from Kiruna to Abisko take an hour.

Need to know: The Northern Lights are sparked when charged particles from the sun hit the Earth's atmosphere. Various websites offer forecasts based on solar activity.

Other months: Dec-Apr – winter, Icehotel's ice rooms open; May & Sep – shoulder, many facilities closed; Jun-Aug – summer (late May–mid-Jul: midnight sun); Oct-Nov – good aurora-watching.

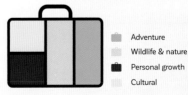

Adventure

Wildlife & nature

Personal growth

Cultural

SOUTHERN AMAZON
PERU

Why now? See red and yellow and blue at Tambopata's macaw clay licks.

Watching wildlife in the Amazon rainforest can be tremendous – the diversity and density of species is unrivalled. But it can also be frustrating, thanks to the thick jungle. Except at a *collpa*, or clay lick, where the Amazon's most dazzling birds gather in huge numbers. Collpa Colorado in Peru's Tambopata National Reserve is reputedly the world's biggest: hundreds of technicolour macaws and parrots gather early each morning to munch the mineral-rich clay. December, early in the rains and peak breeding season for many species, sees numbers of vivid blue-and-yellow and scarlet macaws soar at the *collpa*. Tapir, giant otter and jaguar also roam the reserve, as do harpy eagles, the prehistoric-looking hoatzin or 'stink bird', and dozens of reptiles and amphibians, more easily spotted in the cooler wet season, when tourist numbers are lower.

Trip plan: Fly to Puerto Maldonado, from where multi-day tours and lodges of various levels of luxury offer wildlife-watching opportunities along the Tambopata and Madre de Dios rivers, with trips to the Collpa de Guacamayos Colorado or other clay licks.

Need to know: Expect heavy rain in the afternoon – and bring insect repellent!

Other months: Jun-Aug – dry in highlands and rainforest, busy; Apr-May & Sep-Nov – shoulder, fairly dry; Dec-Mar – wet season.

RAS AL KHAIMAH
UNITED ARAB EMIRATES

Why now? Explore the northernmost emirate.

Pictures of Arabia have morphed over recent decades, from camel trains across the Empty Quarter to high-rise hotels and glitzy shopping malls. Ras Al Khaimah isn't Abu Dhabi or Dubai, though; this small emirate, sandwiched between the Persian Gulf and the Hajar Mountains, has glitzy resorts and sweeping stretches of sand, but retains more than a whiff of its 7000 years of history and tradition. Away from the sands and city, there's camel racing near the village of Digdagga (October to April), hiking, biking, climbing and camping in the mountains, and the chance to visit ancient bastions including the dramatic hilltop Dhayah Fort.

Trip plan: Either fly to Ras Al Khaimah via Doha or Cairo, or to Dubai and then continue by road. A range of hotels and resorts offer high-quality accommodation.

Need to know: Many nationalities receive a visa on arrival. Though Ras Al Khaimah is a relaxed state, it's respectful to cover shoulders and knees in public.

Other months: Oct-May – warm (Nov-Mar: some rain in winter); Jun-Sep – extremely hot.

JASPER
CANADA

Why now? Superb snow and potential savings.

Reliable doesn't have to mean dull – Jasper's Marmot Basin ski resort is as reliable as they come, but also great fun. Its location in the northern Rockies and its high base elevation (the highest in Canada) ensures dependable and delightful champagne powder snow and Alberta's longest ski season, running November to May. There are 86 runs, offering a mix of alpine bowls, bumps, chutes and glade-skiing through piquant pine forest, as well as two terrain parks with jumps and jibs aplenty. Marmot is a beauty too, set in Jasper National Park amid rugged mountains and frozen lakes. Also, the nightlife is exceptional. Not so much the bar scene – though the welcoming 19th-century fur-trading outpost of Jasper Town does have several. It's the natural nightlife that will amaze: Jasper is the world's biggest Dark Sky Preserve, and the stars are out of this world.

Trip plan: Jasper is 217 miles (350km) west of Edmonton; Marmot Basin is 12 miles (19km) southwest of Jasper Town. Stay a week; as well as skiing, consider ice-climbing, wildlife watching, snowshoeing and fatbiking (cycling on snow).

Need to know: Look for bargains – winter is off-season in Jasper, and Marmot Basin is quieter than slopes further south near Banff.

Other months: Nov-Apr/May – skiing; May & Oct – unpredictable; Jun-Sep – warm, best for hiking.

Wildlife & nature
Journey

Relaxation
Wildlife & nature
Adventure

Adventure
Wildlife & nature
Value

TENERIFE
SPAIN

→ **Why now?** Walk the peaks beneath a winter sun.

Tenerife has long welcomed sun-seekers year-round – even in December average daytime temperatures hover around 20°C (68°F). But beyond the beaches there are plenty of reasons, especially for walkers, for a December visit – the rainiest month, November, has passed and the crowded month of January has yet to arrive. At 12,198ft (3718m), Mt Teide is Spain's highest peak and the world's third-largest volcano, and offers a challenging five-hour hike (or breezy eight-minute cable-car ride) to its snow-capped summit. There's a varied array of walking trails – the pine forests of the northwest, ridge walks among the laurels of the Anaga Mountains, the spectacular Masca gorge from the eponymous village down to the sea – and excellent infrastructure for trekkers, with a good bus network and plentiful accommodation around the island. Microclimates can be dramatically different even in adjacent valleys, so if you don't like the weather in one spot, just shift a few miles and you'll probably find sunshine.

Trip plan: Tenerife has two international airports in the north and south. Probably the most convenient base for walking is in Puerto de la Cruz on the north coast.

Need to know: Look out for Canarian salt fish, tapas and *papas arrugadas* (wrinkly potatoes) with spicy and green sauces to fuel your hiking.

Other months: Year-round; May-Jun & Sep-Nov – shoulder seasons, quietest.

BATH
ENGLAND

→ **Why now?** Get into the Christmas spirit in this pretty city.

With its glorious honey-hued Georgian architecture and famous Christmas market, the genteel city of Bath is a top pick for a festive break. The aromas of mulled wine and sizzling sausages waft among scores of stalls that spring up around the abbey and Roman baths, peddling artisan cheeses and chocolates, handicrafts and high-class hooch to locals and visitors alike. The appeal doesn't end with shopping, though. The city is packed with museums and galleries, plus the steaming hot-spring waters of Thermae Bath Spa – soak in the rooftop pool while gazing down at the lights of the market below, graze on gastro fare and bed down in a boutique B&B or one of the upmarket hotels, such as the Royal Crescent.

Trip planner: Hotels are dotted around the city, with B&Bs concentrated around Newbridge Rd and Pulteney Gardens; you can even stay in Jane Austen's old house opposite the lovely Holburne Museum. Leaven city life with a wintry stroll on the Bath Skyline walk, providing sweeping city views.

Need to know: The annual Christmas market runs from late November to mid-December. The abbey hosts carol concerts, advent processions and recitals of Handel's Messiah this month.

Other months: Year-round.

ALTA USA

→ **Why now?** Ski some of the United States' finest powder pistes before peak season.

When it snows in Alta, it really snows. On average, 46ft (14m) of the stuff – most of it the softest powder – dumps here each year, and with 2200 acres (890 hectares) of skiable terrain, there's a lot of options for making the most of it. Alta opens mid to late November, but December is the ideal time to arrive, with deep snow pretty much guaranteed but peak season yet to kick in. There's plenty for everyone at this old-time resort (opened in 1939), with 25% beginner, 40% intermediate and 35% advanced runs. Après is gentle and there's a family friendly, inclusive atmosphere.

Trip plan: Alta is 27 miles (43km) southeast of Salt Lake City in Utah. There are five lodges at the ski area, plus condos and vacation homes nearby and ample accommodation in Salt Lake City.

Need to know: Snowboarders aren't allowed on Alta's slopes – but it's linked at Sugarloaf Pass to Snowbird resort, which almost doubles the terrain area and has plenty for boarders; a joint lift pass is available.

Other months: Mid-Nov– mid Apr – Alta ski area open; Late May – Snowbird closes; Jun-Sep – summer activities.

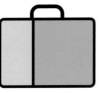

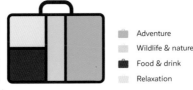

© ostill / Shutterstock

- Adventure
- Wildlife & nature
- Food & drink
- Relaxation

- Cultural
- Food & drink

- Adventure
- Wildlife & nature

Franklin-Gordon
Wild Rivers
National Park is a
phenomenal rafting
destination

The waters of
Mu Ko Similan
National Park are
spectacularly clear
in December

Panoramic view of
San Sebastián's Bay
of La Concha

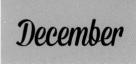

TASMANIA
AUSTRALIA

Why now? Raft the river wild amid dramatic mountains and rainforest.

A couple of words in the name Franklin-Gordon Wild Rivers National Park provide a hint. This wonderful wilderness area in Tasmania's remote central west is a rugged expanse of over 1700 sq miles (4400 sq km) encompassing mountain, rainforest – and those two eponymous roaring waterways. The 80-mile (129km) run down the Franklin from Collingwood Bridge to Sir John Falls on the Gordon River is one of the world's great rafting trips, punctuated by rocky gorges including the aptly named Great Ravine, mighty trees (including 3000-year-old Huon pines) and surging rapids, in the company of native wildlife including platypus, quolls and wallabies. December is prime time to take on the Franklin, in the long, warming days of early summer – though even then only a few hundred tackle the challenge each year. Don't expect luxury or an easy ride; do expect full wilderness immersion and unrivalled thrills.

Trip plan: Several experienced operators offer tours of between five and 14 days, longer trips often including the hike up 4744ft (1446m) Frenchman's Cap for far-reaching views.

Need to know: Weather can change rapidly. Bring clothing for all conditions, remembering you'll be camping for several consecutive nights.

Other months: Dec-Mar – summer, most settled conditions; May-Oct – cooler, often wet; Nov & Apr – commercial trips also run.

- Adventure
- Wildlife & nature
- Journey

SAN SEBASTIÁN
SPAIN

Why now? Indulge in finest Basque cuisine in a beautiful coastal city.

Spain's regional cuisines are astonishingly diverse: Valencia's paella, fine hams in Andalucía, octopus in Galicia, wrinkly potatoes in Tenerife… Many, though, would say the finest is found in the Basque Country, with its *pintxos* (tapas), fish and spicy sauces. San Sebastián, culinary epicentre of northern Spain, has an astonishing number of Michelin-starred restaurants, thanks to chefs such as Andoni Luis Aduriz, Pedro Subijana, Martín Berasategui and the Arzak family. But whether your budget is five-star or five euros, there are countless opportunities to savour fine food in mild December, when low tourist numbers mean accommodation is great value, and snagging a reservation at a top restaurant is easier than in high summer (though some close for winter). Work up an appetite with a bracing walk along Playa de la Concha or up Monte Igueldo (you can cheat with the funicular) for views across this beautiful city on the bay.

Trip plan: Bilbao and Biarritz are the two nearest airports to San Sebastián; journey time from the latter is about 45 minutes.

Need to know: For discounts on transport, attractions, shops, restaurants and tours, buy a San Sebastián Card from the tourist office (www.sansebastianturismo.com).

Other months: Jun-Sep – hot, busy; Oct-Nov – cooler, rainy; Dec-Feb – mild, snow on Pyrenees; Mar-May – spring.

- Food & drink
- Cultural
- Value

SIMILAN ISLANDS
THAILAND

Why now? Experience some of the world's best diving.

Fringed with dazzling white beaches and kaleidoscopic coral reefs, the 11 islands of Mu Ko Similan National Park are endlessly spectacular – and never more so than in December, early in the dry season. At this time of year the water off Thailand's Andaman Coast is clear (visibility is 25m to 40m; 80ft to 130ft) and calm – perfect for snorkelling or diving among marine life large and small. As well as dizzyingly diverse reef fish, expect to swim alongside sharks, barracuda, rays, and green and hawksbill turtles, which nest in this area between November and February. True, this is hardly an unknown paradise – beaches and snorkelling spots can get overcrowded, and park authorities have banned tourists from Ko Tachai to protect the coral – but it's a dream destination for divers.

Trip plan: The national park authority runs basic bungalows on Ko Similan and Ko Miang (Island No 4). Many operators offer day trips to the Similan Islands from Khao Lak on the mainland, but for the best underwater action join a live-aboard dive boat from Khao Lak or Phuket, which has direct flights from Bangkok and several international cities.

Need to know: Prices rise towards Christmas – try to book earlier in December for cheaper deals.

Other months: Nov-Apr – dry, warm; mid-May–Oct – national park closed during rainy season.

- Relaxation
- Adventure
- Wildlife & nature
- Food & drink

The granite peaks
within Torres Del Paine
National Park, Chile

GLACIER EXPRESS
SWITZERLAND

The Glacier Express
winding its way
through a Swiss
winter wonderland

Why now? Ride the world's most scenic railway.

In a country famed for efficiency, the idea of boarding a train that takes over seven hours to travel a mere 180 miles (290km) seems crazy. Yet the narrow-gauge line between Zermatt and St Moritz – billed as 'Europe's slowest express' – does just that, and passengers revel in the pace. The scenery that glides past the picture-windowed panoramic coaches is sensational, starting with the 14,692ft (4478m) Matterhorn, passing snow-clad firs and the lovely Matter, Rhône and Rhine valleys, cute villages and hilltop castles such as Reichenau, and crossing the lofty Landwasser Viaduct before pulling in at chichi ski resort of St Moritz. The magnificent Alps landscape is at its most spectacular in winter – with the bonus of fantastic skiing at both ends.

Trip plan: The Glacier Express departs around 9am daily from both Zermatt and St Moritz. Seat reservations are mandatory, even if you have a Swiss rail pass. Book in advance at www.glacierexpress.ch/en.

Need to know: Keen to continue your Swiss rail odyssey? Board the Unesco-listed Bernina Express at St Moritz, a 90-mile (145km), four-hour ride across 196 bridges and through 55 tunnels to Tirano in Italy.

Other months: Mid-Dec–Apr – winter timetable (one departure daily); May-Oct – summer timetable (three departures).

Journey

Wildlife & nature

Adventure

SOUTHERN PATAGONIA CHILE & ARGENTINA

Why now? Go to the wild ends of the Earth as spring turns to summer. Jagged peaks, gargantuan glaciers, pumas stalking guanacos across vast landscapes – everything is epic in South America's uttermost reaches. Including the weather: you don't want to mess with Patagonia in the austral winter. Come in December, as spring slips into summer but before peak tourist season bites. Top billing goes to Chile's Torres del Paine National Park, which demands to be explored on foot, on the eight-day circuit or four-day 'W' trek for views of the granite towers and Los Cuernos (the 'horns'). In Argentina, 197ft-high (60m) Perito Moreno Glacier calves massive icebergs, while south of the 'Land of Fire', Tierra del Fuego, the Americas finally peter out at Cape Horn.

Trip plan: For a two- or three-week itinerary, fly from Santiago to Puerto Montt and board the Navimag ferry for a four-day cruise through fjords to Puerto Natales. Hike Torres del Paine and gape at the ice giants of Los Glaciares National Park in Argentina, then head south to Punta Arenas (via Magellanic penguin colonies) and Tierra del Fuego.

Need to know: Patagonia gets busier as December progresses; book accommodation and ferry tickets early. Nationals of UK, USA, Canada, Australia and New Zealand currently don't need visas for either Argentina or Chile; however, a reciprocity fee may be payable. Check with an embassy before travel.

Other months: Dec-Mar – warmer, trekking season; Apr-Aug – cold, many hotels closed, trails snow-covered; Sep-Nov – spring.

Wildlife & nature

Adventure

Journey

MICRONESIA

→ **Why now?** Watch mighty manta rays in mating season.

Most people, it's fair to say, have never heard of Yap, Chuuk, Pohnpei or Kosrae – and those who have would struggle to find them on a map. These are the four Federated States of Micronesia (FSM), 607 Pacific islands. Between their traditional cultures, tropical beaches and stupendous snorkelling and diving, they offer the best holiday you never thought of. December brings lower humidity and rainfall to many parts (though it's rarely completely dry), but for divers it has another huge attraction: the mating season of giant manta rays, with wingspans stretching 5m and more. From December these aquatic behemoths get frisky, males chasing females through the submarine channels of Yap. On land, it's the cash that's massive – huge stone coins still used to bank money. There's more great diving off Kosrae and among the wrecks of Chuuk lagoon; on Pohnpei you can kayak among the mysterious ruins of Nan Madol.

Trip plan: Flights link Kosrae, Pohnpei, Chuuk, and Yap via Guam. Take two weeks to visit all four; in one you could dive Yap and Chuuk.

Need to know: FSM spans two time zones: GMT+10 in Yap and Chuuk; GMT+11 in Pohnpei and Kosrae.

Other months: Dec-Mar – rainfall and humidity lowest; Apr-Nov – wetter.

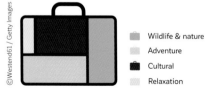
Wildlife & nature
Adventure
Cultural
Relaxation

©Westend61 / Getty Images

WHANGANUI RIVER
NEW ZEALAND

→ **Why now?** Take a spiritual canoe journey.

'Ko au te awa, ko te awa ko au' (I am the river and the river is me). So sing the traditional Māori inhabitants of the Whanganui River, which snakes some 180 miles (290km) south from the slopes of Mt Tongariro. According to legend, the river was first navigated by Tamatea, one of the Māori forefathers in the first waves of migration to New Zealand. Today, the 90-mile (145km) canoe journey from Taumarunui to Pipiriki is designated one of New Zealand's Great Walks; traversing steep-sided gorges lined with tree-ferns and nikau palms, passing sacred Tamatea Cave and Maori kainga (villages), and tackling rapids with just the right level of challenge, it's rewarding for experienced paddlers and delightful for novices and families. The long, warm days of December make it a great month to row with the flow.

Trip plan: Operators offer guided trips of between two and five days, as well as canoe and equipment hire.

Need to know: Various interesting side-trips include the short walk to the Bridge to Nowhere, crossing a valley abandoned by farming settlers in the 1940s.

Other months: Oct-Nov – spring, some rain; Dec-Mar – summer, warm days; Apr-May – autumn, often fine; Jun-Sep – winter.

Adventure
Journey
Wildlife & nature
Cultural

BRECKENRIDGE
USA

→ **Why now?** For a bygone white Christmas.

People were first drawn to Breckenridge for its precious metals – the town was founded by hopeful gold prospectors in 1859. Now, however, people come for its precious powder. Scenically located below the strapping Tenmile Range, Breckenridge offers great skiing, from brilliant baby slopes to tough pistes and some of the best snowboarding terrain you'll find anywhere. A healthy annual snow dump (average: 197in; 500cm) plus substantial snowmaking mean ski season starts reliably early, in November. But wait until December to enjoy fabulously festive skiing. Much of Breckenridge's old centre – including the bright-painted shops and galleries along Main St – is preserved as a National Historic District, and in winter it looks like a Christmas card. The first weekend of December sees the holiday lights switched on, the tree lit, carols sung, and Santas race around the streets. The Victorian-style boutiques offer atmospheric gift shopping, too.

Trip plan: Breckenridge is 90 miles (145km) from Denver; Colorado Mountain Express runs a shuttle between Breckenridge and Denver Airport. Stay a week, mixing skiing with other activities – shopping, ice-skating, sleigh rides, heritage tours.

Need to know: Make time for a Christmas Ale at Breckenridge Brewery.

Other months: Nov-Apr – skiing; May & Oct – unpredictable, quieter; Jun-Sep – warm, summer activities.

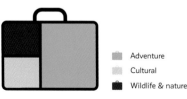
Adventure
Cultural
Wildlife & nature

WEST COAST
MALAYSIA

© Pete Seaward / Lonely Planet

→ **Why now?** Feast on Malaysia's diverse flavours and lounge on gorgeous beaches.

Peninsular Malaysia is a melange of Malay, Chinese and Tamil Indian cultural and culinary influences. The result? A spicy blend of temples and tea plantations, trader mansions and hawker food stalls, sprinkled over a finger of land coated in emerald rainforest and adorned with sumptuous beaches. In December, the northwest coast is in peak condition, warm and dry. The Langkawi archipelago comprises nuggets of forested mountain and brochure-cover beaches; even the largest, Pulau Langkawi, retains a mostly traditional, low-key appeal. Penang, meanwhile, is the peninsula's cultural and culinary hub; in George Town visit restored 19th-century mansions, shophouses and Chinese temples, and browse the countless restaurants and food stalls to discover the best of the five cuisines represented – our pick is Nonya

(Peranakan), typified by spicy laksas (noodle soups). December also sees the streets buzzing with parades, dragon-boat races and music during the Pesta Pulau Pinang festival.

Trip plan: Both Penang and Langkawi have easy connections through Kuala Lumpur and Singapore to international destinations. Regular flights (35 minutes) and ferries (2¾ hours) link the two destinations.

Need to know: Look out for the inventive street art blossoming around George Town.

Other months: Dec-Mar – northwest coast dry; Apr-Nov – northwest coast wet (Nov-Jan: east coast wettest).

The vibrant exterior of a Chinese tea house in George Town, Malaysia

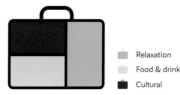

▮ Relaxation
▮ Food & drink
▮ Cultural

SENEGAL

→ **Why now?** Soak up the rays on a wide, white-sand beach.

Three kinds of beat draw visitors to Senegal: the throbbing *mbalax* music of Dakar's clubs; the wingbeats of the diverse birds of the deltas; and the sun beating down on the beaches of Île de Gorée, Ngor and the Petite Côte. Warm, dry December is the ideal time to visit this Francophone nation, when the mangrove swamps of Djoudj and Saloum Delta national parks fill with flamingos, pelicans and dazzling migratory

birds en route south from Europe, and when the swells rolls in off the Atlantic for reliable, big-wave surfing.

Trip plan: Spend a couple of days getting lost in bustling capital Dakar, with regular beach breaks and a boat trip across to explore the colonial buildings and moving slave history of the Île de Gorée (there's good wreck diving here, too). Head north along the coast to the French colonial city of Saint-Louis and the Djoudj National Park, then south towards the Saloum Delta National Park, to drift among

the mangroves in a pirogue (canoe).

Need to know: Check the security situation with your government's foreign office before visiting the Casamance region.

Other months: Nov-Mar – dry, cool; Apr-Jun – getting hotter; Jul-Oct – rainy, hot.

▮ Relaxation
▮ Cultural
▮ Wildlife & nature
▨ Adventure
▯ Journey

LAOS

Why now? Spend warm, dry days wandering ancient temples and sleepy river towns.

For centuries the Lao People's Democratic Republic enjoyed a more romantic moniker: Kingdom of a Million Elephants Under the White Parasol. That ancient epithet evokes the rich heritage and languid charm of this alluring land. Cool, dry December is the ideal time to explore, with the least rain but water high enough for river journeys. Start with the French colonial grandeur and 33 gilt-roofed temples of Luang Prabang, then roam among the mysterious stone funerary vessels of the Plain of Jars, kayak among karst outcrops at Vang Vieng, discover the Angkor-era temple Wat Phu near Champasak, and look for river dolphins near Si Phan Don ('Four Thousand Islands') on the Mekong.

Trip plan: In a fortnight (longer is better) you could fly to Luang Prabang from cities including Bangkok, Chiang Mai, Hanoi, Pnomh Penh and Yangon; drive east to Phonsavan and the Plain of Jars, south to Vang Vieng and on to capital Vientiane, to drive or fly to Pakse for Champasak. If you've more time, explore the forests and meet the hill tribes of the far northwest near Luang Namtha.

Need to know: Unsurprisingly, this is peak season – book accommodation in advance, particularly in Luang Prabang.

Other months: Nov-Feb – cool, dry; Mar-May – hot, humid; Jun-Oct – rainy.

- Cultural
- Journey
- Value
- Food & drink

(L) Wat Si Saket, Vientiane; (R) Wat Xieng Thong, Luang Prabang

SIERRA LEONE

→ **Why now?** Lounge on palm-fringed beaches and spot rare wildlife.

Like its diamonds, so bitterly contested in the 1990s, Sierra Leone is a jewel in the rough. But the sparkle is clear: the beautiful white-sand beaches that lured international holidaymakers in the 1970s are still as lovely, the slavery-era heritage as fascinating, and the pockets of biodiversity as captivating as ever. The warm, dry days of December are ideal for both beach-lounging and exploring, and are an excellent time for spotting the country's dazzling birdlife – David Attenborough came here to film his first-ever nature documentary, about his quest for a rare rockfowl.

Trip plan: Wander the colourful streets of capital Freetown, visiting the bat-hung, 500-year-old Cotton Tree where slaves were once sold, the white-sand beach at River No 2, nearby Tacugama Chimp Sanctuary and the remains of the fort on Bunce Island. Then head east to Tiwai Island in the Moa River, where you might spot chimps, red colobus and Diana monkeys, and – if you're lucky – pygmy hippos. Further east, Gola Rainforest National Park harbours rare bird and mammal species.

Need to know: Though a friendly, largely safe destination, check your government's travel advice before visiting Sierra Leone.

Other months: May-Oct – rainy (Jul-Aug: wettest); Nov-Apr – very hot, dry, windy.

- Journey
- Relaxation
- Wildlife & nature

SAHARA DESERT
MOROCCO

→ **Why now?** For reduced crowds and prettier sights.

Look up into the night sky in mid-December and you could see hundreds of shooting stars. There are few better places to experience the Geminid meteor shower than the Sahara Desert in southern Morocco, where light pollution is nonexistent and camping in Berber tents adds to the allure. December is a fine time to explore Morocco; yes, it's cooler, but crowds are minimal, prices low, and the souks of medieval Fez and Marrakesh as mesmerising as ever – great for families, too. An ascent of snow-capped Mt Toubkal, North Africa's highest peak, is a fine winter challenge.

Trip plan: Fly to Marrakesh and head east across the Atlas to the red kasbah of Aït Benhaddou and on to the desert via Zagora or Merzouga. After gawping at meteors, head north via Todra Gorge to blue-washed Chefchaouen, get lost in Fez's labyrinthine medina and return to Marrakesh and the nocturnal madness of Djemaa el-Fna square.

Need to know: Temperatures can drop by 20°C (68°F) in the desert at night – if camping, bring warm clothes and a good sleeping bag. The Ursid meteor shower hits later in December.

Other months: Mar-May – spring, warm, some showers; Jun-Aug – very hot; Sep-Oct – pleasantly warm; Nov-Feb – cold.

- Wildlife & nature
- Personal growth
- Adventure
- Food & drink
- Value

ANDAMAN
ISLANDS INDIA

→ **Why now?** Sink your toes into the subcontinent's silkiest sand beaches.

A string of emeralds dangling between Myanmar and Sumatra, the Andaman Islands are India's little pocket of Southeast Asia, blessed with delicious beaches, food and submarine wildlife. A limited number of low-key barefoot resorts dot the shores, backed by forest; Havelock Island is the top choice for sand ribbons – the prosaically named Beach No 7 (also called Radhnagar) has been voted the best in Asia – and fine diving on the fringing coral reef. The dry season arrives in December, bringing clarity to the turquoise waters and nesting turtles to the beaches; you might even be fortunate enough to spot the elusive dugong in coastal waters.

Trip plan: Fly to Port Blair, the islands' main town, from Kolkata or Chennai. Boats to Havelock Island take about 2½ hours. If time permits, after a week of lolling, diving and maybe a bit of yoga on the Andamans, add a few days in Tamil Nadu – explore the ornate beach temples and fine rock-carved friezes of Mahabalipuram and the French colonial settlement of Puducherry (Pondicherry) south of Chennai.

Need to know: A Restricted Area Permit is required to visit the Andaman Islands, available on arrival for most nationalities.

Other months: Dec-Mar – warm, sunny; Oct-Dec & Apr-May – more rain; Jun-Sep – heavy rain.

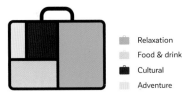

- Relaxation
- Food & drink
- Cultural
- Adventure

HAVANA CUBA

Why now? Sway to its seductive heartbeat in the coolest month. Depending on how you view it, Cuba's capital is a grande dame, her proud good looks fading, or a callow youth rushing headlong into the 21st century. In truth, it's both. Wander the crumbling, pastel-hued colonial masterpieces and turn-of-the-20th-century gems of Habana Vieja (Old Havana) or seafront Malecón, and you'll catch a whiff of past glories, perhaps soundtracked by soulful *son* drifting from a balconied window. Yet after half a century of near international isolation, tourist numbers and development are booming since the entente with the US. Cool December is a fabulous time to roam the streets, sampling rum cocktails, mojitos and Cuba libres in old-time bars (Hemingway loved La Floridita and La Bodeguita del Medio), and soaking up *son*, poetic *trova* or the smooth sounds at Havana International Jazz Festival (mid-December).

Trip plan: Spend a few days in Habana Vieja, Centro and Vedado districts, then roam Spanish colonial forts and peer into Hemingway's house, then catch some rays on the beach at Playas del Este.

Need to know: With the jazz and film festivals, December is a hugely popular month to visit – book transport and accommodation far in advance.

Other months: Nov-Apr – cool, dry; May-Oct hot, rainy; Jul-Aug & Dec – busiest, priciest.

© Mark Read / Lonely Planet

Feel Cuba's rhythms in Havana's streets

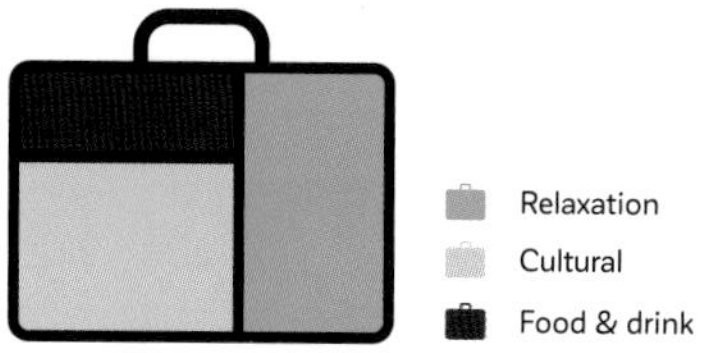

Relaxation
Cultural
Food & drink

BEYOND HAVANA

MATANZAS · 57 MILES (92KM) · Decaying neoclassical grandeur near Varadero's beaches

LAS TERRAZAS · 66 MILES (106KM) · Pioneering eco-village and bird-bustling biosphere reserve

VIÑALES · 115 MILES (185KM) · Tobacco plantations and limestone *mogotes* (outcrops)

TRINIDAD · 198 MILES (318KM) · Well-preserved Spanish colonial town

TALLINN
ESTONIA

→ Why now? Indulge your medieval Christmas fantasies.

Towards the end of the year, plenty of cities in northern Europe play the Christmas markets card. Few, though, are blessed with such a tailor-made backdrop as Tallinn, one of Europe's best-preserved medieval cities. Its walled Old Town and Toompea castle district are enchanting enough at any time, but come December it nestles under a blanket of snow, with candles flickering along cobbled streets and the Old Town Hall Sq sparkling with the lights of the annual Christmas market radiating from the famous tree. The days are short, the nights dark, but the atmosphere is genuinely charming and the traditional festive food – black pudding, gingerbreads – and steaming hot drinks warm the cockles. Shaking off its reputation as a stag-weekend destination, Tallinn is welcoming increasing numbers of boutique hotels and fine eateries, but remains great value.

Trip plan: Spare time to explore the walled Old Town's many Gothic and baroque gems, including the Town Hall, Toompea Castle, ancient Dominican Monastery and the many churches whose spires pierce the sky above the city.

Need to know: The Christmas market runs from late November into early January (www.christmasmarket.ee).

Other months: Jun-Aug – summer, busy; Apr-May & Sep-Oct – shoulder, cooler, quieter; Nov-Mar – cold.

- Cultural
- Value
- Food & drink

Snow dusting the rooftops in the Old Town, Tallinn

ROVANIEMI
FINLAND

→ **Why now?** Visit Santa in his snow-clad grotto.

Christmas comes but once a year – except in Finnish Lapland, where you can immerse yourself in Yule for the full 365 days. The town of Rovaniemi proudly declares itself the 'official' home of Santa, and at nearby Napapiiri (Finnish for the Arctic Circle), there's a village dedicated to the cult of Claus. Naturally, the whole (unsurprisingly commercialised) shebang looks most festive in snowy December, when only those with a heart of ice could fail to be captivated by the magical ambience. And once your kids have met Santa and mailed a card from his post office, there's plenty to occupy the family in and around Rovaniemi for several days: husky sledding, reindeer safaris, cross-country skiing and a trio of interesting museums in the city itself, covering art, Arctic life and Finnish nature. As a bonus, this is a great place to watch the Northern Lights.

Trip plan: Fly to Rovaniemi via Helsinki. Accommodation includes Santa's Holiday Village, igloos of ice and glass, a snowhotel and a range of chalets, lodges and hotels.

Need to know: Temperatures can drop to -30°C (-22°F) in Lapland – bring plenty of warm clothes and thick-soled shoes.

Other months: Nov–mid-May – snowy winter and early spring; Jun-Aug – summer, long days; Sep-Oct – 'ruska', fall foliage.

SOUTHERN
VIETNAM

→ **Why now?** Swim, snorkel, sunbathe and explore the Mekong Delta.

Indochina's southern tip is a lucky dip of the region's best bits: the heady rush of Ho Chi Minh City, moving relics of war, the Mekong Delta's paddies and villages, and beautiful, beach-lined Phu Quoc and Con Dao Islands. Both hosted colonial French prisons – you can visit the haunting remains – but now are better known as chill-out getaways, perfect in December after rain and humidity have eased. Phu Quoc, closer to Cambodia than Vietnam, has varied accommodation, great snorkelling and some lovely, quiet beaches. Con Dao is more remote and rugged, hosting nesting turtles (June to September) and dugongs as well as peaceful resorts on breathtaking beaches.

Trip plan: Both Phu Quoc and Con Dao are accessible by air from Ho Chi Minh City, so it's easy to combine a relaxing stay on an island idyll with an exploration of the compact south. Be sure to visit the Cu Chi Tunnels, a subterranean Viet Cong lair during the war, as well as exploring the Mekong Delta and indulging in fine seafood in Ho Chi Minh City.

Need to know: On Phu Quoc, seek out *bún kèn* – a seafood noodle salad with sweet and sour fish broth. Prices and visitor numbers rise towards Christmas.

Other months: Nov-May – warm, dry; Jun-Oct – humid, wet (rainy season longer on Con Dao).

- Cultural
- Adventure
- Wildlife & nature

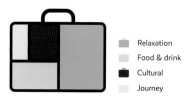

- Relaxation
- Food & drink
- Cultural
- Journey

© Matt Munro / Lonely Planet

The beach at Wreck Bay, one of many dotting the Sapphire Coast

SAPPHIRE COAST
AUSTRALIA

→ **Why now?** Savour seafood, surf, beaches and wild national parks.

The far south of New South Wales is an origami coastline of capes, inlets, lakes and beaches, fishing villages and forests. The Sapphire Coast label may be a tourism marketing ploy, but it's also a fair badge for this offbeat gem, perfect for exploring in early summer. The menu is varied: seafood, especially oysters; the bottlenose dolphins, fur seals and little penguins of Montague Island; coastal trails in Bournda National Park and Goodenia Rainforest; and dozens of beaches, from family-friendly stretches (Eden, Tathra) to surfers' haunts (Merimbula, Tathra) and dramatic coastlines in Mimosa Rocks and Ben Boyd National Parks.

Trip plan: A week-long road trip starts from Narooma, about 200 miles south of Sydney, 130 miles southeast of Canberra. Take a cruise to see the penguins of Montague Island, follow the A1 south to Tilba Tilba and peel off onto the coastal road to the fishing village of Bermagui. Tourist Drive 9 traces the coast south to Tathra, Merimbula and Pambula via Mimosa Rocks and Bournda National Parks; continue south to explore Ben Boyd National Park either side of Eden.

Need to know: Southern right whales migrate past the coast in July and August; humpbacks follow September to November.

Other months: Dec-Apr – warm; May-Nov – cooler, slightly wetter.

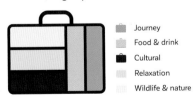

- Journey
- Food & drink
- Cultural
- Relaxation
- Wildlife & nature

Admiralty Bay on Bequia in St Vincent and the Grenadines

© Justin Foulkes / Lonely Planet

TRINIDAD

> **Why now?** Party in the sun to the sound of *parang*.

The southernmost Caribbean island is hardly a shrinking violet. But rather than jumping to calypso, steel pans or soca, December – start of the dry season – is time for *parang*. Traditionally, in the run-up to Christmas *parranderos* toting guitars, cuatros, and castanets toured neighbourhoods to croon Spanish-style nativity songs in exchange for eggnog, rum and sorrel (a drink made from a hibiscus plant, hugely popular at Christmas). Today you might hear *parranderos* touring in Paramin or Lopinot, or performing in a bar or organised show, sometimes with a soca-parang mix-up – but wherever the lilting notes serenade you, it's a unique festive treat.

Trip plan: Most of Trinidad's attractions are on the west of the island. The beach at Maracas Bay and hummingbird-buzzing Asa Wright Nature Centre are north of Piarco International Airport; head south via capital Port of Spain to look for scarlet ibis and silky anteaters at Caroni Bird Sanctuary, enjoy the best nightlife in San Fernando, and sink your toes in the gloopy asphalt of Pitch Lake.

Need to know: Trini food stalls rate as the best in the Caribbean: try rotis with curried meat and vegetables, doubles (curried chickpeas in *bara* flatbreads), or bake'n'shark (fried fish rolls) at Maracas Beach.

Other months: Dec-May – drier season; Jun-Nov – rainy.

- Cultural
- Relaxation
- Food & drink

ST VINCENT & THE GRENADINES

> **Why now?** Get festive (between sunbathing and snorkelling) on these volcanic islands.

This string of emeralds in the southeast Caribbean has two faces in December. In the first half it's the peaceful beach buddy, luring you to relax on palm-shaded sand under post-hurricane-season sunshine. Then, from mid-December, the character changes and the early bird emerges: seemingly the whole population rises at 4am (yes, four in the morning) for the nine days leading up to Christmas to sing, play steel pans, ride bikes, dance, sup callaloo and generally get prematurely festive during the Nine Mornings Festival. This uniquely Vincentian tradition reputedly dates back over a century, and captures the imagination of any visitor with the stamina to enjoy successive pre-dawn choruses.

Trip plan: St Vincent's international airport is at the south of the island. Though there are beaches on St Vincent itself (Young Island is popular), the best are in the Grenadines. Canouan and Bequia, which has a lively Nine Mornings tradition, have gorgeous beaches, while the tiny Tobago Cays boast some of the Caribbean's best snorkelling and sailing.

Need to know: Flights and ferries link St Vincent with the Grenadines, while the Tobago Cays are best visited by sailing yacht or on day-trips from Union Island.

Other months: Dec-May – warm, relatively dry; Jun-Nov – hot, rainy.

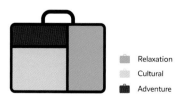

- Relaxation
- Cultural
- Adventure

SCOTLAND

Why now? Celebrate the end of the year in the home of Hogmanay. Forget dropping balls or raising champagne glasses – the most inflammatory new-year shindigs involve blazing balls, barrels or torches paraded through Scottish towns. The traditional Hogmanay conflagrations reputedly stem from ancient Viking celebrations of the winter solstice, though some also claim they were intended to drive away evil spirits. The festivities come in a host of fiery flavours, with unique versions in different parts of Scotland. Inverness throws an alfresco party with music and fireworks; the people of Comrie in Perthshire light tall torches – birch poles topped with birch rags – and Biggar builds a huge bonfire; in Stonehaven a piper leads a procession swinging fireballs, while in Dufftown, the 'malt whisky capital of the world', the annual Hogmanay ceilidh ends with drams of whisky in the town square. But the biggest bang is surely in Edinburgh, with a huge party in Princes St, an outdoor concert and fireworks, and a lone bagpiper tooting in the new year from the castle ramparts.

Trip plan: Book ahead, turn up and be ready to celebrate!

Need to know: The town of Burghead ignores the Gregorian calendar and instead celebrates Hogmanay on 11 January with a parade of the *clavie* – a stave-filled barrel that is then set aflame on a nearby hilltop.

Other months: Apr-Sep – warmest, driest (May-late Sep: midges); Oct-Mar – colder, wetter (Dec-Feb: snow likely at altitude).

Cultural

Food & drink

Fireworks lighting up the Edinburgh sky as part of Hogmanay celebrations

© Chris Hepburn / Getty Images

NEW ORLEANS
USA

A saxophonist absorbs the applause at Preservation Hall, New Orleans

→ **Why now?** Celebrate a bon Noël in the Big Easy.

What – no Mardi Gras? True, if you arrive in Louisiana in December you'll be too early for the parades leading up to 'Fat Tuesday', which begin early January. You'll also arrive before the hordes, while hotels are more likely to find you a room (maybe at a discount). December is drier and cooler than the summer months, but toasty by most standards. And then there's the yuletide charm: wrought-iron balconies and streetcars decked in sparkling lights and garlands, carol concerts in St Louis Cathedral, and restaurants serving four-course fixed-price Reveillon dinners – a historic Creole tradition. The old favourites are as hypnotic as ever, of course: jazz clubs, the creaky elegance of the French Quarter and Garden District, steamboats on the Mississippi – just without the crowds.

Trip plan: For atmospheric accommodation in the French Quarter it pays to book ahead, even in the quiet season.

Need to know: The St Charles Streetcar is reputedly the oldest continuously operating street railway in the world, running since 1835. Today its sage-green cars trace a 13-mile (21km) crescent through the city, offering a US$1.25 slice of New Orleans life.

Other months: Feb-May – warm, lots of music and events; Jun-Sep – hot, rainy, hurricanes possible; Oct-Nov – autumn, pleasant; Dec-Jan – cooler, peaceful.

■ Cultural
■ Food & drink

© Kris Davidson / Lonely Planet

BEYOND NEW ORLEANS

🚗 **BAYOU SAUVAGE NATIONAL WILDLIFE REFUGE · 16 MILES (25KM)** · Alligator-infested swamps

🚗 **EVERGREEN PLANTATION, EDGARD · 51 MILES (82KM)** · The South's most intact plantation complex

🚃 **MOBILE, ALABAMA · 145 MILES (233KM)** · Mini-New Orleans, lively music scene and Mardi Gras

🚌 **MONTGOMERY, ALABAMA · 318 MILES (511KM)** · Civil rights and Hank Williams heritage

INDEX

C

PHOTOCREDITS

LONELY PLANET'S
WHERE TO GO WHEN

Published in December 2016 by Lonely Planet
Global Limited CRN 554153
www.lonelyplanet.com
ISBN 978 17865 7193 9
© Lonely Planet 2016
Printed in China

Written by Sarah Baxter & Paul Bloomfield

Managing Director, Publishing Piers Pickard
Associate Publisher & Commissioning Editor Robin Barton
Editors Simon Williamson, Matt Phillips, Tasmin Waby, Ross Taylor
Art Direction Daniel Di Paolo
Layout Designer Mariana Sameiro
Print Production Larissa Frost, Nigel Longuet

Lonely Planet offices
AUSTRALIA
The Malt Store, Level 3, 551 Swanston Street,
Carlton VIC, 3053 Australia
Phone 03 8379 8000

UNITED KINGDOM
240 Blackfriars Road, London SE1 8NW
Phone 020 3771 5100

USA
150 Linden St, Oakland, CA 94607
Phone 510 250 6400

IRELAND
Unit E, Digital Court, The Digital Hub,
Rainsford St, Dublin 8

STAY IN TOUCH lonelyplanet.com/contact

Although the authors and Lonely Planet have taken all reasonable care in preparing this book, we make no warranty about the accuracy or completeness of its content and, to the maximum extent permitted, disclaim all liability from its use.

Paper in this book is certified against the Forest Stewardship Council™ standards. FSC™ promotes environmentally responsible, socially beneficial and economically viable management of the world's forests.